Disorder

The 21st century has brought a powerful tide of geopolitical, economic, and democratic shocks.

Their fallout has led central banks to create over $25 trillion of new money, brought about a new age of geopolitical competition, destabilized the Middle East, ruptured the European Union, and exposed old political fault lines in the United States.

Disorder: Hard Times in the 21st Century is a long history of this present political moment. It recounts three histories—one about geopolitics, one about the world economy, and one about Western democracies—and explains how in the years of political disorder prior to the pandemic the disruption in each became one big story. It shows how much of this turbulence originated in problems generated by fossil-fuel energies, and it explains why as the green transition takes place the long-standing predicaments energy invariably shapes will remain in place.

The Afterword brings these geopolitical, economic, and political crises up to date by reflecting on the development and impact of the war in Ukraine.

Helen Thompson is Professor of Political Economy in the Department of Politics and International Studies at Cambridge University. She was a regular contributor to the podcast *Talking Politics* and is co-host of the podcast *These Times*. She has written for many publications including the *New York Times*, the *Financial Times*, *New Statesman*, *The Sunday Times*, and *The Nikkei* on subjects such as energy, geopolitics, Brexit, and cultural narratives around energy.

T0020559

Praise for *Disorder*

'There could be no better guide than Helen Thompson to the turbulence of the 21st century, with its successive disruptions, from financial crisis to energy transition, from Brexit to emerging geopolitical conflicts. When history seems to have come for us with a vengeance since the turn of the millennium, this magisterial book brings into focus the key structural forces driving, not only recent events, but also the inevitable changes still to come.'

Diane Coyle, University of Cambridge

'If you want to understand why Russia invaded Ukraine then this book will help.'

Richard Lofthouse, *QUAD*

'Bold and brilliant, studded with insights . . . one of the year's most essential books.'

Christopher Bray, *The Tablet*

'A powerful guide to modern Hard Times . . . any reader will finish it with a deeper understanding of our contemporary challenges.'

Paschal Donohoe, *Irish Times*

'In this absorbing and wide-ranging study Helen Thompson unravels the complex intersections of oil, money, and democracy for understanding the politics of the last century. She provides an indispensable and illuminating guide to our current predicaments.'

Andrew Gamble, University of Sheffield

'Most of us struggle to keep up [with the news], but not Helen Thompson— she doesn't merely grip each strand, but ties them together.'

Tom Clark, *Prospect*

'If you are looking for a well-developed and convincing theory of our time, I advise you to start here.'

Gilles Gressani, *Le Grand Continent*,
'What to read this summer'

'[*Disorder* is] as disturbing as it is thought-provoking.'

Martin Wolf, *Financial Times*, Summer
Books 2022: Economics

Disorder

Hard Times in the 21st Century

HELEN THOMPSON

OXFORD

UNIVERSITY PRESS

OXFORD
UNIVERSITY PRESS

Great Clarendon Street, Oxford, OX2 6DP,
United Kingdom

Oxford University Press is a department of the University of Oxford.
It furthers the University's objective of excellence in research, scholarship,
and education by publishing worldwide. Oxford is a registered trade mark of
Oxford University Press in the UK and in certain other countries

First Published 2022
First published in paperback 2023

Published in the United States of America by Oxford University Press
198 Madison Avenue, New York, NY 10016, United States of America

British Library Cataloguing in Publication Data
Data available

Library of Congress Control Number: 2023938496

ISBN 978-0-19-886501-8 (pbk.)

Printed by Integrated Books International, United States of America

For my niece Florence, and to the memory of my colleague
and friend Aaron Rapport

Time went on in Coketown like its own machinery: so much material wrought up, so much fuel consumed, so many powers worn out, so much money made. But less inexorable than iron, steel, and brass, it brought its varying seasons even into that wilderness of smoke and brick.

Charles Dickens, *Hard Times for These Times*

It is likely enough that, rooted in the woods of France and Norway, there were already growing trees, when that sufferer was put to death, already marked by the Woodman, Fate, to come down and be sawn into boards, to make a certain moveable framework with a sack and knife in it, terrible in history. It is likely enough that in the rough outhouses of some tillers of the heavy lands adjacent to Paris, there were sheltered from the weather that very day, rude carts, bespattered with rustic mire, snuffed about by pigs, and roosted in by poultry, which the Farmer, Death, had already set apart to be his tumbrils of the Revolution. But that Woodman and that Farmer, though they work unceasingly, work silently, and no one heard them as they went about with muffled tread; the rather, forasmuch as to entertain any suspicion that they were awake, was to be atheistical and traitorous.

Charles Dickens, *A Tale of Two Cities*

We see, the Lawes of other Common-weals to alter with occasions, and even those that pretended their originall from some Divinity, to have vanished without trace or memory.

Thomas Browne, *Religio Medici*

Preface to the Paperback Edition

Disorder was published on 24 February 2022, the day Russia invaded Ukraine. That proved a disorientating experience. While I had made Ukraine pivotal to my account of the geopolitical fault lines running through post-Cold War Europe, Russia's all-out war on Ukraine was a different proposition. By upending the Europe-Russia energy relationship and accelerating energy-driven inflation, the war also highlighted the centrality of energy to geopolitics and the monetary and financial world that I had used as the premise of *Disorder*. After 24 February 2022, energy appeared everywhere. In writing an additional chapter, I have tried to situate Russia's war in 2022 within my long history of the disruption of the first two decades of the 21st century while recognizing the war as a point of departure in both the material world and consciousness about energy.

I am very grateful for all their wonderful help in organizing my talks about the book to Anna Silva, Emma Smith, and Samuel Sheldon. My thanks for conversations over the past year that have helped me to clarify my thinking for writing the Afterword to Andrea Binder, Alexander Chartres, Robert Fox, Gary Gerstle, Maurice Glasman, Tom Holland, Hans Kundnani, Demetri Kofinas, Russell Napier, Alice Thompson, and Adam Tooze. I am grateful to Emma Slaughter for her help with the text and to Kayley Gilbert with the production process. Once again, I would like to thank Luciana O'Flaherty for her editing skills; and, for ensuring that I didn't get stuck in *Disorder*, Sarah Chalfant.

London,
March 2023

Contents

Acknowledgements

In retrospect, this book had its genesis in the summer and autumn of
2016. In part, this came from a sense of what I thought I understood.
Over that summer I worked to finish a short book on why oil has
proved so disruptive to Western economies since the turn of the
century and wrote a piece for the magazine *Juncture*, arguing that
whichever way the referendum result had gone, Brexit was in the
long term most likely unavoidable. After I submitted my book manuscript, I began an academic article interrogating the relationship
between what I judged Brexit's eventual inevitability and the contin-
gencies of David Cameron's premiership. As I pursued that argument,
the contingency seemed weaker than I first thought and the structural
forces propelling Britain out stronger. In thinking my question
through, I realized that the long-standing monetary divergence between
Britain and the Eurozone became particularly consequential from 2011
because of the very different responses of the Bank of England and ECB
to high oil prices. In a rather different way, an energy story also seemed
part of the 2016 presidential election, which was the first election for
nearly fifty years that had taken place with the United States as a top oil
producer. To my analytical mind, Trump's election victory seemed an
explicable political phenomenon. If that was not a particularly comfort-
able place to occupy, it gave me some confidence that I could explain to
myself anyway why 2016 had taken the turns it had.

Just as importantly, the impulse to write this book came from a
sense of what I did not understand in the turbulence of that year but
instinctively judged to be geopolitically significant, in particular the
fallout from the attempted coup in Turkey. During my research on
oil, I had begun to think geopolitically. But there was much I still
needed to learn.

My responsibilities in Cambridge meant it was several years before
I pulled my thoughts together and sketched with broad brushes a
version of the arguments in this book. In September 2019, I began a
year's academic leave and started writing. I was two-thirds of the way
through a draft when the pandemic hit. Initially, I wondered if there

was still a book: if I was trying to explain the present political moment, what happened if that moment changed out of all recognition? But, relatively quickly, I concluded that the fallout of the pandemic was not replacing the story I was telling with a different one but in crucial respects deepening it. The additional time I have taken to complete the book in order to include 2020 in my analysis gave me the chance to reflect again on the last decade of the geopolitical story, in particular its relationship to green energy.

In writing a book that looks to *la longue durée* to explain ongoing economic and political change, the vantage point can never be quite right. The book risks trying to explain more than can be seen clearly at this moment in time. There are a lot of moving parts that I am well aware in their interaction may unfold in the future in different ways than my historically driven narrative would suggest. I am generally wary of predictions, and those few I have made in the conclusion I have done with some hesitancy. Getting to grips with the appropriate time frames for political analysis is an inherently troublesome task. The fact that how to think about risks in relation to time has become a central problem of modern politics only compounds this difficulty.

My title is part homage to Dickens and his meditation on industrial civilization pitted against 'the innumerable horse-power' of time in his most schematic novel, *Hard Times for These Times*. It is also a small reminder to myself of the need for epistemological humility: what I was unable to see when I read the novel for the first time as a 16-year-old stupidly deprived me of more than a decade of opportunities to enjoy Dickens' insight and pleasures.

My primary debts are to Sarah Chalfant, Emma Smith, and Luciana O'Flaherty. My agent Sarah and her colleague, at the Wylie Agency, Emma guided me with consummate professionalism through every stage of this book, including the last discussions of my title. Their phenomenal support through the stresses thrown up by events during the first months of the pandemic allowed me to work much more productively that spring and summer than I would otherwise have done. Luciana, my editor at Oxford University Press, has been a huge assistance in helping me improve the text. I try not to dwell on what it might have done to her sanity in the process.

I am also grateful at Oxford University Press for their help to Céline Louasli, Anna Silva, Amy Guest, David McBride, Jocelyn Córdova, and Gabriel Kachuck. For their work on the production of the manuscript, I would like to thank Sindhuja Baskaran, Kalpana Sagayanathan, and Phil Dines.

Hans Kundnani and Dmitri Safronov took the time to read the first draft of the manuscript. Andrea Binder read chapters six and eight, and Gary Gerstle chapter seven. I am very grateful to them all for their suggestions and insight, as I am to a reader for Oxford University Press for their comments.

Since I started thinking seriously about the book, I have had conversations—including in the pandemic virtual world—that have stimulated me to new thoughts or made me stop to reconsider my arguments with Stefan Auer, Chris Bickerton, Andrea Binder, Christopher Brooke, Daisy Christodoulou, Diane Coyle, Gary Gerstle, Tom Holland, Erik Jones, Shashank Joshi, Hans Kundnani, Hjalte Lokdam, Matthias Matthijs, Tom McTague, Anand Menon, Brendan O'Leary, Craig Parsons, Aris Roussinos, Lucia Rubinelli, David Runciman, Tom Runciman, Waltraud Schelkle, Josh Simons, Adam Spielman, Alice Thompson, Robert Tombs, Adam Tooze, Shahin Vallée, Daniel Yergin, and Ayse Zarakol.

A series of long calls with Maurice Glasman during the first lockdown opened my eyes to the importance of Hong Kong to the geopolitical and economic stories I was telling.

As I was finishing my first complete draft of the book with a dawning awareness that my geopolitical story was incomplete, I spent time reading and listening to much of what Adam Tooze wrote and broadcast during the first six months or so of the pandemic. Through Adam's extraordinary erudition, I began to bring into focus what I had hitherto been missing. Some of our disagreements may run deep, but precisely because they do, I learn immeasurably from my engagement with him.

If it were not for Thanasis D. Sfikas, I would not have spent as much time over the past decade trying to understand the Eurozone crisis. Whatever my scepticism about the idea of the European Union as a teleological project, our enduring friendship will always ground my sense of being a European.

The *Talking Politics* podcast has forced me to assemble my thoughts on any number of subjects and has given me the chance to converse with many different interesting people. When, back in 2015,

David Runciman asked me to start talking about politics outside conventional academic formats, neither of us had any idea how much talking we would be doing, nor where what began as conversations, which we might otherwise have had in the departmental corridor, about one British general election would take us. It has been quite an intellectual and existential journey; through the good times and the more difficult times—especially the tragic deaths over the summer of 2019 of our fellow podcasters and friends Aaron Rapport and Finbarr Livesey and Aaron's wife Joyce Heckman—I cannot imagine having taken it with anyone else. My thanks to Catherine Carr for everything she has given to make *Talking Politics* happen and to Nick Carter for making us sound much better than we do.

I am grateful to Jason Cowley for the opportunity to write as a columnist for the *New Statesman*. The latitude he has given me has been a privilege. It is in writing these columns that I worked out some of the book's geopolitical argument, which it took me the autumn and early winter of 2020 to see clearly. My thanks also to Gavin Jacobson at the *New Statesman* for his editorial advice and intellectual engagement.

Sally Chatterton at *UnHerd* commissioned me in 2018 and 2019 to write a number of pieces about the EU and geopolitics that pushed me into sharper lines of argument. In giving me the chance to write about Dickens just as London opened up again after the first lockdown, she also did something to keep me going on this book.

I developed some of my arguments in earlier forms. On Southern Europe and the euro, I did so at the Hamburg Institute of Social Research at the invitation of Clara Maier. On Brexit, I prepared several lectures and papers: for a *British Journal of Politics and International Relations* workshop in Edinburgh at the invitation of Daniel Wincott and the late John Peterson; at King's College London at the invitation of Brian Salter and Peter John; and for the annual British politics lecture for Birkbeck at the invitation of Sarah Childs. On the Fed and the Eurodollar markets, I very much benefited from working with Iain Hardie for an article published in *Review of International Political Economy*.

Delivering the Leonard Schapiro Memorial Lecture in February 2021 helped me improve my second and third geopolitical chapters. My thanks to Katharine Adeney, Laura Cram, Erik Jones, and Rosalind Jones for inviting me to give the lecture and the occasion and, again, to Hans Kundnani for hosting me at Chatham House; additional thanks to Erik and Laura for their incisive comments on the subsequent article for *Government and Opposition*. Alun Michael's prompting, after he asked me to talk on energy to the Economics and Current Affairs Group at the Reform Club, first got me thinking systematically about the geopolitics of gas. I would not have reached my closing argument without the chance to work out my thoughts on the relationship between the climate crisis and our energy future for *Engelsberg Ideas*. My thanks here to Iain Martin and Oliver Rhodes.

John Hall hosted a wonderful weekend in Montreal in March 2019 on Europe and the Habsburg world of yesteryear; Francesco Duina and Frédéric Mérand encouraged me to rework the short paper I had written for that workshop into something more substantial and submit it for an edition of *Research in Political Sociology*. I was ultimately unable in this book to directly pursue several of the lines of argument I articulated there. Nonetheless, it proved a very intellectually fertile endeavour, not least in getting me to read about democratic politics in turn-of-the-century Vienna and allowing me to get my geopolitical story about Ukraine into a sharper focus.

My intellectual debts to John Dunn and the late Geoff Hawthorn are long and abiding. Without their influence, I would not have acquired the intellectual ambition to conceive of a book like this nor would I have found a voice to engage with politics in a historical way. That my gratitude to Geoff can no longer be received still saddens me.

London,
September 2021

Introduction

Disruption

The Covid pandemic hit after a decade of fierce disruption. As 2019 turned into 2020, a sense of democratic fragility was near pervasive in North America and Europe. The House of Representatives impeached Donald Trump for soliciting interference from the Ukrainian president to discredit his eventual opponent in the upcoming election. In Britain, the three-and-a-half-year political contest over whether the Brexit referendum result would be upheld came to an end with a decisive victory for the Conservatives in a winter general election. But Boris Johnson's new government began the new year confronting a Scottish secessionist cause furnished with the devastatingly simple argument that Scotland was being forced out of the European Union (EU) against its will. In the German state of Thuringia, the regional Christian Democrats temporarily joined with the far-right party *Alternative für Deutschland* to elect a new government, an occurrence described by the German chancellor, Angela Merkel, as 'unforgivable' and a 'bad day for democracy'.[1]

Geopolitically, turbulence appeared writ large. In January 2020, the American and Chinese governments were bringing a near two-year trade war to an end. But mass protests in Hong Kong and legislation passed by the US Congress over the city were augmenting Sino-American tensions. Meanwhile, from Syria in the north to Yemen in the south, the Middle East was rife with conflicts. Some exposed long-standing rifts within NATO. In the autumn of 2019, President Trump tried, for a second time, to withdraw American troops from Syria, allowing Turkish soldiers to advance into the north of the country. Furious at this Turkish action and at Trump for enabling it, the French president, Emmanuel Macron, proclaimed that 'what we are currently experiencing is the brain death of NATO'.[2] Soon, Merkel distanced herself, insisting that 'from a German perspective

NATO is...our security alliance'.[3] On 3 January 2020, Trump unilaterally ordered the assassination of the head of Iran's foreign military operations in retaliation for an attack by Iranian-backed Iraqi militias on the American embassy in Baghdad. Putting aside their rows over Britain's imminent departure from the EU, Johnson, Macron, and Merkel issued a joint statement saying that there was 'an urgent need for de-escalation'.[4] Frenzied political and media commentators asked if the third world war was about to begin.

Economically, nearly everywhere over the winter of 2019–20, the prospects for growth were worsening. After three years of trying, the American Federal Reserve—the American central bank—had given up on returning policy to anything approaching monetary normalcy. In September 2019, the overnight money markets where banks borrow from each other froze, as they had first done in August 2007 at the onset of the 2007–8 financial crash. Without quite acknowledging that it was doing so, the Fed turned back to the practice of creating money to buy assets—what is known as quantitative easing (QE). Two months later, the European Central Bank (ECB) resumed its QE programme while still waiting for a long-delayed decision from the German Constitutional Court on the policy's legality in Germany. Even China, which had done much to drive the world economy for a decade, was experiencing significantly slower growth.

In the energy sphere, the world appeared at a turning point. For the first time since 2009, annual world oil production fell. The gap between oil consumed and oil produced reached its highest level since 2007, when prices were hurtling towards a final peak of $150 a barrel. The credit conditions that followed the 2007–8 crash drove a flood of capital into the American shale oil sector. But now, as pressure for action on climate change accelerated, investors were deserting American and European oil companies. What, a decade earlier, would have been perceived as a medium-term disaster for oil was now seen as promising evidence that the world was on a three-to-four-decade path away from fossil fuels to green energy.

It was into this extensive turmoil that the Covid-19 emergency arrived. While it had its own extraordinary effect, it also acted as a window on the decade of disruption that preceded it. Over the course of 2020, many of the fault lines that had already done so much to shape the 2010s shuddered again.

There is no singular explanation of the disruption. Nonetheless, a good number of its causes were interactive in their effects. Take Brexit. It had a particular history in Britain's democratic politics, Britain's absence from the euro, and the EU's unbending constitutional order. But it was also a product of wider changes that on the surface were separate from it. When oil prices surged in 2011, the Fed and the Bank of England did not respond. The ECB, by contrast, raised interest rates twice. While the British economy continued its recovery, the Eurozone plunged back into recession. For the next few years, Britain became an employer of last resort for the Eurozone's southern members while, under Mario Draghi's leadership, the ECB endeavoured to find a means of running an asset-purchase programme that the German Constitutional Court might tolerate. By the time Draghi had persuaded Merkel he had one, David Cameron was at least halfway to concluding he should promise the British electorate the chance to vote on leaving the EU. Then, just as the British prime minister was preparing to hold that referendum, the Syrian refugee crisis made Germany's outsized influence within the EU overt to the voters whom he needed to persuade that Britain should continue with the status quo.

Like Brexit, Donald Trump's successful electoral insurgency in 2016 had a particular history, this time in the long-term fractures in the American republic. But it also occurred in a geopolitical context connecting the United States' re-emergence as the world's largest oil and gas producer to China's post-2015 industrial strategy to the return of Russia to the Middle East. In part, Trump triumphed electorally by asserting to American voters that where the United States was strong its power was not being used and where it was weak it was trapped. What became the geopolitical choice in the 2016 election had a structural logic: in a world in which China and Russia were moving closer together, a confront-China candidate in Trump stood and won against a confront-Russia candidate in Hillary Clinton.

Trump's presidency then served as its own destabilizing force. In starting from the overt premise that Beijing was a strategic rival, it made the Sino-American economic relationship a matter of immediate geopolitical contest, with sharp ramifications for Europe and NATO. But while it prioritized the Chinese technological threat over the Russian military one in the Middle East, the Trump administration also used the American shale boom to confront Russian gas exports to Europe more aggressively than its predecessors. In the face of this overall reorientation of American power, the European countries were left at sixes and sevens, not just with Washington, but, as Merkel's rebuke of Macron over NATO indicated, with each other.

From the beginning, the geopolitical turbulence that made Trump's election possible rebounded back into American democratic politics. Before it even began, the legitimacy of his presidency was contested: some of his opponents were convinced that he was a quite literal product of geopolitics. The unproven allegations that, as Hillary Clinton charged, he was Vladimir 'Putin's puppet' formed the basis of the Mueller inquiry into Russian interference in the 2016 election.[5]

But the contested legitimacy of Trump's presidency went well beyond a projection of resurgent Russian power into the White House, or Trump's boorish disregard for the real and symbolic gravitas of the office. It reflected the fact that a significant number of Americans were unwilling to accept that the 2016 election had settled who the president was for four years. In a more dramatic and dangerous form, the same problem reappeared during the 2020 election, culminating in Trump's demand that his vice president invalidate Congress' certification of the Electoral College results and the violent mob attack on the US Congress on 6 January 2021. What is presently missing in elections in the American republic is what no democracy can function without: losers' consent.

Much has been written and said about the disruption of the last decade. This has often been framed around a populist nationalism, its relation to the 2007–8 economic crash, and the fall of a purportedly liberal international order.[6] But at the systematic level much remains unexplained, not least because energy has largely gone unrecognized as an important cause of the geopolitical and economic fault lines at work.

Casting the pre-pandemic decade as a populist revolt facilitating a return of nationalism has been particularly misleading. Historically, democracy and nationhood have been bedfellows. If the whole idea of national citizens living under common political authority with some sense that they constitute a people is considered only an alien, populist intervention into democracy, the predicaments that always confront representative democracies cannot be understood. As the sharpest early-twentieth-century observers of representative democratic politics saw, the move to full-franchise democracy and nationalism belonged to the same political moment.[7] Seen from this historical perspective, the weakness of losers' consent in the American republic hinges on the fact that American nationhood has been diminished without the need for it disappearing while the political conditions that might make an alternative, more inclusive, American nationhood possible do not seem to exist.

Laments for the breakdown of a once liberal international order betray the same ahistoricism. Structural changes around energy and finance always bring tumultuous geopolitical consequences. The postwar monetary regime constructed at Bretton Woods was anchored in the dollar and conceived by its American architects as a source of American power. It dovetailed with the fact that the United States was the world's largest oil producer and could sharply circumscribe how West European states were able to manage their oil dependency on the Middle East. As the American economy too became reliant on foreign oil imports, President Richard Nixon unilaterally ripped up the entire Bretton Woods exchange rate system over a weekend at Camp David. Now, we live in a geopolitical world shaped by another monetary and energy transformation in the second half of the 2000s, the consequences of which are still playing out a decade later as a green energy revolution is beginning.

In a search for a comprehensive explanation of the last decade's disruption, this book starts from the premise that several different histories are necessary to identify the causal forces at work and a conviction that these histories must overlap. Certainly, there are specific factors that account for the distinctive impact of this disruption on individual democracies, especially for the American republic. Nonetheless, the present disruption can be understood as originating in a set of structurally driven shocks, the effects of which have cascaded from one place to another and between the geopolitical, economic, and domestic political spheres.

A number of large-scale shifts over the past decade explain the causal interaction. The world's economic and political geography is being recast. From the 1980s, industrialization in Asia and computer

technology created an economic space that connected North America
and Western Europe to the more prosperous parts of Asia. But a
simultaneous Chinese infrastructural turn towards Eurasia and to
technological competition with the United States has diminished
that cross-oceanic economic space. As Eurasia takes an overt post-
imperial economic form, the effects of a development in any part of
the world's one supercontinent reverberate across it. The weakening
of a broader Atlantic-Pacific world economy has constituted a shock to
the world's most powerful state. As it occurred, the United States also
simultaneously became the world's largest oil and gas producer and
saw its bid to remake the energy-rich Middle East into an American
sphere of influence break down. Both American strength and American weakness have destabilized the Middle East and Turkey, making
Europe much more politically vulnerable to events in its south-eastern
neighbourhood.

By unsettling the balance of political power within a country,
geopolitical upheaval will always have an impact on domestic politics.
In Europe, this dynamic has singular consequences since the issue of
where the political authority to respond to such change should lie is
still subject to fierce political contest. The EU is a union of nationally
organized democracies that is reliant on an outside power for external
security and to legitimate itself in part appeals to the idea that the
nation state is archaic. This external dependency and internal mut-
ability leaves both the EU itself and its constituent member states
extremely open to disturbance from geopolitical change.

Meanwhile, the post-2008 monetary environment has weak shock
absorbers and is a further source of connective instability. It allows for
historically high levels of peacetime debt at historically low levels of
interest. This situation has proved particularly destabilizing for the
Eurozone, which having been rigidly constructed in a radically different world took considerable time to adapt. In the interim, the Eurozone exported its structural problems into the wider EU.

The interaction between the geopolitical and monetary domains
amplifies the effects of what is happening in each. Most directly, the
debt-driven American shale boom challenged Saudi Arabian and
Russian energy power, unsettling both the Middle East and Europe.
Central bank financing for debt, meanwhile, allowed for geopolitically
destabilizing changes like Brexit to occur unconstrained by financial

market panic. Since the present monetary world enhances American financial power, monetary policy is also now more geopolitical than it has been in some time. The Federal Reserve determines which states have access to dollar credit at times of crisis, and its decisions about interest rates and QE constrain all other economies. This dynamic is a strong countervailing movement to the disintegrative pressures around the old Atlantic-Pacific economic space. As such, even as China's power grows in other respects, the monetary sphere is a source of weakness for China, the consequences of which have spilled over into Europe.

In charting this world, the book's first history is geopolitical and it centres around energy.[8] It starts with the rise of the oil- and capital-rich United States as a geopolitical power during the period when oil began to replace coal as the energy base of military power. This change shaped a contest during the First World War between the European powers to control the fading Ottoman Empire just as Britain and France became financially indebted to the United States. Conflicts around how European countries could secure oil in relation to American financial power were fundamental to the subsequent interwar European crisis, and American oil and money were pivotal to the outcome of the Second World War. After the war, Western Europe was reliant on a hierarchical security alliance with the United States in the form of NATO and oil imports from the Middle East. But from the start, the Middle East and Turkey bedevilled NATO, making Western Europe also dependent on Britain's fading imperial power around the Persian Gulf. From the 1970s, what had been primarily a European foreign energy dependency problem became an American one too, at just the time when Britain withdrew from the Middle East. What followed from these cumulative difficulties set the NATO states on different and divisive paths in regard to all of the Soviet Union, Turkey, and the Middle East.

In their own right, the Cold War years left a lasting legacy. Now, the consequences are playing out in a world in which what China does is much more consequential. Where oil and gas are concerned, the United States has acquired the capacity for more energy autonomy than at any time since the 1960s, and extreme American financial leverage complements this power. This renewed American strength became an agent of geopolitical havoc in the Middle East. It also made China's dependency on foreign oil pivotal in oil markets and gave Russia a serious rival in exporting gas to Europe. This American–Russian competition has pressed against the post–Cold War fault lines around Ukraine and the longer one around Turkey. Since China is both the world's largest carbon emitter and already has large-scale advantages in renewable energy as well as the metals on which it depends, green energy is now a second source of geopolitical instability running concurrently with that generated by fossil fuel energy.

The book's second history is economic. This is a story of monetary, financial, and, again, energy upheaval. It begins in the early 1970s when the Bretton Woods system broke down, under the pressure of dollar banking markets in Europe, and Western countries were hit by high oil prices delivered by Middle Eastern producers.[9] The ensuing difficulties in Europe eventually led to the creation of the euro. By the late 1990s, the monetary, oil, and financial environment had settled into a more benign form, and China's integration into the world economy was deepening. This precipitated a new set of shocks at the same time as oil supply problems returned and the risks around internationalized dollar banking accelerated. In trying to manage these new problems, Western central bankers set off a chain of events that produced multiple economic crashes in 2007 and 2008.

The policy responses in the United States, the EU, and China remade the world economy again. Everywhere, the accumulation of debt ensured that there could be no return to the past. The Fed presided over a credit environment in which debt was extremely cheap, and it acted as a lender of last resort to large banks in other countries. The Eurozone crisis destabilized the relationship between the EU and the Eurozone, unravelling Britain's membership of the EU. The ECB's eventual transformation has left the Eurozone in political limbo. As the last decade progressed, China's economy grew in importance for the world economy, especially for Europe. But it has also been seriously constrained by the Fed's new power and a backlash against Xi Jinping's bid to turn China into *the* high-tech manufacturing superpower. Under these competing pressures, the world economy has become a site of sharper geopolitical conflict.

The book's final history is about democracies. Representative democracy has come to be perceived in Europe and North America as a stable and superior structure for collective political life. But representative democracies, like all other forms of government, are prone to becoming unbalanced through time as the geopolitical and economic conditions in which they were established change. They have also been historically reliant on an idea of nationhood that is as potentially destabilizing as it is necessary.

These vulnerabilities were evident from representative democracies' beginnings, especially in the American republic. They have often manifested themselves at times of economic crisis around debt. While, during the Depression of the 1930s, a number of European democracies fell, in the United States, Franklin Roosevelt's New Deal reconstructed democratic nationhood as shared economic fate. Although this endeavour was compromised by American racial politics, it set a general template for reforming democracies to save them. After the Second World War, Western European governments also started from the assumption that in the name of democracy the state should take responsibility for a national economy, allowing them to finance what democratic states spent through taxes rather than international borrowing.

The geopolitical and economic changes of the 1970s started to unravel this form of democratic politics. Fiscally, governments became more dependent on international capital markets and less dependent on their citizens. Open international capital flows and new trade agreements made it easier for North American and European manufacturing corporations to offshore jobs to countries where labour costs were lower, and highly internationalized financial sectors concentrated wealth more intensely. Everywhere, democracies became from the 1990s increasingly unresponsive to democratic demands for economic reforms that would increase the return to labour.

Under these conditions, democracies became particularly susceptible to their plutocratic tendencies and more difficult to reform. In the case of the American republic, this turn fuelled wider conflicts around democratic citizenship. In the EU, monetary union and a proliferation of treaties hollowed out the stakes at national elections and eroded the EU's democratic legitimacy. Sharp differences emerged between the European democracies and the American republic, which have manifested in distinct forms of disruption over the past decade on each side of the Atlantic. Only in the United States has losers' consent to elections so overtly broken down. Only in France are the old political parties so weak that they struggle to compete in elections; nowhere else has as persistent a protest movement as the *Gilets Jaunes* taken to the streets.

The book's three histories are anything but exhaustive, either in themselves or as an explanation of the present political disruption.[10] The analytical history offered is synthetic interpretation and privileges the schematic over forensic detail. When it comes to democracy, the book has a circumscribed focus on the United States, the long-standing EU members, and Britain. In putting considerable weight on material conflicts and geopolitical power rather than culture or religion, I do not wish to suggest that the political world is reducible to the material realm. Indeed, I emphasize time as a source of instability in democracies precisely because material explanations do not suffice. Since the liberal assumption that history was moving an ever more prosperous and democratic world away from religion was erroneous, there is a very important story to tell that is missing in this book about the political ramifications of the religious and cultural experiences of Europe and North America through the twentieth and early twenty-first centuries.[11]

Perhaps jarringly, at a time when climate change is an urgent reality, the book also makes two fossil fuel energies central to two of its three histories and a part of the third. If it is not quite true, as the physicist Geoffrey West quipped in his popular-science book *Scale*, that 'it's all energy, stupid', twentieth- and early twenty-first-century economic and political history is impenetrable without understanding what has followed from the production, consumption, and transportation of oil and gas.[12]

In understanding the path from the past to the present, oil has a particular significance. Since it powers ships and aircraft, it is the energy source on which military power rests. Oil is also fundamental to daily life as we know it. The food chain, from the fertilizers and pesticides used in commercial agriculture to the distribution of supplies in trucks across land and ships across the seas, depends on oil. Petrochemicals that are obtained from oil are indispensable components of plastic and medical equipment. Problematically for green energy ambitions, they are also presently required to manufacture solar panels, batteries, and electric vehicles.

Hopes for a different energy future cannot attenuate oil and gas' present significance. Quite evidently, oil and gas were important causal factors in the last decade's disruption. In the same way, the politics of this decade will be quite incomprehensible outside the drive for green energy. When energy is the underlying material basis of any civilization, the significance of changes in energy should be self-evident.[13] Thus far in human history, economic development has been a function of using more energy.[14] At the centre of the present bid for green energy is an attempt to change this long-standing relationship through new technologies.[15]

Any analysis that brings together energy and politics runs into a temporal disjuncture. The turn in the industrial revolution to using stored ancient sunlight as an energy source effectively reset economic and ecological time, destabilizing human beings' relationship to the biosphere and making economic life dependent on ever more techno-logical innovation against a backdrop of resource depletion with no a priori guarantee of success.[16] But this transformation also left much about politics as a site of collective material and cultural conflicts in place. If energy were anything like a sufficient explanation of the past decade's political disruption, some of the second part and most of the third part of this book would add little. But politics causes its own problems. It too is burdened with a version of the entropy that occurs whenever energy is made usable: the attempt to establish and main-tain political order necessarily produces the seeds of future disorder.

PART I

Geopolitics

1

The Age of Oil Begins

In May 2018, Donald Trump announced that the United States was withdrawing from the Iran nuclear deal presided over by Barack Obama. In reinstating sanctions against Tehran, Trump denounced the agreement as a betrayal of American power, charging that 'at the point when the United States had maximum leverage, this disastrous deal gave this regime . . . of great terror many billions of dollars', allowing 'the dictatorship . . . to build its nuclear-capable missiles, support terrorism, and cause havoc throughout the Middle East and beyond'.[1] Trump's action invited confrontation not just with Iran but with Britain, France, Germany, the European Union, and China, which, along with Russia, were all party to the agreement. The new American sanctions included extraterritorial provisions designed to curtail their trade with Iran too. By 2019, the United States had successfully sanctioned Chinese firms for transporting Iranian oil and China's Iranian imports fell significantly. The EU pursued means for conducting financial transactions with Iran beyond the reach of the sanctions. But European firms' reliance on access to the American banking system to make dollar payments rendered it near impossible for the European energy companies to work in Iran's energy sector.

Trump called this unilateral display of American power 'maximum economic pressure'.[2] But Trump's action invited an Iranian military response in the Persian Gulf that revealed the brittleness of American military power in the Middle East. As it lines the eastern shore of the Strait of Hormuz—the narrow body of water connecting the Persian Gulf to the Indian Ocean down which around 20 per cent of the world's oil supply travels each day—Iran has the potential to inflict serious damage on the world economy. Fearing imminent Iranian interference with shipping, the Trump administration increased the

American naval and air presence in the Gulf and the Arabian Sea. But when, during the summer of 2019, Iran shot down an American military drone over the Strait, seized a British oil tanker in the Strait, and then attacked, either directly or via proxies, Saudi Arabia's oil processing facilities at Abqaiq—where up to 7 million barrels per day of oil are stabilized—no American military response came.

Meanwhile, NATO's deep disunity on all Middle Eastern matters was conspicuous. When, that July, the Trump administration suggested a NATO joint surveillance operation in the Strait, the European NATO states rebuffed the idea. After Iran seized the British-flagged ship, the British government advocated for a European naval mission to protect tankers. But with EU discussions still ongoing, Boris Johnson replaced Theresa May as British prime minister, and quickly ordered British naval ships to join an American-led mission. Even after Britain left the EU in January 2020, the EU remained divided. That month, the French government, with political support from eight EU states, announced that a European Maritime Surveillance Mission would operate in the Strait. But the German government was unenthusiastic and offered no ships or planes to the mission.[3]

It is the Middle East's oil and gas reserves that makes the Persian Gulf the site of these geopolitical fault lines. In their origins, they go back to the early twentieth century when the energy age of coal became the energy age of coal and oil, fundamentally changing Eurasia as a geopolitical space as well as the relationship between Eurasia and the Western Hemisphere. In the age of coal, Western Europe benefited from what world historian Kenneth Pomeranz has aptly called 'fortunate geographic accidents' that were 'essential to the energy revolution'.[4] But when oil also became a crucial energy source, these European countries, despite their empires, were left at an immense geographical disadvantage compared to the United States and Russia. Some of the oil-poor European states began searching for energy resources in the Middle East. Their successes and failures would shape the twentieth century. At the start of the twenty-first century, with the European empires long gone, China too would turn towards Iran. But the geopolitics of the Middle East is now shaped as much by the two states that in energy terms had little need of the region's resources when the age of oil began. Although the American bid that began in the 1990s to turn the region into a sphere of influence is near exhausted, the presence of the American Navy in and around the Persian Gulf is still the central geopolitical fact about oil security in the world today. In contrast to a decade ago, it now exercises that power in a Middle East where Russia also has a military presence.

The Non-Eurasian Eurasian Power

There is a paradox at the centre of American power: over the course of the twentieth century, the United States became the world's dominant power, even though, to use historian John Darwin's words, the 'centre of gravity in modern world history' was still located in Eurasia.[5] As a non-Eurasian state, the historical formation of the United States as a territorial entity was strikingly singular. After the thirteen states' war for independence, the American republic expanded rapidly and violently westwards across the North American continent, largely untouched by Eurasian power conflicts, meeting significant military resistance only for a relatively short time from Mexico.[6] As a growing continental empire, the United States was able, albeit with some British assistance, to shut out the European imperial powers that had colonized the two American continents.

While establishing its primacy in the Western Hemisphere, the United States, from the middle of the century, began to back its long-standing economic interests in Pacific Asia with military action, intervening in the Second Opium War between Britain and China and using its navy to open Japan to American and European traders. By the 1880s, some American policymakers, often under the influence of the military strategist Alfred Thayer Mahan, saw naval power as the path to Washington greatly increasing the American commercial presence in Eurasia. In 1898, the modernized US Navy won two major battles against Spain, giving the country its first Eurasian territory, in the Philippines. During Theodore Roosevelt's presidency, a 'Great White Fleet' journeyed around the world for more than a year to demonstrate that the United States had arrived as a naval power.

But the Eurasia in which the United States began to assert itself as a naval power was still dominated by the British Empire backed by British naval supremacy. If the size of its territory and population would give the United States a long-term geopolitical advantage over

Britain, the factor that more immediately benefited the United States was oil.[7] Oil geopolitically transformed a state that, in energy scientist and historian Vaclav Smil's words, had, hitherto, been 'an overwhelmingly rural, wood-fuelled society of marginal global import' into an industrial power that by the turn of the century economically and technologically mesmerized Europeans.[8]

In the 1860s, oil began to be extracted for commercial use in Pennsylvania, and by the 1870s one American company, Standard Oil, had acquired pre-eminence in oil refining and transportation. Initially, the demand for oil was for kerosene for light. An *Atlantic* magazine article in 1891 proclaimed that 'we use more kerosene than Bibles' and that kerosene 'has become, by its cheapness, the people's light the world over'.[9]

During these last decades of the nineteenth century, Russia was the only other part of the world where any significant oil production took place. Since Russian oil was largely located in Baku on the landlocked Caspian Sea, initially it could not be exported.[10] But after Russia annexed Batumi—on the south-east coast of the Black Sea—from the Ottoman Empire in 1878, Russian oil could be transported via railway and pipeline from the oil wells in Baku into Europe. Now, American and Russian producers began to compete for consumers. In the 1890s, a fierce competition for European markets ensued between Standard Oil selling American oil and two European businesses—the Nobel Brothers Petroleum Production Company and the Caspian and Black Sea Petroleum Company—selling Russian oil.[11] This commercial rivalry intensified when the companies selling Russian oil used the first oil tankers to take the fuel through the Suez Canal to compete with Standard Oil in Asia. Although at times Standard Oil and the European companies sought to divide world markets between them, each attempt at cooperation collapsed.[12]

For a short time between 1898 and 1902, Russia overtook the United States to become the world's largest oil producer.[13] But the American oil industry retained significant strengths. From 1908, Henry Ford's mass-produced Model T car, made possible by the internal combustion engine, transformed the demand for oil, even though gasoline produced from oil was only one of the fuels on which Ford's new car could run. The gasoline-fuelled car produced in the huge Ford factories in Michigan became the prime symbol of

American technological innovation and industrial consumerism. Although, in 1911, the US Supreme Court ordered Standard Oil to be broken up into competing firms, nothing in American domestic politics could impede the industry's growth. By contrast, Russian politics nearly destroyed the Russian oil industry. Baku and Batumi became revolutionary centres where Stalin learned his trade as a local organizer. During the 1905 revolution, Tatar groups intent on killing Armenians set fire to two-thirds of the Baku oil wells, wrecking the Russian export industry for much of the next decade.[14] Consequently, by the time the First World War began, the preponderance of oil production lay in the Western Hemisphere, with the United States supplying nearly two-thirds of the world's oil and Mexico operating as the world's third largest producer.

American dominance in oil caused intense fear in Europe.[15] Other than Austria-Hungary, the European great powers lacked oil, as did their colonies, with the exceptions of the Dutch East Indies and British Burma. Their hope to compete with the United States lay in the Middle East, which, unlike much of Asia and Africa, had proved relatively resistant to European territorial rule. In 1908, oil had been discovered in Persia, then formally a constitutional monarchy but in practice largely divided into distinct British and Russian spheres of influence. The prospects for oil in Ottoman-controlled Mesopotamia appeared similarly formidable.

The British and German governments wanted to control these Middle Eastern resources. Although British and German firms did cooperate to form the Turkish Petroleum Company consortium in 1912, Middle Eastern oil played a significant part in shaping British–German rivalry before the First World War.[16] If Britain's presence in the southern Gulf and imperial control of India gave it an obvious advantage, Kaiser Wilhelm II began courting a resource relationship with the Ottoman Sultan from the time he assumed the throne. To this end, Deutsche Bank secured the concession from the Ottoman state to build a railway from Konya in Anatolia to Baghdad and Basra that could connect to the line from Berlin to Constantinople. Just as significantly, the right to explore for oil by the track accompanied the concession.

The prospect of oil-fuelled navies encouraged these ambitions. From the late 1890s, naval planners in most of the major powers began to experiment with using oil to fuel their vessels.[17] Initially, this was a far from straightforward technological exercise. As the world's most powerful naval state, Britain had the most to lose if another power made a decisive move, and it was Britain that first acquired the capacity to construct oil-only ships.[18] But committing to them entailed abandoning an energy source Britain enjoyed in domestic abundance for one that could then only be imported from the United States or Burma. In 1911, Winston Churchill, on becoming First Lord of the Admiralty, took the decision that oil should entirely replace coal as the British Navy's energy source. It was, in Churchill's words, 'tak[ing] arms against a sea of troubles'.[19] The only prudent defence in this new world, Churchill believed, was diversity in supply using sea routes that the British Navy could readily protect.[20] To these ends, Herbert Asquith's government, in which Churchill served, bought in 1914 a controlling share in the Anglo-Persian Company, a hitherto privately owned British business with the premier concession in the emerging Persian oil fields and a contract to supply the British Navy.

The First World War accelerated oil's geopolitical importance and reinforced American oil primacy.[21] As the environmental historian Dan Tamir has written, it was during the First World War that 'petroleum became the resource *par excellence* of the twentieth century'.[22] Oil-based navies and the internal combustion engine made access to oil a condition of war. Once the Germans had persuaded the Ottomans to join the Central Powers and the Ottomans shut the Dardanelles, cutting passage from the Black Sea to the Mediterranean, little Russian oil could reach Britain and France. Contrary to Churchill's hopes, Britain found there was one country it ultimately depended upon and one decisive shipping route: the Atlantic. For its part, the German command had largely prepared for a European war fought by moving troops and supplies by coal-powered railways.[23] In a war with oil-fuelled navies and submarines and eventually oil-fuelled trucks and planes, Germany and Austria-Hungary lacked options. Despite the Kaiser's long-standing cultivation of the Ottoman Empire, the only oil the Central Powers controlled in August 1914 was in the Austrian Crown Land of Galicia in north-eastern Austria-Hungary, with no easy means of transporting it to the Empire's naval base in Pola on the Adriatic coast.[24] When Austria-Hungary lost the Battle of Galicia against Russia in 1915, the

Central Powers were left without Galician supply for the best part of a year, ensuring the Central Powers only survived as long as they did by capturing Romania's oil wells.

To counter the Allies' structural energy advantage, Germany had to stop oil coming across the Atlantic. For a while German submarines destroyed countless oil tankers. But once the British Navy finally established a convoy system, Germany could not recover. By late 1917, American-supplied oil ensured that Allied troops were much more mobile than the Central Power forces because they could be moved by motorized transport. In 1918, Germany made a final bid for more oil. Six months after the Brest-Litovsk treaty, the German government struck an agreement with the Bolsheviks for a quarter of Baku's oil production. General Ludendorff drove German troops towards Baku in an unsuccessful attempt to prevent their erstwhile Ottoman ally taking the city.[25] When the war was over, the British foreign secretary pronounced that 'the Allied cause had floated to victory upon a wave of oil'; 80 per cent of that oil was provided by the United States.[26]

The New Financial Emperor Has Few Eurasian Clothes

American financial power in Eurasia reinforced American oil power. Before the war, Britain was the world's dominant creditor. Those responsible for establishing the Federal Reserve System in 1913 saw an American central bank as a means of diminishing British financial power and facilitating the use of dollars for trade in Eurasia.[27] But almost as soon as hostilities began in August 1914, it became clear that Britain and France would require American materials and food to fight the war and American credit to finance their purchases. Soon, gold reserves moved in large volume westwards across the Atlantic, and the American trade surplus in manufacturing goods grew substantially. By the early 1920s, the majority of the world's gold reserveswere in the United States; a few years later, there were, for the first time, more central bank foreign exchange reserves held in dollars than sterling.[28] Britain and France's war debt created severe financial dependency. After Warren Harding won the 1920 presidential election, the British ambassador to Washington wrote a memo bemoaning that the new administration would 'look for the opportunity to treat us as a vassal state so long as the debt remains unpaid'.[29] In 1923, Britain eventually accepted a debt deal that caused the British prime minister, Andrew Bonar Law, to write anonymously to the *Times* newspaper to complain about the harshness of the terms his own chancellor had reluctantly agreed.[30]

Yet despite the massive financial power the United States enjoyed, the actual geopolitical power it could exercise in Eurasia was seriously constrained by geography, ongoing European oil ambitions, and the country's own democratic politics.[31] The legacies of these interwar limits to American power are still pertinent to the geopolitical fault lines at work today, as indeed are the failed bids of the large European states after the First World War to escape dependency on American oil.

The most glaring immediate weakness in American power lay in the Middle East. The principal geopolitical gain available during the First World War was Ottoman territory in the oil-rich Middle East, allied to strategic control of Constantinople and the Dardanelles.[32] But the American president who took the United States into the war, Woodrow Wilson, never declared war on the Ottomans, although this did not stop him in his Fourteen Points for the post-war world pronouncing on the Ottoman Empire and the Dardanelles' fate. After the war ended, the United States was not legally party to any of the treaties pertaining to the Ottoman Empire's dissolution.[33] When, at Versailles, various proposals were floated for an American mandate for administrative rule over various former Ottoman territories without formal annexation, Wilson said that he 'could think of nothing the people of the United States would be less inclined to accept than military responsibility in Asia'.[34]

By contrast, from the summer of 1914, the European powers competed militarily to extend their empires into the Middle East and Anatolia as well as for control of the waters connecting the Black Sea to the Aegean via Constantinople. In taking the Ottoman Empire into the war as a German ally, the Kaiser secured the declaration of an Islamic jihad against Britain, France, and Russia in the hope that a revolt by Muslims from the Middle East to India would procure a German sphere of influence from the Dardanelles to the Persian Gulf.[35] At the start of the war, Britain moved its Indian Army troops to protect the oil refineries at Abadan in Persia and occupied

Basra in Mesopotamia. Later, British imperial forces captured Baghdad and Mosul. During the war, Britain, France, and Russia secretly agreed in the event of victory to divide up the Ottoman Empire, including giving Russia Constantinople, and made other covert agreements to grant Italy much of south-western Anatolia. If Germany had succeeded in its 1918 spring offensive, it would have dominated, in alliance with the Ottomans, the Middle East and the Caucasus and subordinated Persia.[36] As it was, Britain and France forced an armistice on the Ottomans that gave the British control of the Dardanelles and pushed the Ottomans out of the Caucasus, including Baku and Batumi. This proved overambitious: Britain was unable to retain the Dardanelles, the Soviet Union militarily retook the Caucasus, and the British hope that Greece would take Constantinople was dashed by the Turkish National Movement's military success in the Turkish War of Independence. But Britain still emerged from the First World War with the League of Nation mandates to administer Mesopotamia and Palestine, its sphere of influence in Persia not only preserved but more secure from other powers than before, and, by 1923, it had gained the advantage of a demilitarized Dardanelles.[37] Although the Iraqi revolt in 1920 ended the Mesopotamian mandate before it began and Iraq acquired formal sovereignty in 1922, Britain retained control over Iraq as a geopolitical space, leaving London in control of the Persian Gulf from its head to the coastal emirates, which were British protectorates, at its mouth.

Post-war administrations in Washington were acutely aware of the implications of the American absence from the Middle East and the British and French bids for oil independence.[38] Having expended so much oil supplying the Allies, the United States became in 1919 a net importer of oil and remained so for the next three years. Wilson concluded that 'there seemed to be no method by which we could assure ourselves of the necessary supply at home and abroad'.[39] Following the armistice, the British government stopped Standard Oil of New York from pursuing its pre-war claim in Palestine and American geologists moving into Mesopotamia. To American fury, Britain and France then concluded the 1920 San Remo Oil Agreement, giving Deutsche Bank's 25 per cent share of the Turkish Petroleum Company to France.[40] By 1919–20, the reality was that British companies, despite controlling less than 5 per cent of the world's oil supply, now possessed at least 50 per cent of the world's known oil reserves.[41] Subsequently, the US State Department endeavoured to impede negotiations between the Iraqi government and the Turkish Petroleum Company over the pre-war concession granted by the Grand Vizier, claiming it was void.[42] But the Turkish Petroleum Company resecured the concession in 1927, and oil was discovered in Iraq the same year.

Through the second half of the 1920s, the American position did improve. Worries about immediate oil supply were abated by large oil discoveries in Texas. Seeing the benefits of an injection of American capital in the Iraqi oil fields, the British allowed an American consortium—which included Standard Oil of New Jersey and Standard Oil of New York—to join a reconstructed Turkish Petroleum Company that became the Iraq Petroleum Company (IPC). But the American companies remained constrained by Britain and France. The IPC's 1928 Red Line Agreement gave each partner, which meant via the Anglo-Persian Company the British government, a veto on any other independently pursuing oil inside former Ottoman territory as the Ottoman Empire had existed in 1914. This arrangement effectively shut out the American firms in the IPC from exploration around the western Persian Gulf. In 1929, the British government relented enough to let Standard Oil of California drill around the island of Bahrain. When oil was discovered there in 1932, prospects that there was also oil in Saudi Arabia improved. In good part thanks to the duplicitous manoeuvring of the British official Jack Philby who was advising him, the Saudi King granted an exclusive concession for exploration in the kingdom to Standard Oil of California rather than the IPC.[43] In the future, this oil would give Washington leverage over the European governments. But the American commercial presence in Saudi Arabia was first born from American geopolitical weakness and concurrent British geopolitical strength in Persia and Iraq.

*   *   *

Between 1914 and 1941, American democratic politics would also make it impossible for the United States to use its military and financial power to act decisively as a Eurasian power.[44] This domestic constraint was apparent from the start of the First World War. During the war, the American capacity to provide credit to Eurasia emerged independently of the American state. When Wilson was resolutely opposed to American military intervention, the British government turned to Wall Street to finance a transatlantic supply line. One New York bank, JP Morgan, became the purchasing agent and creditor for Britain and France and by extension the rest of the Allies. Wilson's unsuccessful efforts to constrain JP Morgan reflected his knowledge that many voters, especially those in states west of the Mississippi, disliked and distrusted the New York banks. Wilson fought the 1916 presidential election using the campaign slogan 'America First' against a pro-war Republican candidate supported by JP Morgan. When, in April 1917, Wilson did take the United States into the war, he insisted that the fighting would be financed by Liberty Bonds purchased as government debt by millions of American citizens. The republic could not, he believed, be involved in any conflict readily damned as 'a bankers' war' or lacking political support from one coast to the other.[45]

Even the eventual American military entry to the war in 1917 ultimately arose because of a risk that the conflict in Eurasia would spread to the Western Hemisphere. Germany's return in February 1917 to unrestricted submarine warfare in the Atlantic pushed Wilson closer to declaring war on Germany. But one month later, Wilson was still describing the prospect of the United States fighting in Europe as a 'crime'.[46] Only Germany's offer to ally with Mexico against the United States—whereby Germany would support a Mexican annexation of Texas, Arizona, and New Mexico—finally pushed Wilson to declare war, and, even then, exclusively against Germany. This left Britain and France to their war against Austria-Hungary and, rather consequentially, the Ottoman Empire.

When Wilson became a proponent of American leadership in Eurasia, he ignited his own domestic resistance. Anti-war sentiment contributed to the Democrats losing control of both Houses of Congress in 1918. When the new Senate met, Wilson could not ratify the League of Nations provisions of the Versailles treaty. Indeed, the divisions within his own party between more Anglophile Americans on one side and German and Irish Americans on the other demonstrated that any domestic consensus on European matters in the US Congress was near impossible.

Throughout the 1920s and 1930s, the discourse that the First World War was the 'bankers' war' persisted. Members of Congress regularly attacked the New York Federal Reserve Bank President, Benjamin Strong, as a JP Morgan stooge, impeding his efforts to work with European central banks to stabilize European currencies and return them to a fixed value against gold.[47] The 'merchants of death' became a phrase frequently used to describe the relationship between Wall Street and the manufacturing companies that had benefited from JP Morgan's participation in the British and French supply chain. Between 1934 and 1936, a Senate Committee investigated Wall Street's role in the United States entering the First World War, leading Congress to pass neutrality laws in 1935 and 1936, with the second banning loans to belligerents.

Meanwhile, the domestic unpopularity of writing off any Allied war debt shaped the entire Versailles settlement on reparations and made the peace Wilson had supposedly sponsored inherently unstable. The New York Federal Reserve, which was operationally responsible for dealing with the European states' financial obligations and credit requirements, favoured the reduction and perhaps cancellation of Allied war debts.[48] But, again, Congress insisted on curtailing the executive, passing legislation in 1922 for a World War Foreign Debt Commission to negotiate the terms of British and French loan repayments.[49] So long as the American president could not concede on Allied war debt, Britain and France, fiscally enfeebled by the war as they were, could not lessen their demands for German reparations. When, in the early 1930s, most European states finally repudiated these debts, Congress prohibited any state that had defaulted on their loans from borrowing in the United States.[50]

Yet the domestic constraints on American financial power paradoxically ensured there could be no American escape from Eurasian affairs. The French and Belgian occupation of the Ruhr to extract German reparations and Germany's hyperinflation ignited the prospect of war and financial meltdown. Rather than entertain these risks, the Harding administration agreed to use American financial power to end the Ruhr crisis via the Dawes Plan, with JP Morgan making a large loan to France and organizing with the Fed a massive bond issue for Germany, in which the American government encouraged ordinary American citizens to invest. Sustained by American credit, Germany could make reparation payments.[51] But this made American financial stability, as well as American democratic politics around savings, vulnerable to the risk that Europeans had insufficient dollars to service their debt.[52] It also offered a path for Germany to wriggle away from Versailles. Since American politicians could not politically privilege the French and British claim to German money over American bondholders receiving interest from Germany, they had acquired an incentive to shift Britain and France away from reparations, regardless of what consequently ensued for the balance of power in Europe.[53]

Between 1929 and 1932, these American democratic constraints played their part in the end of the financial side of the Versailles treaty. Under depression conditions, Germany could not pay reparations or service dollar debt. When, at the 1932 Lausanne conference, President Hoover finally brokered an agreement ending those reparations in exchange for an Allied debt-reduction plan, Congress rejected the proposal. Since Congress would also not authorize new American credit, this left Germany free from its financial obligations under Versailles and, ironically, free also to repudiate its American debts.[54]

Franklin Roosevelt's response to what by 1933 had become a cross-Atlantic banking crisis weakened American financial power further. For Roosevelt, the domestic corollary to geopolitical financial power was Wall Street's political influence. On his first day in office, Roosevelt closed all the banks and suspended the export or private holding of gold. Contrary to almost all advice he received, he then removed the dollar from the gold standard in the hope of stabilizing the banking system and raising prices for domestic producers. To many this seemed incomprehensible since the United States still possessed the world's largest gold reserves.[55] But Roosevelt was determined to prioritize the domestic economy—for reasons that will be discussed in chapter seven. He dealt the final blow to the gold standard when, from his yachting holiday off the New England coast, he sent a cable for release at the 1933 World Monetary and Economic conference in London telling the American negotiators that they should not concern themselves with the 'old fetishes of so-called international bankers'.[56]

If the First World War had created American financial power, the peace had shattered it. Between 1924 and 1932, American presidents, the Fed, and JP Morgan had endeavoured to use that power to stabilize Europe. But the constraints Congress placed on managing the debt and the sheer volume of American lending to Germany rendered the United States impotent during the economic and geo-political crisis unleashed in Europe by the 1929 crash.[57] The monet-ary instability let loose by the resulting German crisis spread back across the Atlantic. Thereafter, the American president had to choose between domestic politics and the geopolitical sphere. Roosevelt made his America-first choice with some dramatic flair. Yet, given that the American capacity to act coherently in Eurasia had been domestically inhibited from the time the First World War began, that he chose as he did in a national economic emergency could scarcely be surprising.

American Energy Power Returns

The economic and political disorder that materialized in Eurasia after the 1929–33 crisis allowed Germany, Japan, Italy, and the Soviet Union to engage in violent territorial expansion. In this sense, the United States had proved an extremely ineffectual Eurasian power. But in moving the world towards an even more catastrophic war, the first three unleashed American energy power, ultimately making American military and financial power an overwhelming presence across much of Eurasia.

Like its predecessor, the Second World War is inseparable from energy geopolitics. In the technological age of air power, the need war generated for oil was overwhelming. This was overt in the case of Japan's imperial expansion. It was no less consequential in Europe. In the years between 1919 and 1939, all the major European powers wanted to be rid of importing oil from the Western Hemisphere and, in contrasting and conflicting ways, sought energy supplies in Eurasia that they could control.

Unlike Britain and France, Germany did not have an empire or spheres of influence in the Middle East and was near entirely dependent at the start of the interwar years on oil coming from the Western Hemisphere.[58] To try to reverse this weakness, Weimar governments from 1926 actively supported IG Farben's project to develop a synthetic fuel plant at Leuna in Eastern Germany whereby coal would be transformed into liquid fuel through hydrogenation. For Gustav Stresemann, the German foreign minister, this project, helped from 1929 by Standard Oil of New Jersey, represented a German reason of state. Germany had, he said, no foreign policy without the German chemical company and coal.[59]

Wanting war, the Nazis saw ending Germany's foreign energy dependency entirely as an urgent imperative. Hitler believed that the need to import raw materials and oil had brought about defeat in 1918.[60] His 1936 Four-Year Plan presumed that Germany could be fully independent from imported oil by 1940.[61] But Nazi Germany never solved its oil problem. Although the Leuna plant delivered synthetic fuel to the Luftwaffe, Hitler had not achieved German oil independence when he attacked Poland in 1939. With Britain's naval blockade shutting Germany off from importing any more oil from the Western Hemisphere, Germany was instead dependent on supply from Romania, the Soviet Union, and, after June 1940, French reserves.

Militarily, the Nazi strategy required Germany again to use submarine warfare to prevent the United States supplying Britain. But the Germans could make no decisive breakthrough in 1940 and 1941 against British oil supplies via the Atlantic. With Germany's oil supplies from the Soviet Union coming under increasing strain and Soviet troops having captured north-eastern Romania, Hitler gambled on invading the Soviet Union. Hitler's motives have long aroused historical controversy. But Germany simply could not win a war in which the United States was supplying the British Empire without securing control of Soviet oil, 90 per cent of which came from the Caucasus.[62] Whatever other motives, born of his apocalyptic obsession with Lebensraum and hatred of Bolshevism, Hitler brought to bear on Operation Barbarossa, and however far those preoccupations shaped the catastrophe that followed, oil weakness was a near sufficient motive for the invasion. The German failure at Stalingrad set Germany on an inevitable path to defeat. Shortly after, the Allies finally vanquished Rommel's oil-starved forces in North Africa, allowing the Italian campaign to begin.[63]

Britain failed too in its bid for energy independence during the interwar years. British governments expended huge efforts in the 1920s and 1930s on establishing a secure oil supply extracted and transported by British-owned companies from within the British Empire and sphere of influence in the Middle East. A memo to the War Cabinet prior to the San Remo agreement read: 'The overwhelming extent of our dependence on the United

States of America for fuel oil during the War, and the rapidly growing use of oil in the mercantile marine makes it important that every endeavour should be made to open sources of supply under British control.'[64]

But by the mid-1930s, even as it had succeeded in cutting American imports to around 10 per cent of its total requirements, Britain was still receiving more than half of its oil from the Western Hemisphere, notably Venezuela and Mexico. There was limited output from the British Iraqi oil wells and Britain could not by itself militarily protect its Iranian supply. Italy's invasion of Abyssinia in 1935, and the American unwillingness to support oil sanctions against Mussolini, critically exposed Britain's weakness in the event of a European war. So long as Italy, backed by German air power, could close the Mediterranean entrance to the Suez Canal to British tankers, oil from the Anglo-Iranian Oil Company in the Gulf could only reach Britain more slowly, coming around the Cape of Good Hope.[65] After the Abyssinian crisis, the British government started planning for a war in which the Mediterranean would be closed to Britain, an eventuality that ensued between June 1940, when Italy entered the Second World War, and 1943, when the Allies prevailed against Italy. For all the resources invested in energy independence, in the moment of geopolitical revelation Britain had no choice but to pay dollars to American companies for American oil.[66]

Believing that they must not again be dependent on an Atlantic supply in any future war with Germany, the French used the capital procured in the San Remo Agreement to create the entirely French-owned French Petroleum Company (the future Total and now TotalEnergies). They did somewhat better with output from Iraq than Britain but were left dependent on Britain's military position in the country. Unable to protect the only Middle Eastern supply it controlled, France became a significant importer of Soviet oil. In the early 1920s, the Soviet oil industry was in a decrepit state. But from the mid-1920s, Standard Oil of New Jersey helped the Soviet state reconstruct the sector. From 1929 to 1933, the Soviets built up substantial exports to a number of European countries, including Britain.[67] Although Soviet exports peaked in 1933, in 1936 nearly half of French imports still came from the Soviet Union.[68] In the summer of 1939, the discovery of gas in south-west France encouraged the French government to form several state agencies to explore for oil, but it was far too late for the hope of a domestic supply to make any difference.[69]

If the British and French governments were unable to exploit the Middle East as they had hoped at the start of the interwar years, the Second World War also opened up the space for future American influence in the region. At the beginning of the war, the Roosevelt administration judged that, despite the Californian Arabian Standard Oil Company—renamed Aramco in 1944—holding the oil concession, it was for the British to protect the Saudi oil fields.[70] In 1941, Roosevelt turned down a request for financial assistance from the Saudi King, Ibn Saud. But in 1943, the sheer volume of oil being used in the war changed his mind. Although Saudi Arabia was a neutral country, he agreed a Lend-Lease arrangement with King Saud, proclaiming the kingdom 'vital' to the US' defence. Asserting what he hoped was future American supremacy over Britain in Middle Eastern oil production, he also moved to end the Red Line Agreement to allow Standard Oil New Jersey, which was a partner in the Iraq Petroleum Company, to join Aramco.[71]

This new US–Saudi relationship would become a permanent feature of the post–Second World War world. It was also though structurally unstable. For oil reasons, the United States had acquired a strategic alliance with an Arab state, while at home there was strong support for a Jewish state in the territory under the British mandate.[72] Under the conflicting pressures, Roosevelt moved from declaring his commitment to a Jewish state during the 1944 presidential election campaign to accepting Arab opposition to it after his meeting in February 1945 with King Ibn Saud.[73] Later, the State Department and the CIA advised Roosevelt's successor, Harry Truman, against recognizing Israel because they feared that a Jewish state would be a geopolitical burden.[74] When Truman rebuffed them, the strategic predicament of trying to maintain both Arab and Jewish support, which had previously bedevilled imperial British strategy in the Middle East, moved to Washington.[75]

The Shape of Things to Come

Much has obviously changed around American geopolitical power since the period between the two world wars. Yet the peculiar trajectory of the United States' first projection of power in Eurasia has left a lasting legacy. Notably, American democratic politics remains a significant constraint on American commitments in Eurasia. Economically, the European commercial and political interests that separated Wall Street from voters west of the Mississippi during the First World War were partly replicated in the divergence between corporations that constructed supply chains that ran through China and those manufacturing workers in the Rust Belt whose jobs disappeared during the 2000s. Franklin Roosevelt's monetary nationalism was born in a domestic political space with some similarities to Trump's trade war with China in the name of rebuilding a national manufacturing economy. Militarily, the Middle Eastern wars have been sharply domestically contested like American participation in the First World War. Congress has constrained American presidents over the so-called 'forever wars' in the Middle East as it once did war in Europe.

For the large European states bereft of domestic oil, the failed bids for energy independence constituted a perhaps decisive part of how European-dominated Eurasia came to an end. The age of oil would not allow for a European world power or a European continental empire. Now, one attraction of green energy in Europe is that foreign oil and gas dependency in the decades after the Second World War was a world where American presidents and the US Congress used American financial power to constrain European politicians' ability to act around that reliance. For nearly four decades from the 1970s, Washington reluctantly tolerated Germany's dependency on Russian oil and gas because the United States had neither the domestic supply nor enough wherewithal in the Middle East to offer an alternative to it. But during the 2010s, in a world where both American and Russian oil and gas were resurgent, this connection became a significant geopolitical fault line tied to Ukraine's independence, NATO enlargement, and Germany's weak military capability. The Russia–China–Iran relationship has complicated the fallout from these issues further because all three European NATO members that were party to the 2015 Iran nuclear deal want a gas relationship with Iran.

The origins of the United States' present engagement with the geopolitics of European energy dependency lie in what happened after the Second World War. There was one overriding caveat to American geopolitical power in mid-twentieth century Eurasia: victory in the war in Europe depended on a military alliance with the

Soviet Union, a state that, like Germany, had invaded Poland in 1939 before turning aggressively on Finland, the Baltic republics, and parts of Romania. The Soviet Union was for a while anyway a formidable geopolitical rival. As Soviet oil exports in the late 1920s and early 1930s showed, it also potentially offered the European states energy options that would strengthen that geopolitical power.[76]

Prior to Hitler's invasion of the Soviet Union, the risk existed that an axis between Eurasia's two most powerful land powers could carve up Europe and the Middle East between them. This geopolitical relationship had a history. Soviet–German cooperation preceded Hitler and Stalin taking power. Under the 1922 Rapallo Treaty, Germany used the Soviet Union for some rearmament and military training, and recultivated economic relations. Earlier still, Bismarck had seen the value of an accommodation between Germany and Russia and secured the secret 1887 Reinsurance Treaty. Although Kaiser Wilhelm did not renew the treaty that, among other provisions, guaranteed German neutrality if Russia bid for the Bosphorus and the Dardanelles, he offered Russia during the 1904–5 Russo-Japanese war 'a continental alliance' against Britain in the Far East, suggesting it could be a prelude to a 'United States of Europe'.[77] In his 1904 essay 'The geographical pivot of history', the British geographer Halford Mackinder warned that railways stretching from the western Russian border with Germany to Vladivostok on the Pacific coast could conceivably lead Russia, if allied to Germany, to become 'the empire of the world'.[78] Oil had the potential to reinforce this geographical logic by tying German markets to Russian resources. Hitler destroyed that convergence for an impossible and hideous vision of conquest and genocide. But to prevent any Soviet–German axis re-emerging in the post-war world, the United States would have to take responsibility for securing West Germany an oil supply from the Persian Gulf.[79]

2

The Impossible Oil Guarantee

In November 2014, oil prices had been sliding for five months. Contrary to its usual response to falling prices, the producer cartel OPEC decided to maintain production levels. Now, prices crashed. Having stood above $100 a barrel in the summer of 2014, by early 2016 oil prices had collapsed to not much more than $30.

Saudi Arabia drove OPEC's move. Saudi motives were complex and potentially contradictory. Saudi Arabia's first problem was the American shale oil boom. Shale oil is the principal form of oil that is inaccessible by conventional drilling. It is largely extracted by hydraulic fracturing, known colloquially as fracking. After three decades of overall, albeit far from linear, decline, shale oil and gas restored the United States' position as a major energy producer. In 2010, the United States produced a total of 8.6 million barrels of crude oil, natural gas plant liquids, and other liquids a day; by 2014, that output was 13 million and, by 2019, it would be 18.4 million.[1] Between 2010 and 2014, American oil imports from OPEC countries fell by a third; in 2019 they would be half their 2014 level.[2] Meanwhile, American exports grew by around three-quarters between 2010 and 2014; by 2019 they would be around 360 per cent higher than the start of the decade and outpace Saudi Arabia's.[3] For the Saudis, an American oil industry with a growing export-capacity was a commercial rival in Asian markets, complicating the entire US–Saudi relationship.

But Saudi Arabia's problems in late 2014 were also more local to the Middle East. Despite strong Saudi support for the Syrian rebels, the Syrian regime backed by its Iranian rival and Russia remained intact. Since the Russian and Iranian governments were dependent on oil revenues, lower oil prices opened a path to pressurizing each to retreat in Syria. One Saudi diplomat, quoted by the *New York Times* in early 2015, declared that 'if oil can serve to bring peace in Syria, I don't know how Saudi Arabia would back away from trying to reach a deal'.[4]

Whichever Saudi motive mattered more, falling prices achieved neither objective. Although shale output fell, many loss-making shale companies had sufficient access to cheap credit to keep going. In Syria, Russia and Iran were undeterred. Indeed, Russia intervened militarily in Syria ten months after OPEC's decision. Iran's oil revenues were, meanwhile, given a significant boost when the Iran nuclear deal, about which Saudis had grave reservations, removed many sanctions on Iran's oil exports.

Unsurprisingly, this conjunction of an oil-price war, the shared failure in Syria, and disagreement over Iran inflamed US–Saudi relations. In April 2016, the Saudi government threatened to sell its portfolio of Treasury assets if Congress passed a bill allowing US citizens to sue the Saudi government over 9/11. When Congress passed the bill, Obama vetoed it, only for Congress to override his veto. Back in Saudi Arabia, Mohammed Bin Salman (MBS), soon to become the crown prince, announced a plan to end what he called the country's 'addiction to oil'.[5] As if to warn Saudi Arabia that its previous indispensability might be ending, the next month the US Treasury published details about Saudi Arabia's dollar assets, having for four decades declined to do so.

By contrast, from the latter part of 2016, Saudi–Russian relations markedly improved. With shale having proved an immovable part of oil markets, both OPEC and Russia wanted a return to higher prices. In September 2016, Vladimir Putin and the Saudi King struck an agreement to cooperate on oil. Three months later, OPEC and Russia agreed to act in a new cartel, dubbed OPEC Plus, and cut production. In October 2017, the Saudi King went on an unprecedented state visit to Moscow, where the two leaders agreed among other things on Saudi investment in Russia energy projects and that Russia would sell anti-aircraft missiles to Riyadh.

However, this alliance was always vulnerable to its perverse logic. By allying together in the face of shale to push prices back up, Saudi Arabia and Russia helped shale oil producers too. The two governments also did not share gas interests. Whereas Saudi Arabia does not export gas, Russia is the world's leading gas exporter. American shale gas exports transported by sea compete with Russian gas carried both by pipelines and shipping. Predictably, Putin's willingness to tolerate the collateral advantages OPEC Plus delivered to American oil producers was conditioned by how American politicians acted towards Russia's gas interests in Europe. For Putin, a line appeared to be crossed when, in December 2019, the US Congress imposed new sanctions on companies involved in building a second Nord Stream pipeline under the Baltic Sea between Russia and Germany, which led the main contractor to suspend work with around 150 kilometres of the 1,230-kilometre pipeline left to build.

Beginning just weeks later, the Covid-19 crisis quickly unravelled the Saudi–Russian oil alliance. When Chinese demand fell and oil prices started sliding, Putin saw an opportunity to inflict severe damage on the shale oil industry and reduce shale gas firms' ability to compete in European markets. But for the Saudis, China was their single largest customer and a rapid increase in price was essential. Rebuffed by Putin, MBS decided over the weekend of 7–8 March 2020 to flood the market with Saudi oil to try to secure what demand remained. With that decision, the oil price crashed, jeopardizing the future of the American shale industry. For the first time, the US, Saudi Arabia, and Russia agreed a collective approach to realizing some kind of floor. In forcing MBS to back down, Trump reportedly told the Saudi crown prince in a phone call on 2 April that if he did not, Congress would legislate to withdraw military support from the kingdom.[6]

Geopolitically, the world has in part become more unstable over the past decade because, as the United States has acquired more energy power, relations between the world's three principal oil producers have become more complex. Meanwhile, the United States and Russia have begun to compete to supply gas to Europe, as they had done over oil at the end of the nineteenth and beginning of the twentieth centuries. To see the disruptive force of this structural change in American power, we need to resume the story of that power through the Cold War years. Here, we can see why, even at the height of its military power, the United States struggled to exercise coherent geopolitical influence in the Middle East and why Russia's energy power is a persistent feature of the geopolitical landscape that structurally divides NATO.

Eurasia Divided

If nuclear weapons, a navy that could maintain open shipping for trade, an international reserve currency that other states needed to use for imports, and domestic oil constituted power in the post-1945 world, the United States had them all. In deploying this power to stabilize the post-war Eurasian world, the Roosevelt and Truman administrations initially counted on the dollar. During the Second World War, the Roosevelt administration sought to establish a dollar-based international monetary system.[7] At the Bretton Woods monetary conference in 1944, Harry Dexter White—the senior American negotiator—insisted that the dollar alone be convertible into gold and other currencies be pegged to the dollar. In demanding a metallic basis for the dollar's pre-eminence, he wanted to stop other states engaging in significant currency devaluations without American consent.[8] Indeed, in providing credit for other states to maintain their currency parities via the International Monetary Fund (IMF), he thought the United States would control the terms on which other states accessed dollars.[9] He also wanted that access to dollars to be restricted by geopolitics: the Soviet Union would have a credit line but Germany, which the American Treasury wanted industrially annihilated, and Japan would not.

However, this reliance on financial power took little account of military realities in 1945. Not wishing to see permanent American military engagement in Eurasia, Roosevelt promised that American troops would leave Europe within two years. He wanted, he said at that year's Yalta conference, to see a world free of alliances, spheres of influence, and the balance of power.[10] Instead, there would, he hoped, be a security structure whereby the war's premier four victorious allies—the United States, the Soviet Union, Britain, and China—would collectively police world affairs. Yet this principle of collective security offered no means to force a Soviet withdrawal from Eastern Europe. Nor did American financial power, since once Harry Truman became president and discontinued lending to the Soviet Union, Stalin had no incentive to continue with IMF membership.[11]

Unable to prevent Soviet expansion, Truman and his successors chose to contain the Soviet Union as a competitor without recourse to war. For the first years of the Cold War, this meant accepting Soviet rule in Eastern Europe and a divided Germany, defending Western Europe and the division of Korea at the 38th parallel, and preventing Soviet entry into the Mediterranean as a gateway to the Middle East, where Washington feared Iran would fall under Soviet influence.[12] For Truman, even this seemed too much militarily and economically for the United States to bear alone. The Mediterranean was supposed to be Britain's responsibility. But by early 1947, Britain could no longer afford to continue economic and military aid to the Greek and Turkish governments. In justifying taking over these commitments to Congress, Truman expounded the Truman Doctrine, pronouncing that any 'free peoples' could expect the United States to defend them with economic aid.

As the practical basis of post-war West European security, the Truman administration initially relied again on economic aid, here provided through the Marshall Plan, not a military alliance. Allied to the American nuclear umbrella, financing Western European economic reconstruction would, Truman hoped, vanquish any Soviet military threat and turn the tide against the Communist parties in Italy and France. But his hope rested on Western European political conditions that did not yet exist. For the Marshall Plan to succeed, Western Europe had, the Truman administration judged, to unify economically around an independent and prosperous West Germany. In this respect, West Germany was to be treated entirely differently from Germany after the First World War, or indeed from how Roosevelt's Treasury had envisaged Germany's position. The United States would provide financing via direct aid, not loans, and protect West Germany against reparation demands and debt repayment. It would also use its financial power to push the other West European states to join West Germany in an economic federation or confederation centred around a customs union.[13] In this political logic, the West European states were economically and geopolitically weak and confronted with a common enemy; the historical remedy for such political disorder was, as the Americans themselves had shown in 1776, confederation leading to federation.[14]

Realizing any such political move on American terms proved impossible. Although the West European states were obliged as a condition of Marshall aid to draw up plans for an economic federation, they got little further than an agreement to reduce trade barriers and organize payments. Since they had trading interests outside Europe that were not dollar-based, both the British and French governments were deeply reluctant to acquiesce. For them, West European security depended not on economic federation but on a military alliance with Washington that acknowledged a German as well as a Soviet threat to peace.[15] In 1948, Britain, France, and the Benelux governments agreed to establish a Western Union as a mutual defence pact in the hope they could eventually persuade the Americans to join too. They were vindicated when the Soviet blockade of Berlin caused Truman to change his mind. The result was NATO, committing the United States, along with Canada, to a treaty obligation to respond to any attack not just on the five Western Union states but also Denmark, Iceland, Italy, Norway, and Portugal.[16]

NATO represented a massive American departure. For the first time, the United States was committed to a peacetime Eurasian alliance. NATO's very name—the *North Atlantic* Treaty Organization—rather obfuscated this geopolitical shift by collapsing the distinction between the Western Hemisphere and one part of Eurasia. Yet Italy and Portugal's membership belied any notion that the Monroe doctrine had been redefined to include the North Atlantic. From the start, NATO also raised hard questions about who would pay for the alliance's military commitments, including American military bases in Europe. In principle, each member state was required to make payments as a proportion of GDP. In practice the near bankrupt West European states promised more money than they actually contributed.[17]

As well as its long-term geographical and fiscal fault lines, NATO left the immediate matter of West German security unresolved. The creation of the European Coal and Steel Community (ECSC) in 1951 had established some basis for a Franco-German rapprochement. Indeed, for its strongest proponents the ECSC was supposed to make war between France and West Germany impossible by establishing supranational control over Germany's coal resources and steel industry in the Ruhr. This though left the question of West Germany's position in regard to the Soviet Union unresolved. Here, the Korean War convinced Truman that West German rearmament was necessary. But NATO's structure ensured that taking West Germany inside it required a national army for a fully sovereign West Germany. Finding that option unpalatable, the French government offered as an alternative the abortive European Defence Community (EDC).[18] Yet this option entailed each member state immediately placing its national military force under a supranational command with a long-term objective of moving to political union, which Britain would not contemplate. In 1952, the French government finally agreed with the five other ECSC members to establish an EDC. But, despite enormous American pressure, the French Parliament refused to ratify the treaty. Since Eisenhower was not prepared to back down on West German rearmament, West Germany instead had to enter NATO.

By 1955, NATO provided the framework for West European security, yet its foundations were shaky. There were too many internal European geopolitical tensions for a West European security federation, considerable costs for the Americans in a financially skewed NATO, and significant risks for Western Europe in accepting the American nuclear umbrella when the Cold War was spreading well beyond Europe. Inside Europe, if security was the strongest rationale for federation, whether as a customs union or a defence community, NATO made this political logic redundant. Yet if the American security commitment were to prove unreliable, the only basis left for European federation would be economic. In the 1960s, de Gaulle would try to overturn this conundrum and fail. Consequently, when the European Union did emerge from the 1990s as something akin to an economic federation—via the single market and a partial monetary union—it remained dependent on outsourcing its security to an inherently unstable NATO.

* * * *

It was in these decades after the Second World War that oil became the world's most important energy source. In 1950, oil constituted around 20 per cent of total world energy consumption. By 1960, that proportion had risen to 27 per cent. By 1970, it had jumped to 40 per cent.[19] In the United States, oil had replaced coal as the single biggest energy source by 1950, and between 1950 and 1970 total oil consumption doubled.[20] In France, oil represented more than three-fifths of total energy consumption by 1970; in Italy that proportion was almost three-quarters.[21] While oil mattered during the two world wars and the interwar years for military power, from the 1950s onwards it came to matter for domestic economies and everyday life, not least in relation to transportation. Although the United States had moved towards high levels of car ownership in the 1920s, only in the 1960s did European countries reach comparable levels.[22]

Well before this massive expansion in consumption, the question of from where the West European countries, all lacking a domestic supply, could import oil was a crucial geopolitical concern. As the Cold War began, the Truman administration encouraged West European governments towards using more oil since with Poland under Soviet control they could not depend on Polish coal exports. But increasing West European peacetime oil dependency came with risks. Truman and his advisers wished to control the sources of West European supply. They did not want Western Europe or Japan to accept Soviet oil, and, in 1949, the administration imposed an embargo on Soviet imports.[23]

But nor did Truman wish Western Europe and Japan to recreate any of their previous dependency on Western Hemisphere imports, preferring to preserve American and Venezuelan supply for American use in a world where the largest reserves lay in Saudi Arabia, the Soviet Union, Iran, and Iraq.[24] Consequently, Western Europe was left to rely on oil from the Middle East, with the United States acting only as a supplier of last resort.[25]

This strategy relied on American support for infrastructure that would transport oil from the Middle East to Europe as well as to Japan. In Japan's case, tankers moving down the Persian Gulf were the only option. But for Western Europe, the Truman administration also supported the construction of a new pipeline—Tapline, also known as the Trans-Arabian pipeline —to take oil from Saudi Arabia to Sidon on the Lebanese coast via Syria. Once built, Tapline complemented the Iraq Petroleum Company's old pipeline network running from Iraq to the eastern Mediterranean coast.

Oil supplied to Western Europe from the Middle East also raised issues around the dollar's primacy. Britain could buy oil in sterling from the British companies in Iraq and Iran, and British politicians were acutely aware that sterling oil was a significant cushion for the British balance of payments.[26] Given the dollar shortage in Western Europe, sterling oil was also attractive to others. If the West Europeans were to buy oil from the American companies in the Middle East, they needed dollars. Consequently, providing dollars for oil was one part of the rationale for the Marshall Plan: perhaps around 20 per cent of Marshall aid went in one way or another on oil payments.[27]

But a fundamental fault line ran through this American conception of post-war Eurasia. Even though they thought of the Middle East as a site of the Cold War, American presidents from Truman to Johnson were unwilling to station American troops in the Middle East or commit the American Navy to heavy-duty service in the Persian Gulf. Fearing both an overstretch of American military commitments and domestic unpopularity, they, consequently, needed Britain to maintain its empire in the Middle East, even as India's independence had stripped Britain of military resources that it had historically relied upon to police the Persian Gulf.[28] During these early Cold War years, American planning for a war with Moscow required air attacks deployed from Britain's military bases in Egypt.[29] To this end, Truman financially supported Britain developing the Abu Sueir base at Suez. But Washington also worried that Britain's ongoing imperial presence in the Middle East was destructive. Accordingly, Truman's immediate successor, Dwight Eisenhower, wanted to accommodate Arab nationalism directed against Britain. After Gamal Abdel Nasser came to power in Egypt in 1953, Eisenhower used American financial power to push Britain to withdraw from the Suez Canal zone and close the Abu Sueir base.[30] When Nasser then turned Egypt towards the Soviet Union, Eisenhower could only encourage Britain to form an anti-Soviet military alliance with Iran, Iraq, Pakistan, and Turkey. He refused to contemplate American membership of this Baghdad Pact.

Turkey too posed awkward issues in the 1950s for the American approach to Eurasia that retain their purchase today. After Stalin had given the Turkish government an ultimatum in 1946 to allow joint Soviet–Turkish control over the Dardanelles, Truman had ordered American ships into the Mediterranean and authorized plans for air operations. Whatever Truman's rhetorical grandiosity about why aid to Greece and Turkey was necessary, in practice energy realism prevailed; as Truman said in private about these Mediterranean commitments, 'look at a map'.[31] For Truman, Greece and Turkey had to be defended as bulwarks against the Soviet Union turning to the Middle East for oil, even as, in fact, Stalin offered little to the Greek communists. Not uncoincidentally, on the same day Truman asked Congress to finance Greece and Turkey, the four big American oil companies signed a collective agreement to participate together in Aramco.[32]

Yet when the Cold War stretched to the Middle East, Turkey's absence from NATO exposed the limits of a security alliance focused on Western Europe. In 1952, the Truman administration resolved this contradiction with Turkish and Greek accession to NATO. But this move produced sharp internal NATO divisions, with some European members preferring a clear demarcation between Western European and Middle Eastern security. Ever since—as will be discussed in the next chapter—there have been persistent questions about a number of European states' willingness to defend Turkey as a NATO member.[33]

For all this incoherence, the American military absence from the Middle East did not mean an eschewal of American coercive force in the region. Indeed, it could not. Consequently, the Central Intelligence Agency (CIA), established by Truman with authority to engage in covert action against other states that could plausibly be denied, became active in the region. After the Syrian Parliament chose not to ratify the agreement to route Tapline through Syria, the CIA engineered a coup to ensure a government that would proceed with the pipeline.[34] The CIA also proved the means for extending American assistance to Britain in Iran. When a new Iranian prime minister, Mohammad Mosaddegh, nationalized the Anglo-Iranian Oil Company in 1951 and terminated the concession, Britain enforced a blockade in the Persian Gulf against Iranian oil exports. While the Truman administration tried to broker a compromise, Eisenhower was persuaded that the CIA should act with British intelligence to remove Mosaddegh from power.[35] In the short term, this intervention required the Eisenhower administration to push American companies into a new consortium with an Iranian national company to rebuild the Iranian oil sector. In the long term, it acutely damaged American relations with Iran, and turned the Middle East into an even bigger strategic burden for the United States.[36]

Atlantic Splinter

In 1956, the inherent tensions of the United States acting as an oil guarantor for its allies via a supply coming from a part of the world where it lacked military power produced a profound geopolitical crisis whose monumental consequences still reverberate.[37] Too often seen primarily as a story about post-war British power, the Suez crisis shattered the idea that the United States would always act as an oil supplier of last resort to its allies, reintroduced Soviet oil into Western Europe, and ended the illusion American presidents held that they could keep the United States militarily out of the Middle East.

The crisis began when Nasser nationalized the Suez Canal and shut it to Israeli shipping. In 1956, around 70 per cent of Western Europe's oil passed from the Persian Gulf up through the Canal. Immediately, Anthony Eden, the British prime minister, told Eisenhower that he believed that if Nasser did not back down force should be used to stop him, and in the event of the Canal being closed 'supplementary [oil] supplies for a time from your side of the world' might be necessary.[38] Eisenhower replied to Eden's letter by saying that unless it was absolutely demonstrated that all peaceful means had been exhausted 'there would be a reaction that could very seriously affect our people's feeling towards our Western Allies' with quite possibly 'the most far-reaching consequences'.[39] When, in October 1956, Britain, France, and Israel launched unilateral military action against Egypt, Eisenhower, just days away from a presidential election, reacted furiously. With the Canal shut, the Iraq Petroleum Company pipeline sabotaged by the Syrian army, and Saudi Arabia embargoing exports to Britain and France, Eisenhower refused to release supplies from the American emergency programme.[40] 'They can', he said, 'boil in their own oil so to speak.'[41] Used to purchasing oil in sterling, Britain was now confronted with dollar-denominated imports from the Western Hemisphere. When Khrushchev then threatened, albeit as a bluff, nuclear attacks on Britain and France, Eisenhower's Treasury prevented Britain drawing dollars from its IMF quota.[42] Immediately, the British government terminated its military action without consulting the French or Israeli governments.

The crisis necessarily exposed the incoherencies in the American approach to the Middle East, which simultaneously encouraged West European oil dependency on the region, relied on British military power, and accommodated the Arab nationalism that was pushing the British Empire in the Middle East towards its end. Afterwards, Eisenhower tried to reconstruct American influence via the more conservative Arab states. Under the Eisenhower Doctrine, the Saudi King, in alliance with Iraq, was supposed to become the regional leader and provide an alternative Arab pivot to the burgeoning Egypt–Syria axis.[43] But radical Arab nationalism could not be contained within state borders. In February 1958, Egypt and Syria formed a political union—the United Arab Union. Over the following months, the Saudi King was forced to appoint the more radical crown prince as a prime minister, and a group of military officers toppled the Iraqi monarchy and allied the country with the new Egyptian–Syrian state. With the British military having now lost its bases in Iraq, it could no longer reach the Gulf by air from Turkey and had to rely on an operational base at Aden at the eastern entrance to the Red Sea.[44] As the British position deteriorated, Eisenhower became the first American president to use military force in the Middle East by ordering troops into Lebanon to prop up the pro-American government in Beirut.[45] But this did not represent a change in strategy, only a reaction to the chaos of events. For the next decade, American policy became ever more focused on keeping Britain committed to its small Gulf protectorates and position at Aden.

Suez also inflicted severe long-term damage on NATO's cohesion. West European dismay at American action was widespread. The West German chancellor, Konrad Adenauer, described the British and French military action 'as an act of European raison d'état'.[46] Eisenhower's actions during the Suez crisis accelerated the intergovernmental conference about creating what became the European Economic Community (EEC) and the European Atomic Energy Community (EURATOM). In the belief he could secure a decisive French commitment to proceed with the EEC and EURATOM, Adenauer went to Paris to offer his support to the French premier, Guy Mollet. After the British prime minister, Anthony Eden, called Mollet to say that he had succumbed to Eisenhower's pressure, Adenauer told Mollet, 'we have no time to waste. Europe will be your revenge.'[47]

But Suez also exposed West European divisions around security that made confederation or federation difficult. The last Fourth Republic French governments concluded that France needed nuclear weapons to lessen French security and technological dependency on the United States.[48] By 1956, France had already started a nuclear programme and saw in EURATOM a means to complete it. Adenauer, by contrast, wanted to strengthen European defence capacity without jeopardizing NATO, which meant enticing Britain into any new European confederation or federation. But the British government, under Harold Macmillan, wanted to preserve NATO and still did not wish to join a European customs union.

These post-Suez conflicts could not be resolved. Under Charles de Gaulle's leadership, French policy became ever more confrontational. De Gaulle wanted geopolitical, as well as economic, distance from both the United States and Britain, culminating in him withdrawing France from NATO's integrated military command in 1966 and twice vetoing British applications to join the EEC. He also wanted to move the EEC states towards a security confederation. In this he failed for reasons that have endured. For de Gaulle, there could be no European security so long as the Cold War left Europe at the mercy of an American–Soviet nuclear confrontation. But for Adenauer, and the other EEC member leaders, there could be no security without NATO and the American nuclear umbrella. Consequently, the EEC in the 1960s remained trapped between its existence as a customs union with a common agricultural support system which de Gaulle tolerated, and its security dependency on NATO, which de Gaulle did not accept.

The French contribution to this impasse was matched in reverse by the British. The Macmillan government responded to Suez by trying to repair relations with Washington. It too drew a lesson about the necessity of nuclear weapons but sought the answer in bilateral cooperation with Washington to secure them. As far as the EEC was concerned, Macmillan believed the British interest lay in a free trade agreement between the EEC and the British-led European Free Trade Area. Repeatedly threatening between 1958 and 1961 to withdraw British troops from Western Europe, he erroneously assumed that the EEC could be coerced via its security weakness into agreeing one.[49] During John F. Kennedy's presidency, these two post-Suez problems for Britain came together. Fearing de Gaulle's ambitions, Kennedy enticed Macmillan to apply for accession to the EEC.[50] But in granting submarine-launched Polaris missiles to Macmillan in the 1962 Nassau agreement, Kennedy gave de Gaulle a ready justification for damning Britain's EEC application as a 'trojan horse' for American interests in Europe.

With France out of NATO's command structure and Britain excluded from the EEC, by the mid-1960s Western European geopolitics had become even less coherent than it had been before Suez.[51] The EEC was left a partial economic federation structurally incapable of internally resolving security issues, and dependent on an external security alliance one member had in part repudiated. After de Gaulle departed the French presidency, the path to Britain's accession to the renamed European Community (EC) opened. But France stayed outside NATO's military command structure for the rest of the Cold War.

* * *

The implications of Suez for energy were just as momentous. The American veto drove France to make another bid for energy independence. Ever since 1945, French governments had strongly supported oil and gas exploration in the French Empire in Africa. In 1956, oil was found in Algeria. For a time, the French hoped that Algerian oil could move the entire EEC away from Middle Eastern dependency and its relation to American power, even though France's capacity to maintain French rule in Algeria through strength of force required tacit American consent.[52] While the French had not asked that Algeria as a juridical part of France be included in the ECSC, they insisted that Algeria and the other French overseas territories be included in the EEC. This would have allowed Algerian oil produced by French companies to have open access to the EEC, and gave other member states an interest in France maintaining its North African colonies.[53] Although France's forced withdrawal from Algeria in 1962 thwarted this hope, de Gaulle did protect French energy interests in the Évian Accords on Algerian independence, which granted French control over the Saharan oil field.

The British government too looked for new energy options after Suez, beginning Britain's first nuclear energy programme and encouraging what was now British Petroleum, the former Anglo-Iranian Oil Company, to engage in oil exploration in the Western Hemisphere, including Alaska.[54] Nonetheless, Britain still had a stronger position in the Middle East than any other European country. By 1957, half of Britain's oil came from Kuwait, a British protectorate, and those imports were, crucially, denominated in sterling.[55] As Arab nationalism spread and American involvement in South East Asia deepened, the British military presence in the Middle East became more, not less, important in Washington. Suez had not demonstrated that the British were dispensable in upholding the Western oil guarantee. Rather, it had demonstrated the immense vulnerability of Britain's ability to act militarily in the region to sterling's weakness. When the next crisis came, the risk would be that the Americans could not rely on the British. In sanctioning an emergency loan to support sterling in late 1964 in tacit exchange for a British commitment to stay in the Persian Gulf, Lyndon Johnson foresaw just the eventuality that would arise at the decade's end.[56]

Most consequentially for the long term, the Suez crisis definitively broke Western European governments' acceptance of the prohibition on Soviet oil imports. Even before Suez, the Italian state oil company ENI had seen an opportunity in Soviet premier Nikita Khrushchev's determination to rebuild an export-centred oil industry. In 1958, ENI began negotiations for a large-scale oil deal.[57] Italy was soon joined in this new Soviet market by Austria and West Germany.[58]

The West European turn to Soviet oil produced another NATO crisis. When the Soviets began building the Druzhba (or Friendship) pipeline that took Soviet oil first to Eastern Europe and then to Central Europe, they needed wide-diameter steel pipes from Western European companies. Eisenhower decided against embargoing these exports via NATO. But the greater Soviet export capacity became, the more American politicians became alarmed. In the Senate, Hubert Humphrey, later the 1968 Democratic presidential nominee, declared that Soviet oil exports were 'one of the major threats that face us ... perhaps even more dangerous than the military offensive threat'.[59] In late 1962, Kennedy used the Cuban Missile Crisis to demand Western companies stop selling the wide-diameter piping the Soviets needed. Procuring the Italian government's partial cooperation with this policy required the administration to push American companies to offer Italy cheaper oil.[60] Although the American military presence in West Germany made the government in Bonn easier to pressurize, it still took every Christian Democrat member of the Bundestag walking out to stop a vote that would have forced the government to reject the embargo.[61] Even the British government, which had less immediate interest in Soviet oil, was extremely reluctant to accept the American diktat.[62] The embargo was also unsuccessful, slowing down the pipeline by perhaps a year, before being abandoned by the Johnson administration.[63]

These Soviet oil exports to Western Europe destabilized the Middle East. Faced with losing market share in Western Europe, the American oil companies in the region cut their prices without consulting the Arab governments.[64] The ensuing fury led Saudi Arabia, Iran, Iraq, Kuwait, and Venezuela to form OPEC as the Organization of the Petroleum Exporting Countries.[65] Although OPEC's ability to force prices back up with production cuts was initially limited, not least by new oil discoveries, the three large Middle Eastern producer states now had a platform for collective political action that would reconfigure oil markets from the 1970s.

The 1967 Arab–Israeli war brought the post-Suez fault lines into sharp relief. De Gaulle used the war to insist once again that France would not be constrained by Washington and dropped France's previous support for Israel for a pro-Arab policy.[66] By contrast, American policy was more accommodating to Israel and more hostile to Egypt than it had been in 1956. This reorientation encouraged the Johnson administration to act as a direct supplier of last resort to Western Europe as Eisenhower had not.

Nonetheless, the logistical problems around Western European access to Middle Eastern oil would now become permanently more difficult. The Tapline pipeline carrying Saudi oil went through the Golan Heights, and this Syrian territory was now under Israeli occupation, making it a Palestinian target. The Suez Canal remained closed until 1975. Above all, the 1967 war finally destroyed Britain's position in the Middle East. The year before the war, the British government had already announced that it would leave Aden as a Nasser-backed insurgency grew. The war then intensified the uprising, producing a mutiny in the South Arabian Federation army and the Aden police. In November 1967, the beleaguered British military withdrew, leaving behind an independent republic of South Yemen, which by 1970 was run by a Soviet-backed regime. By 1967, British military weakness was compounded by sterling's. A closed Suez Canal and the Arab embargo on oil to states that supported Israel left Britain buying dollar-denominated oil, triggering another balance of payments crisis.[67] With the practical basis of British power having crumbled, the Wilson government soon announced that Britain would, by 1971, end all military commitments east of Suez. Britain's exit from the Persian Gulf produced an immediate crisis for Washington.[68] But Johnson could no longer use American financial power to change Wilson's mind. Any hope he had of offering Britain the option to reduce its troop commitments in Western Europe, as Dean Rusk had suggested to Wilson in 1965, in exchange for keeping them in the Persian Gulf had evaporated with France's withdrawal from NATO's common military structure the year before.[69]

This impasse turned Saudi Arabia and Iran into the anchors of Western energy security in the Middle East. As Walt Rostow, Johnson's national security adviser, wrote in a memo to the president, 'we don't want to have to replace the British, and we don't want the Russians there. So we must count on the Shah and Faisal.'[70]

From the outset, this new approach was fraught. The whole presence of the big American and European oil companies in the region was increasingly politically contested. When, in 1969, Colonel Gaddafi seized power in Tripoli under a pan-Arabism banner, he immediately shut down American and British military bases in the country and soon asked for Soviet military aid. With an increasing proportion of non-Soviet oil exports to Western Europe coming from Libya, he also began a fight with the oil companies about prices and revenue share. Other OPEC states soon followed in pushing to reverse the balance of power between the oil-producing countries and the oil companies, yielding new agreements that gave them greater revenue and control. Some OPEC members went further. Between 1971 and 1974, Algeria—which had joined OPEC in 1969—took majority ownership of the French oil companies' interests in Algeria, the pro-Soviet Ba'athist government in Iraq nationalized the Iraq Petroleum Company, and the Saudi government procured a majority share of Aramco. By the end of the decade, Aramco would be entirely owned and run by the Saudi state.

Meanwhile, the internal geopolitics of the Middle East remained unconducive to any external power looking for stable allies. Elevating Iran tied American credibility to a country where strong anti-American sentiments already prevailed thanks to the 1953 coup. It also encouraged Iran's territorial ambitions in Iraq and the southern Gulf. Leaning more heavily on Saudi Arabia meant dependence on a monarchy contending from the mid-1960s with defections within the military to Egypt. Indeed, the CIA warned Johnson and then Nixon that the kingdom was vulnerable to a radical nationalist coup. After the 1967 war, King Faisal reached an accommodation with Nasser and vigorously embraced the cause of a Palestinian state. The relationship between Iran and Saudi Arabia made matters worse: this new American strategy embroiled Washington in the rivalry between the two large Gulf states over oil prices and output institutionalized in OPEC.[71]

A little more than a decade after Suez, the purported American oil guarantee to Western Europe was incoherent and in part unwanted. American presidents could not use military power on any sustained basis in the Middle East, had been unable to use financial threats and extraterritorial sanctions to stop the West European states from turning towards Soviet oil, and had failed to prevent Britain from ending the military commitments on which the American expectation that Western Europe would import oil from the Persian Gulf ultimately rested. With Iraq moving towards the Soviet camp after 1968, Soviet influence in the Middle East had, meanwhile, grown. Far too much now hinged on the fate of the Iranian Shah, whose ambitions only incentivized Iraq to look for military help from Moscow.

Détente

These fractures were one part of a bigger geopolitical cataclysm around American power. The immediate cause was Vietnam. In its own terms, the war was an American disaster and created sharp, new domestic political constraints on American power. But it also intersected with the Middle Eastern and energy fault lines, as well as those inherent to Bretton Woods, to change American Cold War strategy with consequences that continued into the post–Cold War world.

Like the Suez crisis, Vietnam revealed NATO's divisions. Once American ground troops were committed in Vietnam, the Johnson administration failed in its attempts to use American support for sterling to take Britain into the war. Even though it threatened to withdraw American military protection from West Germany, it also proved unable to make Bonn help finance the war. Indeed, American pressure succeeded only in precipitating the end of Ludwig Erhard's

Christian Democratic–Free Democratic coalition government over the issue. The subsequent formation in 1966 of the first German grand coalition between the Christian Democrats and the Social Democrats opened the path to West Germany's turn in the 1970s towards accommodation with the Soviet Union, entrenching politically the prior German turn to Soviet energy.[72]

Meanwhile, the demands Bretton Woods placed on American dollar policy made it near impossible from 1968 for the United States to continue to fight the war as anything but a damage limitation exercise. What in 1947 had been a shortage of dollars had by the 1960s necessarily become a shortage of gold—as will be discussed in chapter seven. Faced with a gold crisis in March 1968, Johnson judged that since, in his words, the American 'fiscal situation' was 'abominable', he could not meet the request made by the American military generals for a large increase in troops.[73] Having accepted this gold-generated constraint, Johnson announced in March 1968 a radical curtailment of the air campaign against North Vietnam and that he would not seek re-election.

The Vietnam failure shattered the relative domestic political consensus about security that had allowed the United States to exercise power in Eurasia since Pearl Harbor. In the early Cold War years, Truman had won congressional support for the Marshall Plan, NATO, and peacetime conscription without anything like the domestic difficulties presidents had faced during the interwar years over Eurasian commitments. Over Vietnam, Johnson had won in 1964 a blanket authorization from Congress to deploy troops with only two dissenting voices. But without victory ever being in sight, Vietnam exhausted American voters' willingness to fight in, and pay for, Eurasian wars. Recognizing that reality, Richard Nixon campaigned in 1968 to abolish conscription, although it took him five years to realize his promise. After Vietnam, the United States would have a volunteer army and an electorate with a very low tolerance for any Eurasian commitments that risked body bags.

Fearing a period of Soviet ascendancy would follow an American retreat from Indochina, Nixon and his national security adviser, Henry Kissinger, wanted to freeze the strategic conflict with the Soviet Union as it was in the early 1970s. This required not only an accommodation with Moscow over some issues, including arms limitation treaties, but establishing diplomatic relations with Communist China in the hope that China would serve as an instrument of anti-Soviet containment.

Although détente followed from Vietnam-driven problems, it also had an energy logic. By the end of the 1970s, American energy power was waning and Soviet energy power was rising. American crude oil production reached a peak in 1970 that it would not hit again until the eighth year of the shale boom in 2018. Without a surplus capacity, American producers could not, even in principle, act as a supplier of last resort to Western Europe, and, requiring its own imports, the United States acquired a direct interest in oil bound for NATO members passing through the Persian Gulf.[74] Meanwhile, discoveries during the 1960s in Western Siberia boosted further the Soviet oil industry. In 1968, the Soviets completed an extension of the Druzhba pipeline to the Baltic coastal city of Ventspils, increasing export capacity to Western Europe. By 1974, the Soviet Union had replaced the United States as the world's largest oil producer.[75] The huge Western Siberian hydrocarbon basin also contained large quantities of gas. Exporting this gas to Western and Central Europe was Moscow's opportunity to develop these fields with European money and equipment. In the long term, these gas exports would prove even more consequential than Soviet oil exports, not least in providing an economic foundation to the Soviet–German accommodation, just as West German politics acquired the most significant green movement in the world that would strongly constrain the growth of nuclear power.[76]

With American energy power weakened, Nixon edged towards American–Soviet cooperation. He sought commercial opportunities for American consortiums in developing the Western Siberian fields, and loosened NATO's rules on energy-related exports.[77] The communiqué after an American–Soviet summit in June 1973 noted 'a number of specific [energy] projects involving the participation of American companies, including the delivery of Siberian natural gas to the United States' and that the two governments had 'signed an agreement to expand and strengthen co-operation' over nuclear fusion.[78]

But energy matters also seriously strained détente, which was already bitterly domestically contested, not least since neither the

State Department nor Pentagon supported much of Nixon and Kissinger's approach. Energy trade with the Soviet Union required Moscow to have Most Favoured Nation status and Congress made that outcome dependent on human rights, especially Soviet Jews' liberty to emigrate. It also required the Soviet Union to have some access to American capital, which Congress restricted.[79]

Most immediately, détente could not prevent a full-scale crisis in the Middle East, the ramifications of which spread around the world.[80] When Egypt and its Arab allies attacked Israel on Yom Kippur 1973, the Arab oil-producing states had advantages unavailable to them in 1967. In the 1973 war, the line between Soviet-supported and American-supported states dissolved, with Saudi Arabia actively participating in the military coalition Egypt assembled. American OPEC imports also exposed the United States to Saudi Arabia's oil weapon. The Saudis were frustrated by the dollar's devaluation in 1971 and saw higher prices as a necessary compensation, especially when Washington was also strengthening their rival Iran.[81] Although King Faisal was initially reluctant to break with Washington and asked the American oil companies to put pressure on Nixon to change course, once the war turned in Israel's favour, he did embargo exports to the United States. Coming on top of the pressures on prices and supply already in play from American production having peaked in 1970 and OPEC's ascendancy, the American and Western Europe an economies and democracies experienced an intense collective oil price shock—as will be discussed in chapters four and eight.

With most West European governments reorienting their policy towards the Arab states or neutrality, the Yom Kippur War shattered any lingering remnants of NATO unity over the Middle East. The British government joined most of its fellow EC members in eschewing American support for Israel, prompting Kissinger to suspend American intelligence sharing with London.[82] In the political scientist Ethan Kapstein's words, the Arabs in 1973 'divided and conquered the Western alliance' by deciding who got oil and who did not.[83] When it appeared that the Soviet Union might enter the conflict, most West European governments told Washington that the American military could not necessarily expect to use their bases in the event of a Middle Eastern war with the Soviet Union, and Britain refused to let the Americans launch reconnaissance flights from Cyprus. Left without allies, Washington sent American warships to the Indian Ocean near the entrance to the Gulf.[84]

Kissinger later complained that the West Europeans had largely acted 'as if the alliance did not exist'.[85] But NATO was not conceived, and, beyond Turkish membership, had not been adapted, to deal with the Middle East. At times, Kissinger and other American officials talked as if the United States had the requisite unilateral power to seize oil fields in the region. On one occasion Kissinger told journalists that unless the Arab states learned to cooperate again with the oil-consuming states they would 'go the way of the Greek city states'.[86] In reality, Washington lacked the power to demand Arab acquiescence, and its Vietnam-consumed domestic politics could not have accommodated a Middle Eastern war. Indeed, diminishing oil power made it the supplicant state.

The crisis was not an operational failure for NATO but a reckoning. NATO was devised as a European-focused military alliance in a bipolar world in which its European members' energy security interests depended on the Middle East. One NATO state, whose military power was severely financially constrained and whose imperial presence ignited resistance, had been primarily responsible for defending those interests. With Britain's military exit, NATO had for several years been entirely absent from the Persian Gulf, at a time when the United States itself was becoming dependent on imports through those waters and the Moscow–Baghdad alliance had taken the Soviet Navy into the Gulf. Instead, Saudi Arabia and Iran were supposed to protect the oil interests of NATO members, although they would only refrain from harming them on conditional terms that divided the military alliance.

Confronted with this actuality, Kissinger demanded the Europeans come to an energy summit in February 1974. He framed the Washington Energy Conference around the collective interests of the industrial oil-consuming countries in relation to producer countries. But there was now an incentive for beggar-thy-neighbour bilateral oil deals, and the French government refused to join the International Energy Agency (IEA) the Nixon administration pushed to increase international energy cooperation. Under conditions of declining domestic production, American consumer-oil interests competed with those of the Western European states. Caught in this tension, Nixon resorted to threatening to remove American troops from Europe unless the West European states agreed a collective approach.[87] But throughout the 1970s, West European governments had an option to reduce Middle Eastern dependency: they could import more oil from the Soviet Union. In practice the United States could not. Although Kissinger tried again, when serving Gerald Ford, to establish a basis for future Soviet exports across the Atlantic, the preliminary agreement reached with Brezhnev fell apart.[88]

Strategically exposed by the 1973 crisis, the Nixon administration repaired relations with Saudi Arabia, strengthened its alliance with Iran, which had supported the price rises but not the embargo, and sought to broker an Arab–Israeli peace via Egypt. For the future, Nixon told Americans in a national address in November 1973, the country had to wean itself off Middle Eastern oil and embrace what he called 'Project Independence' to be realized by the decade's end, including through the development of shale oil.[89]

A Strange Victory

If American energy power diminished throughout the 1970s, the revolution in Tehran at the end of the decade and the ensuing Iranian hostage crisis deepened the blow, creating some of the central political dynamics presently at work in the Middle East. What had been the American fear of the Egyptian–Soviet axis became the fear of an Iran–Soviet alliance. Given the Persian Gulf's importance, American policy became much more confrontational.[90] For Western European governments, this created a further Middle Eastern predicament. Now on top of the risk that the Arab states and Iran could embargo oil exports, they confronted a world in which American sanctions against Middle Eastern regimes would threaten the supply of moderately priced oil.

The fallout of the Iranian revolution soon spread to the western side of the Persian Gulf. Once again, events elsewhere in the region left Saudi Arabia vulnerable to anti-Western sentiment. In late 1979, fundamentalists wanting to overthrow the Saudi monarchy seized control of the Grand Mosque in Mecca, and the Saudi regime had to fight to regain control. Thereafter, it upheld stricter Islamic rules and proved more open to religious conservatives. Iran also quickly proved willing to support Shi'ite groups in Arab countries, beginning in Lebanon where the Islamic Revolutionary Guard Corps established a base in the Syrian-controlled part of the country out of which Hezbollah grew.

Like Nixon before him, President Carter saw recreating energy independence as the United States' only way out of this geopolitical morass. In what was dubbed his 'malaise' speech, Carter declared:

> This intolerable dependence on foreign oil threatens our economic independence and the very security of our nation...Beginning this moment, this nation will never use more foreign oil than we did in 1977—never. From now on, every new addition to our demand for energy will be met from our own production and our own conservation.

Practically, he put his faith in a federally backed Synthetic Fuels Corporation and shale, telling Americans that 'we have more oil in our shale alone than several Saudi Arabias'.[91]

But once more the aspiration to restore energy independence could change nothing in the present. The Soviet invasion of Afghanistan in late 1979, which seemed to open a Soviet path to the Strait of Hormuz, and then Iran's ascendancy in the Iran–Iraq war, which appeared from 1982 to conjure the spectre of Iranian troops reaching the Saudi and Kuwaiti oil fields, deepened American vulnerability in the Middle East. Carter's defence secretary said that the loss of Persian Gulf oil would be 'a blow of catastrophic proportions' and 'Soviet control of this area would make economic vassals of much of both the industrialized and the less developed world.'[92] His energy secretary, James Schlesinger, went further, saying that 'Soviet control of the oil tap in the Middle East would mean the end of the world as we have known it since 1945.'[93] But after Vietnam there was no possibility of committing American troops to Afghanistan, leaving the Carter administration to arm the Islamic Mujahideen through Pakistan, or to Iran, leaving the Reagan administration to restore diplomatic relations with Iraq and the CIA to provide covert support to Baghdad.

Although the Carter administration announced a military strategy for the Middle East—the Carter Doctrine—committing the United States to use military force against any outside force seeking control in the Persian Gulf region, it and its successors lacked any decisive wherewithal to act upon that doctrine.[94] Carter did order the US fleet into the Gulf and established a rapid deployment force to operate outside West Europe and East Asia. But the United States lacked the military capacity to impose regional order in the Middle East. What military power it could bring to bear also caused problems for its remaining regional allies, such that when the Reagan administration established the US Central Command in 1983 as a permanent unified combatant command for American operations in the Middle East, no Gulf state would host it. Consequently, the logistical headquarters for American military power in the region was located in Florida and remains there.[95]

The Persian Gulf crisis that began with the Iranian revolution also reactivated NATO's discord. Only Britain participated in joint man-oeuvres in the Indian Ocean after the Soviet invasion of Afghanistan, and again the French government flirted with its own solution by contemplating an accommodation with the Russians in the Gulf.[96] During the early period of the Iran–Iraq War, France did join Britain in contributing convoy ships to protect tankers around the Strait of Hormuz, but the West German government refused to participate in the operation.[97]

For the long term, the Carter Doctrine's use of the term 'outside' begged the question of what would happen if Iran attacked Saudi Arabia and were supported by the Soviet Union.[98] Revolutionary Iran has proved a significant military power. In 1988, Iran sued for peace in the war with Iraq, after the American Navy and Air Force launched a massive attack on Iranian ships in Iranian waters. But the Iran–Iraq war still ultimately consolidated the Iranian regime, and the American intervention made the regime's political legitim-acy even more dependent on anti-American hostility. Iraq's partial victory then produced Iraq's invasion of Kuwait, and Saddam Hussein's attacks on the Kurds. Although George Bush Sr issued a national security directive in 1989 to clarify that the United States would use force against a regional actor as well as an external actor, this has in practice proved more material in relation to Iraq than Iran.

* * *

Back in Europe, the Cold War's emphatic return after the Soviet invasion of Afghanistan deepened NATO's schism over energy. In 1981, the Soviet government struck an agreement with a German banking consortium led by Deutsche Bank to provide credit to build a new gas pipeline. The Trans-Siberian pipeline would eventually run from the Urengoy gas field in the West Siberian basin to Uzhhorod in what is now Western Ukraine, where the gas was transported to central and Western Europe. The Reagan administration opposed the Trans-Siberian pipeline, and, after the Soviet-controlled Polish government imposed martial law in December 1981, it imposed tough extraterritorial sanctions on European companies involved in the project. These sanctions prompted a furious reaction among West European governments. Helmut Schmidt, the West German chancellor, insisted that whatever the Americans thought the pipeline would go ahead. The British trade secretary, Lord Cockfield, raged that the American embargo constituted 'an unacceptable extension of American extraterritorial jurisdiction in a way which is repugnant in international law'.[99] But for the Reagan administration, this was more than simply a replay of Kennedy's confrontation over the Druzhba pipeline, as senior advisers believed that hard currency earnings from energy exports allowed the Soviet Union to project military power abroad such that their absence would have strategic consequences.[100] Reagan backed down on the pipeline after the West Europeans agreed that no more than 30 per cent of their gas imports would come from the Soviet Union.[101] But the European–American conflict within NATO over energy appeared inescapable as long as the Cold War continued.

Of course, at the end of the 1980s the Cold War did draw to a close, and, paradoxically, energy played its part in hastening that resolution. High oil prices in the 1970s made possible what would have otherwise been prohibitively expensive: production in the North Sea. In the Western Hemisphere, more oil was discovered in Mexico and the end of regulations on domestic American oil prices—which will be discussed in chapter eight—spurred BP and several American oil companies to pursue high-cost supply in Alaska. This increase in non-Middle Eastern and Soviet supply sapped OPEC's capacity to control prices, as did the creation of exchanges in New York and

Chicago for futures contracts—which gave the right to buy oil at a specified date at a specified price—by encouraging speculative movements in the price driven by investors with no interest in receiving actual oil. Confronted with these developments, Saudi Arabia initially led OPEC into production cuts to try to maintain prices. But when the dollar began to slide in 1986, causing the kingdom's dollar revenues to fall, it reversed course to fight for market share, crashing prices.

Saudi motives in letting prices plummet in 1986 have been subject to much subsequent speculation. Some former Reagan officials have claimed that the administration encouraged the Saudis to act in order to heap pressure on the Soviet Union.[102] There is no decisive evidence that this was the case.[103] Nonetheless, the Reagan White House welcomed the fall, proclaiming that it was 'one of the most beneficial things that happened to mankind in 13 years'.[104] For America's Texan producers, by contrast, it was anything but. For them, the 1986 reverse oil price shock was a disaster, and as the 1980s Texas oil economy crashed, Texas became the epicentre of the American savings and loan crisis.[105] In not stepping in to protect the Texas oil companies, the Reagan administration acted differently from any of its predecessors.[106] Even before the 1986 crash, Reagan had shown much less interest in restoring American energy independence than Carter or Nixon, not least by letting the Synthetic Fuels Corporation wither.[107] When the Saudi shock then arrived, any prospect of reducing American oil imports from the Middle East ended, until high prices and extremely cheap credit after the 2008 crash facilitated the shale boom.

Whatever the Saudi motivation, the oil price collapse was geopolitically transformative. In 1986, the Soviet Union was by some distance the world's largest oil producer. But the Soviet state was so dependent on revenues from energy exports that it could not function without them. Low oil prices brought the long-standing military crisis in Afghanistan to a head, as the dollar had for the Americans in Vietnam, and made Soviet food imports dependent on Western credit. Oil is far from a sufficient explanation for the imperial crisis that engulfed the Soviet Union in 1989. But when the Eastern European rebellions exploded that year, the oil-caused immediate economic crisis left Mikhail Gorbachev in no position to try to defend Soviet rule.[108]

As the Ottomans' demise had done earlier in the century, the Soviet Union's collapse in 1991 left a geopolitical energy prize, this time around the Caspian Sea. For two decades, Soviet energy production had been dominated by Western Siberia. But in the Soviet Union's last years, geological engineers discovered the Azeri-Chirag-Gunashli fields off the Azerbaijan coast and oil and gas in Kazakhstan. This opened up the prospect of another source of Eurasian supply. But it also meant the Americans and Europeans could disagree once again on where NATO members had shared energy security interests.

* * *

Today, NATO's old energy fault lines formed during the Cold War interact with these new ones that began to take shape as the Cold War ended, as well as those generated by the United States' return in the 2010s as a top-tier oil and gas producer. As the American need for oil imports has lessened, the end result has been a partial American strategic withdrawal from the Middle East. But the American naval commitment in the Persian Gulf and a strategy to deter Iran by means falling short of war remain in place, in part because China too now needs Middle Eastern energy resources. For the European NATO members, this tension in American policy has created harder versions of old disagreements. In Emmanuel Macron's eyes, the Middle East is Europe's 'neighbourhood', replete with risks. In his judgement, the United States cannot share these European interests and, consequently, NATO cannot be fit for purpose as a military vehicle for the protection of those interests. Here, there is a clear echo of the Suez crisis, with the added complication that neither the British nor the French possess anything like the military power they did in 1956 and can still be constrained in the Middle East, especially in regard to Iran, by American financial power.

But the European Union has scarcely worked as geopolitical revenge for Suez. It could not in energy terms because the West European countries could not end oil imports from the Middle East and Algeria's integration into the EEC did not last. Nor could the EEC states break with NATO. Although France pulled away from NATO's command structure, French governments were never able to realize de Gaulle's ambitions for an independent European security confederation.

So far as Suez marked a decisive geopolitical change in Europe, it was through the European turn back to Soviet energy exports. From the 1970s, the Soviet–German gas relationship became a defining feature of the European geopolitical landscape and the structural division within NATO created by the absence of comparable energy interests across the Atlantic. Despite the part oil revenues played in the Soviet Union's fall, this was a construction from the Cold War that would endure into the post–Cold War world. There would though be a crucial difference between a Soviet–German energy relationship and a Russian–German relationship: after 1991 the territory to Germany's east through which the gas was delivered would be constituted by independent states that were neither part of the Soviet Union nor subject to its rule. This geopolitical change would simultaneously make NATO militarily important for security in Eastern Europe and make NATO, as well as EU, unity over Russian energy exports impossible, especially as new supplies were opening up from the Caspian Sea. Even before the United States acquired the means both to compete with Russian gas exports and to use its financial power over European states to force a change in energy policy, this conundrum would prove, as the next chapter will show, extremely disruptive.

3

Eurasia Remade

In September 2015, warships from Russia's Black Sea Fleet moved through the Bosphorus into the eastern Mediterranean, and the Russian air force launched airstrikes against groups of US-backed Syrian rebels. The Obama administration made no response. As one senior State Department official briefed, 'if the Russians are going to be more engaged in this theatre, we have to de-conflict militarily'.[1]

As Russian intervention turned the balance of power back to Bashar al-Assad's regime, in the summer of 2016 Obama decided to work with Russia to try to end the Syrian civil war. On 9 September, his secretary of state, John Kerry, and the Russian foreign minister, Sergey Lavrov, announced an impending ceasefire and said that if it held for a week, Washington and Moscow would begin to plan joint airstrikes against Islamic State (ISIS). But nine days later, American and British planes mistakenly killed around sixty Syrian soldiers in north-east Syria, prompting the Syrian government to repudiate the ceasefire. After Syrian and Russian aircraft then struck an aid convoy near Aleppo, Obama suspended American–Russian cooperation.

As, not for the first time, Obama was reversing course in Syria, Donald Trump and Hillary Clinton were exchanging blows about American geopolitical priorities. For Clinton, Russia had to be confronted in Syria. In the second presidential debate, she said that 'what is at stake here is the ambitions and aggressiveness of Russia. Russia has decided it is all in in Syria.' For Trump, Russia was still a potential partner in fighting ISIS. Each argued that the Russia issue made the other unfit for the presidency. Clinton portrayed Trump as a Russian stooge: 'they've . . . decided who they want to see become President of the United States too and it's not me'. Trump charged that Russia had gained power in Syria and in Iran 'because of our weak foreign policy' and that, as Obama's first secretary of state, Clinton bore responsibility.[2]

Clinton and Trump also disagreed about the relative importance of Russian power. For Trump, China was the United States' primary geopolitical problem. He painted a picture of a Chinese assault on the American manufacturing sector and complained that 'there's nobody in our government to fight them'.[3] For Clinton, China was still a net economic asset. She would not, she insisted, rip up the multilateral trading order that sustained the American economy. Again, each saw in China a means to attack the other's personal competence to be president. Trump regularly reminded voters that Bill Clinton had been responsible for bringing China into the World Trade Organization (WTO). Trump, Clinton retaliated, regularly used cheap Chinese steel to construct Trump buildings across the country.

But if, geopolitically, the 2016 presidential election became a confront-China challenger candidate versus a confront-Russia incumbent candidate, this juxtaposition also distorts. When, alarmed by China's rise, the Obama administration had made a Pivot to Asia, Hillary Clinton was the policy's principal architect. Until six weeks before the election, Obama had been pursuing much the same policy of cooperation with Russia against ISIS advocated by Trump. After Trump won, the Obama administration imposed new sanctions on Russia. Whatever Trump's hopes of moving towards accommodation with Putin, he assumed the presidency under the accusation from his opponents that he and his advisers had colluded with Moscow to win it. In August 2017, the US Congress imposed more sanctions on Russia and placed legal restrictions on the president's authority to remove them. Paradoxically, the 2016 election ended with a domestic politics that drove a confrontation with both Russia and China.

Yet the difficulties of changing Russian behaviour had already been proven by earlier events in Europe. When Russian warships entered the eastern Mediterranean, Moscow had been subject to sanctions for eighteen months, prompted by Russia annexing Crimea from Ukraine in 2014 and Moscow's subsequent support for anti-government forces in Ukraine's Donbass region. These sanctions had some consequences for individuals. But since they did not prevent Russia selling oil and gas, they gave Putin little motive to retreat.

Here, American geopolitical choices ran into the European Union's (EU) geopolitical weaknesses around its borders. It was European dependency on energy imports from Russia that made any serious sanctions impossible. Having set the Ukrainian crisis in motion by insisting the Ukrainian government—whose NATO membership France and Germany had earlier vetoed—choose between an economy oriented towards Russia and a formal economic relationship with the EU, the EU was powerless to act when, in February 2014, Russian soldiers seized control of the Crimean Parliament building.

Russian influence in Syria, meanwhile, exposed the EU to another border problem, this time with Turkey. As Russian ships moved through the Bosphorus, the EU was already immersed in a crisis generated by the plight of Syrian refugees who had been living in camps in Turkey. At the beginning of September 2015, Angela Merkel declared that there was no limit to the number of refugees Germany would take. Hundreds of thousands of people headed out of Turkey across Southern and Central Europe. But her new policy rapidly proved unsustainable. Only weeks later, the EU struck a provisional deal with Turkey to stem the flow. In March 2016, Merkel's bilateral diplomacy with Turkish premier Recep Tayyip Erdogan turned this provisional agreement into a more substantial accord, where, in exchange for a Turkish commitment to reduce further the number of refugees entering Greece and Italy, the EU agreed to a large aid package and to accelerate the stalled negotiations on Turkey's accession to the Union.

If this moment in early 2016 appeared a turning point in the EU's relations with Turkey, Turkey's geopolitical alignment was dramatically reconfigured through the rest of the year. On the night of 15 July, Turkish army officers tried and failed to seize power. In the aftermath, Erdogan made it clear he felt better supported by Putin than Obama or any EU leader. Erdogan's post-coup purges and threat to reinstate the death penalty led some European capitals to cast public doubt on Turkey's suitability for EU membership. By the year's end, Erdogan had sent Turkish forces across the Syrian border to attack American-backed Kurdish militias and joined with Russia and Iran to launch a counter peace process for Syria to the one operating under the United Nations' auspices.

These events that made Russian power a major issue in the 2016 American presidential election and so pressurized the EU on its borders arose from geopolitical fault lines long present in the post–Cold War world. Those around Ukraine existed from the start since the Cold War's end had uprooted the European geopolitical environment in which NATO and the EU's predecessors were born without settling a new one. Those around Syria could partly be traced back to the long-term incoherencies in American policy in the Middle East. Those around Turkey and European energy imports from Russia had their origins in the Cold War and continued beyond its end. Even though few imagined in the 1990s that they could prove so disruptive, each would have been recognizable as a geopolitical challenge. By contrast, that China's economic development should feature as a contested geopolitical issue in the 2016 American election and help a businessman who had never previously run for any office was experienced as a profound shock. In the late 1990s, the US–China trade relationship was not supposed to be a geopolitical issue, or any longer a partisan one, only an engine of growth for a singular world economy run under American leadership.

A decade that was often disingenuously hailed as the dawn of a new American-led universal order turned out instead to be the prelude to a geopolitically dangerous world that has recast Eurasia and connected old fault lines running across it. For all China's importance, understanding this geopolitical turbulence must begin in Europe. It was Europe's geopolitical map that was rewritten by the Cold War's denouement in relation to both Russia and Turkey.

Where is Europe?

After the Soviet Union's dissolution in 1991, the questions of where Europe ended, whether any part of Europe could still be threatened by Russia, and, if so, who would provide security still remained. This massively complicated the already difficult relationship between NATO and, what from 1993 became, the EU. If the EU claimed to realize an ideal of European unity, it could not end on the Eastern German border at the Oder–Neisse line. But since centuries of instability in Europe had arisen over states and empires in the geographical space between Russia and Germany, bringing the former Warsaw Pact states into the EU begged the question of their military security. If the East European states joined the EU, Cold War logic said they should also join NATO. But if they were indeed to enter NATO, then NATO would be asserting that Soviet power had been little more than a new version of old Russian power and a security guarantee to these states would not be a cosmetic exercise. In the Maastricht Treaty, agreed in December 1991, the Eastern European question went unaddressed. But, by creating a Common Foreign and Security Policy, the EU did make a move towards becoming a security confederation, albeit without any assumption being made that NATO was thus dispensable.

The EU's subsequent inability to substitute for NATO in the Yugoslav wars of succession was matched by its inability to resolve the security implications of Eastern enlargement. Three non-NATO members—Austria, Sweden, and Finland—joined the EU in 1995, the same year that France rejoined NATO's Military Committee, albeit not its command structure. Meanwhile, the leading Eastern European states that wished to join the EU pressed the Americans for NATO admission. By the mid-1990s, there was an impasse. Fearing the EU would become more dependent on NATO if Poland and others joined, and that Germany would lose interest in security matters if NATO were entrenched in Eastern Europe as a buffer between Germany and Russia, France became averse to EU and NATO enlargement.[4] Later in the decade, it tried to reinvigorate the EU's formal security confederation structure. In Tony Blair, the French president, Jacques Chirac, found an unprecedented British advocate for the EU having some military capacity independent of NATO. In the 1998 Saint-Malo Declaration, the two governments agreed that the EU should have an autonomous military capability and a decision-making structure around it. This bilateral Franco-British agreement facilitated a European Security and Defence Policy and a 2002 agreement that the EU could access NATO assets for operations in which NATO did not participate.[5] A year later, EU troops were for the first time deployed in a peacekeeping mission in Macedonia. But giving the EU some military capacity was again no answer to the Eastern European question.

That involved confronting what it would mean for the EU to have a border with Russia. When, by 1996, it became clear that for the EU Eastern enlargement was urgent, the Clinton administration decided that NATO accession for Poland, Hungary, and the Czech Republic should be an American priority. This led to these three former Warsaw Pact members joining NATO in 1999, followed in 2004 by, among others, the former Soviet republics, Estonia, Latvia, and Lithuania. In moving eastwards before the EU did, NATO became a supposed symbol of democratic values.[6] But the question of whether there was sufficient political will in Europe, let alone among American voters, to defend the Baltic republics was not answered.[7]

In 2004, the EU did finally welcome eight new members, including Poland. But Eastern EU enlargement was still bedevilled by security matters. If the French feared it would compromise the EU as a security confederation, they took the second Iraq War as vindication of their apprehension. In the weeks before the war began, Chirac described the East European governments' support for the American position on Iraq as 'infantile', and said they were 'missing an opportunity to shut up'.[8]

These tensions were near inevitable. For the East European states, the old logic that made NATO the security wing of the EU remained a self-evident reason of state. For France, a post-1989 accommodation with NATO could be contemplated because for at least some French politicians in a post-Soviet world NATO was in the long term irrelevant.[9] Nor was the cause only Eastern enlargement. On the side of the Eastern European members over Iraq were Britain, Italy, the Netherlands, Denmark, Spain, and Portugal. On Middle Eastern matters during the Cold War, the West European states had bitterly disagreed with Americans, not least over Suez, but in nothing like this way with each other. This new scope for conflict pitched France and Germany against Britain, destroying the British–French security rapprochement. For the EU to become a security confederation, France and Britain needed to be closer on geopolitical questions than France and Germany since a reunified Germany had cut defence spending by nearly a third during the 1990s. But if the EU were still to rely on NATO, France took risks in attacking East European governments for accepting American leadership over Iraq and siding with Russia when a NATO that was not in Europe an alliance against Russia would lose any reason for existence.[10]

Ukraine was pivotal for these EU–NATO fault lines.[11] Ukraine formally became an independent state with the Soviet Union's dissolution in 1991. But its strategic importance around the Black Sea made for an uneasy separation. In 1997, Russia and Ukraine agreed to divide the former Soviet Black Sea Fleet based at Sevastopol in

Crimea. Under this treaty, the new Russian Black Sea Fleet was able to use Sevastopol for twenty years and station troops on the Crimean Peninsula. If this treaty effectively guaranteed Ukrainian independence subject to Russian military rights in Crimea, it lacked meaningful external support since neither EU nor NATO membership was on offer to Ukraine. Indeed, the EU formally ruled out EU entry when, after its 2004 enlargement, it set out a 'European neighbourhood' policy for relations with the states between the Baltic republics and the Black Sea, the Caucasus, North Africa, and the Middle East that excluded further accessions.

The 2004–5 Orange Revolution brought the Ukraine dilemma to its first crisis.[12] Massive demonstrations after the presidential election in November 2004, which appeared rigged in favour of the pro-Russian candidate, led the Ukrainian Supreme Court to order a rerun, then won by Viktor Yushchenko on a pro-EU platform. On taking office in January 2005, Yushchenko promised that securing EU membership would be the 'alpha and omega' for his government, and that he would take Ukraine into NATO.[13] The enlarged EU was now beset with a geopolitical divide around Ukraine. A Union that included Poland, Slovakia, and Hungary—states that border Ukraine—ensured there would be persistent internal pressure to offer a substantially closer economic relationship. But since an EU that took Ukraine into its economic orbit would have to endure more confrontational relations with Russia, and thus this move would need to be coupled with NATO accession, France would continue to resist.

Back to the Caucasus and Turkey

Aside from producing an independent Ukrainian state, the Soviet collapse unravelled the post–First World War settlement around the Black Sea and the Caspian Sea, as well as the Caucasus that separated these waters. This returned Eurasia to aspects of the pre-1914 geopolitical world, including Russian–Turkish competition in the region.

This change was intensified by the late Soviet oil discoveries around the Caspian Sea. When Azerbaijan and Kazakhstan declared their independence, George Bush Sr's administration sought to make them American energy allies. But since the Caspian Sea is landlocked, Azerbaijan is bordered by Russia to the north as well as Iran to the south, and Kazakhstan shares a long border with Russia, transporting future oil and gas from the two countries would pose serious logistical and geopolitical difficulties.[14]

For the remainder of the 1990s, the Clinton administration prioritized avoiding new pipelines from Azerbaijan that went through either Russia or Iran. Eventually, it supported an expensive oil pipeline from Baku through Georgia to the Turkish coastal port of Ceyhan. In Europe, Caspian gas was an opportunity for the Central, Eastern, and Southern EU states to reduce their Russian energy dependency. In 2000, the European Commission published a green paper on the importance of European states acquiring new energy supplies, which translated as fewer Russian imports. From 2002, companies from Austria and four EU-applicant Central and Southern states, including Turkey, formed a consortium to develop a pipeline, named Nabucco, to take gas already transported to Turkey northwards via Bulgaria, Romania, and Hungary into Austria. But from the outset, the Nabucco consortium was caught in a geopolitical bind: it needed an agreement with Azerbaijan to supply gas for onward transit from Turkey, and since this was not a given, the EU was open to Iranian imports through the pipeline, which antagonized Washington.[15]

In endeavouring to contain Russia and Iran, Clinton and Bush Jr made Georgia geopolitically important and amplified Turkey's long-standing significance.[16] Consequently, many in Georgia saw an opportunity for moving the country into NATO and the EU and the 2003 Rose Revolution brought a pro-Western government to power. For Turkey, the new and proposed pipelines offered the chance to become a strategically crucial energy transit state.[17] Turkey's reinvigorated geopolitical importance added to the eastern stresses between NATO and the EU. Since 1964 Turkey had enjoyed associate membership of the EU, and an EU–Turkey customs union was finally completed in 1995. Two years later, the EU declined to give Turkey applicant status, unlike the East European, Balkan, and Mediterranean states that eventually acceded in 2004.

This decision did have a geopolitical rationale. Taking Turkey inside the EU would leave an extremely underdeveloped security confederation with borders with Iran, Iraq, and Syria. But leaving Turkey out, while more recent applicants were included, appeared to make Europe's borders cultural. After the decision, the Christian

Democrat parties in the European Parliament issued a statement stating that 'the European Union is a civilization project and within this civilization project Turkey has no place'.[18] Helmut Kohl, the German chancellor, added that the EU was based on Christian principles.[19] By contrast, Clinton's advisers had no patience for civilizational rhetoric. In the words of one State Department paper, they saw Turkey as a 'democratic secular nation that draws its political models from Western Europe and the United States'.[20] Under this logic, since NATO and the EU were geopolitically complementary, Turkey belonged inside the EU.[21] Serious pressure from Washington and a new Social Democrat–Green government in Berlin led the EU to relent, giving Turkey candidate status in 1999. But still there was little political will inside the EU actually to move towards Turkish accession.

Russian energy only exacerbated the Turkey part of the EU–NATO fracture and tied it to the Ukraine conundrum. During the 1990s, Russian gas and, in particular, oil output fell. Caspian Sea energy would mean competition for post-Soviet Russia to supply European markets. The Soviet Union's dissolution also geopolitically reconfigured Europe's gas transit geography. Gas imports into Germany and Central Europe principally came via a set of pipelines, including the Trans-Siberian (Brotherhood) pipeline, running from the west Siberian fields through eastern to western Ukraine into what was then Czechoslovakia and soon Slovakia. Managing transit through an independent Ukraine and later Belarus was now a strategic burden for Moscow, where it had to regulate transit fees with two states with an opportunity to divert supply to themselves. How Russia handled these relations left an external border problem for the EU.

On the Russian side, Turkey offered potential solutions. In 1997, the two governments struck an agreement to build the Blue Stream gas pipeline under the Black Sea. Blue Stream, which opened in 2003, allowed Russia to increase exports to Turkey and to divert some gas for European consumers away from transit through Ukraine and Belarus. But this pipeline sowed more seeds for long-term European division around both Turkey and Russia. In part, this was driven by commercial interests. Operationally, Blue Stream was a joint venture between the part-state-owned Italian energy company ENI and the Russian energy behemoth Gazprom. Unsurprisingly, when formal accession negotiations for Turkey finally began, the Italian government was rather more sympathetic to Turkey's case than the German. But in time, as Russia made moves to counter increased market competition and break its transit dependency on Ukraine, the EU states would divide too on which route their Russian energy imports would take.

For Turkey itself, the post–Cold War energy environment was both an opportunity and a reopening of historical wounds. Turkey was, and remains, heavily dependent on imported oil and gas. But with the new oil and gas discoveries in Azerbaijan, it could act as an energy hub connecting the Caspian Sea and the Middle East to Southern European consumers. This network of gas and oil flows would join up what had once been the Ottoman Empire, the end of which had left Turkey shut out of both the energy-rich Middle East and the Caucasus. Over the next three decades, however, this Eurasian energy geography would also create considerable incentives for Turkey, notwithstanding its position in NATO, to reach an accommodation with Russia.

The Middle East Weakness Persists

In the Middle East, the Cold War's end and Iran's defeat in the Iran–Iraq War appeared to strengthen the United States' hitherto weak geopolitical position at a time when Nixon and Carter's aspiration to restore oil independence lay shattered by low prices and Reagan's indifference.[22] For a short time, American success in preventing Iraqi troops from reaching the Saudi oil fields and then forcing them out of Kuwait appeared to show that American military power could act as a geopolitical foundation for American and some European countries' ongoing dependence on energy imports from the Middle East. As James Schlesinger—Nixon and Ford's defence secretary and Carter's energy secretary—commented at the time, the United States had 'made a choice to secure access to oil by military means'.[23] Moreover, in mobilizing an international coalition to fight this war with authorization from the United Nations, Washington had been able to count on European (including French), Arab (including Saudi and Egyptian), and Turkish participation.

But the war's fallout soon showed that the old reasons that limited American military power in, and NATO's coherence around, the

Middle East were not about to disappear. Bush Sr backed away from a longer war to depose Saddam Hussein largely because he feared the likely American casualties would be domestically intolerable. Meanwhile, the war coalition Bush assembled could not disguise NATO's internal divisions. Twelve out of NATO's then sixteen members provided forces, but they did not fight under NATO command. Turkey was logistically crucial to the war, providing air bases and closing Iraq's oil pipeline to enforce sanctions against Baghdad; it also had to deal with the refugee problem the war caused on its southeastern border with Iraq. But Turkey's proximity to Iraq also raised the delicate question of whether all NATO's European members were committed to defending Turkey, and it was far from clear they were.

Having eschewed regime change, the United States was left with what looked like permanent military commitments in the Persian Gulf to restrict Iraq. These entailed maintaining no-fly zones over both northern and southern Iraq, the first to defend the Kurds and the second the Strait of Hormuz, as well as an oil sanctions regime that had to be enforced by the US Navy and a weapons inspection regime that had to be implemented inside Iraq. The new American military commitment in the Persian Gulf expressed the Carter Doctrine. But a direct response to a direct attack in the Gulf, as Iraq had made against Kuwait, was not the same as a permanent military watch over the Gulf. Operation Southern Watch became an American–British–French air operation, with Saudi assistance, using Turkish air bases. Militarily, it lasted until the second Iraq War. But the political coalition underpinning it came apart five years earlier when, as disagreements mounted, the French government withdrew from enforcing the no-fly zones.

In exercising this degree of military power in the Persian Gulf, the United States deepened its long-standing predicaments in the region. Retaining American land forces anywhere in the region required movement on the Israeli–Palestinian conflict if their presence were not to re-establish Arab unity, and retaining them in Saudi Arabia, where the holiest sites in Islam stand, was likely to destabilize further Saudi domestic politics. Through the 1990s, American politicians and officials tried to contain the conflict between Israel and the Arab states and support the Israeli–Palestinian peace process set out in the 1993 Oslo Peace Accords. But the ongoing American military presence in the Middle East, allied to the failure of the peace process by 2000, strengthened the religious and political forces seeking confrontation. Whether al-Qaeda was driven primarily by political or religious motives and whether or not it was responsive to American actions remains open to question. But al-Qaeda's attacks on 11 September 2001 demonstrated that nuclear weapons were no protection against a direct assault on the American homeland from non-state militias originating in Eurasia.

* * *

As by the turn of the century, the Middle East became less susceptible to American military power and Franco-American disagreements in the region mounted again, oil stresses returned with a vengeance. With oil discoveries falling sharply, supply prospects were deteriorating. Of the world's twenty largest oil fields in 1999, seventeen had been found between 1928 and 1968; the last to be discovered was Azerbaijan's Azeri-Chirag-Gunashli field in 1986. Oil sanctions on Iran, Iraq, and Libya, meanwhile, restricted production from existing reserves. As these supply constraints tightened, Asian demand, generated most forcefully by China's spectacular economic growth, accelerated. Although China would continue to use much more coal for energy in relation to oil than Western countries, China's oil consumption more than doubled between 1997 and 2006.[24]

By 2005, an oil crisis was beginning to materialize. That year, as Asian demand rapidly increased, crude oil production stagnated. Predictably, between 2005 and mid-2008, oil prices rose rapidly.

From taking office, George Bush Jr's administration treated oil as a systemic problem. Its Energy Task Force, led by Vice President Dick Cheney, concluded that the country confronted an 'energy crisis' arising from the 'fundamental imbalance' now at work between supply and demand, which threatened national security. To allow for more production from the Middle East and North Africa, it recommended reviewing the sanctions regimes in place against Iraq, Iran, and Libya.

The fear in Washington of an impending oil crisis was an important context for the second Iraq War. An Iraq not ruled by Saddam Hussein would not need to be subject to oil sanctions. Regime change in Baghdad also appeared to Bush and his advisers to offer military advantages. Without oil sanctions, Operation Southern Watch could finally end as, without the need to protect the Kurds, could military operations in northern Iraq. A post-Ba'athist Iraq would then allow the withdrawal of American troops from Saudi Arabia, a move that Bush made just days before he declared 'mission accomplished'. In this sense, the second Iraq War constituted a reversal of the energy logic of the first: Iraq was stopped the first time because it appeared to aspire to control oil reserves in the Gulf; Iraq would be attacked the second time because containing it on a long-term basis restricted oil supply, had burdensome military costs, and ignited too much resistance in the region.[25]

Whatever the decisive motive behind the war, Bush chose to justify the war both as a military necessity—the threat of weapons of mass destruction—and in Wilsonian terms about democracy.[26] Behind each rhetorical argument lay a presumption that American air and land power could still reshape the Middle East, and that the domestic constraint on casualties that Vietnam created had been substantially lessened by 9/11.

In the event, the second Iraq War turned into another story of geopolitical failure and domestic political disaster. Again, American democratic politics precluded mobilizing an army and fiscal resources commensurate to the task.[27] Far from achieving its energy aim, the war did the opposite.[28] The post-war chaos in Iraq ensured that oil production there took the best part of a decade to recover simply to where it had been in 2000. It also created the conditions for ISIS as a cross-border Sunni insurgent movement with ambitions for a caliphate. While Hussein's Iraq had been a check on Iran, the Iraqi government that came to power after the December 2005 parliamentary elections was dominated by an alliance of Shi'ite parties. This strengthened Iran at a time when high oil and gas prices were augmenting the state's revenues, it had begun a nuclear programme, and Hezbollah's influence in Lebanon was growing.

Within NATO, the war was exceptionally destructive. The Turkish Parliament voted down an agreement struck between the first government formed by Erdogan's party, Justice and Development, and the Bush administration to allow Washington to use Turkey to launch an attack on northern Iraq. Meanwhile, the German chancellor, Gerhard Schröder, made clear that Germany would not support the war even if it were authorized by the UN Security Council.[29] Germany, France, and Belgium vetoed NATO plans to defend Turkey if attacked by Iraq. The then US ambassador to NATO described the disagreements over the war as a 'near death experience' for the alliance.[30] As if purposely to antagonize the French government, Bush's defence secretary, Donald Rumsfeld, happily extolled the 'new Europe' in the East, not the 'old Europe' of France and Germany, as NATO's European centre of gravity.[31]

Russia too emerged with geopolitical advantages. The energy environment in which the war took place had already made Russia a resurgent power. Rising oil and gas revenues had allowed Putin to pay off the money Russia borrowed from the International Monetary Fund in the 1990s, ending the American capacity to influence Moscow via debt. China's rapidly growing energy demands had amplified the opportunity. As China became a large oil- and gas-importing state, Russia had the chance to become its primary supplier.

The Iraq War amplified this burgeoning Russia–China energy relationship and prompted a strategic reassessment in China. For the Chinese leadership, it seemed self-evident that the American motive in Iraq was foreboding about future oil supply.[32] The fact that Washington was willing to commit serious military power to energy security, consequently, appeared a reason to strengthen China's capacity to defend its own foreign supply. In November 2003, China's President Hu Jintao set out what he called Beijing's 'Malacca dilemma' whereby the United States—as the naval power in practice responsible for maintaining open navigation in the maritime commons—could block Chinese oil imports through the Strait of Malacca, the narrow body of water that connects the Pacific and Indian oceans down which most of China's oil imports passed.[33] The fear behind the 'Malacca dilemma' encouraged the Chinese leadership to look for options that would reduce the volume of oil imports coming through the Strait. Under Xi Jinping, this desire would produce a land route out of the Persian Gulf. But in the short term, the Chinese leadership's heightened security fears drove it to strike a formal agreement with Moscow to build the Eastern Siberia–Pacific Ocean pipeline. Since China had become a net oil importer in 1993, it had considered a more land-based oil supply. But while it had reached an agreement with Kazakhstan in 1997, previous negotiations with Russia had proved inconclusive. Now, even before the pipeline was built, Chinese oil imports from Russia accelerated.[34]

Russia Abides in Europe

In the same year that crude oil production stagnated, a significant shift in the geopolitics of natural gas transit in Europe occurred. In 2005, the pipelines through Ukraine still carried around 75 per cent of the EU's Russian gas.[35] This dependency on Kyiv had frustrated Moscow since the Soviet Union's dissolution. During the early 2000s, the Social Democratic–Green coalition government in Berlin sought alternative transit too. In his last weeks in power, Schröder signed an agreement with the Russian government to construct the North European Gas Pipeline under the Baltic Sea to take gas from Vyborg, near Russia's border with Finland, to Greifswald on the north-east German coast. This pipeline became Nord Stream 1, and began operating in 2012.[36]

From the start, Nord Stream pulled in the opposite direction to what was supposed to be European energy diversification away from Russia. In much of Eastern Europe, it provoked a furious response, made worse by Schröder becoming the chairman of the Nord Stream company almost immediately on leaving office. The Polish defence minister compared the pipeline to the Nazi–Soviet pact, which handed over Polish-ruled Ukraine to the Soviet Union.[37] But on the German side, it was the Ukrainian problem that justified Nord Stream. When in January 2006, after a dispute between Moscow and Kyiv, Russia cut off gas going through Ukraine for three days, this fear appeared vindicated, even though it was not German imports that were hard hit.

Nord Stream also divided the EU on a north–south axis. For Southern European governments, Nord Stream was no remedy for the Ukrainian risk. Their interests were better served by the Nabucco project with Turkey on which there was little progress. With Putin judging this transit route for Caspian and Middle Eastern gas a threat to Russian dominance in European gas, Gazprom and the Italian company ENI signed a memorandum of understanding in 2007 to build a South Stream pipeline for redirecting Russian gas into Southern Europe away from Ukraine. This underwater pipeline would have taken gas from a port on the Russian Black Sea coast to Varna in Bulgaria—which joined the EU in January 2007—and then, on one route, through the western Balkans into Hungary and Austria and on the other through Greece and under the Adriatic Sea to Italy. ENI's central role in a second pipeline project with Gazprom echoed the deal struck back in the 1950s between the Italian company and the Soviet Union.[38] But while all the then EEC states and eventually Britain had seen Soviet energy's post-Suez utility, the post–Cold War EU could never agree about Russian gas or its transportation. Indeed, the competition between South Stream and Nabucco at a time when Germany had made an independent commitment to Nord Stream rendered any common EU energy strategy hopeless.

Deteriorating Russian–Ukrainian relations exposed the post–Cold War NATO–EU fault line in Europe. Seeing Putin as ever more confrontational from 2007, the Bush Jr administration pushed to take Ukraine and Georgia into NATO.[39] Whether such a security guarantee would have been redeemable on the American side was doubtful. But the principal EU states were simply unwilling to consider it. In April 2008, the German and French governments vetoed the two countries' NATO entry. Instead, one month later, as a concession to Poland, they agreed to begin serious talks with Ukraine on an associate EU membership to bring about the country's economic convergence with the EU.[40] This move upended the de facto formula that emerged in the late 1990s whereby the former Warsaw Pact and Soviet states joined NATO first or NATO and the EU at the same time. Committing to Ukraine on economic association, breaking with it on gas transit, and keeping it at bay on NATO would dramatically expose the EU–NATO misalignment over the next decade.[41]

Ukraine's position as an energy transit state ensured these stresses had systemic consequences in Europe. For a few days in January 2009, Russia stopped any gas going through Ukraine. The ensuing European gas crisis was later described by the Commission as a 'stark "wake-up" call'.[42] Predictably, it refocused European attention back on energy diversification and Nabucco. In 2009, Turkey signed an intergovernmental agreement, supported by the EU, with Austria, Hungary, Bulgaria, and Romania to build this pipeline. After the signing ceremony, the Commission president, José Manuel Barroso, described Nabucco as a 'truly European project'.[43]

Inescapably, Nabucco reopened the issue of Turkish EU member-ship.[44] In the decade after granting Turkey applicant status in 1999, the EU had acted with little alacrity to expedite Turkish entry. Formal accession talks only began in June 2005. Three months later, the German general election brought the Christian Democrats, some of whom were still happy to cast Turkey's future in civilizational terms, back into office. If Merkel herself demurred from making religious arguments, she had repeatedly stated when in opposition that Turkey should have only a 'privileged partnership'.[45] Now, some within the Turkish government thought that a reinvigorated Nabucco made membership inevitable.[46] Yet a Turkish pipeline to provide for more non-Russian gas did not represent a common EU energy strat-egy. Neither the German nor French governments were invested in it, and the British government under Gordon Brown was not prepared to spend political capital on it.[47] Even the Italian government, which did support Turkish membership, was on gas transit strongly commit-ted to Nabucco's South Stream rival. With no possibility of EU unity about gas, what had appeared to Ankara a path for Turkey to enter the EU quickly closed. It would remain shut until the 2015 refugee crisis.

American Power Waxes and Wanes at the Same Time

Across the Atlantic, the second Iraq War reactivated sharp democratic political constraints on how American military power could be deployed in the Middle East. Before 9/11, there had been a broad domestic consensus about using American power to bring about regime change in Iraq. Congress had passed the Iraq Liberation Act in 1998, committing Washington to support endeavours to remove Saddam Hussein from power. Since the Iraqi regime allowed no opposition, this meant some kind of American intervention, albeit not necessarily military.[48] But, as in Vietnam, the Iraq War eventually shattered the domestic support necessary for an American president to engage in significant new military action anywhere in Eurasia. In the 2006 mid-term elections, the Democrats used the war's unpopularity to win control of both houses of Congress. When, in January 2007, Bush announced a troop increase, labelled the Surge, members of the new Congress made a legislative bid to stop him. Although they failed, the following year Bush agreed a schedule with the Iraqi government to complete an American exit by 31 December 2011.[49] The Surge provided a central context for the 2008 presidential election. As a senator, Barack Obama opposed it. He then forcibly exploited his opposition to the war when an Illinois state senator in defeating Hillary Clinton for the Democratic nomination and John McCain in the general election.[50]

Having won as an anti-war candidate, albeit one who would remain committed to American combat operations in Afghanistan until 2014, Obama wanted to transfer American strategic attention towards China in what he termed a 'Pivot to Asia'.[51] The United States, he told the Australian Parliament in November 2011, was 'a Pacific power' that was 'here to stay'.[52]

Since successive American presidents had treated China's deep integration into the world economy from the late 1990s as a matter not of foreign policy but of mutual economic gain—as will be discussed in chapter five—this move in part constituted a significant change. But it also widened what was always the geopolitical fault line in the post–Cold War Sino-American relationship. This tension was, at least tacitly, acknowledged around climate change in Washington and energy in Beijing. Bill Clinton was unable to ask Congress to ratify the 1997 Kyoto Protocol because almost every congressional member rejected the idea that the United States should be subject to commitments on greenhouse gases that did not apply to China. For China, from the time it joined the WTO, its economic growth involved a massive increase in energy consumption, not least for manufacturing production. In the two decades between 1980 and 2000, China's primary energy consumption increased by around 240 per cent; in the one decade between 2000 and 2010 it would increase at the same rate.[53] The Chinese leadership never believed that China's economic development should be circumscribed by American power. Consequently, from the moment, in 1993, China began to need oil imports, it treated energy security as an inexorable geopolitical imperative, even if for the short to medium term it would take advantage of the US navy's presence in the maritime commons. What changed in China prior to Obama's Pivot to Asia was a military shift around naval energy security: in 2010, Beijing declared that the South China Sea, through which around one-third of world maritime trade passes, was a 'core' Chinese interest.[54]

Even in its own terms, the Pivot to Asia was difficult to exercise. Obama pushed for a new regional trade bloc—the Trans-Pacific Partnership (TPP)—that the United States could lead and from which China would be excluded. But he could not procure congressional support even to discuss ratifying the TPP. During the 2016 election, the trade treaty would be opposed by both Hillary Clinton and Donald Trump, as well as Bernie Sanders, most of the Democratic Party, and some of the other Republican candidates. Militarily, the Obama administration enhanced American naval resources in the Pacific, developed an operational doctrine for a possible military confrontation with China, and improved bilateral security relations with other Pacific states. But this brought a strategic Chinese response, especially after Xi Jinping's ascendancy. Announced in 2013, Xi's Belt and Road Initiative sought to reorient China's economy from the Pacific towards Eurasia, what one Chinese general described as China's 'strategic hinterland'.[55] If the United States was moving farther east and increasing the likelihood of an eventual maritime confrontation in the Pacific, China would turn westwards over land.[56]

Predictably, oil and gas security appeared fundamental to Xi's strategic recalibration. In 2013, China acquired the Gwadar port on Pakistan's Arabian Sea coast and struck an agreement with Islamabad to construct the China–Pakistan Economic Corridor. With a deep-sea port just beyond the Strait of Hormuz and an agreement to build pipelines through Pakistan to the Xinjiang province in the north-west of the country, China would have an alternative to transporting all oil from the Middle East and Africa through the Strait of Malacca.[57] In May 2014, Xi also secured an agreement with Putin for a gas pipeline from western Siberia to north-eastern China, backed by a thirty-year gas deal with Gazprom. The Power of Siberia, which became operational in December 2019, was Russia's first eastward-directed gas pipeline. In 2016, China began work on a naval base in Djibouti, in the waters connecting the Red Sea and the Gulf of Aden, which, via the Suez Canal, allows passage from the Mediterranean to the Indian Ocean. As a sea, as well as a land, project, Belt and Road required military change too: China's 2015 defence White Paper stated that China aimed to become 'a world-class maritime power' and that it needed a bigger navy because 'China's overseas interests have gradually expanded to every corner of the globe.'[58] By 2020, China's navy had become the largest in the world, albeit the US navy remained the most powerful.[59]

Confronted with this strategic Chinese turn, the Obama administration struggled to respond. It was unable to stop a good number of European and Asian governments from joining the Asian Infrastructure Investment Bank launched by China to support Belt and Road. It was slow to act when, in 2014, China began reclaiming large tracts of land to build artificial islands in the South China Sea, even as China proceeded to turn these islands into military bases equipped with anti-aircraft and anti-missile systems.

Indeed, rather than attempting to put a further brake on China's ambitions after Xi's arrival, Obama sought cooperation over climate change, an imperative driven by a large increase in Chinese coal consumption between 2008 and 2013. In November 2014, in an agreement laying the foundations for the Paris climate accord the following year, Obama and Xi announced in Beijing that China would reduce emissions from 2030 and that the United States would make significant cuts to achieve emissions 26 to 28 per cent below the 2005 level by 2025. In September 2016, Obama and Xi coordinated American and Chinese ratification of the Paris Treaty in a ceremony in Hangzhou.

As Obama's presidency came to an end, US–China relations had structural dynamics pulling in opposing directions. On the one side, Washington had moved towards a containment strategy in the Pacific, and China was seeking to diminish the Malacca dilemma by turning much of Eurasia into an economic sphere of influence. On the other hand, climate was now a matter of bilateral US–China cooperation. Neither could these dynamics be separated around energy. If climate change created a logic for Sino-American détente, Belt and Road involved huge carbon-intensive projects, and added gas to the China–Russia oil relationship.

That the confront-China candidate in 2016 could use geopolitical issues more effectively than the confront-Russia candidate, in part, reflected the immediate political problems posed by accommodating China. Indeed, Trump's presidency revealed that there was in fact a broad, largely bipartisan consensus in Congress favouring a more confrontational policy towards China, even among those taking climate change much more seriously than Trump. Although Trump's style of confrontation elicited persistent censure, there was—as will be discussed in chapter six—little substantive criticism of using tariff pressure to try to reconstruct the US–China trade relationship or, crucially, making technological competition a matter of national security.

* * *

Obama's confidence that he could strategically prioritize China over the Middle East and then work with China over climate change could not have arisen without the seismic change wrought by the American shale oil and gas boom. Without shale oil, Obama could not have embarked upon a strategic approach to the Middle East that wrote off the failure in Iraq. Without shale gas, he could not have made a serious offer to China on American emissions that substituted domestically produced gas for coal in electricity generation. This resurgent American energy power yielded immense geopolitical disruption in Europe around gas and in the Middle East around oil. Paradoxically, it also made American strategic choices harder.

The shale gas sector's rapid development allowed the United States to become a gas exporter at a time when an international market for sea-transported liquid natural gas was already growing. Immediately, this further politicized energy in the EU and heaped more pressure on all the strains gas imports and transportation place on the EU–NATO fault lines. For Poland and Lithuania, American gas imports were a geopolitical lifeline. When the first ship carrying American gas arrived in 2017, the Polish prime minister declared that Poland could now say 'it was a safe and sovereign country'.[60] For Germany, by contrast, American imports were unattractive. By the early 2010s, the German–Russian gas relationship was three decades old. In committing in 2011 to eliminate nuclear power within a decade, Merkel ensured that in Germany's *Energiewende* gas consumption would increase, at least until there is a technological breakthrough on renewable storage.[61] Liquid natural gas imports are more expensive than pipelined gas, and they require constructing technologically sophisticated port infrastructure. For European countries, they are also at the mercy of ships changing direction and heading to Asia where prices are higher since, except to China, there are few pipelines. Rather than welcoming the new American export capacity, Merkel's government doubled down on Russian gas and Baltic transit by supporting a second Nord Stream pipeline.

With Russia facing a fight with both the United States and Azerbaijan for its European markets, the existing conflicts around gas imports to Southern and lower Central Europe intensified. In 2013, Nabucco collapsed when Azerbaijan's state energy consortium declined to sign a supply contract.[62] This appeared to render South Stream the winner of the conflict between the two projects. But after Russia annexed Crimea in 2014, the Obama administration sanctioned the Russian company contracted to build the Bulgarian part of the South Stream pipeline and pressurized those EU member states committed to South Stream to withdraw. In June 2014, the Bulgarian government buckled and suspended work on the pipeline.[63]

Of course, American pressure on EU members over Russian energy dependency was nothing new. But Washington could also now point to an alternative, and American energy companies stood to gain from the trade. The European Commission's active support for Obama's moves to stop South Stream also showed just how deep geopolitical disunity now ran within the EU. The Commission had long insisted that Gazprom's role in South Stream did not comply with EU regulations, and had launched legal proceedings against Bulgaria. But in framing energy supply as a matter of competition law, the Commission infuriated those EU governments that stood to benefit from South Stream and were better equipped than Bulgaria to resist Washington. In defiance of the Ukrainian round of sanctions on Russia, the Austrian government signed an intergovernmental agreement with Russia over the Austrian part of South Stream two months before Bulgaria retreated. The Italian prime minister, Matteo Renzi, also made known his anger that the Commission had moved to end South Stream but had not acted decisively on Nord Stream.[64]

Defeated over South Stream, Putin simply reinvented it. In December 2014, he agreed with Turkey to build TurkStream, taking this version of a Black Sea pipeline to the Turkish rather than Bulgarian coast. One month later, Gazprom wrote to the Commission to say that once TurkStream was complete Russia would send no more gas to EU states via Ukraine.[65] This was part idle threat. Against all its protestations that it would do no such thing, Gazprom struck a new deal in December 2019 with the Ukrainian state energy company to keep the gas pipelines through Ukraine open until at least 2024. But TurkStream, nonetheless, succeeded by bypassing the EU's legal authority in its construction. It would also join Nord Stream in dividing NATO: in January 2020, gas started to arrive in Bulgaria and Greece, just one month after the US Congress imposed sanctions against companies working on Gazprom's next project, TurkStream 2. For both the EU and NATO, internal disunity about energy had initially arisen after the Soviet Union's dissolution around Turkey and Ukraine. But what during the Cold War was a cross-Atlantic NATO division became over Ukrainian and Turkish transit an intra-EU problem as well.

For the EU, this dilemma was exacerbated by the logic of Merkel's position on Nord Stream 2, which was to insist, in her words, that 'it is first and foremost an economic project' and that 'Ukraine must continue to play a role as a transit country.'[66] This could only mean that it is Southern EU states that should accept transit via Ukraine, even as much Russian and Azeri gas comes into Southern Europe via Turkey. But the difficulties for NATO went beyond the strategic ramifications of pipeline routes to the source of European imports: so long as the United States can compete with Russia to export gas to Europe, the large founder EU states' dependency on Russian gas makes NATO unstable.

* * *

Shale oil's geopolitical consequences began in the Middle East. Fears about its own oil supply after the First World War had driven the Americans to establish a foothold in the region in Saudi Arabia. A desire to protect access to Persian Gulf oil for Western Europe and Japan had shaped the incoherent American commitment in the post–Second World War Middle East, a stance that then had to be refashioned in the early 1970s in service of its own need for foreign oil. After the Iranian revolution, the Carter Doctrine led to increasing amounts of American military power being deployed there, as one problem cascaded into another without stability ensuing. Consequently, from the start of shale oil's rise, the apparent prospect of renewed energy independence appeared to Obama and his advisers an attractive portal out of Middle Eastern wars, as well an opportunity to confront Iran's nuclear ambitions. Both shale and the strategic calculations that the new supply brought in Washington proved a disruptive shock.

Before these dynamics began to play out, the Middle East and North Africa were thrown into tumult by the 2011 Arab Spring rebellions, compounding their eventual effects. With some American troops still in Iraq, Obama sent the American Navy and Air Force back into action in Libya in a NATO-led coalition of the willing joined by several Arab states. As with the second Iraq War, this military action divided NATO. But there were also crucial differences. On the European side, the big three EU states split differently. While the British and French were heavily involved in the Libyan war, the Germans did not even support the military action at the UN Security Council. In Washington, meanwhile, Obama appeared to conceive of the Libyan intervention as lending American services to France and Britain as the front-line NATO states responsible for what happened in North Africa. Indeed, retrospectively at least, he presented the war as a test case for whether the Europeans could stop 'free-riding' on Washington and take responsibility where geography meant their interests alone were directly at stake.[67]

With higher stakes, similar dynamics were at work over Syria. Obama did want to see regime change in Damascus, and his administration offered substantial support to the Syrian opposition. But his actions towards Syria were still premised on an assumption that what happened on the western side of the Persian Gulf was more a European, Turkish, and Arab problem than an American one. For him, the American relationship to Eurasia had changed, and if, in his words, the Washington 'playbook . . . that Presidents are supposed to follow' had not caught up, he, as a self-consciously 'Pacific President', had.[68] When his moment of decision came in September 2013 about whether to uphold the redline he had previously articulated over chemical weapons and order the planned airstrikes in Syria, he backed down.

For Obama, as an interview in *Atlantic* in 2016 revealed, this was the decisive choice of his presidency, the point at which he asserted the primacy of his judgement free from the old assumption that the Middle East is a shared European–American neighbourhood.[69] But whatever Obama's retrospective musings, it was the democratic backlash against the second Iraq War more than resurgent American energy power that shaped this political moment. The chain of events that led to Obama pulling the airstrikes began when British prime minister David Cameron decided he needed to seek parliamentary authorization for British participation and lost a vote in the House of Commons. Only then did Obama ask Congress for its support for military action, and only when it became clear that the House of Representatives might well not pass a bill did he take Putin's offer to make Assad eliminate the regime's chemical weapons.

An Eisenhower fearful of the 1956 presidential election had detonated Britain's war against Egypt and America's own post–war Middle Eastern strategy. Now, sixty years later, the British Parliament inadvertently played its part in an American president retreating in the Middle East. On the European side, Obama's U-turn on Syria then left the French government adrift as it had been in 1956. Over Libya, the French had come to accept NATO as a necessary structure for European military action in North Africa, only to find that Washington would not preserve the credibility of its own military threats in the Middle East. They were left with no military vehicle beyond unilateral French power for any decisive action in a region that they still saw as a matter of vital interest.

In reality, Obama did not dispense with Middle Eastern wars any more than Eisenhower could dispense with Britain after Suez. During 2014, Obama took American forces into action against ISIS in Iraq and Syria, after the Islamic group captured large swathes of territory in Syria and Iraq and the Iraqi government fell apart. Since the Global Coalition to Defeat ISIS was centred around NATO members and included Germany, this intervention placed less strain on the European side of NATO. But this new Middle Eastern war did re-exhibit the fragility of the American commitment to military action in Eurasia. Again, American democratic politics constrained an American president. Fearing Congress would withhold authorization for the war, Obama did not seek it for his air strikes against Syria in 2014, only for his parallel move to provide more logistical military support to the Syrian rebels. He also promised he would not place American troops on the ground in Syria. By limiting the military commitment to some air cover and special forces, Washington had to find local militias on the ground to do the heavy fighting, and chose the Kurdish People's Protection Units (YPG). Immediately, this tactical imperative set up an inescapable conflict with the Turkish government, for which the YPG is a terrorist organization. Where the rift over Iraq had been the Turkish Parliament's unwillingness to host American military action in a border state and some NATO members' unwillingness to defend Turkey, in Syria it became an American willingness to subordinate Turkish security concerns to the domestic impossibility of committing American soldiers to another Middle Eastern war, regardless of the fact that American airbases in Turkey were being used for attacks on ISIS.

The war again also made explicit the geographical chasm in NATO around non-energy matters in the Middle East. In justifying the intervention, Obama distinguished between Europe where ISIS had launched direct terrorist attacks and 'our homeland' that was less threatened.[70] After the 2015 Paris attacks, Obama warned against the dangers of 'an exaggeration of the risk' emanating from groups in the Middle East.[71] But for France, the war against ISIS was an entirely different proposition. From 2014, France was subject to a series of deadly assaults, and had to contend with thousands of Muslim French citizens answering the Islamic caliphate's call to jihad. Beleaguered, France began its own independent military action in Iraq in September 2014. This air war constituted France's first direct military action in the Middle East itself since withdrawing from Operation Southern Watch. Neither, for France, did the war against ISIS and other Islamic groups end in the Middle East. In 2013, President François Hollande sent French troops to Mali, and, thereafter, made further deployments across the Sahel region in Africa. In French, but not American, terms the Sahel poses some of the same problem as the Middle East, and NATO is ill-equipped to deal with either.

On the energy side, a more distant relationship with Saudi Arabia and an ultimately less confrontational relationship with Iran were supposed to be the geopolitical rewards from renewed domestic American oil capacity. It was because Jimmy Carter wanted to be freed from his own Carter Doctrine that he wished to restore energy independence. Carter heralded shale oil as one part of a future that did not arrive. Now shale was financially viable and with it came the hope that time could be called on the Carter Doctrine.

On Iran, Obama hoped that a display of power to curtail Tehran's nuclear ambitions would serve as the precondition for a reset. To realize this shift, Obama had first to move the EU towards confrontation. In the 1990s, the EU had reacted furiously to American extraterritorial sanctions against companies that invested in the Iranian energy sector. During the 2000s, the EU's sanctions against Iran did not restrict Iranian energy imports, and several EU states were reliant on them. In December 2011, Obama asked Congress to pass new extraterritorial sanctions. These used American dollar power to stop non-American companies that dealt with the Iranian central bank, through which Iranian oil revenues pass, from accessing the American financial system.[72] This time what would have been an oil shock could be palliated by shale supply, and the EU quickly agreed to ban Iranian oil imports. With Iran for the first time under sanctions directly curtailing its ability to earn hard currency from oil exports, Tehran now had an incentive to negotiate on its nuclear ambitions.

Yet Obama's deployment of American energy power could only go so far. Although the 2015 nuclear deal did temporarily restrict Iran developing nuclear weapons, it was silent on Iran's regional activities. The reality that an Iranian nuclear bomb was only delayed, and that Iran could continue to operate in Syria as well as support Hezbollah and Hamas, fuelled acute disquiet in the US Congress. Realizing there was little chance the then Republican-controlled Senate would ratify a treaty, Obama framed it as an executive agreement that did not require legislative consent, ensuring any future president could straightforwardly undo it. Since all the leading candidates for the Republican nomination were against it, the Iran nuclear deal had little chance of surviving the Democrats losing the presidency.

In the EU, the calculations around the Iran nuclear deal were rather different. For the European governments, curtailing sanctions on the Iranian energy sector was an opportunity for a new economic relationship with Tehran, not least to pursue gas diversification in the Middle East, as the European Commission acknowledged in 2014 in declaring that a 'hard-headed strategy for energy security' was urgent.[73] Consequently, whether Washington and the EU could maintain a unified position on an accommodation with Iran was always dependent upon the outcome of the 2016 American presidential election.

Russia's military entry into the Syrian war, effectively ensuring that Iran and Hezbollah would remain a military presence in the country, then wrecked any hope that rapid Iranian economic growth would lead Iran to retreat from the west of the Persian Gulf. As Obama acknowledged in heralding the deal, Russia played its part in bringing Iran to the nuclear negotiating table.[74] But its military arrival in Syria upended the Middle Eastern geopolitical environment that had made some rapprochement with Iran conceivable.

Both the Obama administration's moves on Iran and its approach to Syria shook Saudi Arabia. Each occurred on the premise that shale energy allowed a partial American strategic retreat from the region. But it was the sheer volume of new oil that was most disruptive in its consequences for Saudi Arabia. In late 2014—as described at the start of chapter two—the Saudis drove already falling prices to extremely low levels. Immediately, this dramatically weakened the already beleaguered Iraqi government, augmenting Iranian influence in the country at the same time as the Iranian-backed Houthi rebels took power in Yemen. The Saudi failure to dislodge the American shale sector led Riyadh to seek cooperation with Moscow, making OPEC Plus more important than OPEC. Soon, the Western oil majors in Iraq found themselves subject to production limits part determined in Moscow on top of ISIS attacks on their infrastructure. By 2019, all but TotalEnergies were seeking a way out from at least some of their investments.

This Saudi-centric disruption then flowed back to the United States. When Saudi Arabia militarily intervened in Yemen in 2015, the Obama administration entangled the United States in another Middle Eastern conflict by providing logistical support. Being the one major oil producer outside the new cartel was advantageous for American shale firms, allowing them, from late 2016 to March 2020, to benefit from the higher prices secured by cuts in production made by OPEC Plus. But Saudi weakness also left prices for American consumers dependent on Russian decisions. If the Carter Doctrine had been conceived to keep the Soviet Union out of the Persian Gulf, then a Saudi–Russian oil axis, a Russian military presence in Syria, and Russian support for the Iranian regime were a near exact inversion of the point.

The Trump administration was even more trapped by the Carter Doctrine's failures than Obama had been after 2008.[75] The candidate who engaged in freewheeling attacks on Saudi Arabia became the president who made the Saudi capital the location of his first official visit abroad. In part Trump's excesses hastened this reversal, allowing him to suppose that his and his family's relationship with King Salman and the Saudi crown prince, Mohammed Bin Salman (MBS), could substitute for a new Saudi strategy and lead to personal gain. Consequently, when, in 2017, MBS purged the Saudi government and had members of the royal family tortured, Trump's relationship with the crown prince only fuelled the domestic political toxicity of the US–Saudi relationship from which Trump once profited. But the problem was also structural: the United States could neither impose order nor exit the region. Early on in the Persian Gulf crisis, Trump tweeted 'we don't need to be there'.[76] But, after withdrawing American special forces from northern Syria in 2019, Trump sent them to Saudi Arabia.

Like Obama before him, Trump's immediate problem lay in Iraq's instability. In October 2019, large-scale domestic protests erupted in Iraq and continued through the whole of 2020. They were initially driven by resentment against Iran's activities in the country and Iraq's post-2014 economic crisis. As the violence escalated, fuelled by Iranian militias and the Iranian-backed security forces, Trump ordered air strikes as well as the drone strike that in January 2020 assassinated General Soleimani, the commander of Iran's extraterritorial forces. Now, the protests took on a strong anti-American character as well. After the Iraqi parliament voted to expel all foreign soldiers, another incomplete withdrawal of American troops began.

Resurgent American energy production did not provide a path away from the Carter Doctrine. In 2019, American oil imports through the Persian Gulf were 250 per cent lower than their first peak in 1977, before the Iranian Revolution, and around 290 per cent lower than their second peak in 2001.[77] But American energy independence is an illusion even if the United States were to stop importing oil entirely, which it will not any time soon since American refineries have a circumscribed capacity to process shale oil. What happens inside OPEC Plus is consequential for American consumers if prices rise too high and for American producers if they fall too low. This puts American presidents and Congress at the mercy of both Saudi-Russia relations and Iraq's instability.

Indeed, the shale-shaped energy world that led to China replacing the United States as the world's largest oil importer paradoxically amplifies the strategic case for the Carter Doctrine.[78] Most of the oil now passing through the Strait of Hormuz is destined for China and other Asian countries. Since acquiring the port at Gwadar, China can monitor shipping through the Strait of Hormuz. While China has no permanent naval presence around the Gulf, the Chinese leadership treats Iran as a country of critical geopolitical importance. On land and at sea, Iran is central to the Belt and Road. China conducted joint naval exercises with Iran near the Strait of Hormuz in 2017 and trilateral exercises with Russia and Iran in 2019 after the Persian Gulf crisis began. It is far from clear that the Chinese government has any desire to use Chinese naval power to take direct responsibility for China's energy security in the Gulf. But, under the accelerating Sino-American geopolitical rivalry, it would be a risk for any US president to let China become the predominant naval presence there, even if remaining in the Gulf seemingly to protect oil imports to China will always be open to domestic political challenge.

*   *   *

The pandemic's fallout pressurized the fault lines around American power in Eurasia and dramatically showed how they have come to interconnect. Although the Trump administration and China in January 2020 reached a preliminary agreement to end the trade war, this step back from decoupling was short-lived. With Chinese demand crashing in the first quarter of the year, China was in no position to buy the volume of American exports it had promised. When, in May 2020, China imposed national security legislation on Hong Kong, effectively terminating the governance arrangements agreed in the 1984 Joint Declaration with Britain, US–China relations deteriorated further.

Meanwhile, Putin's initial willingness in early 2020 to ditch temporarily OPEC Plus and retaliate against Washington over the Nord Stream 2 and TurkStream sanctions imposed in December 2019 demonstrated how American–Russian gas competition in Europe could spill over into oil matters. Even the subsequent accommodation between the world's three leading oil producers in April 2020 to put a floor under prices could not stabilize the underlying geopolitical dynamics around fossil fuel energy. With oil prices slumping as far as they did in March and April, China bought large quantities of oil to stockpile. Apparently emboldened by the belief that American shale producers had taken a severe hit, a Gazprom vessel arrived in May 2020 at the German port of Mukran with the aim of completing the last stretch of Nord Stream 2. Against a backdrop of congressional pressure, Trump ordered more sanctions. Days later, Trump announced that a quarter of the American troops in Germany would be withdrawn.

After Trump lost, Congress moved to ensure that Trump could not implement the troop removal before he left office. During his first six months in office, Biden waived the sanctions on Nord Stream 2. But, in an age of seaborne liquid gas and OPEC Plus, American politicians are unlikely to accept as a given European countries importing large quantities of Russian gas, especially while German governments expect NATO to act as anti-Russian bulwark in Eastern Europe. What looks like the Trump shock to Germany was far more structural. If it were not, it would not be possible to explain why Obama's advisers spent time worrying that Merkel sometimes appeared rather keener on Russian and Chinese company at the United Nations than American.[79] What Trump made explicit in deeds is that the American commitment to resolving security dilemmas for Germany in Europe is coming to an end.

Nonetheless, the events of 2019 and 2020 have weakened American energy power. Shale oil companies were battered by the price collapse in March–April 2020 and the slump in investment in oil firms. Although output cuts made by OPEC Plus pushed prices back above $60 a barrel in February 2021, a wave of shale bankruptcies had already occurred, and American production at the end of 2020 remained around two million barrels per day lower than at the start of that year. Albeit temporarily, the United States once again, in May and June 2020, imported more oil than it exported.[80] From the start of his presidency, Joe Biden's climate agenda meant he could not be seen to be encouraging shale producers. But without a recovery of the shale sector, the United States will be back to having a substantial foreign oil dependency, including from the Middle East. Appositely, as the prospects for shale oil faltered, another incomplete withdrawal of American troops from Iraq was handed off in January 2021 from a Republican to a Democratic president. Macron greeted Joe Biden's inauguration by calling for greater American military involvement in the Middle East.

American liquid natural gas exports proved more robust during the pandemic. By the beginning of 2021, they had reached a new monthly high.[81] But they did so as climate became another source of tension in American–European gas relations. In the autumn of 2020, the French government asked the French energy company Engie, in which the French state has a stake, and which is a financial backer of Nord Stream 2, to refrain from signing a long-term contract for American imports on the grounds of the high methane emissions in shale.[82]

The geopolitics of climate change now also intersects with Sino-American rivalry and its consequences for Europe. If the EU and individual EU states, as large fossil fuel energy importers, treat China—the world's largest carbon emitter—as more of a partner on climate than the United States—the world's largest oil and gas producer—green ambitions are likely to destabilize further the American–European energy relationship. Moreover, the more the United States acts to improve its weak economic position on green energy, the more Sino-American rivalry will intensify. Joe Biden began his presidency promising billions of dollars of investment to the green energy manufacturing sector while his climate czar John Kerry expressed his desire to decouple climate from the rest of the Sino-American relationship. But China's dominance of renewable energy manufacturing and the metals necessary for it ensure that these aims are incompatible. Green energy in the United States cannot empower the Chinese manufacturing sector without starting off the cycle of resentments that helped bring a confront-China political outsider to the presidency.

The Centrifugal EU

For Europe, the disruption in the Middle East over the 2010s has made the region much more than an energy-rich neighbourhood on which it economically depends. The millions of refugees driven out of Syria produced a political, as well as humanitarian, crisis for the EU. Although the Merkel–Erdogan deal in 2016 to stop the movement of people into the EU was supposed to expedite Turkish accession talks, Merkel's rationale for pursuing the agreement was also the reason why Turkish membership was untenable for the EU. Indeed, that there would be no resolution was soon made explicit by Merkel herself when, during the 2017 German general election campaign, she said that 'the fact is clear that Turkey should not become a member of the European Union'.[83] Yet, since the EU still required Turkey's cooperation over migration across the EU's land and sea borders, bringing a formal end to accession talks proved another matter.

This muddle was part of the geopolitical context in which the Brexit referendum occurred. Regardless of party, British governments since the 1990s had consistently supported Turkish membership of the EU. For David Cameron's government, the EU's 2009 gas crisis had made it more urgent.[84] Shortly after becoming prime minister, Cameron, on an official trip to Ankara, said that he was the 'strongest possible advocate' for Turkish accession.[85] A year later, his government signed a new bilateral military cooperation treaty with Turkey. But the bipartisan geopolitical consensus in Britain around Turkish membership hid a domestic legitimation problem: public support was low and only a little above the EU average.[86] Apparently fearful of letting the issue become entangled in British democratic politics, Cameron's coalition government excluded the accession of new states from the 2011 EU Act—which guaranteed a referendum before any more powers were transferred away from Westminster—despite the fact that France and Austria were already legally committed to referendums on any agreement for Turkish membership.

In these circumstances, it was always reasonably likely that Turkey would feature in a referendum on whether Britain's own EU membership should continue. But the 2015–16 refugee crisis and Merkel's actions gave the Turkey issue an acute additional potency. This was in part a simple function of large numbers of people arriving in Europe in the months preceding the referendum. But Merkel's role as the arbitrator of the EU's response to the crisis also demonstrated Britain's political weakness inside the EU. Even where Britain had an opt-out, as with asylum, EU decisions driven by other states had consequences. Once put under direct pressure from the Leave campaign's lines of attack, Cameron conducted a large U-turn, claiming that his referendum opponents were fear-mongering since Turkey would not be ready to join 'until the year 3000'.[87] But, as it had done in the French referendum on the EU constitutional treaty in 2005, the Turkey issue, quite probably, hurt pro-EU arguments with enough voters to influence the referendum outcome.

Elsewhere, the structural impasse around Turkish membership was deepened by new Franco-German differences. For the German government, Turkey's economy had to be treated as a sphere of risk for Germany and the EU. When the Fed raised interest rates in 2018, Turkey experienced a financial crisis. This reflected a structural vulnerability in the post-crash Turkish economy, with Turkish banks having acquired a high volume of dollar debt without the Turkish central bank possessing a swap line to provide dollars in an emergency. This financial hit was intensified by trade sanctions imposed by Trump. Fearing a Turkish economic meltdown would end the 2016 EU–Turkey agreement, the German government began to contemplate economic aid to Ankara. But for Macron, Turkey had become a French antagonist in the Middle East. He judged the Turkish military intervention in Syria, which began in 2016, as contrary to European NATO interests in the war against ISIS. Asked whether his comments in 2019 that NATO was 'experiencing a brain death' suggested he believed that Turkey did not belong in NATO in the long term, he answered, 'I couldn't say.'[88]

These disagreements necessarily pressed upon the EU's fault lines around energy. By 2018, any idea that Turkey would become an energy hub for the southern EU independently of acting as a transit state for Russian gas was exhausted. Indeed, Turkey and several EU states were now competing over the rights to energy sources lying in the eastern Mediterranean. These tensions had first surfaced in 2010–11 over gas discoveries in the Levant basin around Israel, Egypt, and Cyprus, where Turkey alone recognizes Northern Cyprus as a state. They were intensified in the same summer as the 2015 refugee crisis by a large discovery in Egypt's waters by the Italian firm ENI. With the prospect of a partially internal new gas supply, the Commission backed a project for a new pipeline to take offshore gas from Cyprus and Israel to Greece and Italy and onto wider European markets, and in early 2020, the Cypriot, Greek, and Israeli governments signed an agreement to build it. Shut out of all the gas developments in the eastern Mediterranean, the Turkish government began aggressively to assert what it claims are Northern Cyprus' legal rights. In early 2018, Turkish warships stopped ENI drilling off Cyprus, and in 2019 Turkish vessels began their own operations, prompting the EU to sanction Ankara. Erdogan responded with what from 2016 became his standard retaliatory threat, saying 'these doors will open and these Daesh (ISIS) will be sent to you'.[89] Seeing Turkey as encircled, Erdogan struck an agreement in November 2019 with the beleaguered Libyan government to demarcate new maritime boundaries between the two states, which the EU denounced as violating Greek and Cypriot sovereignty. Soon after, the Turkish Parliament authorized troop deployments in Libya, pitting Turkey militarily against the Russian-backed rebel army, prompting a furious reaction from Macron but not Merkel.

The growing Franco-German schism over Turkey cut through the old EU–NATO misalignment at a time when in principle Brexit offered a path to the EU ending its security dependence on NATO. The post–Cold War ambition to make the EU akin to a security federation had never recovered from the Franco-British estrangement over the second Iraq War. But after the 2008 crash, bilateral relations between London and Paris improved significantly. In 2009, France rejoined NATO's integrated military command. A year later, motivated in part by a mutual desire to cut defence spending, the British and French governments agreed to enshrine bilateral military cooperation for fifty years outside any EU frame-work. Although this new collaboration continued into Libya, it came apart when the American retreat in Syria in the autumn of 2013 reactivated the question in Paris of European strategic autonomy. As the idea that the EU should acquire more authority in the security sphere regained some momentum, David Cameron opposed pro-posals to develop a separate EU military headquarters and joint EU defence assets. In the same month as the British referendum, the EU High Representative published the EU's first security strategy since the beginning of the Iraq War. Over the next year, without having to worry about British objections, the EU agreed measures to deepen defence cooperation and allow for a subset of member states to develop joint military capabilities.

For Macron, this appeared an opportunity to move the Franco-German axis into the security sphere so that Europe could, as he later put it, 'regain military sovereignty'.[90] In the 2019 Franco-German Aachen Treaty, he did persuade Merkel to accept more bilateral integration on security. But the EU could only move towards strategic autonomy if Germany were to replicate the security guarantee NATO provides to the EU's Eastern member states as well as support French commitments in the Middle East and North Africa. In reality, the post–Cold War German military has lacked the most basic operational capacity: fewer than half of its tanks and a third of its fighter aircraft were fit for action in early 2018, and at the end of 2017 it did not have a single submarine in operational order.[91]

As the distance between Macron's geopolitical ambitions and German preferences became clearer, the EU's structural incapacity on security issues came to press ever more strongly against the NATO–EU fault lines. In 2019, the French president began arguing for reappraising relations with Russia. Here, Macron was replaying de Gaulle's Cold War strategy. But de Gaulle failed in a more propitious geopolitical environment. This EU has borders with Russia, and consequently members that will never contemplate repudiating NATO's command, as France did, or reaching an accommodation with Moscow, as West Germany did. The Middle East and North Africa are much more distant neighbourhoods for parts of the EU than they were for an EEC that initially included Algeria and where a third of the original members were Mediterranean states.

Frustrated, Macron resorted to unilateral action. Most dramatically, in October 2019 he vetoed EU accession negotiations previously promised to North Macedonia and joined others in blocking Albania's, declaring that the EU could not develop a strategic identity or decision-making capacity if it continues to expand. This only deepened the Franco-German impasse. It was after his veto that Merkel reportedly told him that she was 'tired of picking up the pieces' of his 'disruptive politics' and 'glue[ing] together the cups [he] ha[d] broken'.[92]

Meanwhile, Merkel prioritized containing the risk posed to NATO from an American president exceedingly willing to pontificate out loud on the incoherencies of the EU–NATO relationship. Her tactic was to play for time. But in defending the German commitment to Nord Stream, she could only amplify EU differences about gas dependency on Russia. When, in late 2019, the US Congress passed its new sanctions on Nord Stream 2, the German finance minister attacked them as a 'serious interference' not just in Germany's 'sovereignty' but in Europe's too, ignoring the fact that other EU governments thought about sovereignty very differently.[93] Then, in late August and early September 2020, the protests in Belarus over the country's presidential election and the attempted murder of Russian opposition leader Alexis Navalny pushed these EU divisions into German politics. What had been a relative consensus within the grand coalition parties in Germany appeared to shatter, leaving Merkel subject to unprecedented domestic criticism about her commitment to Nord Stream, including from fellow Christian Democrats.[94]

In their origins, these disputes reach back to the energy issues at the heart of the Suez rupture and Europe's longer history since oil became a part of geopolitics. For five decades, Central and Southern European energy dependency on Russia has been a geopolitical fact of life. Indeed, since the First World War's end, the periods in which Germany has eschewed Russian/Soviet oil and later gas have been short. In their entirely different ways, it is Hitler's turn to Russian conquest and the first decade of the Cold War that have been the aberrations. The present German-Russian gas relationship was constructed with the Soviet Union. Since it has endured three decades into a post–Cold War world where Moscow uses gas as an instrument of power, Germany cannot escape responsibility for what happens to states with borders with post-Soviet Russia whether they are inside the EU or, as in Ukraine's case, they are not.

Erdogan's push to contest the Ottoman Empire's end in Europe and the Middle East also makes the present geopolitical environment much tougher for the EU to navigate than the one that prevailed during the 1950s. By June 2020, the Turkish military intervention in the second Libyan civil war had helped the government in Tripoli force the Russian- and French-backed rebels out of the north-west of the country, giving Turkey the chance to develop naval and air bases on the southern Mediterranean coast. Over the next months, Erdogan made a further series of confrontational moves in the eastern Mediterranean.[95] Turkish survey vessels, guarded by Turkish naval ships with Ottoman names, moved into Cypriot and Greek waters. Explaining the Turkish government's actions, Erdogan's deputy pronounced that 'we are throwing away the maps of the eastern Mediterranean that imprison us on the mainland'.[96] The same summer, Erdogan issued a decree reconverting Hagia Sophia and other former Byzantine churches from museums to mosques.

Fearing a breakdown of relations with Turkey, Germany pursued mediation. But from inside the EU, it was constrained by the Greek government, which, in August 2020, unilaterally struck an agreement about maritime sovereignty with Egypt. By contrast, Macron pushed for confrontation, sending French ships and jets to the eastern Mediterranean against a fellow NATO member while offering an effective bilateral security guarantee to Cyprus. Later in the year, France, supported by its Greek and Cypriot allies, pressed for substantial EU sanctions against Ankara, including ending the EU–Turkey customs union, only to be thwarted by the German government, backed by Italy and Spain, insisting on much milder measures.

This Franco-German disagreement has rendered a collective EU response to Turkish strategic ambitions impossible. For Macron, Erdogan's neo-Ottomanist rhetoric is evidence of revisionist territorial ambitions. If that judgement disregards the two countries' shared NATO membership, in Macron's eyes that only throws more doubt on NATO's usefulness. If the EU also proves an inadequate vehicle for checking Ankara, France has non-European allies in Saudi Arabia and the United Arab Emirates, where France has a naval air station.[97] By contrast, Germany is Turkey's largest trading partner and foreign investor. As it is more oriented towards Russia for oil and gas than France, it is less dependent on facilitating future imports from North Africa or the east Mediterranean.

These are not accidental differences. Rather, they reflect the EU's broader geopolitical fault lines generated by its post–Cold War Eastern and Southern borders, ongoing oil and gas energy dependency, and need for, but misalignment with, NATO. If the fracturing of the US–Turkey relationship means that the EU can now deal with Turkey without Washington's pressure to negotiate accession, Turkey's reorientation also makes it a geopolitical competitor in the EU's southern neighbourhood, as well as a source of division about that region's relative importance.

* * *

To varying degrees, all the geopolitical predicaments of the past three decades have been amplified by economic problems. In a world economy in which dollar credit became central to growth, and where corporate access to the American banking system is often indispensable, the United States has enormous financial power. That the political disruption of the past decade is structurally interconnected is in part a function of this power. But the substantial economic changes that have occurred since the 1970s have also played an independent role in destabilizing politics in Western democracies, including in ways that constrain geopolitical choices. These start with the breakdown of Bretton Woods. This is not because the years between 1945 and 1973 can be reduced to something usefully summed up as the Bretton Woods era. Rather its collapse cannot be separated from a host of interconnected factors: the decline of American energy power, the American move to détente, the growing importance of an international dollar credit environment, and much higher levels of debt.

Since the Bretton Woods fixed exchange rate system was replaced with floating exchange rates in 1973, there has been no return to an international monetary order, or a metallic basis for money. Only in a world without dollar–gold convertibility could there be quantitative easing and could such easy credit conditions have renewed American energy power. The international economy into which China became integrated had no rules about exchange rates, and it was China's currency management that became the first source of significant Sino-American trade tensions in the 2000s. Without Bretton Woods' end, there would not have been the monetary problems to which the Eurozone became a remedy and German power inside the EU would not have taken the particular form it has. The dollar, monetary policy, debt, and energy are the points where economic change, geopolitics, and democratic politics decisively intersect. It is in the 1970s where the economic origins of the present political disruptions lie, and the book's second story begins.

PART II

Economy

4

Our Currencies, Your Problem

In the early summer of 2011, yields on Italian government bonds were rising to the point at which Italy would be unable to borrow without a bailout that the Eurozone had no capacity to provide. On 5 August, the outgoing and incoming presidents of the European Central Bank (ECB)—Jean-Claude Trichet and Mario Draghi—sent a letter to the Italian prime minister, Silvio Berlusconi. They demanded action in six policy areas that 'in view of the severity of the current financial market situation' should be made 'as soon as possible with decree laws, followed by parliamentary ratification by end-September 2011'. It further stated that 'a constitutional reform tightening fiscal rules would also be appropriate' and concluded with the sentence that 'we trust that the government will take all the appropriate actions'.[1] Within twenty-four hours, Berlusconi promised action. On 7 August, Trichet issued a statement welcoming Berlusconi's move and revealing that the ECB would indirectly purchase Italian sovereign debt. Later that month, Berlusconi asked the Italian Parliament to pass an austerity budget and bills providing for structural reforms. But, as it became clear some of this legislation would fail, Berlusconi backtracked. During September and October, the market pressure on Italian bonds, which had fallen after 7 August, mounted and the ECB made only a small volume of purchases to counter it. At the G20 summit on 3–4 November, the German chancellor and French president then gave Berlusconi an ultimatum to act decisively or lose their support.[2] After the summit, the ECB stopped buying Italian bonds and Angela Merkel rang the Italian president, Giorgio Napolitano, to suggest he find an alternative government.[3] A few days later, Berlusconi resigned, and Napolitano appointed an entirely technocratic Italian Cabinet led by former European Commissioner Mario Monti. From that political moment until September 2019, no minister of economy and finance in Italy was an elected politician.

In the first general election held after Monti's installation, the insurgent Five Star Movement took a quarter of the vote. Five Star, which claimed that the entire Italian political class was undemocratic and corrupt, refused to share power with the centre-left grouping led by the Democrats, which had the largest number of seats. Italy was left with a grand coalition government formed between the centre-left, Berlusconi's centre-right grouping and two centrist parties. Five years later, at the following general election, Five Star won the single largest share of the vote of any party. Afterwards, it formed a coalition government with *Lega*, a right-wing Eurosceptic party that had begun life as *Lega Nord*, at times advocating northern Italy's secession. During that election campaign, Matteo Salvini, *Lega*'s leader, said that 'it is clear to everyone that the euro is a mistake for our economy' since the euro was really 'a German mark which they have called the euro'.[4]

In between Berlusconi's exit and the arrival of the Five Star–*Lega* coalition, Italy's debt was made sustainable by Mario Draghi, the man who in November 2011 took over at the ECB and would, in early 2021, himself become Italian prime minister. Speaking in London in July 2012, Draghi, without having consulted anyone else at the ECB, declared that 'within our mandate, the ECB is ready to do whatever it takes to preserve the Euro'. He paused, and continued: 'Believe me, it will be enough.'[5] This speech did not immediately end the Eurozone crisis. Indeed, Draghi could not have done so: there was no agreed ECB policy behind his words and, just as importantly, no acceptance by the German government that the ECB should take radical action at all. Accordingly, Draghi had to spend the summer constructing a new bond-purchasing programme that would be acceptable to Merkel.[6] The solution he arrived at was Outright Monetary Transactions (OMT). Although Draghi's words and their acceptance by Merkel bought Italy time, they could not fix the Eurozone. Indeed, nothing that was politically possible could: the Eurozone, both as it was conceived and as it materialized, contains a series of insoluble problems, some of which pre-exist its creation.

Bretton Woods Ends

Like much else in the present world economy, the story of the Euro-zone begins in the 1970s, and, in particular, in Bretton Woods' end. As a dollar order, Bretton Woods had made the American currency the only currency convertible into gold and the currency for much international trade. This system offered obvious benefits to the United States since European states could not easily engage in competitive devaluations, and through the International Monetary Fund (IMF) Washington could insist on economic policy changes when lending to them. It did though also provide the West European states access to dollar credit to finance small balance of payments deficits and gave them the right to control the flow of capital from their countries into the United States. For John Maynard Keynes—Britain's chief negotiator at Bretton Woods—by diminishing the problem of capital flight and allowing governments to set interest rates in relation to unemployment, this monetary system was crucial for the prospects of democratic political stability in Europe.[7]

In practice, Bretton Woods proved both inadequate to the problems of recovery in a world short of dollars and unpalatable to the Roosevelt administration's successor. During the 1947–48 European economic crisis, Harry Truman eschewed the Bretton Woods institutions in providing dollars to the West European states; instead, he initiated the Marshall Plan. He also made little effort to stop the New York banks receiving illegal capital outflows from Europe, although he accepted that Europe's currencies would for trading purposes remain non-convertible for some time.

The 1947–48 European economic crisis also revealed a fundamental fault line around the dollar–gold relationship that would persist until Bretton Woods ended. In his search for a solution that would give the dollar primacy and yet still rely on gold, Harry Dexter White—the chief American negotiator at Bretton Woods—had created a system where a national currency served as a physically bound international reserve asset. The result was a system that had to function with either too few dollars, as it did between 1947 and 1948, or too little gold, as would be the case in the 1960s.[8]

The second of these problems was hugely intensified by the rise of Eurodollars as an offshore currency. They ensured that by the late 1960s there were many more dollars in the world economy that were not backed by gold than those issued by the Federal Reserve.[9] Eurodollars began in the early post-war years as dollar deposits held in banks outside the United States that were not subject to American banking controls.[10] By the end of the 1950s, banks were trading and lending these offshore dollars in London.[11] In these London markets, capital moved free from the post-war capital controls deployed by the European governments, or the controls on interest rates operated by the US Treasury. By the mid-1960s, a significant Eurodollar credit market had emerged. It was increasingly dominated by American banks that established London branches to participate, and it allowed European firms to borrow in offshore dollars. Quite how these Eurodollar credit markets worked to generate an accelerating quantity of dollars was far from transparent. In a seminal article about the Eurodollar system, the monetarist economist Milton Friedman commented upon 'the mystifying quality of money creation' and suggested that Eurodollars were 'mostly the product of the bookkeeper's pen'.[12] In December 1968, the Fed discussed the risk that it might come to be seen as the lender of last resort to these credit markets.[13] But what happened in the Eurodollar system was ultimately beyond any central bank's control or authority. As the American political economist Jeffry Frieden has neatly expressed the point: 'who was going to supervise the dollar deposits in a German bank's branches on British soil? The answer came quickly: nobody.'[14]

With the Eurodollar markets rendering even the principle of dollar–gold convertibility incoherent, American decision-makers could not make Bretton Woods work as it was designed. From 1965, their geopolitical priorities worsened the dilemma. In deciding to send American combat troops to Vietnam, President Johnson increased American borrowing and, abetted by the Federal Reserve, allowed inflation to rise. This overt disregard for the dollar's external value infuriated the French president, Charles de Gaulle. From 1965, de Gaulle demanded gold for France's dollar reserves, and charged that the system allowed the United States to run up 'enormous debts' to finance its wars for which others had to 'suffer'.[15] His anti-dollar stance and Johnson's de facto anti-gold stance created an unresolvable structural conflict.[16] Johnson's decision in March 1968 to change course in Vietnam during a gold crisis—discussed in chapter two—demonstrated just how constraining dollar–gold convertibility had become.

From the 1970s, oil made these American choices harder. Since domestic pre-shale oil production peaked in 1970, the United States imported growing quantities of oil through the decade.[17] Rising oil imports structurally widened the trade deficit. Bretton Woods was designed for a world where the dominant economy with a strong domestic oil supply had a large trade surplus, not one in which the world's largest oil consumer was on a path to becoming the world's largest oil importer.

This pressure oil placed on the American trade deficit amplified a problem that predated it. Dexter White was wrong to assume that the system necessarily protected American export competitiveness. By the late 1960s, it did not require currency devaluation for West Germany and Japan to benefit from the exchange rate parities in operation; they only had to resist significant revaluation. In response, American politicians could only threaten trade tariffs to protect those sectors, starting with textiles, most imperilled by international competition. This dynamic created a choice between maintaining the international monetary system and maintaining the international trading order.[18] In one way, it was the same choice that American politicians in the early 1930s had confronted, albeit without the added complications around German reparations. Then, Hoover and Congress had supported tariffs while Roosevelt had preferred to remove the dollar from gold.[19] This time, the politically tumultuous year of 1968 ensured that the burden of decision fell upon Richard Nixon, a man who took office convinced that the Fed's monetary caution at the decade's start had lost him the 1960 election to John Kennedy.

In August 1971, President Nixon dramatically ended dollar–gold convertibility and imposed tariffs on imports that would stay in place until other states agreed to a dollar devaluation. Four months later, Nixon secured that devaluation as part of the Smithsonian agreement. This agreement could have reset Bretton Woods. But while some in the Nixon administration did want to reform the international monetary system, Nixon wanted to end it. Indeed, in 1972, his Treasury indicated it wished to liberalize capital from laws that restricted its movement in and out of the United States. With oil imports widening the American trade deficit, the American economy now needed an overseas supply of dollars to finance that deficit. Without even the appearance of American restraint, the exchange rate parities became ever more strained. In March 1973, all attempts to maintain fixed exchange rates were abandoned. Thereafter, currencies would float, their value being determined by daily transactions in the foreign exchange markets. At the beginning of the next year, the Nixon administration removed all American capital controls. What could have been a trade war became instead a several-decades-long competition about exchange rates and who should bear the monetary burden of what Washington and the Fed wished to do with the dollar.[20]

In the post–Bretton Woods monetary world, the Eurodollar markets and oil became the basis of American financial power. Preserving the dollar's international position at as little domestic cost as possible was made much easier by the Eurodollar system: these offshore markets made the dollar the premier currency for banking and credit. Then the 1973 oil price shock—as the next chapter will discuss— boosted Eurodollar activity.[21] It also engineered a flow of the dollar earnings of the Arab oil-producing states in OPEC back into the United States.[22] To reduce any temptation Saudi Arabia might have had to lend those dollar revenues to European countries, Nixon's treasury secretary in 1974 procured an agreement that Riyadh would buy US Treasury bonds outside the normal auctions where government debt was sold and without any requirement that the volume of purchases be publicly released by the Treasury. In exchange, Saudi Arabia received increased military aid and access to new arms purchases.[23] Nixon's successors maintained this petrodollar recycling. In the second half of the 1970s, the dollar's weakness incentivized Saudi Arabia and other OPEC states to peg oil prices to a basket of the world's major currencies. But the Carter administration brokered an increase in the Saudi quotas and voting rights in the IMF to bind OPEC to dollar pricing, a deal probably sweetened by more military aid.[24] In this sense, Saudi Arabia's emerging utility to American energy security in the Persian Gulf in the 1970s was paralleled by the part Riyadh played in allowing the United States to import oil denominated in its own currency at a moment when OPEC state-run companies were taking over from the big American and European companies in the Middle East.

* * *

This post–Bretton Woods world in which no currency was convertible into a metal—the world of fiat money—was an unprecedented monetary phenomenon in human history. Allied to the oil shocks, these hitherto untried monetary conditions produced profound economic changes. Public and private debt exploded, with total world debt more than doubling as a proportion of world GDP between 1974 and 2016.[25] Inflation, in the past associated with war, accelerated. Unemployment, which Keynesian economists were convinced should fall when inflation rose, increased across virtually all Western economies.

The political implications of this new inflationary and debt-shaped world were complex. Indeed, who politically benefited and who lost, and why they did became bitterly contested. One familiar narrative makes the 1970s the beginnings of the political rise of an anti-state approach to the organization of economies and economic policy.[26] This telling renders Paul Volcker's appointment as president of the Federal Reserve Board in 1978 followed by Margaret Thatcher's arrival in power in Britain a year later and Ronald Reagan's 1980 election win watershed moments. Each—and in Thatcher's and Reagan's cases their advisers—is then cast as attracted to the arguments of the Austrian economist Friedrich Hayek and the American monetarist Milton Friedman that the state's post-war interventions were responsible for the surging inflation and weak growth that marked the 1970s. The unemployment that arose from their policies in the late 1970s and 1980s led critics to charge that the American and British economies were sacrificed to ideological dogma. Much later the ideology was given the name neoliberalism, even though the origins of ideas that can coherently be labelled neoliberalism are to be found in the Habsburg Empire's demise and what its defenders saw as the post-inflationary onslaught of a destructive nationalism tied to democracy replacing constitutional monarchy.[27]

But making the economic story of the 1970s one of any ideological ascendancy necessarily downplays the structural material causes of the decade's crises that played out regardless of the prior dispositions of politicians and central banks.[28] In particular, energy casts a huge shadow over the apparently ideological debate in the 1970s about what the state could and should do.[29] Politicians on both sides of the Atlantic had an acute incentive to retreat from regulating capital flows because they needed easy access to dollars to pay for larger oil import bills. In the United States, those who advocated economic deregulation in the 1970s were first and foremost arguing for an end to federal government agencies regulating energy prices and allocating oil to individual states for specific uses—as will be discussed in chapter eight.[30] The first executive order Ronald Reagan issued as president lifted all remaining federal controls on oil prices and allocations, pronouncing that 'the 1970s were the Dark Ages of America's energy history'.[31] Milton Friedman, frequently taken to be a leading proponent of neoliberalism, was obsessed with the energy question, charging that governmental controls on prices and effective federal oil rationing were entirely responsible for the energy shortages.[32] Indeed, Friedman's intellectual insistence that inflation was always a monetary phenomenon, and hence unaffected by energy shocks, might politically be seen as the corollary of his belief that oil prices needed to increase to end the supply shortages. Quite simply, without taking energy seriously there is no persuasive story that can be told about the trajectories of economies from the 1970s through to the 1980s, or their political consequences, including those that led to the euro's creation.

Dwelling on neoliberalism as a principally Anglo-American phenomenon also obscures the fact that the strongest and most powerful proponents of anti-inflationary discipline in the 1980s were to be found not in Washington, New York, or London but in Frankfurt and Bonn. Nor, as will be shown, are these separate matters: it was precisely because the West German central bank did not treat the 1986 oil price slump as an end to the inflationary era that the French government began to turn back to the idea of European monetary union that had flickered and fallen during the last years of Bretton Woods.

The Twin European Monetary Burden

The West European governments were, to use Paul Volcker's word, 'stunned' at Nixon's actions in August 1971.[33] Afterwards, they expected Bretton Woods to be repaired, not put on a path to destruction. But their common adversity could not disguise crucial differences in their perceptions of the crisis, their capacities to respond to it, and the prospects for their currencies in a new floating world.

German politicians and officials framed the Bretton Woods crisis around the Eurodollar markets. If higher interest rates could be avoided by banks and companies borrowing dollars in London, the Bundesbank could not in practice tighten credit conditions. For the West German chancellor, Willy Brandt, the Eurodollar markets compromised European monetary autonomy, by which he meant German autonomy. His solution was a European central bank. For French policymakers, Bretton Woods' problems primarily arose from the cavalier American attitude towards gold. Indeed, just days before Nixon's decision, French president Georges Pompidou had ordered a French warship to cross the Atlantic to retrieve France's gold in New York.[34]

These different political judgements were compounded by material differences. The West German Deutsche Mark had an anti-inflationary credibility that the franc lacked. The German monetary advantage in part arose from the West German trade surplus and in part from the Bundesbank's independence from democratic control at a time when in most of Western Europe governments, not central banks, decided interest rates. Over time, these two phenomena reinforced each other: the German central bank prioritized domestic price stability, making the West German economy export oriented.

Notwithstanding the divergence, the European Community (EC) began in 1969 discussing monetary cooperation. The 1970 Werner report proposed a three-stage transition to monetary union, while avoiding the question on which the French and Germans probably most disagreed, namely who would decide European monetary policy.[35] By early 1971, there was massive upwards pressure on the Deutsche Mark's parity against the dollar, with German firms borrowing dollars at high volumes in the Eurodollar markets, where interest rates were lower than those prevailing in the domestic economy, and then selling them for Deutschmarks.[36] In May 1971, just two months after the EC states formally adopted the Werner Plan, West Germany and the Netherlands unilaterally floated their currencies. Pompidou denounced this currency appreciation tactic as a violation of 'Community morality' since by default it also changed the German and Dutch currencies' value against those of other EC currencies.[37] As one German official commented, unilaterally floating the Deutsche Mark had 'brought the Community near to breaking point'.[38] Although there was simply no policy available to deal with the Eurodollar and intra-European exchange rate instability problems simultaneously, French fury over the unilateral floating episode pushed Brandt to try to find a European solution anyway. In 1972, the EC adopted a collective exchange rate arrangement known as the Snake in the Tunnel. This pegged EC currencies against each other within margins narrower than their Bretton Woods parities. Consequently, their fluctuations against each other would be less than their individual movements against the dollar. Its participants were the six original Community states together with the three states—Britain, Denmark, and Ireland—that would join the EC in January 1973 plus Norway.

But the Snake in the Tunnel soon graphically demonstrated a slightly different version of the twin exchange rate dilemma at work around the dollar and the Deutsche Mark. After Nixon ended dollar–gold convertibility, most EC currencies faced upward pressure against the dollar, which affected export competitiveness against dollar-based producers, and downward pressure against the Deutsche Mark, which drove up inflation. This dynamic then left the West German government facing Deutsche Mark appreciation against both other European currencies and the dollar as well as demands from their EC partners for the Bundesbank to cut interest rates. When, in March 1973, fixed exchange rates ended, these conflicting tensions came to a head. After Nixon once again devalued the dollar and Japan floated the yen, the EC states suspended foreign exchange markets to deliberate as to what to do. Still scarred by the European divisions in May 1971, the West German government wanted commonality. Indeed, Brandt saw an opportunity to move towards monetary union. But the Snake in the Tunnel had already shown that stabilizing the EC currencies against each other required the weaker currency states to make policy changes that their governments could not politically contemplate. Consequently, any nominally collective approach could not include all nine EC currencies. The temporary solution divided the EC into two monetary groups. One, led by West Germany, reformed the Snake, pegging its members' currencies against each other. The other, which included Britain, Ireland, and Italy, had currencies that floated against both the dollar and the Deutsche Mark.

This division left France in the West German monetary bloc. But it was an outcome driven by the necessity of Franco-German political agreement, not, as was soon evident, macro-economic compatibility.

Unable to follow the Bundesbank's monetary policy, the French government removed the franc from the Snake in January 1974, returned it in May 1975, demanding reforms from the Bundesbank, and quit again in March 1976 when none was forthcoming. As early as 1974, the French finance minister, Valéry Giscard d'Estaing, told President Pompidou that 'ultimately we will not be able to prevent the franc and the DM from drifting away from each other'. By 1976, Brandt's successor as chancellor, Helmut Schmidt, saw in the divide between the Snake around Germany and the larger group outside a 'two-tier Community'.[39]

Only their common dollar problems could push the EC monetarily back together. But, necessarily, the price was institutionalizing West Germany's intra-European monetary privileges. A prolonged bout of dollar weakness in 1977–78 exasperated Schmidt. For Schmidt, West Germany could not simultaneously adjust to more Asian trade competition, buy US Treasuries to finance American deficits, absorb more Deutsche Mark appreciation against the dollar and the non-Snake European currencies, and control domestic monetary conditions while the Eurodollar markets provided offshore credit. Although there was nothing in the short term that could be done on the dollar side, France and Germany could not, he told the Bundesbank in 1978, continue in 'two different monetary areas' if in the medium term the impact of the dollar on European economies was to be diminished.[40]

Schmidt pushed for a European Monetary System (EMS), with an Exchange Rate Mechanism (ERM) as its centrepiece. He found an ally, albeit a somewhat nervous one, in the French president, Valéry Giscard d'Estaing. Giscard perceived the choice for France to be between allowing ever-higher inflation and accepting German-led monetary discipline, and he chose the latter. All parties to the new European fixed exchange rate system tried to disguise the monetary power structure it entailed, pegging currencies against an artificial currency, the ECU, which financial historian Charles Kindleberger called 'the Deutsche Mark with a French name'.[41]

As it would later do in the euro's creation, Italy's position revealed that little had changed around the European monetary hierarchy since the last years of Bretton Woods. The ERM had to allow for singular arrangements for Italy, so the lira could fluctuate within wider margins around its central parity than the other currencies.

The West German, French, and Italian governments all wanted to treat Italy's membership principally as a matter of EC unity. If the EC was to become a single monetary area, Italy had to be inside. If it were not, the EC would have tiers of membership.

*   *   *

Whatever the aspirations to EC commonality, the ERM did not include Britain. From the start, Britain became detached from EC monetary cooperation. This was not because the Heath government, which took Britain into the EC, had a strong political objection to future European monetary union. Indeed, Heath and his chancellor talked during the March 1973 crisis as if this was the desired future.[42] But the economic and domestic political costs of defending any sterling parity with the Deutsche Mark were near insurmountable.

From the first British application to join the EEC, Britain's Sterling Area had proved an impediment to membership. Originating in the 1930s, the Sterling Area was a monetary and exchange rate arrangement whereby former British colonies and states closely associated with Britain pegged their currencies to sterling, maintained large sterling balances as reserves, and aligned their capital controls to Britain's. Believing that sterling's international use made Britain's interests within Bretton Woods more akin to those of the United States than the West European countries and fearing that in any currency crisis the sterling balances would become an EEC problem, de Gaulle had not wanted the Sterling Area inside the EEC. Indeed, it was Wilson's 1967 decision to devalue sterling that pushed de Gaulle into his second veto. On this occasion, de Gaulle said that 'the state of sterling would not allow it at present to become part of the solid, interdependent, and assured society in which the franc, the mark, the lira, the Belgian franc, and the guilder are joined'.[43] In order to pre-empt the issue derailing the third application, Heath gave an assurance to Giscard that the sterling balances would be gradually eliminated as the states that held them turned to dollars.[44] But ending the Sterling Area was likely to cause severe capital outflows. Allied to the fact that Britain's rate of inflation was more akin to Italy's than Germany's, this made the prospect of defending any new currency parity with interest rate increases electorally unappealing, even to a government like Heath's that wished to preserve Britain's Community credentials.

Although Heath did place sterling in the Snake in the Tunnel in May 1972, he took it back out again the next month at the first sign of difficulty. During the discussions in March 1973 about the Snake, Heath, well aware that the French had told the Germans that they were only willing to move to a joint float with all nine EC states on board, did endeavour to return to a European approach.[45] But once it became clear that the burden of maintaining sterling inside the Snake would fall on British politicians, not the Bundesbank, and that the French government would not tolerate a unilateral German float, Heath was left with a choice that would largely haunt British governments for the next two decades: the macro-economic and domestic political price for joining a European monetary arrangement was too high to contemplate, but staying out cost Britain political influence inside the EC. When Schmidt began to push his ERM plan, the Labour prime minister, James Callaghan, hoped the French reluctance would leave the two EC monetary areas in place, with Britain and France on the same side. But after Giscard decided that France should accept more monetary discipline, the costs on the EC side of exclusion increased. With Italy and Ireland deciding to join, Britain was left in a monetary group of one.[46]

The Volcker Shock

If the ERM represented an attempt to protect the EC from the dollar's weakness, the source of European fear was American inflation. But, as the ERM began, the Fed was already beginning to worry about how far and for how long this inflation could be accommodated. After Carter appointed Paul Volcker to lead the Fed, American monetary policy took a radical turn. In October 1979, Volcker reconceptualized it towards systematically eliminating inflation by restricting the money supply.[47] The ensuing high interest rates, which remained for the most part in double digits until autumn 1984, produced a much stronger dollar between 1981 and spring 1985.

The Volcker shock caused the EC states many problems. Even after dollar oil prices gradually fell from the second oil price shock of 1979–80, the strong dollar made oil imports more expensive. Jacques Delors, who served as French finance minister from 1981 to 1984, termed the years between 1981 and 1985 the third oil shock.[48]

High American interest rates, meanwhile, created conditions for capital flight at the same time as several European states, led by Britain and West Germany, were removing their capital controls.

Again, American monetary decisions reverberated divisively. In 1981, the Bundesbank tightened interest rates, and pushed for a wage freeze. By preventing Schmidt's government opening up a credit line from Saudi Arabia, the German central bank played a big part in ending the Social Democratic–Free Democratic coalition government without an election taking place.[49] This coalition switch by the Free Democrats brought the Christian Democrats back to power where they remained for sixteen years.

In France, by contrast, there was no independent central bank that could force a monetary response on politicians. Under any political conditions, this demarcation would have strained the ERM. But when François Mitterrand won the 1981 presidential election, and then the Socialists won a majority in the National Assembly—the first political victories for the Socialists in the Fifth Republic—it risked breaking up the mechanism entirely. Even without the Bundesbank's monetary tightening, Mitterrand and his ministers would have baulked at the constraints Giscard had agreed to institutionalize. But Mitterrand became president when ERM membership required particularly high interest rates. After devaluing the franc several times, he was confronted in March 1983 with a moment of decision. Either his government accommodated itself to tracking the Deutsche Mark, and in so doing accepting that it was the Bundesbank that determined how to manage the dollar constraint, or it decisively broke monetarily with West Germany. After toying with both options, Mitterrand chose to retain ERM membership. His new *franc fort* (strong franc) approach subordinated the entirety of French macro-economic policy to maintaining the franc-Deutsche Mark parity. Henceforth, French politicians had to support the Banque de France's monetary alignment with the Bundesbank, achieve wage discipline in the export sector, and aim for a current account surplus.

Being outside the ERM, Britain was in a different position when the Volcker shock hit. Indeed, the Thatcher government had already moved to a monetary policy rather like Volcker's. In the same month Volcker prioritized inflation, the Thatcher government removed capital controls, amplifying the fallout for Britain of

Thatcher and Volcker's policies. Consequently, in the period between 1979 and 1981 before the dollar's general rise accelerated, sterling sharply appreciated. As in the United States, high interest rates and a strong currency had a devastating effect on manufacturing and employment. For much of 1981, as the Bundesbank pushed the ERM states to higher interest rates, the Thatcher government was wrestling with how to steer sterling down without reigniting inflation.

But since dollar appreciation was now gathering speed, this strategy only moved Britain closer towards the ERM states' dollar-generated currency problems. From autumn 1981, the Thatcher government had to keep raising interest rates to try to abate sterling's decline. This imperative occasioned the first serious debate within the Thatcher government about ERM membership. From 1985, the debate became an incredibly acrimonious dispute between Thatcher and her senior colleagues, right up to the point when Britain joined in 1990.[50] But neither in 1981 nor in 1985 did anyone in Thatcher's Cabinet particularly see the issue as a matter of Britain's position within the EC. In good part, this reflected the sheer difficulty that fiat money and exchange rates under conditions of open capital flows generated. When economic conditions eased from 1986, and the European issue did resurface, the Thatcher government used its macro-economic flexibility to differentiate the British economy further from the ERM states. Consequently, a geopolitical argument and a macro-economic argument for Britain joining never realigned.

A Not Quite German Single Currency

The end of the Volcker monetary shock and the second Reagan administration's concerns with the impact of a strong dollar on American exports provided a temporary monetary respite for the EC. Just as Nixon had ultimately chosen dollar devaluation over tariffs, so Reagan decided to approach the burgeoning American trade deficit first and foremost as a monetary matter, albeit in the face of a Congress—controlled in both houses after the 1986 mid-term elections by the Democrats—that legislated for some protectionism.[51] In aiming to depreciate the dollar, the Reagan administration sought cooperation from West Germany, Britain, France, and Japan. In the 1985 Plaza Accord, these five governments agreed to act collectively to bring the dollar steadily down. Adding Canada to their group, they followed Plaza with the 1987 Louvre accord to put an effective floor under the dollar's depreciation.[52]

But Louvre reopened the American-German monetary divergence. The American trade deficit benefited little from the dollar's fall. If this deficit was to be dealt with as a monetary problem, US treasury secretary James Baker believed, other governments and central banks would have to pursue policies that would encourage higher domestic consumption to create demand for American exports. While the Japanese government could agree a monetary accommodation to which the Japanese central bank would adhere—one that had disastrous consequences for the Japanese economy—the West German government could not bind the Bundesbank to any Atlantic assurances. Since the Bundesbank was unwilling to loosen monetary policy—indeed in October 1987 the Bundesbank raised interest rates—the Plaza–Louvre period of exchange rate cooperation broke down.

This turbulence then reignited the Franco-German monetary disagreement at a time of rapidly falling oil prices. The reverse oil price shock in 1986 was in part, but only in part—see chapter two—a product of dollar depreciation.[53] Whatever its complex causes, it was a structural force driving inflation down. For the Bundesbank, it allowed for zero inflation. For the French, by contrast, this should have been an opportunity to lower interest rates to support higher growth, particularly since the Fed's monetary policy was so much more accommodating than it had been earlier in the decade. But the ERM ensured the Banque de France had to follow the Bundesbank.

From a French perspective, the German-shaped constraints inside the ERM were now remorseless. In late 1987, Mitterrand persuaded the West German chancellor, Helmut Kohl, to accept a Franco-German Council to coordinate macro-economic policy, including monetary matters. But, once it realized what Kohl had surrendered, the Bundesbank rendered the agreement redundant. The French finance minister, Edouard Balladur, then took a proposal for monetary union to an EC finance ministers' meeting in January 1988, setting in motion a path that would eventually lead to the Maastricht Treaty and the euro.[54] This French push for a single currency marked a departure from previous European monetary moves. The Werner Report and the ERM had been responses to the problem the dollar caused European states. By contrast, Balladur's case was a response to the internal European problem posed by the Bundesbank.[55]

That monetary union was conceived as a move to end the Bundesbank's monetary power and required West Germans to relinquish the Deutsche Mark ensured there was plenty of opposition in Germany to the project. Helmut Kohl's government decided to focus on the advantages of a single currency, which were primarily the prospect of an end to competitive devaluations by other ERM states and an opportunity to repurpose and reform the EC. Even after German reunification could have provided a pretext for retreat, Kohl persisted with that choice.[56] Nonetheless, given the sacrifice, there was no possibility that the German government would ever allow a monetary union that did not meet fundamental German concerns.

In straight monetary policy terms, this meant that the proposed ECB had to be another version of the Bundesbank, legally committed by a European Union (EU) treaty to price stability as the sole purpose of monetary policy, and free from any democratic political control. Whether the ECB could in practice be like the Bundesbank would, of course, be another matter. The Bundesbank's de facto political authority to set interest rates for Germany came from a strong domestic political consensus that price stability should prevail in monetary policy.[57] A similar consensus was not in evidence in the EU by the time the Maastricht Treaty establishing the ECB was ratified. Indeed, had there been a European consensus behind a Bundesbank-like monetary policy, there would not have been a political demand for monetary union in the first place. When monetary union did begin, the dissensus was soon made apparent by attacks on the ECB's treaty-guaranteed independence.[58]

Although this judgement could not be made explicit, the German government, to all intents and purposes, also insisted that monetary union could not include every member of the EC. To this end, the Maastricht Treaty, agreed in 1991, included strict convergence criteria—on inflation, exchange rate stability, budget deficits, and state debt—for states to qualify for the single currency.[59] Drawing lines to establish ins and outs took Germany to a position quite different from that adopted by Brandt and Schmidt. When the push for monetary union began in 1988, of the then Southern EC states, only Italy was in the ERM, and it still used the wide bands with which it entered the system. It would have seemed implausible then to think that Italy, let alone the others, could maintain a permanently fixed exchange rate with West Germany without disastrous economic consequences.[60] In contrast to 1978–79, any case for treating Italy as if it were France would appear to have required either significant support from the ECB for Italy's debt, or a fiscal union that redistributed revenues to Italy, both of which were political non-starters in West Germany. Accordingly, the German path to monetary union set out in the Maastricht Treaty appeared to offer a two-tier EU.

In practice, the Maastricht convergence criteria could not resolve the question of ins and outs. Initially, there was no uniformity of opinion between the German government and the Bundesbank about who the convergence criteria might exclude. The smallest monetary union possible might have suited the Bundesbank's overriding anti-inflationary concerns. But it risked German exporters facing ongoing devaluations from those outside the single currency.[61] Meanwhile, the convergence criteria could not straightforwardly be directed against the Southern European states. If the budget deficit criterion had been applied in 1991, Belgium would have been out, and, although it might have seemed that there was no chance of Italy qualifying, the same could not be said for Spain. In the treaty, the German government looked to have the advantage over the Bundesbank via a clause whereby the European Council could exercise a 'flexible' interpretation as to whether a state had met the conditions or not.[62] But since ERM membership without a devaluation for two years was a convergence condition, the Bundesbank had the means to push out the Southern European states.

Indeed, nine days after the Maastricht summit ended, the Bundesbank raised interest rates in response to the inflationary effects of German reunification. This move led to eighteen months of turbulence within the ERM, during which Britain permanently left, Italy made a temporary exit, the Spanish, Portuguese, and Irish currencies were devalued, and, in July 1993, all currency bands except those between Germany and the Netherlands were suspended. For a while it seemed as if monetary union would not happen. Then it appeared as if a select group of states would go ahead, dividing the EU into a core and the rest. Instead, the Eurozone began in 1999 missing only those with legal opt-outs—Britain and Denmark—and temporarily Greece.

This large monetary union lacked broad political support in Germany. Opposition to it first appeared in a set of legal challenges to the Maastricht Treaty in the Federal Constitutional Court. In 1993, the Court, in ruling that the treaty's ratification was constitutional, also asserted, among other things, that it was for the German Parliament to decide whether a state had qualified to join. This left monetary union's size to be contested within German democratic politics. The Social Democrats fought the 1994 German federal elections on a platform to shut out Southern European states from the single currency, and for some time it looked like they would win.[63] In trying to rescue that election, Kohl turned monetary union into something it had hitherto not been: a symbolic issue of European unity. The following year he went further, saying that monetary union was a matter of 'war and peace in the twenty-first century'.[64] Although the Christian Democrat–Free Democratic coalition did retain power in 1994, the election did not settle the euro's composition. In 1995, Kohl's finance minister, Theo Waigel, declared that Italy would not meet the convergence criteria. This belief that Italy did not belong in a monetary union persisted inside the German government well into 1997.[65] But Waigel and the Bundesbank lacked the means to impose their will since Germany's own fiscal difficulties, caused by reunification, ensured that the convergence criteria on state debt and budget deficits could not strictly be enforced. So long as there was no clean technical way of determining exclusions from the single currency, Kohl's argument that what mattered was European unity had a force it would not otherwise have possessed.

Nonetheless, the risks around a large monetary union drove the Kohl government to revisit the Maastricht terms for relinquishing the Deutsche Mark. By the mid-1990s, it wanted legal fiscal rules for monetary union once the euro began and proposed what became the Stability and Growth Pact. This move left French ministers nonplussed, particularly since their attempts to bring the French budget deficit down in accordance with that convergence criterion was meeting fierce domestic political resistance. When the Gaullist president Jacques Chirac decided to hold early parliamentary elections in May 1997 to strengthen his ability to pursue Maastricht-driven reform, he succeeded only in giving the Socialist Party a majority in the French National Assembly, just two years into his presidency. Chirac's new Socialist prime minister, Lionel Jospin, was sceptical about monetary union—as will be discussed in chapter nine—and he had opposed the Stability and Growth Pact during the election campaign. But, in office, he concentrated on preventing a small monetary union in which France would have been one of the weakest members, accepting the Pact's fiscal rules in exchange for German acquiescence to Italian membership.[66]

In consenting to the Maastricht Treaty, the Southern European governments imposed a large burden upon themselves. They agreed a legal obligation to endeavour to join a single currency that would be harder to manage than the ERM and of which Greece and Portugal had no experience at all; and they did so in the knowledge that, whatever they politically sacrificed in the effort, other states could still exclude their participation. In part, Italy excepted, they were appeased with side payments in the form of an increase in EU structural funding.[67] But, realistically, they had little choice. Conceding non-membership would have risked currency instability, higher inflation, and higher interest rates. Attempting to qualify also bought anti-inflationary credibility in foreign exchange markets and delivered much lower interest rates, which, in reducing interest payments, made hitting Maastricht's 3 per cent budget deficit limit somewhat easier.

For Italy, the difficulties ran deep with profound democratic political consequences—as will be discussed in chapter nine. Italy did not rejoin the ERM until November 1996. Between its exit in September 1992 and its return, the lira lost nearly a quarter of its value.[68] Average Italian growth between 1992—the year its attempt to qualify for monetary union began—and 1999, the year it entered monetary union, was only just over 1 per cent. Unemployment, which had been under 10 per cent for the whole of the 1980s, rose significantly.

Italian governments were prepared to accept such a growth-restrictive commitment because the alternative was acquiescing to the EU's separation into monetary blocs. As the then Italian prime minister, Romano Prodi, declared in February 1997: 'If we are not in the first group, our currency would come under assault, our economy would be defenceless, our international credibility would be diminished.'[69] His appeal to Germany to interpret the convergence criteria generously was a version of Kohl's to German voters: 'Europe is not just about a currency. It is impossible to think of Europe cut off from its great Latin culture.'[70]

Italy's struggle to join the single currency revealed much about how the Eurozone has since unfolded. Monetary union's French-centric justification was macro-economic and directed at the Bundesbank. But the Maastricht Treaty rid the euro of its macro-economic purpose by giving the ECB the same mandate of price stability as the Bundesbank's. Its consequent German-centric structure required a small monetary union. Yet in practice, as German monetary power diminished through the 1990s, the Eurozone's Southern-European- friendly size led it to become a test of states' commitment to the EU, even as the macro-economic policies it required to participate were economically and politically destabilizing.

*   *   *

Britain's absence from the euro was a different matter, although, at the point in early September 1992 when both the British and Italian governments were battling to save their ERM membership, this reality might have seemed otherwise. Britain's ongoing singular monetary trajectory as an EU member went back to the reverse oil price shock. From 1986, the Thatcher government, like the Reagan administration and the Fed, saw no reason to continue to prioritize controlling inflation when inflation was falling and unemployment remained high. Not having subordinated British monetary policy to the Bundesbank's, it then lacked the French incentive to pursue a single currency, even without Thatcher's instinctive dislike of the idea of dispensing with monetary sovereignty.

This did not mean the exchange rate problem for the British economy went away. Indeed, by the time when, in June 1989, the EC states agreed to proceed with monetary union, sterling's weakness required British interest rates to be significantly higher than those in most ERM states. But sterling's weakness at this time arose precisely because, unlike the ERM states, the Thatcher governments had used the counter oil price shock to dispense with anti-inflationary policies. Consequently, when, in October 1990, Thatcher finally conceded ERM membership, she only did so as a short-term macro-economic expediency to stabilize sterling. Yet as her concession came at a time when the intergovernmental conference on monetary union was shortly due to begin, it strengthened her Cabinet critics who feared that definitively shutting the door to monetary union would relegate

Britain in the EC's hierarchy. Horrified by her remarks that autumn that she would never support relinquishing sterling or monetary authority, her former chancellor, Geoffrey Howe, resigned from the Cabinet, setting in motion the sequence of events that led to Thatcher's resignation.

Nonetheless, finding a macro-economic path that would prevent British monetary isolation was much more difficult. For the Maastricht Treaty, John Major constructed what appeared an opt-out; in structure, it was in fact an opt-in to buy time to join. But since the Bundesbank was tightening monetary policy when the British economy was in recession, ERM membership was not sustainable. Its collapse on Black Wednesday in September 1992 turned the opt-in into a real opt-out by wrecking any possibility that an even stronger European monetary commitment could be sold to the parliamentary Conservative Party and the British electorate.[71]

For a short while, sterling's weakness might have tempted the Major government to gamble on rescuing the opt-in, but in mid-1995 the dollar turned upwards and took sterling with it. Consequently, Major's successors were effectively freed for more than a decade from the pressures on sterling that had with very little interruption constrained British governments since the First World War's end. A large monetary union helped Britain too, making the other non-members by 2001 only Denmark and Sweden, which had also chosen to opt out, not a club of weak currency states. Despite Tony Blair's frustrations at what influence non-membership cost inside the EU, uninterrupted non-inflationary growth from 1993 until 2008 proved too useful for the Labour government to relinquish. In part this economic performance was dependent—as the next chapter will show—on anti-inflationary forces from China that were nothing to do with Britain or the euro. But the absence of inflation separated the macro-economic problem around sterling from the geopolitical problem of Britain's position in the EU. Moreover, after the Eurozone began, the fear that London would lose its position as the premier European financial centre that had motivated, and part served as pretext for, Thatcher's removal unravelled. Instead, London quickly emerged as the Eurozone's financial centre.[72]

* * *

The competing charges that the euro is too German to serve Italy and too Italian to be tolerated by Germany can be traced to the beginning of the Eurozone's history. The monetary union that began in 1999, requiring the reinvention Draghi presided over in 2012, was never intended. In conception, the Eurozone was a French-led project to find solutions to a set of problems unleashed by the West German response to the breakdown of the Bretton Woods dollar-based monetary order. The German government reluctantly accepted monetary union on German terms just as long it did not include heavily indebted Italy. In practice, such a monetary union was thwarted. Instead, it became a currency bloc incorporating Italy with rules enshrined in European law that were not designed to accommodate the burden constituted by Italy's debt. In reforming the ECB by fiat, Draghi effectively sought a way out of this predicament without reopening the treaty through which monetary union was established.

The ECB's eventual move to quantitative easing in 2015, whereby the central bank directly bought euro states' debt, represented a momentous transformation. It completed the conversion of the monetary union laid out in the Maastricht Treaty on German terms into one that it would have been inconceivable for the German government to have agreed as the price for relinquishing the Deutsche Mark. In 1986, the Bundesbank had driven German inflation below zero. Thirty years later, the ECB presided over below-zero interest rates. In 1993, the German Constitutional Court ruled that the Maastricht Treaty's ratification in Germany was constitutional. In 2020, against a backdrop in which the Covid-19 crisis had caused the Commission to suspend the single market's rules, the Court judged that the German government and Bundestag violated German citizens' rights by failing to challenge the ECB. But the ECB's transformation into a central bank that could act as a lender of last resort also opened a question about which states' debt and which parties in government could be supported, as both Italian and Greek politicians would discover.

If the original ECB was supplanted after 2010, it had already lost the anti-inflationary rationale in which it had been grounded. By the 2000s, the German economy no longer operated in an economic world where policymakers had to protect it from inflationary pressures coming from elsewhere. Indeed, the structural dynamics of the world economy and inside Germany pressed in the opposite direction. Chinese imports acted as an anti-inflationary force, even as another oil price shock was under way, and the German financial sector could now not be conceived as a source of stability to be guarded from tumult in the Eurodollar markets. That the top German banks were massively involved in these markets would become part of why the ECB responded to the Eurozone crisis by transforming itself. How these structural changes in the world economy came about around China and the Eurodollar system is what must be considered next.

5

Made in China, Need Dollars

By May 2015, the federal funds rate—the Federal Reserve's primary interest rate—had stood at a quarter of one per cent for seven and a half years. In a speech in Providence Rhode Island that month, Fed chair Janet Yellen said that assuming the economy continued to improve as she expected, the Fed would finally raise the federal funds rate before the year ended.[1]

What Yellen termed 'normalizing monetary policy' would mean trouble for states with pegged exchange rates to the dollar: attracted to higher interest rates, capital would flow into American assets.[2] For China, where some firms had binged on Eurodollar credit markets after 2008, disaster beckoned. China's economy was already growing at its slowest rate for twenty-five years, and its exports, the bedrock of its economic rise, were declining. Pre-empting any move by the Fed, the Chinese central bank dramatically devalued China's currency, the renminbi, on 11 August 2015, sending share prices in China and much of the rest of the world tumbling, and causing exchange rate havoc in emerging markets.[3] In an effort to stave off capital flight, it devalued the renminbi again and over a fortnight liquidated around $100 billion of China's dollar reserves.

Most observers had expected the American interest rate increase to come at the Fed's September meeting. But the financial conditions generated by the chaos in China caused a retreat. In her press conference, Yellen said that 'growth concerns' in China had 'led to notable volatility in financial markets' and that 'in light of the heightened uncertainties abroad', as well as 'a slightly softer expected path for inflation'—meaning falling oil prices—'the Committee judged it appropriate to wait for more evidence' before raising rates.[4]

As the year came towards a close without a rate increase, US–Chinese monetary tensions arose again. On 11 December, the

Chinese central bank announced it would establish a new renminbi peg against a basket of currencies, not just the dollar. At its meeting on 15–16 December, the Fed finally raised the federal funds rate by a quarter of one per cent. In response to the ensuing capital outflow carnage in China, the Chinese central bank let the renminbi depreciate further. Concerned that this was but the prelude to a major Chinese currency shift, Obama's treasury secretary persuaded the Group of 20 central bank heads and finance ministers in February 2016 to sign up to the Shanghai Accord in which each government pledged to 'refrain from competitive devaluations'.[5] Upward pressure on the dollar abated for a few months, but the Fed would not risk raising the federal funds rate again until December 2016.

If the last year of Obama's presidency saw attempts to manage US–China monetary and currency relations through cooperation, Donald Trump's first year began what would become a full-scale assault on the US–China trade relationship. In August 2017, Trump instigated an investigation of China's trade practices. In early 2018, he first announced tariffs on Chinese solar panels and washing machines and then extended them to more than 1,300 categories of Chinese imports. A month later, China retaliated. Talks to restructure the terms of trade began twice only to break down. After the second termination, the US Treasury deemed China a currency manipulator.

Trump's policies were matched by a shift in geopolitical rhetoric on the Sino-American economic relationship. The US National Security Doctrine published in December 2017 said that 'great power competition' had 'returned'. It declared that Washington had shown 'a great degree of strategic complacency' under the mistaken 'assumption' that 'global commerce' would turn 'rivals' into 'benign actors and trustworthy partners'. Henceforth, the United States would, it promised, 'pursue an economic strategy that rejuvenates the domestic economy, benefits the American worker, revitalizes the US manufacturing base, creates middle-class jobs, encourages innovation, preserves technological advantage, safeguards the environment, and achieves energy dominance'.[6] Just under a year later, Vice President Mike Pence gave a speech in which he insisted that China was bent on 'international domination' and lamented 'Beijing's malign influence and interference in American politics and policy', which, he claimed, was orders of magnitude higher than Russia's.[7] After the speech, one Chinese official remarked that a 'bamboo curtain' had replaced the former Iron Curtain.[8]

Unquestionably, Trump's strategic reset commanded support across the American political spectrum. If some Democrats criticized his inflammatory rhetoric, few were willing to defend the status quo. But this American turn against China would prove another matter for the EU. Asked, in July 2018, why he had not sought to work with the EU against China's trade practices, Trump retorted that 'the European Union is possibly as bad as China, just smaller'.[9] When, in 2019, Trump turned aggressively on the Chinese technological company Huawei, he demanded that the EU and Britain follow; they refused.

How the Fed's monetary decision-making came to be constrained by China's dollar problems, and why Trump declared a trade and technological war on China originate in what happened in the decades leading up to the 2007–8 crash, as much as the years after. There are two big stories to tell, one about the consequences of China's economic growth and one about the emergence of a global dollar credit market in Eurodollars. Together, they spawned a seismic shift in international monetary and financial conditions, a huge oil price shock, and far-reaching dislocation in the American economy. Out of the interaction of the first two phenomena came the 2007–8 crash, and from the third arose one part of the political conditions that allowed a confront-China insider-outsider like Donald Trump to win the presidency.

The China Shock

China's spectacular economic growth between 2000 and 2007, reaching an annual rate of 14 per cent at its peak, reverberated across the world economy. Much of this China shock showed itself in trade. With the Chinese government doing everything it could to keep the renminbi pegged at a competitive rate against the dollar, China practised export-led growth. The opportunity for it to do so was accelerated by the US Congress agreeing to the permanent normalization of trade with China in 2000 as a prelude to China entering the World Trade Organization (WTO) in 2001. China's exports in this new trading world were primarily manufactured goods. As a result, the United States and a number of European countries were left with large trade deficits with China; the American trade deficit in goods with China rose by nearly four-fold between 1999 and 2008.[10]

This surge in Chinese manufacturing exports had consequences for both North American and Western European labour markets, especially the American.[11] The scale of this shock is a matter of dispute, but it was, undoubtedly, sizeable in those sectors where Chinese exports were concentrated, and it spread into local supply chains.[12] From 2001, American manufacturing employment began to crash, falling from 17.2 million in December 2000 to 11.5 million in December 2009. This was a dramatic change compared to the recent past. These jobs had peaked at 19.5 million in mid-1979. At the end of 1989, there were still 17.9 million people employed in the sector, and at the end of 1999 there were 17.3 million. Much of the subsequent rapid fall came in the early 2000s. During 2001, manufacturing employment tumbled from 17.1 million to 15.7 million, and by December 2003 it was down to 14.3 million.[13] Regardless of exactly what proportion of these job losses were attributable to China trade, the scale of the change and its timing ensured that normalizing trade relations with China was perceived by those afflicted as a disaster.[14]

An employment shock was not what the Clinton administration had promised would follow from permanently normalized trade relations with China. In 2000, Bill Clinton said that 'this is a hundred to nothing deal for America when it comes to the economic consequences'.[15] His agricultural secretary said of the permanent normalized trade relations legislation that 'this deal is really a no-brainer' and that since American markets were already open to China 'all the concessions are on their side, and all the benefits are on ours'.[16]

The disjuncture between this promise and the reality quickly yielded a backlash in Congress. Much of this anger was directed at China's exchange rate policy. If China had let its currency float, China's expanding trade surplus would have pushed the renminbi upwards, making Chinese imports more expensive. But, since 1994, China had operated a fixed peg against the dollar. Rather than allow the renminbi to appreciate, the Chinese central bank engaged from 2003 in large-scale intervention to stop that happening. That same year, anger about China's trade-centric approach to the renminbi began to be articulated by influential members of the Congress. The Democratic senator Chuck Schumer and the Republican senator

Lindsey Graham introduced the first of a succession of bills to impose substantial tariffs on Chinese exports unless China revalued the renminbi.[17] Their efforts reached a climax in the first half of 2005 when it appeared that they had sufficient votes in the Senate to pass legislation.

But the post-2000 US–China trade relationship had quickly become politically entrenched in Washington. Schumer and Graham's legislative push lacked support from George Bush Jr's administration. Since there was no security dependency to exploit, Bush could not demand change from China as his three predecessors had done from Japan. China had also become the United States' largest state creditor. Indeed, China's determination to preserve the currency parity had incentivized its central bank to buy large volumes of US government debt as a macro-economic strategy. Concerned that the Schumer–Graham legislation could still pass, China repackaged its exchange rate stance in July 2005. On the surface, these moves ended the renminbi–dollar peg and allowed the renminbi some latitude to float. But in practice, China conceded only a 2 per cent revaluation against the dollar. The following autumn, Bush's treasury secretary, Hank Paulson, persuaded China to accept an institutionalized framework for discussing exchange rate and trade issues. His expressed aim was to procure a meaningful renminbi revaluation.[18] But, again, only a minimal adjustment was forthcoming. In May 2007, China agreed to widen the bands within which the renminbi floated. Thereafter, the renminbi did appreciate, but the effects were diluted by the dollar's depreciation against other currencies too.

On the surface, the political stand-off in Washington looked like a replay of past congressional protectionist pressure on the executive from Hoover to Reagan. But the degree to which some American corporations were advantaged from the scale of transnational production and supply chains around China represented a substantial difference. Tech and electronic manufacturers massively benefited by assembling their goods in China, as did large discount retailers, like Walmart, from selling cheap Chinese imports.[19] Once upon a time, Apple, for example, made almost all its products in the United States. Indeed, Steve Jobs, the company's co-founder, boasted in the 1980s the Apple computer 'was a machine that is made in America'.[20] But, from 2004, almost all Apple products were manufactured abroad, mostly in China. As one Apple executive put it to the *New York Times*, 'What US plant can find 3,000 people overnight and convince them to live in dorms?'[21] In part, these selective rewards reduced the resonance of confrontational anti-China rhetoric: manufacturing iPods in China might have added to the American trade deficit, but most of the value of the product was still being captured in the United States.[22] But they also spurred class conflict in American democratic politics: those who gained were shareholders and extremely well-paid executives; those who lost were factory workers.[23]

*   *   *

Although trade became its visible face in American politics, the China shock dramatically extended to oil. China was self-sufficient in oil production until 1993. This oil independence distinguished China's early trajectory in industrial development from those of other East Asian states, not least Japan's. Only in the mid-2000s did rising Chinese oil consumption have an impact on the rest of the world. By 2008, China was using the equivalent of 70 per cent of Saudi production. With demand from other Asian countries, especially India, also accelerating, world oil consumption soared from 68 million barrels per day in 1994 to 77 million in 2000 to 87 million in 2008, despite falls in some European economies. (By contrast, in the two decades between 1973 and 1993, it rose only from 57 to 67 million.[24]) In 2005, as the China demand shock took hold, oil production stagnated—as discussed in chapter four–until the shale boom began.[25] Consequently, after more than a decade of low prices, from the mid-2000s the world economy experienced unprecedentedly high prices. By May 2006, oil prices reached $90 a barrel, around 80 per cent higher adjusted for inflation than they were in March 1974 when the first oil price shock ended. At their peak in June 2008, they were around $150, more than a third higher in real terms than their previous peak during the second oil price shock.[26]

This oil price shock was rather different from the two in the 1970s, the 1981–85 shock the dollar delivered, or the mini price spike that stemmed from Iraq's invasion of Kuwait. None of those had a significant demand side component. Nor had they had such structural causes. The Arab oil embargo was temporary. Iranian output, at least partially, recovered after the revolution, as did Iraq's until the post-1990 sanctions. The dollar fell from 1985, and so spectacularly, from 1986, did oil prices. But this time, additional large-scale demand from China and India became a permanent feature of the world economy. Only new supply, or significantly lower levels of economic growth, could prevent much higher prices becoming a normal state of affairs. Paradoxically, the conditions for additional production to meet accelerating consumption turned out to run through the 2007–8 crash, even as—as will be discussed later in the chapter— the very problem oil prices caused played its part in that crash occurring.

Eurodollar Banking

The Eurodollar banking story begins back in the 1970s. The Euro- dollar markets that had played their part in ending Bretton Woods were given a large boost by the two oil shocks. Fuelled by the dollars earned by Middle Eastern oil producers, American and European banks had huge dollar deposits to lend. The need for oil-importing states, including those in developing countries, to finance large trade deficits made the Eurodollar markets extremely useful, especially since the International Monetary Fund was ill-equipped to deal with such sizeable and structural deficits. Banks became the mechanism for providing dollars to those who needed them through Eurodollar loans.[27] In part as a consequence, finance, and internationalized banking in particular, would assume a significantly larger part in the American and West European economies than it had done in the three decades after the Second World War.[28] But the size of the European banks' Eurodollar operations raised the old question of who regulated this activity, and who would serve as the lender of last resort to these markets, even more emphatically than in the 1960s.[29] In practice the only answer to the second question could be the Fed. But spelling out this reality was a step too far. When, in 1974, the Group of Ten (G10) central bank governors discussed the problem, they could only express confidence that at the moment of crisis a solution would be forthcoming.[30]

That definitive crisis would arrive in August 2007. In the interim, the Eurodollar markets grew beyond recognition. As they expanded, the means by which banks funded their operations in these markets became increasingly dependent on repurchase (repo) agreements: a form of short-term—often overnight—collateralized borrowing in which one party sells securities in exchange for cash and agrees to buy them back in the future at a slightly higher price. By the 1990s, what had been the Bundesbank's earlier frustration that the ability of banks to create dollars to lend in Eurodollar markets undermined national interest rates had spread to the Fed. In a speech in 1996, the then Fed chairman Alan Greenspan noted that 'unfortunately, money supply trends veered off path several years ago as a useful summary of the overall economy' and 'we cannot in the future expect to rely a great deal on money supply in making monetary policy'.[31] In this world, Greenspan continued, monetary policy would have to be conducted by assessing banks' balance sheets and asset prices.[32]

This was, however, much easier said than done. As he said in the same speech, there was an 'irrational exuberance' that was 'unduly escalat[ing] asset values'.[33] Even regulating banks' balance sheets was difficult. Under the Basel Accords, agreed by the G10 states from 1988, bank regulation was concentrated on the asset side of banks' balance sheets. Yet by the late 1990s, banks, as well as other financial corporations, had figured out how to use derivatives to disguise the size of their balance sheets. Moreover, the European banks were big players in the Eurodollar markets and the Fed was in no position to regulate the balance sheets of foreign banks.

Neither did Greenspan actually wish to make interest rate changes in response to movements in asset prices. The years from the mid-1980s had seen ever-larger fluctuations in asset prices.[34] These had been most manifest in the developing countries and emerging markets, culminating in the 1997–98 Asian financial crisis. But they had also been evident in Western economies, including the 1987 share market crash. By the time of Greenspan's 'irrational exuberance' speech, there was already a growing bubble in US share markets driven by the dot-com boom where investors piled into internet start-up companies. But even after it burst in March 2000, Greenspan still proclaimed that bubbles could be neither identified in advance nor contained once they emerged.[35]

As for banks themselves, their internationalized operations grew from the late 1990s to another level. Again, this deepening internationalization was driven by European banks, and in the first instance German banks.[36] These ever bigger and ever more inter-nationalized bank balance sheets contributed very significantly to a massive increase in international capital flows from the turn of the century.[37] A good proportion of these flows were generated by the Eurozone. Once monetary union created apparently unified credit conditions across much of the EU, Northern European banks lent large volumes of money to corporations and governments in the Southern Eurozone and Ireland.

These same Northern European banks also massively increased the international assets on their balance sheets by lending in the United States, through both loans and bond and security purchases. This lending was financed by short-term dollar funding from money markets, including repo and Eurodollar markets, leaving these banks with large liabilities in a foreign currency and a mismatch between their longer-dated American assets and their short-term dollar bor-rowing.[38] After this same dynamic played out disastrously during the Asian financial crisis, the East Asian central banks, not least China's, had responded by amassing large-scale dollar reserves through the 2000s. But the European Central Bank (ECB) and the Bank of England acted as if the huge currency misalignments with which their banking sectors operated could never actually require them to provide foreign currency support, apparently trusting instead in the 1974 assumption that if and when a crisis arrived the Fed would provide a solution.

The Great Moderation, for a While

In the decade before the 2007–8 crash, the combined consequences of China's rapid economic growth and ever more internationalized banking appeared to deepen the benign monetary and credit envir-onment that had first emerged for the United States in the mid-1980s from lower interest rates and oil prices. In a speech in 2004, future Fed chair Ben Bernanke described what he called the Great Moderation as 'a substantial decline in macro-economic volatility', which trans-lated into much lower inflation compared to the 1970s and early 1980s.[39] The causes of this change were disputed. Some, including Bernanke, thought that economic policy decision-making, particularly on monetary issues, had significantly improved.[40] Others pointed to the good fortune of the fall in oil prices, or structural economic changes, including financial innovation and the reduced importance of manufacturing sectors.[41] But, whatever their relative causal weight, China's exports after 2001, by reducing the costs of clothes and other consumer goods, served as a crucial anti-inflationary force, especially as China's rising oil demand was simultaneously inducing inflationary conditions via energy prices.[42]

At least from the 1990s, the Great Moderation also brought across the world a decline in interest rates that could not be explained simply by changes in inflationary expectations.[43] This looked like a historical anomaly. In the twentieth century, there had been periods before of low real interest rates, but not under conditions when inflation was low and banks were lightly regulated.[44] Again, the causes of this apparently structural monetary easing of credit conditions were disputed.[45] Some, including Greenspan and Bernanke, were convinced China's monetary and exchange rate policies were decisive. China was, Bernanke alleged in 2005, in good part responsible for a 'global savings glut' that was driving interest rates down.[46] Certainly, by any standards, China, and other East Asian countries, did provide a massive flow of capital into the United States at low rates of interest. China acquired a huge portfolio of US Treasury bonds, and eventually bonds and securities issued by the two congressionally chartered mortgage corporations, Fannie Mae and Freddie Mac. These purchases allowed the Fed to let the effective federal funds rate fall below 2 per cent in 2001 and remain there until the second half of 2004. This easy credit environment financed a swift increase in the American budget deficit during George Bush Jr's first term in office, albeit it left the country more fiscally reliant on a single state than it had ever been before.[47] It also furnished conditions in which the tech companies like Amazon, Google, and eBay that had survived the bursting of the dot-com bubble could grow without business models that generated profits.

The United States' monetary gains and the trade advantages China acquired in the early twenty-first century world economy appeared to some to establish a de facto new international monetary order that would keep interest rates low for the foreseeable future. Some presented this order as a semi-resurrected Bretton Woods.[48] Economic historians Niall Ferguson and Moritz Schularick labelled this economic world 'Chimerica'.[49] If President Clinton's former treasury secretary Lawrence Summers saw instead a fear-driven 'balance of financial terror' held together by the devastation each would experience if the dollar were to collapse, he still judged there was 'enormous, short-run functionality and comfort' in the Sino-American economic relationship.[50]

In actuality, there was considerable short-term instability that would work its way through the entire world economy. Above all, oil ensured that China's economic growth was far from straightforwardly creating a benign credit environment. Indeed, from the mid-2000s, Chinese oil demand, allied to the growing supply constraints, had monetary repercussions, beginning in June 2004, when the Fed tightened monetary policy in response to what it feared might be the inflationary effects of rising oil prices.[51] For the top central bankers, the return of high oil prices was a decisive turning point. For Alan Greenspan, trying to avoid them had justified the Iraq War.[52] Removing Hussein had been 'essential', he told the *Washington Post* in an interview, for oil markets to function.[53] More pessimistically, in a speech in 2005, the then governor of the Bank of England, Mervyn King, pronounced that rising oil prices had ended what he termed NICE, a period of non-inflationary consistently expansionary growth that had begun in 1992. In this new environment, King argued, inflation and growth would be more volatile than they had been in the recent past. After the end of NICE, King continued, it was an illusion to think central banks could use monetary policy to achieve stability.[54] Three years later, the president of the European Central Bank (ECB), Jean-Claude Trichet, went further, pronouncing that a 'transfer of income from commodity-importing to commodity-exporting countries' was occurring and this change had to be 'accepted' by Western governments and their populations.[55]

Yet internationalized dollar banking complicated this picture. In King and Trichet's telling, the economic world was returning in part to the 1970s, albeit with higher global returns to capital and lower returns to labour in North America and Western Europe. But central banks already could not achieve their stated monetary purposes. As Greenspan told a Senate committee in February 2005, there was a 'conundrum' at work: the Fed's oil-driven tightening from June 2004 had had no impact on long-term rates.[56] Indeed, the ten-year bonds the US Treasury issues were, as he spoke, yielding less than before the Fed moved the federal funds rate upwards. Whether this was quite as an unusual occurrence as Greenspan claimed, or could be explained by Chinese and other Asian central bond purchases, is open to question. But his remarks that credit conditions were not what might have been expected from the Fed's monetary policy was indicative of something consequential about this period of oil-induced monetary tightening: although higher interest rates did have considerable effect on the non-financial economy, especially housing, they had little effect on credit conditions in the financial sector. In part, credit default swaps and other credit derivatives acted as a buffer between monetary policy changes and the availability of credit by providing de facto insurance to financial market participants against their risk-taking. But at least as significantly, whatever effect the Fed's tightening had on dollar credit arising from American banks operating in the United States, it had little effect on Eurodollar credit, and this dollar credit readily found its way back into the American banking system.[57] Not having found a remedy for the problem of aligning monetary policy with the international dollar-credit markets, Greenspan handed over the problem at the beginning of 2006 to his successor, Ben Bernanke.

The Multiple Crashes

The 2007–8 crash was the culmination of the complex interaction between China's economic rise, its effects on oil prices as production stagnated, the Eurodollar markets, and the fallout of each on credit conditions. The immediate framing of the 2007–8 financial crisis around American subprime borrowing, post-1980s financial sector deregulation, and East Asian central banks was always misleading. In Europe, this distortion was also self-serving, hiding what has since been shown to be the pivotal role of Northern European banks through the Eurodollar markets.[58] What Bernanke presented as a 'savings glut' financial crisis made in China was more a 'banking glut' crisis made in Europe, and one in which there is little distinction to be made between German, French, and British banks.[59] But neither is the 2007–8 crash causally reducible to this binary. Indeed, the 2007–8 crash was not one crash, but several.

The first was the American housing market crash. Prices in a boom that had begun in 1997 peaked in early 2006 and remained on a downward trajectory for the next six years, with particularly sharp falls through 2007, 2008, and early 2009.[60] This housing boom had driven a considerable amount of the growth in the American economy in the first half of the 2000s at the same as manufacturing employment contracted.[61] Subprime lending, whereby those previously deemed uncreditworthy were able to take mortgages, was a significant, although far from exclusive, cause of this boom. With the Fed tightening rates from June 2004 into 2006 in response to oil prices, more subprime borrowers found it difficult to make their interest rate payments. Subprime lending rested on the assumption that so long as prices continued to rise, borrowers could refinance at any time. But once prices began to fall, that safeguard fell away. Ever more subprime borrowers defaulted and banks foreclosed on their homes, pushing prices down further and putting still ever more mortgage holders under water. By late 2007, a national foreclosure crisis had begun.[62]

Through the early stages of the housing crash, the Fed was unresponsive. As foreclosures escalated, the Fed was still preoccupied with oil prices, even as it knew that tighter monetary policy had a negative impact on the housing market and that oil prices were themselves creating recessionary conditions, deepening the pressures on mortgages. When it did start to bring interest rates down in September 2007, it was just as the oil price shock accelerated. But in lowering interest rates that autumn, it showed itself well aware that it was ignoring the inflationary risk from oil that had in good part triggered the mortgage crisis. Quite simply, by 2007, the Fed could not set monetary policy to deal with two opposite problems.[63]

The second crash was a recession. It began in the United States in the last quarter of 2007 and in the Eurozone and Britain in the second quarter of 2008. These recessions originated in the oil price shock and central banks' policy responses to it. Higher interest rates slowed growth. Then as oil prices accelerated through the second half of 2007 and first half of 2008, consumer confidence and consumer spending fell.[64] These recessions caught European policymakers, in particular, by surprise. Indeed, when the ECB raised interest rates in July 2008 to try to deal with what it saw as oil's inflationary potential, the Eurozone economy was in fact already in recession.

That summer, King's verdict about NICE ending appeared correct. The spectre haunting central bank policymakers the summer before Lehman Brothers' bankruptcy sent more dramatic shockwaves through the world economy was stagflation: simultaneously rising inflation and unemployment. For the Eurozone, this was a political as well as an economic tribulation. If the 1970s were any precedent, this could only mean intra-European disagreement about whether to prioritize the immediate risks to inflation or to growth. Of course, the very existence of the Eurozone was supposed to have settled the conflict in favour of price stability. Even before the July 2008 tightening, when the Fed, and then the Bank of England, loosened policy in 2007, the ECB had not followed suit. Adamant that policy had to be adjusted to rising oil prices, Trichet stuck to the central bank's anti-inflationary mandate enshrined in the Maastricht Treaty.[65] But his insistence that price stability had to prevail met considerable objection from the Spanish and French governments.[66] After oil prices crashed in July 2008, this profound Eurozone rupture about monetary policy temporarily fell away. But the structural monetary fault line that oil caused inside the Eurozone was now—as the next chapter will show—once again dangerously exposed.

The third crash was the banking crash. It began on 9 August 2007 with a run in the repo markets. Starting with the French bank BNP Paribas, banks were unable to use mortgage-backed security assets as collateral for funding, and the cost of borrowing for all banks in inter-bank markets spiked. That mortgage-backed securities precipitated this bank funding crisis appeared to tie the 2007–8 banking crash more to the American housing crash than was really the case. As Bernanke would tell the US Financial Crisis Inquiry Commission in 2010, 'judged in relation to the size of global financial markets, prospective subprime losses were clearly not large enough on their own to account for the magnitude of the crisis'. Rather, 'the system's vulnerabilities' were, as he said, wide open to 'a sea change in money market conditions'.[67] The European banks had a singular difficulty: they needed funding in a foreign currency, and the Eurodollar credit markets on which they relied stopped functioning and could not be repaired. After 9 August, the effective Eurodollar interest rate LIBOR stopped following the federal funds rate, ensuring that the monetary measures the Fed undertook in response to bank funding pressures did not alleviate conditions in the offshore dollar credit markets.[68]

The fact that the Fed could not rectify the Eurodollar credit markets with monetary policy brought the Eurodollar system to the moment of crisis envisaged three decades earlier by the G10 central bankers. For the rest of 2007, Fed policymakers became preoccupied with the wide spread between LIBOR and the Federal Funds Rate. By December 2007, they effectively accepted defeat using their existing policy tools. Instead, they moved to provide dollar swaps to the ECB, the Bank of England, and the Swiss National Bank to pass onto European banks engaged in the Eurodollar credit markets. This provision of dollar liquidity began a Fed bailout of major European banks, and provided the answer, in practice the only one possible, to the 1974 question as to whether the Fed was the lender of last resort to the Eurodollar markets.

However, dollar swaps could not prevent the financial crisis spreading. The line of East Asian funding into American mortgage markets via Fannie Mae and Freddie Mac brought the American housing crash, the bank funding crisis, and the oil-induced recessions together. China's search for a higher return on dollar investments drove China to establish a sovereign wealth fund in early 2007. During the second half of that year, this fund made investments that recapitalized a number of American banks, including Bear Stearns, one of the big five American investment banks. But when the funding crisis at Bear Stearns deepened in early 2008, it withdrew from discussion of any further capital injections, precipitating the forced sale of Bear Stearns to JP Morgan. The fall of Bear Stearns then led to a rapid deterioration of conditions in the repo markets. The Chinese and Japanese central banks responded to this increase in liquidity risks by selling Fannie Mae and Freddie Mac bonds, pushing the two mortgage corporations towards insolvency. In September 2008, the US Treasury and the Federal Reserve Board took Fannie Mae and Freddie Mac into federal trusteeship, explicitly guaranteeing their entire debt.

This rescue saved the world economy from a monumental blow-up of 'Chimerica' and what would otherwise have been a full-scale dollar crisis. But, given the size of Fannie and Freddie's mortgage-backed securities portfolio, it also produced more turbulence in bank funding and in Eurodollar markets. This new turmoil escalated the growing crisis at Lehman Brothers, the American investment bank that was the principal conduit for recycling Eurodollars back into American credit markets.[69] Having only days earlier assumed massive new liabilities, the American government could scarcely have deemed bailing out Lehman anything other than a huge political risk. But when it allowed the 158-year-old investment bank to go under, bank funding markets completely froze. In the frenzy, the Bush administration and European governments were forced to rescue not just banks, but other financial corporations too, including the American insurance conglomerate AIG.

To cope with renewed crisis conditions in dollar bank funding markets, the Fed doubled the size of the swaps available to European central banks. A month later, it said that its swap arrangements with the ECB, the Bank of England, and the Bank of Switzerland would be increased to accommodate in its words 'whatever quantity of US dollar funding is required'.[70] As the Fed tried to stabilize these markets, the banking crash hit the oil-induced recessions. Across North America, Europe, and some Asian economies, output and employment fell further. With very weak demand now pervasive, international trade rapidly contracted, battering China's export sectors. Fearful for Chinese growth and political stability, the Chinese government in November 2008 embarked upon a debt-financed near $600 billion stimulus package focused on domestic demand for manufactured goods and raw materials and packed full of coal-fired projects.

It Didn't Stop

Growth did resume after the multiple crashes of 2007–8. Indeed, during 2019, the American economic recovery from the 2007–9 recession became the longest on record, going back to the 1850s. But the recoveries were stilted, in some cases slow, and odd. There was not one year during that decade of recovery where the American economy grew by 3 per cent, despite the large boost provided by the shale boom. (By comparison, after the 1991 recession, the American economy saw several years where growth was higher than 4 per cent, and it had been growing at nearly 4 per cent in 2004 before the impact of higher interest rates and oil prices took effect.) The labour participation rate—which measures the active workforce, including those looking for work—kept falling until late 2015, and at the point the Covid-19 crisis hit it still remained several percentage points below its level in 2007.[71] More starkly, Italy experienced two more recessions, and its recovery after its 2018 recession had stalled some time before the economic shutdown began in 2020. Prior to the pandemic, Italian GDP per capita still stood significantly below what it had reached in 2007.

Yet through all the decade, monetary policy had been extraordinarily accommodative first in the United States and Britain, and then after 2011, in the Eurozone too. Whatever the reasons why this easy monetary environment did not drive higher growth, by allowing American firms to extract shale oil, it did abate the energy crisis. This reconnected monetary policy to oil at the same time as the Fed's monetary decision-making became a financial constraint on China, reversing the pre-crash dynamics when the Fed was raising rates between 2004 and 2006 to cope with the consequences of rising Chinese oil demand.

The interaction would prove to have a new set of disruptive consequences. In a speech in 2019, the retiring governor of the Bank of England, Mark Carney, noted that the whole world economy had come to struggle when the Fed even marginally increased interest rates.[72] The Bank's research suggested, he continued, that the continual spillover effects of Fed tightening were now twice that of their average between 1990 and 2004, despite the fact American gross domestic product as a share of the world's had significantly shrunk.[73] He argued that the dollar's long-term primacy was 'making it increasingly difficult for monetary policy makers to achieve their domestic mandates to stabilize inflation and maintain output at potential'.[74]

Structurally, such scepticism at what monetary policy could achieve was the same judgement his predecessor, Mervyn King, had offered fourteen years earlier when he pronounced NICE over. For King oil, not the dollar, had been the problem. He was both wrong and right. He had missed that monetary policy could serve to increase the supply of oil. Since that oil came from the United States, Trichet's parallel assumption that oil was driving a power shift away from Western countries was also erroneous: both

146 *Disorder*

American energy and financial power increased after 2008. The trouble was—as the next chapter will show—that both oil and the dollar would cause new economic problems on top of their geopolitical havoc, not least for the monetary policy instruments on which American policymakers bet everything in late 2008.

6

We Are Not in Kansas Any More

Over the weekend of 7–8 March 2020, Mohammed Bin Salman made his fateful decision to flood oil markets just as demand was falling rapidly. On the Monday morning, tumbling oil prices took share and bond prices down with them, and banks and corporations outside the United States that are dependent on dollar credit markets scrambled for funding. By any historical standards, the ensuing financial crash was spectacular. Only the share market crash in October 1987 was larger than the percentage fall in the Dow Jones index on 16 March, and the fall on 12 March was also significantly bigger than any witnessed in 2008. Two weeks into the crash, the S&P 500 stock market index was down nearly 30 per cent from its all-time peak a month earlier.[1] Between 9 and 18 March, the yields on long-term US Treasury bonds rose more than 250 per cent.[2] At any moment of crisis, these bonds are supposed to serve as safe assets. Instead, they too were part of the panic.

Confronted with another financial crash, the Fed returned to the playbook it had established in 2007–8. During the evening of Sunday 15 March, it sought to calm investor nerves before the markets reopened by cutting interest rates to zero, initiating a fifth quantitative easing (QE) programme, and reactivating swap lines for those central banks with which it had sanctioned permanent swap arrangements. Its actions were to no avail: investors continued to sell pretty much everything they could, even gold. Dollar cash alone would do.

In Europe, a sense of déjà vu also descended during the first week of the crisis. On 12 March, Christine Lagarde, the European Central Bank (ECB) president who had taken office only five months earlier, remarked in a press conference that 'we are not here to close spreads'.[3] In her words, Lagarde repudiated the 'whatever it takes' rhetoric of her predecessor Mario Draghi that back in the summer of 2012 had begun to convince investors that the Eurozone was irreversible. Italian bond yields spiked, as did Italian anger. But the ECB Draghi created could not be brushed aside with Lagarde's disastrous choice of words. Less than a week later, the ECB announced its own new €750 billion QE programme—the Pandemic Emergency Purchase Programme.

As the world's central banks grappled with the disarray, the dollar climbed against virtually all other currencies. China's 2015–16 financial crisis had shown the vulnerability of emerging-market countries to capital flight into dollars. But such exchange rate constraints were no longer supposed to be the experience of advanced economies. Now, in the second week of the pandemic financial crisis, the euro, sterling, and the Canadian dollar scarcely looked different from developing-country currencies under siege. On the same day that the ECB acted, sterling fell so sharply that chaos ensued in British bond markets. The Fed offered swaps to more central banks. But the dollar credit markets continued to deteriorate, and the turbulence in foreign exchange markets did not abate.

Apparently defeated, the Fed now turned to even more radical policy tools. On 23 March, it announced QE 'Infinity': a balance sheet purchasing programme covering pretty much every investor asset, including corporate debt. This calmed American financial markets and the exchange rates of those states with access to dollars from the Fed. But the Fed's moves still left one big question unanswered: if necessary, could the Fed extend a dollar swap line to Beijing? The answer was fudged but consequential: China received no swaps, but on 31 March, the Fed announced that states without swap lines could borrow against their US Treasury holdings of which China has a huge portfolio.[4]

In part, the March 2020 financial crash compressed the 2007–8 financial crash, the 2009–12 Eurozone crisis, and the 2015–16 Chinese financial crisis into a matter of days. It also massively magnified the responses of the different central banks. The Fed began to buy every investor asset going. The ECB worried about its mandate only to reach for QE just three days after the Fed and one day earlier than the Bank of England. The Chinese central bank used its dollar reserves to protect the renminbi and had to rely overtly on assistance from the Fed.

But these juxtapositions only tell part of the story of what was at stake in March 2020 and the economic and geopolitical changes that had occurred over the previous twelve years. China and Europe's relationship to international banking had in part inverted. Indeed, Chinese banks had so grown in importance that they had eclipsed European banks. In 2007, nine of the ten biggest banks in the world ranked by the size of their assets were European; none were Chinese.[5] By March 2020, the largest four measured by assets were Chinese. In the top ten ranked by market capitalization, five were Chinese, and there was only one European bank, HSBC, which had a strong presence in Hong Kong.[6] This growth in Chinese banking ensured that at the same time as the Sino-American economic relationship became more geopolitically contested, China became more integrated into the international financial world where the Fed acts as a lender of last resort.

In the weeks after the March 2020 financial crash, a political crisis in Hong Kong threatened to collapse the distinction between China's financial integration into the world economy and the Sino-American trade and technology war. Hong Kong was the international financial centre that connected China to the rest of the word. In the second half of 2019, the city had been consumed with, at times violent, pro-democracy protests. Then, Donald Trump had been dismissive, saying Hong Kong was China's business.[7] But, in May 2020, when the Hong Kong protestors returned to the streets, Hong Kong became part of the general discord in US–China relations. In imposing national security legislation on Hong Kong, China effectively terminated the governance arrangements for the city agreed with Britain in 1984. In response, the Trump administration declared it would revoke Hong Kong's trading status, meaning that henceforth the United States would treat Hong Kong economically as part of China.

From oil to dollar swaps to Hong Kong's status as an international financial centre, the world economy was geopolitically hypercharged before the pandemic struck. Against this backdrop, the post-2008 monetary world reached a reckoning in March 2020. But the ability of central banks in this world to support debt also allowed governments at the very same time to shut down much of the world economy for several months. To understand the disruptive flows arising from the post-2008 economic world and their advantageous fallout during the pandemic, we need to start with the Fed's response to the 2007–8 financial crash: without it the present economic and energy world could not exist.[8]

The World the Fed Made

The 2007–8 crash proved no ordinary crisis. In a functional credit environment, the Fed would have been able to reinvigorate credit markets by substantially loosening monetary policy, allowing a path back to growth in the real economy. But the Eurodollar markets had deeply complicated how the financial system worked. The fact that cutting interest rates alone was nowhere near sufficient to stabilize bank funding markets pushed the Fed to become the lender of last resort to the Eurodollar markets. The Fed's actions prevented major European banks from collapsing. But it also created a geopolitically charged financial and monetary hierarchy. In the post-2008 monetary world, the Fed selected which countries' banks' dollar borrowing it would back.[9] Notably, in Asia, it supported the Singaporean and South Korean central banks but not the Indian or the Chinese.[10]

In saving the Eurodollar markets, the Fed did not restore them to their pre-August 2007 functionality.[11] At the aggregate level, the international credit environment shrank. As a proportion of world GDP, international capital flows in 2019 were substantially lower than they were in 2007. But this truncation was primarily European in origin, particularly around British banks. For emerging markets, not least China, cross-national credit flows increased.[12] Consequently, after 2008, the Chinese economy became more susceptible to the dollar credit environment, even as China was left outside the Fed's support structure for foreign dollar debt.

The Fed's three QE programmes and seven-year zero interest rates policy detached the monetary and financial world even more profoundly from the one that preceded it.[13] QE1 was driven by the American mortgage crisis. In November 2008, the Fed began purchasing debt and mortgage-backed securities issued by Fannie Mae and Freddie Mac.[14] Over the next six years, the Fed purchased $2.3 trillion worth of mortgage-backed securities.[15] These purchases pushed nominal long-term rates for mortgages tied to these corporations to an all-time low. But QE could not end the foreclosures crisis.

Indeed, QE support for Fannie Mae and Freddie Mac created a deep division between American mortgage holders. Those with loans already backed by the two congressionally-chartered mortgage corporations, or those who could qualify for one, had access to a refinancing mechanism via lower interest rates that other borrowers, who had taken subprime loans, did not. This—as will be discussed in chapter nine—had serious implications for American democratic politics.

QE quickly became a means also to support the federal government's borrowing. The Fed added Treasury bond purchases to QE1 in March 2009. In the second QE programme—which began in November 2010 and ran to June 2012, and the third, which started in September 2012 and concluded in October 2014—Treasury bonds took centre stage. These purchases allowed the American government to run a much bigger deficit than it had before 2008.

Whatever its macro-economic utility, QE had systemically disruptive consequences. Some arose from asset-price inflation. In pushing bond yields down, the Fed necessarily pushed asset prices up. This improved banks' balance sheets, provided an easy source of cash, and kept interest rates for their borrowing near zero. But by simultaneously providing support for asset prices and cheap credit, it created strong incentives for corporations to borrow to buy back their own shares rather than invest in productive capacity. As the International Monetary Fund (IMF) warned in its 2019 Global Financial Stability report, the sharp increase in share buy-backs also led to a surge in financial risk-taking by many large American corporations. When the pandemic hit, their cash reserves were, consequently, low.[16] More generally, rising asset prices obviously benefited those already owning assets.[17] Since older people are more likely to own assets, QE increased wealth inequality between generations.[18] Both phenomena soon became evident in housing markets. In some countries, house prices in large cities rose formidably, as property increasingly became an international investment asset. With prices rising and mortgage lenders often requiring much higher deposits than before 2007–8, levels of home ownership among younger people fell.[19] With more people stuck in rental markets, rents too accelerated upwards in cities where rapid house price inflation occurred.

QE also shaped investment capital flows. Extremely low yield on US Treasury bonds produced a hunt for a return elsewhere. In the immediate years after 2008, this desire sent large quantities of money to emerging markets.[20] It also ignited the corporate junk bond market, where to compensate for the greater risk of default interest yields are higher.[21] The primary beneficiaries in the productive economy of this search for yield were shale energy companies, which acquired a supply of easy cash.[22] It was this credit that made shale oil production financially viable when, even with the high prices that prevailed between 2011 and late 2014, there was no prospect of firms actually making a profit. Back at the time of the first Gulf War, James Schlesinger—Nixon and Ford's defence secretary and Carter's energy secretary—had said about shale that 'we have not found a mechanism for overcoming the cost barriers to these new technologies and as a nation we are not prepared to pay higher prices for energy in order to have a larger domestic supply'.[23] Now, the Fed's post-crash monetary accommodation, at a time when Chinese demand ensured a quick recovery for oil prices, proved the inadvertent remedy for still largely stagnant conventional—oil produced by traditional drilling methods—production.

If QE was originally conceived as temporary, in practice returning to any measure of monetary normalcy proved impossible. In May 2013, the Fed chair, Ben Bernanke, told a congressional committee that if the economy continued to grow, the Fed might over the next months' meetings decide to taper its bond purchases. Panicked, financial investors responded by selling bonds, sending the interest rate on Treasury bonds upwards. This 'taper tantrum', as the markets' extreme reaction became known, encouraged the Fed at its 17–18 September meeting to decide against reducing purchases. Three months later, it did begin to taper. But caution now prevailed: QE3 continued until October 2014.

Almost immediately, oil prices created a new constraint on monetary policy. The oil crash in late 2014 induced by shale—as described in chapters two and three—accelerated an already downward trend in inflation. By mid-2015, the IMF was warning about a debt-deflation spiral while the Fed, now desperate to normalize, was seeking to raise interest rates.[24] When the Fed finally did act in December 2015, American inflation stood at just 0.1 per cent and another recession was a distinct short-term possibility.

This belated retreat from QE and zero-interest rates also constituted a geopolitical and economic shock for the rest of the world economy. For some states without emergency access to dollar swaps, the Fed's attempt to reverse course was a disaster, bringing as it did the prospect of higher yield for investors on American Treasury bonds. Some of these states' difficulties had massive geopolitical ramifications. Nowhere was this more so than in Ukraine. As soon as Bernanke suggested tapering was a possibility, investors sold Ukrainian bonds. This made it impossible for Viktor Yanukovych's government to roll over its debt in bond markets, pushing it to turn to Moscow in search of financial assistance and cheaper gas, an imperative fuelled by the weak support offered by the IMF and the EU.[25] For others, not least China, the problem was financial instability and slower growth. In the summer of 2015, the Fed's preparation to make its first post-crash increase in interest rates plunged China into a financial crisis. Since China responded to huge capital flight by selling dollar reserves, China's financial instability then made it harder for the Fed to continue to raise rates. By devaluing the renminbi, China also fuelled protectionist anger in the US Congress, just as the primaries for the 2016 presidential nomination races began.

The Europe the Eurozone Made

If the Fed remade the economic world by its monetary and financial actions in 2007–8, the ECB remade the EU first by what it did not and in part, at least, could not do.[26] Although not well understood at the time, the Eurozone crisis began with the European banking crisis in August 2007 and the need for the Fed to provide large-scale financial support for various North European banks.[27] Once the severity of Greece's fiscal problems then became apparent from late 2009, a double Eurozone crisis emerged. On the one side, bond market contagion left the Southern European states and Ireland with drastically increased borrowing costs. On the other, largely the same banks that had acquired vast dollar assets and depended on short-term dollar funding were now exposed by their large-scale lending to Southern Europe and Ireland. The risk of default on these assets became a reason why investors and other banks did not want to lend to Northern European banks. Consequently, between mid-2010 and the summer of 2012, any time that Southern European governments and corporations were unable to rollover their debt in bond markets there was a parallel problem faced by Northern European banks in dollar funding markets.[28]

The crisis severed the Eurozone as a monetary bloc. For investors, the notion that lending to Germany was essentially the same as lending to any other Eurozone member disappeared. Accordingly, each government needed to keep what was now the 'spread' between the rate at which it could borrow and the rate at which Germany could borrow as low as possible. At one point, the French prime minister, François Fillon, said that 'the first thing' he looked at 'every morning is the spread differential between France and Germany'.[29]

Structurally, the spread returned the Exchange Rate Mechanism's (ERM) asymmetry in a new form. This was reinforced by what had become another divergence between the German economy—again as with the ERM matched by the Dutch—and the rest of the Eurozone around Germany's trade surplus. In 2004, the German current account surplus surpassed its previous peak in 1989. Henceforth, it swelled until it would become in absolute terms the largest in the world. This outcome was not accidental. Rather, it was the consequence of labour market reforms made by the 1998–2005 Social Democrat–Green coalition government in Berlin, culminating in 2005 with an end to the old German welfare state that largely protected citizens' prior incomes from unemployment. The corollary of this structurally large German trade surplus was a trade deficit in many other Eurozone states.[30]

For the weaker Eurozone states, the ensuing dynamics were worse than the ERM. In dealing with the spread, governments needed to defend their credibility in financial markets. But they no longer had national central banks that could take monetary decisions aimed at reducing bond market pressure. Moreover, as the Maastricht Treaty forbade the ECB from directly purchasing the debt issued by member states, the ECB could not readily act as a guarantor of any sovereign bonds either. Without a national or European lender-of-last resort capacity, differential borrowing costs could not be stopped.[31] Those shut out from capital markets—as at different points in 2010–11 were Greece, Ireland, and Portugal—then needed bailouts, even though the Maastricht Treaty also forbade bailouts.

In 2010 and 2011, Greece, Ireland, and Portugal all agreed credit programmes with the European Commission representing the

Eurogroup (the finance ministers of Eurozone states), the ECB, and the IMF. These three creditors became known collectively as the Troika. The loans from the Troika came with German-driven conditions that forced these governments into public expenditure cuts, tax increases, and labour and welfare reforms in the name of replicating the German trade surplus. Since what was expected in outcome was in fact impossible without Germany pursuing policies to shrink its trade surplus, these dynamics could only in practice reinforce the spread problem that threatened the Eurozone's existence.[32]

For the Eurozone to survive, the ECB had to change. Immediately after the first Greek bailout was agreed in May 2010, it began to do so by establishing a Securities Market Programme (SMP) to buy sovereign bonds indirectly in secondary markets. But in reforming itself, the ECB immediately ran into political difficulties: no one could seriously pretend this purchasing programme was compatible with the intent behind the Maastricht Treaty.[33] If this issue could be ignored in some Eurozone countries, it could not be, in Germany. The Bundesbank voted against the SMP. Later, the Bundesbank president and the German representative on the ECB Executive Board resigned over the issue. Most lethally, improvising reforms to the Eurozone without changing its legal structure had to ignite the hitherto dormant political tension created by the German Federal Constitutional Court's 1993 decision that further extending EU authority should be compatible with German Basic Law. The resulting need for prudence around German politics ensured that, having established a purchasing programme, the ECB quickly became extremely tentative in using it. Notably, the ECB stopped buying Greek debt within a few weeks of starting to do so.[34]

Before Mario Draghi broke this impasse, escalating oil prices in 2011 deepened the Eurozone crisis and aggravated the long monetary disagreement that preceded it. Driven by still growing Chinese demand and the absence yet of large-scale shale output, prices went back over $100 a barrel again in early 2011 and by and large stayed there until mid-2014. Even with the prospect of higher inflation, the Fed decided against increasing interest rates. In sharp contrast, the ECB prioritized its legal mandate to pursue price stability. Indeed, in justifying two interest rate increases in 2011, Jean-Claude Trichet deployed much the same arguments about oil's inflationary dangers that he had in July 2008. This time, there could be no doubt that several Eurozone economies were badly struggling: when the ECB made its first move, Greece, Spain, and Portugal were in recession, and when it made its second, Italy, Slovenia, and Cyprus had joined them.[35] The ECB's moves made growth even harder. By the year's end, the aggregated Eurozone economy was in recession. It would remain so until early 2013.

If the ECB could not decisively support government debt and remained bound to a price stability mandate, then the corollary had to be a Eurozone with strong treaty constraints on sovereign borrowing and populated with governments that accepted anti-inflationary discipline. Neither existed. The Stability and Growth Pact had set out fiscal rules for the Eurozone. But its credibility had been fatally damaged in 2003 when the French and German governments broke them without sanction.[36] Moreover, the last thing that governments presiding over economies in recession wished to consider were policy changes likely to impede short-term growth.

When, in the summer of 2011, Italy and Spain appeared to be heading into the same territory as Greece, Ireland, and Portugal, something had to give.[37] The bailout framework established for Greece was inadequate to support these larger economies, and the size of French and German banks' exposure to Italy and Spain reignited their dollar funding problems. That August, the ECB changed tack. By writing to the Italian prime minister, Silvio Berlusconi, to demand policy changes, Trichet and the incoming ECB president Draghi set in motion the train of events—set out at the beginning of chapter four—that culminated in the Italian president appointing Mario Monti's cabinet of technocrats to office.

The brutal Eurozone logic behind Berlusconi's removal was later spelled out by Obama's treasury secretary, after Merkel and Sarkozy asked for his help in dealing with Berlusconi. 'The German public', he wrote in a note to himself, was 'not going to support, like, a bigger financial firewall, more money for Europe, if Berlusconi was presiding over that country'.[38] Put simply, if the ECB did have to act as a meaningful lender of last resort to save the Eurozone, it needed German consent, and that meant it having an implicit veto over who issued the debt and for what purpose.

Less dramatically than in Italy, the ECB's actions in the summer of 2011 also kept economic policy from being contested in Spanish democratic politics. On the same day as Trichet and Draghi despatched their letter to Berlusconi, Trichet and the governor of the Bank of Spain wrote to the Socialist Spanish prime minister, José Luis Rodríguez Zapatero. They requested that various policy actions, most contentiously on labour markets, be taken by the end of August. Having already announced that there would be an early general election in November that the opposition People's Party appeared very likely to win, Zapatero presided over a lame-duck administration.[39] As the ECB deadline approached, it was clear that he had nothing like the parliamentary votes to deliver the labour market changes the ECB demanded. Searching for a way out, he agreed with the People's Party leader, Mariano Rajoy, to use an emergency legislative procedure to set a constitutional cap on future budget deficits. After the People's Party did indeed win the election, Rajoy was left with the labour market problem, and, like Zapatero, not having the votes to legislate, he resorted to decree to do as the ECB asked.[40]

These overt political interventions in national democracies were tantamount to 'emergency' politics.[41] The Eurozone simply could not function in 2011 as it was constitutionally supposed to under the Maastricht Treaty. A Eurozone in which the ECB set monetary policy and elected member state governments decided on the rest of economic policy was a Eurozone heading towards its death. Nonetheless, if the ECB had to keep intervening in national democratic politics to achieve the economic policies it deemed necessary, the Eurozone would be in permanent political trouble, a reality of which the ECB was well cognizant. What the ECB lacked, in Trichet's words, was 'a solid democratic anchor' for making demands of member states.[42] But at the same time, the German Constitutional Court could rule at any time that its actions to buy member states' debt was unconstitutional under German Basic Law or illegal under EU law. Consequently, German consent cut both ways. If the ECB were to be allowed to buy debt to prop up Italy, Merkel could not tolerate Berlusconi. But in pushing the Italian president to remove Berlusconi, the ECB was likely to send more petitioners to the German Court to charge it with abusing its authority.

The only way the Eurozone could resolve its monetary–economic mismatch was by changing EU treaties. But any such ambition would run into counter political realities. A new treaty meant involving the non-Euro members in discussing changes necessary only for Eurozone members. Any treaty revision that changed the legal mandate of the ECB was also politically untenable in Germany. For Merkel, the only way forward was a treaty that forced member states to take responsibility under their own domestic laws and constitutions for fiscal probity. In late 2011 and early 2012, she persuaded all except the British and Czech governments to agree such a treaty in what became the Fiscal Compact. But this treaty stood in awkward relation to EU law: with two member states absent, it was an intergovernmental treaty and not a treaty of the EU as a legal entity. Even more problematically, entrenching balanced budgets nationally supposed a Eurozone-wide political consensus about economic policy that simply did not exist, not least in France. This was potentially explosive. The French president, Nicolas Sarkozy, reluctantly gave his support to the Fiscal Compact, but his Socialist opponent in the 2012 French presidential election was staunchly opposed. In that election, François Hollande campaigned on a pledge to renegotiate the Fiscal Compact—as will be discussed in chapter nine—and won. Although he eventually did preside over its ratification, this French president showed no urgency in complying with it.

Eventually, Mario Draghi and Angela Merkel ended the existential Eurozone crisis over the summer of 2012. Between them they convinced investors to expect a large Eurozone to endure. In this respect Draghi's crucial words were not 'whatever it takes'; they were 'we think the euro is irreversible' and '[irreversible] is not an empty word now'.[43] What then gave those words content was not so much the fact that Draghi constructed a new bond purchasing programme—Outright Monetary Transactions (OMT)—but Merkel and her finance minister Wolfgang Schäuble's public acceptance of OMT. As one Polish diplomat had explained the problem prior to Draghi's speech: 'Regarding Germany, the danger is that they will dump the child with the bathwater and destroy the euro. The markets still need a clear signal that Germany will do what it takes to save the euro.'[44] In acceding to OMT, Merkel and Schäuble gave it.

But for the Greek government, a de facto reformed ECB backed by the German chancellor and finance minister was nowhere near enough to extricate the Greek economy from the catastrophe that

.had engulfed it, or end doubts about Greece's future inside the
Eurozone. By the summer of 2011, the ECB was buying few if any
Greek bonds and Greece needed another bailout.[45] In November
2011, the Greek prime minister, George Papandreou, announced
there would be a referendum on the proposed terms of a second
Greek bailout. Merkel and Sarkozy promptly told him that the bailout
could not proceed if such a referendum took place. Instead, they said
he should hold a referendum on Greece's membership of the euro and
the EU. Behind the scenes, European Commission officials worked
with the opposition New Democracy leader to form a national unity
government led by a former ECB vice president, Lucas Papademos.[46]
After Papademos took office, the ECB set up a Grexit working group
without Greek government or central bank representatives.[47] The
following year, just days before Greek voters were due to head to
the polls, Merkel reportedly told the Greek president that Greece
should hold a referendum on continuing euro membership with its
general election.[48] No such referendum took place. Still unsatisfied,
Merkel spent the summer months consulting about Greek expulsion.
She decided against it only after determining there were too many
unknowns in play.[49] But without ECB support, Greece was still
floating away from the Eurozone.[50] When Draghi indicated that
Greece would not be eligible to participate in OMT, the reality that
'whatever it takes' did not apply to Greece could scarcely have been
clearer.[51]

   The political resolution of the Greek crisis in the summer of 2015
played out against the backdrop of Draghi moving the Eurozone to
QE. In June 2014, around the same time as the Fed was eyeing the
end of QE3, the ECB announced it was intensifying its preparations
for an asset-purchase programme. Six months later, the Greek government fell, and new elections were called for 25 January 2015.
A victory for the radical left party Syriza would have risked the spread
problem returning to Italy and Spain.[52] Now QE had to serve as a
means to stimulate higher growth and one to prevent contagion
from Greece to the rest of Southern Europe. On 22 January, the
ECB announced that it would begin a QE programme in March
2015. Three days later, Syriza became the largest party in the
Greek Parliament. The ECB immediately indicated that Greece,
along with Cyprus, would not be eligible for inclusion in QE.[53]

It also restricted Greek banks' access to emergency assistance in the event of liquidity problems.

The Syriza-led government's predicament was how to stay in the Eurozone now that those within Germany who wanted to expel Greece from it had a renewed opportunity to act. It was not, as Yanis Varoufakis, the first Syriza finance minister, judged it, a matter of how to leverage the threat of a Greek default to secure a restructuring of Greek debt or a reform of the Eurozone. This was a matter of Greek survival, a reality that became palpable after Greek voters rejected the terms for a third bailout in a referendum in June 2015. Rather than offering concessions, Wolfgang Schäuble led his fellow finance ministers to propose severe additional measures as a condition of the loans on the assumption that the Greek prime minister, Alexis Tsipras, could not possibly accept them and would embark on withdrawing Greece from the euro. Greek choices were, however, harder than Schäuble supposed. Even with the tacit offer of more loans or even the prospect of debt restructuring to facilitate an exit, there was no orderly path out of the Eurozone: Greece would have been left with enormous debts in a foreign currency and huge questions about its future inside the EU. Staring into that abyss, and aided by some small concessions by Merkel, Tsipras conceded what Schäuble had deemed impossible, leaving Greece's Eurozone membership intact.[54]

The Greek experience went straight to the fault line inherent to a large monetary union from the start. In Schäuble's judgement, Greece should never have been allowed to join the euro, and what membership required was largely incompatible with Greek democracy. Greece then survived its expulsion crisis because the same symbolic imperatives around European unity that had taken Italy into the euro still resonated. Nonetheless, Greece remained trapped in the pre-OMT monetary union. When Greece exited its bailout programme in the summer of 2018, Draghi made clear that it still would not be eligible for QE.[55] A year later, when the ECB reactivated QE, it again left Greece outside the programme.

Yet there remained a paradox that went beyond the EU and Eurozone's own fault lines. Despite the absence of direct ECB support, Greece exited its third bailout programme on schedule in August 2018, and in March 2019 it sold ten-year bonds again in international capital markets. The ECB's commitment to the euro's irreversibility had not applied to Greece. But the international credit environment created by the Fed ensured that any positive rate of return would attract investors, allowing Greece to borrow at rates that prior to 2008 would have seemed absurd for a state carrying debt worth nearly 180 per cent of GDP. Soon, this had consequences for Greece's formal position inside the Eurozone too: when the ECB announced its Pandemic Purchasing Programme, Greece was included, ending the country's near-decade-long exclusion from the ECB bond-purchasing debt support structure.

* * *

Quite differently, the Eurozone crisis set in motion a path that led Britain out of the EU. Of course, the crisis did not determine Brexit. But it interacted lethally with the existing fault lines around Britain's EU membership. Most directly, it pressed upon the relationship between Britain's exclusion from monetary union, its inclusion in the single market, and London's position as the Eurozone's financial centre. Wanting more regulatory discretion over euro trading, the ECB hoped to end the London Clearing House's predominance as the intermediary in the buying and selling of euro-denominated financial instruments, especially derivates. For the British government, the ECB's proposals in 2011 for new euro clearing rules violated single market law by discriminating between Eurozone and non-Eurozone members. It took a case to the European Court of Justice and eventually won. But in passing judgment, the Court did not adjudicate on the principle of non-discrimination on which rested the long-standing British assumption that the single market and monetary union could be compartmentalized.[56]

As the single market and the Eurozone interacted to yield different outcomes under crisis conditions, the dominant political currency for exercising influence inside the EU also changed to Britain's disadvantage. Via bailouts and tolerance for missed fiscal targets, Germany acquired a new array of de facto side payments to dispense. By contrast, the British government struggled to find allies on economic issues even among the non-euro states, since it alone had a London problem, and Sweden and Denmark—the two other North European non-euro members—largely aligned their monetary policy with the ECB after the crash.

How far the Eurozone crisis had weakened British political influence was on overt display at the EU summit in December 2011. It was here that the EU states minus Britain agreed the substance of what became the Fiscal Compact.[57] David Cameron saw Merkel's desire for a new EU treaty as an opportunity to establish new safeguards for British financial services within the single market against Eurozone- driven regulatory decisions. But, for Merkel, British participation in a new EU treaty was the disadvantage of such a treaty since, under the 2011 EU Act passed by the British Parliament, in transferring powers to the EU it would necessitate a British referendum.[58] Unable to secure his demands to protect London's position, Cameron vetoed the proposed Union-level treaty. Unwilling to make Eurozone necessity hostage to British democratic politics, Merkel moved to an intergovernmental treaty that did not require British consent.[59]

It was Cameron's failure in December 2011 that set the context for his decision in January 2013 to commit a future Conservative-majority government to renegotiate the terms of Britain's membership and then hold a referendum on whether Britain should remain in the EU. But by the time the Conservatives won the 2015 general election and could honour Cameron's promise, the problems for Britain generated by the Eurozone crisis went further than exposure to Eurozone-driven financial regulation.

The Eurozone crisis had reinvigorated the macro-economic differences between Britain and Eurozone members. In the months after the financial meltdown in the autumn of 2008, the Bank of England had acted much more like the Fed than the ECB. It began a QE programme in March 2009. It also did not raise interest rates in 2011 in response to rising oil prices, even though British inflation was several percentage points higher than that within the Eurozone. With these decisions, a clear divergence between the British and Eurozone economies emerged. Recovery in Britain from 2012 and recessionary conditions in the Eurozone saw significant numbers of people from Southern Europe coming to work in Britain. With the long-standing monetary difference between the Bank of England and the ECB now spilling over into the labour side of the single market, Britain had effectively become, with Germany, an employer of last resort for the Eurozone. This shattered any chance that the Conservative–Liberal Democrat coalition government could achieve the immigration target it had adopted in accordance with the Conservatives' 2010 manifesto promise to reduce migration to Britain. Against this backdrop, the United Kingdom Independence Party began in 2012 to climb in the opinion polls, heaping pressure on Cameron within the parliamentary Conservative Party on all EU matters. By the time Cameron began his negotiations with the other EU states after the 2015 general election, he wanted significant concessions on freedom of movement, as well as on financial services regulation, even though what he wished for in this area was incompatible with EU law and Merkel had already indicated it could not be contemplated.[60]

There was now an impasse. Freedom of movement could not be kept out of British democratic politics because there was insufficient political support for constitutionally guaranteed migration rights from EU countries. Only a British economic downturn could alleviate the political pressure, and then only if the Eurozone recovered. Nor was any British government likely to allow the single market to become a sliding door into governance arrangements made between the Eurozone states. Stabilizing British membership would have compromised the single market and required the Eurozone states to accept they could never vote for financial regulations that discriminated against London. Consequently, Cameron could only ask British voters whether they accepted that the alternative of leaving was worse than the problems of the status quo after his own renegotiations had shown the British government lacked the political wherewithal inside the EU to address them.[61]

* * *

Ultimately, the 2009–15 Eurozone crisis reshaped the EU without politically stabilizing it. The crisis drew sharp lines around the question of who was in and outside both the EU and monetary union.

Of those acceding to the EU in 2004 or after, Cyprus, Malta, Slovenia, and Slovakia had joined the euro before the crisis began. By embarking on fierce fiscal tightening, Estonia, Latvia, and Lithuania entered the Eurozone between 2011 and 2015. Of the Eastern European states, this left the Czech Republic, Hungary, and Poland outside monetary union. All were legally supposed to terminate their national currency. In the Czech case, it was evident well before the crisis that this was unlikely to happen with any alacrity. But for Poland and Hungary, there was a plausible path to relatively imminent euro membership that the crisis made much more politically difficult. By the time of the British referendum, neither Viktor Orbán's government in Budapest nor the Law and Justice government in Warsaw wished to proceed to entry. Yet as Britain was the most politically awkward non-euro-member, Brexit offered an opportunity to force a resolution of the conflict between an EU formally committed to ever closer union and its practical existence as a multi-currency Union.

For the Commission president, Jean-Claude Juncker, this chance had to be taken. In his 2017 State of the Union speech, he declared that 'the euro was meant to be the single currency of the whole European Union' and it was time to act to make it so.[62] His rallying call inevitably raised questions about the structure of the monetary union those outside could be asked to join. Italy and Greece had already shown there were 'which' state and 'which' government questions around asset purchases. Any enlargement of the Eurozone to include Poland and Hungary could only harden those questions and increase the chances of German dissent when QE had still not been legitimated constitutionally for Germany by the German Constitutional Court. Moreover, some governments wanted the Eurozone to carry debt directly. A few weeks after Juncker spoke, Emmanuel Macron outlined his vision of reforming monetary union to include a common budget, a finance minister, a parliament, and common bank deposit insurance.[63] In sharp contrast to the Commission president, Macron assumed that a debt-bearing Eurozone would entail hierarchical tiers of EU membership structured around whether states were in or out of the euro.[64]

Neither would prevail. There was no move to force non-member entry to monetary union. Meanwhile, the political asymmetries of the Eurozone crisis, the Eurozone's enlargement, and Britain's impending exit from the EU in good part doomed Macron's reform project. In response to the proposals Macron laid out in September 2017, a new political bloc of EU states dubbed the New Hanseatic League formed. It consisted of several original Eurozone members—the Netherlands, Finland, and Ireland—the recent entrants—Estonia, Latvia, and Lithuania—and the two long-standing non-Eurozone members—Denmark and Sweden—left without their sometime British ally.[65]

These states avowed that the Eurozone should retain the Maastricht monetary–economic distinction. They also insisted that extending supranational authority further over debt would not command political support in their countries. Although the Eurozone governments did agree some small reforms in October 2019, the New Hanseatic League gutted Macron's radical agenda without the German government being put to a decisive test on its stance.

A decade after the Eurozone crisis, the EU remained what it had been before the crisis: a multi-currency Union with stronger EU than Eurozone institutions. The explanation for this outcome is the reality that there was no available political resolution: muddling through proved the decisive response because it was much less difficult than pursuing remedies.

* * *

Nonetheless, when, in 2020, Italy became the first European country to face the Covid-19 crisis, there appeared a reckoning for the inaction. Even after the ECB initiated pandemic QE, Italy's existing debt set some limits on how much new debt it could plausibly issue. By contrast, in early March 2020, the German government abandoned the constitutional brake on its budget deficit and agreed a large national fiscal stimulus. For Macron, the crisis appeared an opportunity to reopen the matter of Eurozone common debt. In late March 2020, he organized eight other Eurozone governments, including the Italian, to write to the European Council president to demand the creation of a European institution with the power to issue a common debt instrument dubbed 'coronabonds'. Openly joining several New Hanseatic League states, the German government dismissed the idea as unthinkable.[66] But the German position was only tenable so long as there was no question that the ECB could deepen its support for Italy's debt. Less than two months after the ECB announced its pandemic purchasing programme, this certainty ended when the German Constitutional Court delivered a final verdict on the first QE. In a startling statement, it ruled that in accepting the ECB's action, the German government and Bundestag had acted unconstitutionally. What's more, for the first time, it declared that a judgment made by the European Court of Justice lacked legal authority in Germany. Across the case, its reasoning strongly suggested that when legally challenged in Germany pandemic QE would also fall foul of its stipulations.

For the German government, the tactic of muddling through the disjuncture between the monetary union legally established in the Maastricht Treaty and the practical imperatives created by keeping the Eurozone together appeared exhausted. Having repudiated Macron in the early spring, the German chancellor changed course. Just a few weeks after the Court's decision, Merkel made a dramatically staged proposal with the French president to create a new EU collective borrowing capacity.[67] Confronted with a decision as to whether openly to accept German constitutional limits on Eurozone decision-making and what that would entail for some other Eurozone states' debt, she chose instead to, as she put it, 'advance integration'.[68] Some New Hanseatic League states tried to resist. But, in July 2020, Merkel and Macron were able to secure an agreement from the whole EU to establish an EU Recovery Fund, whereby the Commission could borrow in the EU's name to give to member states money to fund national recovery projects.

The EU Recovery Fund appeared a breakthrough, even to some a 'Hamiltonian moment' akin to the point when, in 1790, the American federal republic became a debt-sharing Union.[69] Without any parallel move on taxes, this interpretation was overblown—as will be discussed in chapter eight. This final German turn away from the constitutionalized Maastricht commitments was another muddle-through move. Merkel's insistence that a Recovery Fund primarily conceived to support Eurozone members should run through the EU budget could only exacerbate the fault line that rendered the EU a multi-currency union. By eschewing new Eurozone institutions, Merkel gave non-Euro zone members a formal veto over debt being issued to facilitate stimuli for Eurozone states burdened by past debt. This allowed the Hungarian and Polish governments to drive hard bargains about non-Eurozone matters in return for their compliance. Consequently, the terms of the Fund's operation took months to finalize, ensuring that no money was available to member states by the scheduled start of January 2021.

The pandemic emergency also demonstrated that the residual tension between Eurozone dynamics and those generated by the single market had not ended with Britain's departure. To deal with the 2020 economic crisis, the Commission suspended some single market rules, including those for state aid. But states with much lower debt, like Germany, were in a much stronger position to benefit from these rules being suspended than those like Italy that relied on ECB support to borrow cheaply.[70]

This fresh disruption structurally spreading out from the 2020 Eurozone crisis into the wider EU order paralleled what happened when the first Eurozone crisis began in earnest in 2010. Then German power in the EU increased and fear of the German Constitutional Court became the arbiter of what the ECB could do. Via the single market, this caused a specific set of problems for British politics. Neither the British government nor the Eurozone states could readily do anything to diminish their impact, and the stasis made the British government's political weakness inside the EU transparent. A decade later, the most pressing issue has become the relationship between Poland and Hungary and the Eurozone states. This time around, German decision-making has served to make secession less likely by strengthening the non-Eurozone states' veto power rather than, as with Britain, weakening it. But this move has created a sense of frustration elsewhere in the Eurozone at the slow pace of reform.[71] Even more ominously, it has tied the fault lines in the EU between Eurozone and non-Eurozone members to some of those around NATO.

Made and Undone in China

Between the beginning of the Eurozone crisis in 2009 and its return in March 2020, the EU's cohesion and ability to avoid hard choices became deeply complicated by China's post-2008 strategic turns. In the immediate years after 2008, China tried to acquire an international currency, restructure its economy towards higher value-added manufacturing, increase domestic consumption, and reorient its economy geographically towards Eurasia. Each in good part was conceived in terms of entrenching China's economic development and enhancing Chinese power. Nonetheless, it is too simplistic to present the post-2008 China story as an inexorable Chinese rise that invoked an American-led attempt to reset relations for geopolitical reasons. In part, albeit only in part, this version of China's rise destabilized the world economy because China became financially exposed in the world the Fed made. After 2008, the world economy absorbed China's monetary weakness as well as China's manufacturing strength and energy ambitions. As the decade progressed, these competing dynamics played out against a growing crisis in Hong Kong. Their interaction proved disruptive, especially in Europe.

After the crash, the Beijing leadership concluded that the country was stuck in a 'dollar trap', whereby China held large dollar reserves and conducted its trade almost entirely in dollars while Washington could allow the dollar to depreciate.[72] In March 2009, the then Chinese central bank governor called for the dollar to be replaced by a 'super-sovereign reserve currency'. In a provocative essay, Zhou Xiaochuan complained about the problems caused when 'national currencies' served as the international reserve currency and said that the world needed a currency with 'stable value'.[73] But China could not possibly change the position of the dollar.[74] It could only hope to moderate the dollar trap by facilitating the renminbi's use outside China, allowing China to transact more of China's trade, including oil and gas imports, in its own currency.[75] To achieve this, it had to open up its bond markets to allow foreigners to buy Chinese government debt and allow offshore renminbi trading.[76]

China had some partial success: renminbi-denominated payments for foreign trade rose from zero to 30 per cent by 2016.[77] In March 2018, Beijing issued renminbi-denominated oil futures contracts on the Shanghai International Energy Exchange to try to establish an Asian oil price benchmark independent of the American and European benchmarks, whereby Chinese traders could transact some crude oil futures in renminbi.

But these attempts to internationalize the renminbi came with a price. Permitting offshore renminbi trading increased the economic premium on Hong Kong. The city had long served as the financial portal for foreign investment capital to enter China and for Chinese companies to raise dollars.[78] Its great advantage over Shanghai and Shenzhen was common law. As the legal scholar David Donal has neatly summarized, Hong Kong worked as a 'foreign offshore financial centre operating a British-origin legal system within the Chinese state'.[79] But at the same time as China sought to make Hong Kong into a centre for renminbi trading, the city was becoming more politically contested than at any time since the territory's return to China on the one-country, two-systems principle in 1997. In 2014, the Chinese government announced that it would restrict candidates in the 2017 chief executive election, and the Umbrella protest movement, driven by young Hong Kong citizens, erupted in response. This political situation then began to compromise Hong Kong's position as China's international financial centre, with the protests causing temporary panic in Hong Kong's financial markets.

More generally, far from escaping 'the dollar trap', China plunged further into it.[80] As the then retiring governor of the Bank of England, Mark Carney, explained in his speech in 2019, the post-2008 monetary world the Fed made tightened the dollar constraints around all economies, including China's.[81] After China's debt-driven fiscal stimulus, China's banking system grew much faster than its GDP. That banking system and Chinese corporations became much more integrated into the international dollar credit environment than they had been before. By 2014, China's gross external debt— according to official figures that might well be an underestimate— was more than 450 per cent higher than it had been in 2008.[82] A large majority of this debt was denominated in dollars. In the summer of 2015, the massive capital flight out of China induced by the prospect of the Fed increasing interest rates confronted Beijing with a choice between domestic financial instability and protecting the renminbi's reputation as an international currency. The Chinese leadership decided to prioritize the former and tightened capital controls. Consequently, after 2015 renminbi trade payments and offshore renminbi debt market issuances sharply declined.[83]

These cumulative financial risks became a significant constraint on China's growth. It first slowed in 2011 when the ongoing risks around dollar shortage problems in Eurodollar markets became manifest for European banks. It then slowed further from the second half of 2015 through 2016, and again from the second half of 2018. Reflecting a fear that China's dollar debt vulnerability had trapped the country in a lower growth paradigm that threatened the country's future economic development and political stability, an anonymous writer, believed to be Xi Jinping's chief economic adviser, published in May 2016 an article in the *People's Daily*, which serves as a newspaper for the Communist Party, warning that 'trees cannot grow to the sky'.[84]

From at least 2015, and probably earlier, the pace of growth in the world economy appeared vulnerable to these financial conditions in China. When the Chinese economy recovered in 2017 and the first half of 2018 on the back of another credit stimulus, the IMF began to talk of 'synchronized global growth' and said growth prospects were better than at any time since 2010.[85] But this optimism soon dissipated. When Chinese growth fell in late 2018 and 2019 to its lowest level for three decades, the IMF judged that 'the global economy is in a synchronized slowdown', despite the Fed easing monetary policy.[86]

By 2019, Hong Kong too had descended into crisis. That June, new and larger protests began in response to a proposed law allowing extradition to the mainland. They continued for the rest of the year, even after the extradition bill was withdrawn. Meanwhile, the Trump administration began to talk about delisting Chinese tech firms from New York. In November 2019, the Chinese e-commerce and artificial intelligence corporation Alibaba made a secondary listing in Hong Kong without any obvious need for more cash. For the Chinese government, this was an assertion of faith in Hong Kong as China's financial centre and its hope that Chinese corporate dependency on New York could be reduced.[87] But by the year's end, Hong Kong had moved into recession, with business confidence sinking. In May 2020, the protestors came back on the streets. The same month, the US Senate unanimously passed a bill to delist Chinese companies from American stock exchanges and prevent them raising capital in the United States. Two days after the Senate vote, the Chinese government imposed national security legislation on Hong Kong.

By contrast, as the 2015–16 financial crisis and Hong Kong pushed China inwards and slowed growth, Xi Jinping's ascendency enlarged China's economic and, in particular, energy ambitions. In May 2015, the Chinese leadership set out a *Made in China 25* strategy, a state-led development plan to turn China into a high-tech manufacturing power. By aiming to make China into a world leader in ten sectors, including robotics, green energy, and electric vehicles, Made in China 25 changed China's industrial orientation towards the rest of the world. This version of industrial China would be significantly more protectionist than pre-crash China and would attempt to insert Chinese high-tech manufacturing into global supply chains.[88] For both Germany and the United States, this constituted an industrial shock.

For the German economy, it meant direct competition with industrial Chinese producers in sectors where the most prestigious German manufacturing firms had a strong presence. For the United States, it made China's supply-chain ambitions in sectors close to its defence industry a matter of national security. Consequently, even before Trump began his campaign for the presidency, Made in China 25 geopolitically charged the Sino-American trade relationship. Once it opened up a future of high-tech manufacturing competition, American defence officials and the intelligence agencies grew much more critical about deep economic engagement with Beijing. On the campaign trail, Trump frequently returned to the matter of American manufacturing job losses in the 2000s. But the new consensus he established after winning the 2016 election came from Made in China 25's implications for American geopolitical power in an age of high-tech economic competition.

In his own terms, Xi Jinping also sought to recalibrate the Chinese economy geopolitically. He intensified China's pivot away from American export markets towards Eurasia. This geographical turn had begun with moves towards more trade with, and investment in, Europe. Before 2009, there had been scarcely any direct Chinese investment in European countries; afterwards it rose rapidly until 2016, considerably exceeding that going to the United States.[89] In 2013, Xi announced—as outlined in chapter three—the Belt and Road project. Here, China would principally focus on developing and protecting energy routes from the Middle East and Central Asia. But there was also a strong European component to the Belt and Road. To carry its exports to Europe, China sought new train links and ports. It also encouraged European states to join a new Asian Infrastructure Investment Bank, launched in 2013 to fund Belt and Road infrastructure projects.

China's Eurasian turn proved divisive in Europe. In part this was institutional: in 2012, China brokered a new Eurasian forum called Cooperation between China and Central and Eastern European Countries (otherwise known as 17 plus 1 until Lithuania withdrew in 2021), constituted on the European side by a mix of a subset of EU members and non-EU states. But it also became about the reach of Chinese economic engagement. From 2016, Chinese capital controls, imposed in response to the Fed-induced 2015–16 financial crisis, drove Chinese foreign investment in Europe sharply down, but far from evenly.[90] In the western Balkans, Greece, and Italy, it increased. Some of the Southern European states still benefiting from Chinese investment joined the Belt and Road. As a result, the EU increasingly appeared economically factionalized by China. It was one thing that Serbia, sitting outside the EU, set up China as an alternative external economic support structure.[91] It was quite another when Italy joined the Belt and Road in March 2019, and the German and French governments directed sharp criticism towards Rome.

Yet this Franco-German censure also drew counter accusations of hypocrisy that went to the centre of the EU's economic fragmentation. If Germany was not a formal member of the Belt and Road, in practice it was very much part of China's Eurasian trade routes: the German city of Duisburg had become the rail and river port hub for Chinese exports coming to Europe; the German port of Mukran, used by the Russians to construct Nord Stream, is the end point of a new railway route running from Central China. Indeed, the scale of increased trade and supply chains with China was changing the relative importance of the European single market to Germany. Since the 1980s, Germany had enjoyed a singular economic relationship to China. Unlike other European countries, Germany's exports to China grew before 2008. German carmakers became dependent on China's large auto market, with production chains that involved both China and the United States. Although as a region, Europe still dominates German trade, a significant change took place over the 2010s with China becoming Germany's single largest overall trading partner. When the Eurozone crisis began in 2009, German trade within the Eurozone was worth much more than that with non-EU countries. By 2012, non-EU trade had overtaken it, a position that remained until 2017.[92]

By the middle of the decade, this German singularity rendered the Eurozone susceptible to asymmetric shocks. From 2015, Germany was disproportionately hit by the growth fallout of the 2015–16 Chinese financial crisis, the US–China trade war—which left German car manufacturers exporting to China from their American factories subject to Chinese tariffs—and Made in China 25. In 2018 and 2019, these shocks left the German economy hovering around recession while most other Eurozone economies were experiencing higher growth.[93]

Rather than retreating from China, the German government responded by doubling-down on Germany's commercial presence in China. In the same month that Italy joined the Belt and Road, Merkel decided, with Macron, that the EU should complete negotiations on an EU investment treaty with Beijing, which after six years of discussion were stalled. They hoped such an agreement would open China to investment from European companies to balance the capital still moving in the other direction to Southern and Eastern Europe. The beneficiaries were likely to be German and French firms rather than those of any of the 17-plus-1 EU members. Since Merkel appeared particularly interested in advancing the close commercial relationship between Europe's largest telecommunication's company, Deutsche Telecom, and the firm Huawei that by 2019 Trump was pressurizing all European capitals to ban from 5G networks, this move opened the prospect of interjecting the conflicts about NATO into the future of EU–China relations.[94]

The geopolitical ramifications of this German decision to protect the Germany–China relationship after 2015–16 were amplified by what happened to the Britain–China economic relationship from 2016. Between 2010 and 2018, Britain took the largest share of the Chinese foreign investment coming into the EU.[95] Most significantly, David Cameron's government saw an opportunity to make London the international centre of renminbi trading, in good part by leveraging the financial networks between the City and Hong Kong.[96] Trumpeting the British–Chinese relationship, Cameron proclaimed that 'there is no country in the Western world more open to Chinese investment, more able to meet the demands of Chinese consumers'.[97] At the time of Xi Jinping's state visit in 2015, when he was taken in the royal carriage down the Mall, the British chancellor and Chinese officials spoke of a 'golden era' of Britain–China relations.[98]

From the start, Cameron's courtship of China was a geopolitical risk. When, in early 2015, Britain joined the Asian Infrastructure Investment Bank, before any other European state had taken the same step, the Obama administration was dismayed. Trump's trade and technology war against China then raised the stakes further at a time when Theresa May and Boris Johnson's governments were hoping for a post-Brexit trade agreement with Washington. The intensification of the Hong Kong crisis that began in June 2019 further exposed Britain's high vulnerability to events in its former colony. When the protests in the city started, the British government was much more critical than other EU states, prompting China to denounce Britain's interference in vociferous terms. That autumn, Johnson's government began to face demands from some democracy activists for full citizenship rights for those with British overseas passports.

During the first months of the Covid-19 crisis, this shift became complete in ways that hardened British choices. For a moment in January 2020, Johnson made a last-ditch attempt to salvage something of the Sino-British economic relationship by deciding that Huawei could be included in developing Britain's 5G network. Faced in May 2020 with China's actions and Trump's response, the Johnson government reversed its earlier decision on Huawei and offered 3 million Hong Kong citizens with British national overseas passports a path to British citizenship.[99]

The collapse of Britain's pre-2016 China policy created a new schism around China in Europe. The EU adopted only modest sanctions in response to China ending Hong Kong's autonomy. Merkel came under strong domestic criticism for her stance that Hong Kong could not be a matter warranting cooling relations with Germany's largest trading partner. But she, again, responded to a potential crisis in the Germany–China relationship by entrenching it within a collective EU framework.[100] Notwithstanding what was by December 2020 the impending transfer of power in Washington to the Biden administration, she worked with Macron through the last weeks of 2020 to complete an EU–China Comprehensive Agreement on Investment. For her, this was commercial realpolitik: it opened up the prospect of German tech firms establishing a market presence in China, as the old industrial corporations with productive capacity and market share there struggled. For Macron, the investment agreement served at least as much as a statement of European strategic autonomy from the United States at a time of technological competition. But after the agreement was announced, several EU governments immediately made known their unease, including some members of the Belt and Road that now saw a clear tension between the benefits of Chinese capital pouring into their infrastructure and a rupture with Washington. There were complaints also that Merkel and Macron had acted unilaterally to settle the negotiations and make a symbolic statement about the EU's future relationship with China.[101] In many ways, they had. As this was not an agreement that the British government could have contemplated after China's move against Hong Kong seven months earlier, they had also made a statement about an EU that no longer included Britain.

Seen as a whole, the fate of the China–Europe economic relationship after 2008 became part of several of the other big stories of economic and geopolitical disruption. Both China's Eurasian turn and post-2016 retreat behind tighter capital controls economically dissected Europe. Each reinforced the singularity of Germany's economic position within both the EU and the Eurozone. Meanwhile, as 'Chimerica' became US–China strategic rivalry and Hong Kong's portal capacities unravelled, this economic factionalism acquired a sharp geopolitical edge: China had joined Russia as a source of divisions over NATO within the EU, and it had created an overt geopolitical rationale for Britain's divergence from the EU.

We Can't Go Home Again

At the start of this decade, the pandemic, not least through its origins in China, brought all the previous decade's disruptions into sharp focus. That spring of 2020, the Fed rescued the monetary and financial world it had constructed after the 2007–8 crash, in good part by acting, once again, as a lender of last resort. Unlike in 2008, it sought indirectly to include China in its orbit, even as much of the rest of the Sino-American relationship was unravelling. This change was the logical consequence of how Eurodollar markets work. At the systemic level, when everyone in offshore dollar credit markets in the moment of crisis is scrambling for dollars, there must be a lender of last resort, and, regardless of geopolitics, China had become too vulnerable a player to be left without any protection.

In other respects, what the Fed did recharged the conditions for disruption created by its post-2009 monetary policies. With QE Infinity, the Fed, effectively, took over credit markets. One commentator quipped that the Fed was now 'the lender of all resorts'.[102] Given the legacy of its past actions, the Fed had little choice. Corporations with high debt levels and without cash reserves that faced collapsing revenues could not survive without easy access to more credit. But the very dynamics that had encouraged corporations to issue debt via corporate bonds, including to fund share buyback programmes, were now hugely amplified when the Fed was a buyer itself of corporate bonds. Predictably, in the first months after 23 March, there was a huge increase in corporate debt issuances.[103]

As a consequence, much of the aftermath of 2008 was repeated during the pandemic. Assured that there was almost nothing the Fed would not buy, share markets soon detached themselves from any non-monetary economic and political risks beyond the Fed's own utterances on future monetary action. As American unemployment surged to around 15 per cent in April 2020, the jobs data month by month had little effect on equity markets. The Fed's 'lender of all resorts' activities also sharpened the hierarchies between those large businesses able to issue cheap debt via bonds and those small firms that could not.

Among those corporations desperately needing access to more credit in the spring of 2020 were the shale oil companies. Since the Fed included corporate junk bonds in its purchasing programmes, the Fed moves in principle bailed them out. But the future of oil production now represented a big change from the world that emerged in the first years after the 2007–8 crash. Then the oil and gas industries, and the shale sector especially, had absorbed a disproportionate amount of investment capital. Combined with the high prices that prevailed between 2011 and 2014, QE facilitated the shale boom. By contrast, before the Covid shock hit, prices were scarcely above the level that would finance most shale producers' debt, and oil companies had been partially shut out from capital markets by investors privileging green energy. Despite the Trump administration's efforts to push prices back up and the Fed's new purchasing programmes, three of the large shale companies still entered bankruptcy in the middle of 2020.

If oil were on a rapid way out as an energy source, this hit to the American shale industry would have fewer structural consequences. But it is not. Weak growth in the world economy in 2019, not least in China, ensured that there was relatively little fallout from the fall in oil production that year. But as winter came in late 2020 and early 2021, prices climbed to their 2019 peak, even with much of Europe remaining in some form of lockdown and restrictions still in place in much of the rest of the world. This time, the American shale sector is much less well placed to rescue the world economy from permanently high oil prices at any reasonable level of growth. What will come after the pandemic crash may well be a version of the world economy prior to mid-2008 where central bankers worry about the simultaneously deleterious effect of rising energy prices, for gas and electricity as well as oil, on inflation and consumer demand.

Modest inflation would provide some temporary relief to central bankers who since 2014 have desperately searched for it to diminish the real value of debt. But in creating pressures for higher interest rates, accelerating energy-driven inflation would also leave many debtors struggling to service their debt. Where government debt is concerned, the only option left would be for central banks to provide interest-free direct financing to governments.

Whether the shale industry will be temporarily resurrected will be as much a political and geopolitical matter as an economic question. The future of oil is now part of a complex and disruptive energy world where the old geopolitics and commercial competition around oil and gas coexists with the intense commercial and geopolitical rivalry around manufacturing production in the renewable and electric vehicles sectors. Near the centre of this competition lies an ongoing contest for private investment capital that a decade ago was readily won by energy companies in the shale sector.

* * *

As geopolitics now permeates the entire world economy, the EU faces the fundamental question as to whether the gains in scale from a regional approach to this competition compensate for the disadvantages of collective compromise for individual national economies.[104] It does so in circumstances where a sharp divergence has already occurred between the EU's largest economy and the rest of the EU around China.

Structurally, the EU struggles with these geopolitical predicaments because it simultaneously is constructed around democratic nation states, attracts aspirations to replace them, and provides opportunities for the most powerful member states to shape their immediate external environment. The creation of the Eurozone compounded this difficulty. Its institutionalized commitments make it harder for European democracies to adapt to economic change and circumscribes acceptable party competition over economic strategy. Its incompleteness within the EU unsettles the relationship between euro members and non-euro members. When the Eurozone crisis destabilized Britain's position, what began in the economic sphere quickly moved into a politically unmanageable problem for the British democratic nation state. It did so because the European single market works by protecting some economic policy matters from national democratic politics by constitutional law. Contesting the ensuing fallout then necessarily became a question of Britain's very participation in that constitutional order since democratic consent to that order must come from inside the nation state.

Here, Brexit was indicative of a much wider story about democracies. They are destabilized by geopolitical and economic change and risk their future as democracies unless they can adapt to it. At the same time, they must reconcile those who lose from the changing balance of power within them to accepting the democratic state's authority to make decisions. The story of why this is so difficult shapes the beginning of the book's final section about just how democracies work through time and their complex relationship to nationhood.

PART III

Democratic Politics

7

Democratic Time

In the pandemic's early months, the British Cabinet minister and veteran of the Leave campaign Michael Gove gave a lecture on public service. Beginning at the end of the age of 'economic globalization' and 'aristocratic liberalism' in the 1930s, he heralded Franklin Roosevelt's conviction that the future would belong to 'democratic nation states with welfare systems'. Possessing 'a bias to experimentation', the American president had, Gove said, 'managed to save capitalism [and] restore faith in democracy'. For Gove, a Roosevelt-style mantle for democratic renewal was the one the post-Brexit Conservative government had assumed, after a majority of British voters had four years earlier expressed their dissent from 'almost every arm of Government and those with powerful voices in it'.[1]

Gove's argument about Brexit oversimplified. He was, after all, a member of the British government when he campaigned for Leave, and more than a third of the parliamentary Conservative Party was on his side. But Brexit did indeed represent a democratic rebellion, in part against the constraints of representative democratic politics. British voters were given the chance in a referendum to decide on a majority basis a matter that would simultaneously change the United Kingdom's constitutional order, geopolitical orientation, and economic relations with the rest of the world. The result where 52 per cent of UK voters opted for Leave while more than 70 per cent of Members of Parliament supported Remain revealed a serious gulf between enough citizens and enough of those who represented them to constitute a democratic crisis.

That in the aftermath of such a crisis Gove should turn to Franklin Roosevelt for inspiration, lining up the longest-serving American president on the side of the 'democratic nation state' against both 'aristocratic liberalism' and 'economic globalization', is not particularly surprising.[2] Roosevelt's New Deal stands as the political archetype of democratic renewal because democracies have more often than not proved hard to reform in any substantial way. It took Roosevelt throwing aside the gold standard to pave the way for the post-war future of 'democratic nation states with welfare systems'. But the Roosevelt story about the American democratic nation state is also rather more complicated than the one Gove told. Indeed, the American republic is still burdened by the path of racially restrictive economic nationhood that Roosevelt trod in renewing American democracy, as it is by African Americans' longer historical exclusion from the material and political rewards of American citizenship from which Roosevelt's approach was born.

Democracies exist in particular places in particular times. Since they function through changing geopolitical and economic conditions, they, like any other form of government, experience time as a source of instability. This change in conditions is often what produces the impulse to reform, sometimes, as with Roosevelt, to try to restore the balance between the material interests of different citizens that through time has become distorted. But democracies that have retained a constitutional form while becoming more democratic through a widened franchise—as the American republic has done—also face a problem when they engage in this kind of democratic renewal: the demands to restore a lost political balance between citizens by returning to a democracy's origins must run into the reality that the citizenry constituting that democracy will have radically changed over time.

That democratic politics is prone through time to instability would have surprised scarcely any political observer for much of the twentieth century. Only from the 1990s did liberal democracy come so much to be treated as a universal, timeless ideal.[3] This discourse has distorted political analysis, including accounts of the present political disruption, by making nationhood a uniform threat to democratic norms and shaping a narrative of democracy around universal progress detached from the historical complexity of individual democracies. To understand the instability in present Western democracies, we need to begin with the historical relationship between democracy and nationhood and the problem of political time.

Nationhood

The historian Benedict Anderson described the nation as 'an imagined community' formed by some notion of a shared past with a distinct starting place.[4] In some cases, imaginative claims to nationhood told a collective story about ethnicity. But there is no reason why nations need understand themselves in these terms. Indeed, language, accompanied by a literary culture, was often the stronger affirmation of commonality in Europe because it was through a common language that stories about shared historical experience were rendered.[5] Imagined communities attached to the word 'nation' existed long before representative democracy emerged, including in places where the term was deployed to constitute a political identity. But with the French Revolution, a new political language about nationhood gathered force. Thereafter, the European states generally justified their authority and power at home in the name of a nation and claimed to represent its unity. Those who wanted to free themselves from empires, whether subject to British, French, Russian, or Ottoman rule, almost all demanded statehood in the name of the nation. Although since the nineteenth century, nationhood as an idea for legitimating political authority has also regularly been attacked, outside the Islamic world no other basis for this task has yet emerged. As the historian Michael Howard observed, nowhere did a Communist revolution destroy an existing nation state.[6] The Cold War ended with an emphatic assertion of nationhoods against the Soviet Empire. When, after the Berlin Wall fell, the West German chancellor, Helmut Kohl, issued his plan for German unity, he directly invoked the language of nationhood, saying that the German Federal Republic had had 'to keep alive and sharpen consciousness for the unity of the nation' and that his government was working so that the 'German people can regain their unity in free self-determination'.[7] If the EU undoubtedly constitutes an attempt to construct considerable political authority beyond the nation state in the name of a multinational continent, those who are directly elected to executive power within the EU are, nonetheless, still chosen by electorates of national citizens.

Representative democracies have not historically existed without the political resources that nationhood has provided.[8] Conceptually, nationhood serves as 'the people' in any representative democracy.

Just as ancient democracies required a people who could rule themselves, so representative democracies require a people who collectively
can choose representatives and, when necessary, authorize a constitution. The historical answer to whom these peoples were became
nations. Indeed, for some time the words 'nation' and 'people' were
interchangeable.[9] The democratic political nation did not have to
correspond with cultural claims to nationhood. Some democracies,
for example the Swiss, have historically worked without an idea of
shared cultural nationhood, or a common language. But for the
nation to serve as the people in a representative democracy, it did
have to be defined via criteria for inclusion and exclusion. In practice,
this has meant national citizenship.[10]

The resulting idea of a democratic people who share citizenship
stops the contests inherent to representative democracy unravelling a
state's authority. Representative democracies need a political means
to procure losers' consent. Alone as a form of government, they ask all
adult citizens to decide who should govern and then give only some
subset of these citizens the representatives they chose. Consequently,
exchanges of power via elections require tacit justifications for those
who lose elections that enable them to accept the outcome without
resort to violence or secession. Nationhood provided the historical
answer to this crucial political problem.

Viewed schematically, the absence of a serviceable belief in
American nationhood precipitated the American Civil War. Although
the constitution began with the words 'We the people of the United
States of America', it created a federal republic with profound conflicts of economic interests between its component states, a racial
divide between citizens and slaves, and a moral chasm around slavery.
Whereas in the Roman Republic the language of the people and the
practice of slavery had readily coexisted, there was no chance they
long would in the American republic, saturated as many of its citizens
were in Protestant Christianity and equipped as they were with an
imaginative founding story proclaiming the divinely bestowed equality of human beings.[11] Leaving unresolved the question of whether
the union established in 1788 was supposed to be permanent, the
constitution did not represent a definitive agreement between the
republic's citizens to be a people subject to the same political authority
regardless of their sectional political influence within it. As in time the

slave-owning states' political power deteriorated, the fact that most whites in the South thought of themselves as Southerners before Americans became a huge political problem. Every accession to the Union became a site of conflict about whether the slave or non-slave states would win more electoral influence. After the 1860 election, the eleven Southern states seceded from the Union to protect slavery from electoral defeat.

If nationhood has substantial political uses for representative democracies, the two also emerged in historical tandem. This language of the nation fuelled the first moves towards representative democracy. Where, as in England, a monarchy coexisted with a legislature that enjoyed some independent authority, reformers demanded that political rights be extended to more classes in the name of the nation.[12] In 1789 in France, nationhood was mobilized to claim sovereignty against the monarchy. The French Declaration of the Rights of Man and of the Citizen proclaimed that 'the principle of all sovereignty resides essentially in the nation'. Although, hoping for a cosmopolitan revolution, the Jacobins began as anti-nationalists, they soon became nationalists, seeing in nationhood the path to a citizen French army that would be much more powerful than its European counterparts.[13]

By tying nationhood to conscription, the Jacobins began a political relationship with lasting consequences.[14] In using nationhood to mobilize citizen armies in 1914, European governments ensured that by the war's end democracies would have to be reconstituted. As Athens' need for a citizen navy had driven Athenian democracy, so citizens who were asked to die and kill for their states could not afterwards be excluded from voting in elections.[15] In contrast to non-belligerents like Spain and Portugal, virtually all the belligerent states legislated during or after the war for a full male franchise. Where women were central to the economic war effort, women gained the vote too.[16] In France, military service allowed North African Muslim migrants to France to attain French citizenship and voting rights.[17]

*   *   *

But if nationhood became necessarily entangled in representative democracies, it also proved dangerous to them. In one sense, nationhood worked similarly to the older mytho-historical stories told about territorial entities to justify political authority. Contrary to Thomas Hobbes' assumption that a state's power can most readily be justified by a present-tense fear of death, nationhood connected democratic authority to the past and a past with a beginning.[18]

In ancient Rome, considerable imaginative effort was, likewise, expended on locating first the republic and then the imperial monarchy's authority in the mythological origins of the Roman people as refugees from Troy and the city's founding by Romulus and Remus.[19] But historically, storytelling around nationhood has proved to be much more literal than the mythical Roman origins stories and, consequently, much more perilous. Since Europe was not territorially divided into cohesive groups of people with a shared language, historical memory, or mythos, nations had to be created politically by states' actions and the non-mythical stories that could be told about them.

On occasion, the 'patriotic spirit', as Alexis de Tocqueville called it, could be cultivated in ways that were relatively benign towards most of their own citizens, albeit emphatically not those subject to European empires.[20] In the late nineteenth century in the newly unified German state, Bismarck began to use the state's power to provide some economic protection to national citizens via a welfare state. Rather than needing foundational origins in the past, this rendered a nation a present community of shared material fate.

But, in practice, the imperative for nationhood often led to states' using their coercive capacity against their own citizens. Where existing cultural nationhoods were weak, conjuring a political nationhood required the state to try to homogenize populations and shape a collective view of the past.[21] Governments sought citizens who spoke the same language, were commonly educated including in national history, shared religious beliefs and practices, and from the 1890s disavowed transnational political commitments like international socialism.[22] This meant using the law to impose linguistic and religious uniformity and mark out political subversion. French governments forced Basques and Bretons to speak French and prohibited non-French literature. In the United States, those of English-Scottish descent, whose ancestors were understood to have brought with them a passion for the liberties of Magna Carta, saw themselves as the ethnic, and not just political, heirs of the republic's founding.[23] After the Mexican–American war, English soon became an enforced national language.[24] At times in a number of countries, this coercion brought violence against ethnic and national minorities, forced emigration, mass transfers of population, and on occasion genocide.[25]

Coercion and constructed stories about the past were not contradictory sides of nationhood. Abraham Lincoln reunified the American republic by mobilizing the federal government's coercive power to defeat the Southern confederacy militarily, destroy slavery, and impose constitutional terms for re-entry to the union. But he also sought in the Gettysburg Address to take the blood spilled in the war and imaginatively recast the story of the American republic's founding into one of shared democratic nationhood. In the new story, there always was an American 'nation', founded by present generations' ancestors, 'dedicated to the proposition that all men are created equal'; accordingly, it was the present generations' responsibility to ensure that their inheritance of 'government of the people, by the people, for the people' should not 'perish from the earth'.[26]

Attempts to strengthen nationhood where it was weak, or create it where it was absent, could entail more coercion than a democratic state could bear. Without any serious prospect of absorbing Irish Catholics into an idea of British nationhood, the British democratic state ultimately could not accommodate Ireland into its constitutional order. In the decades leading up to the First World War, the so-called Irish question dominated Westminster politics, producing a severe constitutional crisis between 1910 and 1914. In passing in 1918 a bill introducing conscription in Ireland and attempting to coerce citizens who largely did not recognize the British state as having national legitimacy into the army, the British government went a long way to making some form of independent Irish state inevitable.

The sheer difficulty of realizing nationhood in a form of politics that required a concept of the people placed deep and ongoing burdens on democracies. The term 'the people' as 'the nation' became indispensable, too readily available, and evanescent.[27] Where the nation as a people was supposed to be a source of unity allowing losers' consent, as a piece of rhetoric it could just as readily be deployed to deny that everyone subject to a democratic state's authority should have the same political rights. Those who displayed non-national identifications, or who were suspected of other loyalties regardless of how they behaved, could be excluded.[28] Indeed, during elections there were votes to be won in redescribing the nation as those who shared something other than national political citizenship.

This dynamic encouraged a new form of antisemitism that deemed Jews racially suspect and deficient in national loyalty. Antisemitism became an electoral weapon in democratic politics, especially when it could disingenuously be tied to class grievances against those who habitually exercised power and prospered. Nowhere was this political phenomenon on clearer display than in turn-of-the-century Vienna. There, the Christian Social Party, led by the charismatic Karl Lueger, won electoral victories in 1895 and 1896, ending the Liberal Party's thirty-year dominance in the imperial capital, by combining municipal socialism, Catholicism, a loyalty to the Habsburgs, and antisemitism. Although, as mayor of Vienna, Lueger did not act to deprive Jews of their legal rights, his rhetoric imagined a Christian Austrian people that excluded Jews, and he promised Christian Social voters he would distribute the municipal spoils, including jobs, to those who constituted the Austrian people.[29]

By 1914, there was abundant evidence that nationhood was the language of the emerging democratic politics and was useful in making elections peaceful contests for power, but that it also generated divisions that weakened citizens' consent to states' authority. Democracies were simultaneously inexorably bound up with nationhood and at risk from it.

Time and Excess

Leaving aside this structural tension within democratic nationhood, the passage of time necessarily destabilizes all claims to nationhood. Even where a relatively strong belief in national citizenship emerges in a particular democracy, the alignment between the state and a population willing and able to identify politically with the imagined community the state purports to represent will not remain a constant. Significant changes in geopolitical and economic conditions through time often lead to groups and individuals migrating from one state to another. Where democratic states move to restrict such movement, they then undermine the languages of nationhood used to include past migrants in the idea of national citizenship.

The idea that time, to use the historian John Pocock's words, is 'the dimension of instability' in politics was once a commonplace in political thinking.[30] In Europe, conceptualizing forms of government through the lens of temporal decay began with Polybius and reached its intellectual zenith under Machiavelli. Polybius was a Greek historian writing in the second century bce about the Roman Republic's rise. He thought that the fact 'that all existing things are subject to decay is a proposition which scarcely requires proof, since the inexorable course of nature is sufficient to impose it on us'.[31] In the beginning, there is always chaos, brought about by a cataclysm. When established, 'every kind of state' was 'liable to decline from two sources, the one being external, and the other due to its own internal evolution'. Externally, there was no discernible pattern to this decay. But internally decay followed, he believed, 'a regular sequence': after chaos there comes monarchy, kingship, tyranny, aristocracy, oligarchy, democracy, and the mob rule of ochlocracy before out of the chaos a single demagogue claims power and starts the cycle again.[32]

For Polybius, each form of government is destroyed by its own excess.[33] The only way to check the cycle and allow for a long middle—what he called 'a state of equilibrium'—is to balance the three positive forms of government—kingship, aristocracy, and democracy—and have them counteract each other.[34] Increased external power and rising material prosperity, he continued, especially threaten any constitutional balance. For Rome, he foresaw the move from aristocracy to oligarchy to democracy occurring against a backdrop of external success and 'long-established prosperity'.[35] Under the weight of personal competition for wealth and office and 'the spread of ostentation and extravagance', there would be, he anticipated, a 'period of general deterioration' driven by the masses 'who at some moments will believe they have a grievance against the greed of other members of society, and at others are made conceited by the flattery of those who aspire to office'.[36]

If Polybius was prophetic about Rome, political time has certainly not always fitted the pattern he identified. But forms of government in any particular place do in time end, and, as the French *Ancien Régime* graphically demonstrated, their own excess under the pressure of geopolitical and economic change is part of the reason why they do. We do not need to follow Polybius' cyclical schema to see that the notion of accumulating aristocratic or democratic excess might help us understand how forms of government become unstable through time.

The matter of where the risk of excess lies in representative democracies raises a fundamental question about them: are they primarily a democratic or an aristocratic form of government? As representative democracies historically first emerged, they were obviously largely aristocratic in Polybius' terms. In Europe, parliamentary government was grafted onto monarchies, and the franchise was restricted, as was the chance to stand in elections, by property qualifications. In some cases, as in Germany, the monarch retained the de facto as well as de jure authority to appoint and remove governments. Meanwhile, the American federal republic coexisted with slavery, and its constitution placed buffers between the people and their representatives since state legislatures chose senators and the electoral college to decide upon the president.

Representative democracies also look like they became more democratic through time. Monarchies disappeared in France, Germany, and Austria. Slavery was ended in the United States, and the wealth of the slave plantation–owning class destroyed. Everywhere, the franchise eventually became universal, and legislatures began to authorize taxes on individuals' income and wealth designed to make the rich pay more tax so as to redistribute income towards the poor.

Nonetheless, a temporal story where representative democracies evolved towards being refounded as 'full' democracies is at least partially misleading. Since representative democracy was a form of government of the modern state—albeit complicated in the American case by federalism—representative democracies had from the start the coercive capacity to tax the rich, whether those who governed them decided to use that power or not.[37] Moreover, political moves that appeared to make constitutional polities more democratic did not in practice always do so. The 1832 Reform Act in Britain that extended the franchise actually reduced some of the more democratic components of British constitutional politics by taking the vote away from working class men in some long-standing English boroughs, as well as those propertied women who enjoyed it, while making Parliament less responsive to petitioning from those without the vote.[38] In the United States, African Americans gained the vote through the constitutional amendments passed after the Civil War and thousands were elected to office across the South, only for Southern states, supported by the Supreme Court, systematically to remove their franchise. Consequently, the American federal republic operated until the 1960s with a separation between citizens with political rights and citizens in name only.

Economically, widening the franchise did not necessarily lead to economic reforms benefiting the poorer classes. In ancient Rome, the reforming Gracchi brothers tried to end the republic's aristocratic excess by restoring earlier agrarian laws that restricted the amount of public land the senatorial class could own and distributing the reclaimed land to landless soldiers. But in Britain, expanding the electorate through the four voting reform acts from 1832 to 1918 did nothing to restore the common land lost during the previous three centuries to the enclosures.[39] In the United States, the Civil War years and the continuing appropriation of western lands from Native Americans did bring reforms that distributed land to around 1.5 million American citizens. But land reform in the South after the Civil War did little to change the vast racial imbalance in land ownership.[40]

Far from proving economically redistributive, representative democracies have long coexisted with forms of economic organization that frequently produce high levels of material inequality. Indeed, at times the balance of power within democracies furnished the political conditions that sustained this inequality.[41] Early reforms directed to reduce the political power of the wealthy often failed. In 1894, the US Congress voted for a tax on income for the first time in peacetime.[42] This tax was only to be levied on the wealthy. A year later the Supreme Court struck down the legislation. In 1913, ratification of the Sixteenth Amendment allowed for an income tax to be introduced. During the First World War, Congress used this authority to levy significant taxes on the incomes of the rich, as well as on war profits and inheritance. But the political manoeuvring of the richest Americans ensured that after the war income tax became less of a burden.[43] Historically, it is war, not elections on full franchises, that has proved the necessary condition for taxation systems that levy high taxes on the rich as well as increasing the share of income going to labour.[44]

Although representative democracy's aristocratic propensities are often rhetorically disguised, they generally dominate. Representative democracies distinguish between the large number of the represented and the much smaller number of representatives; they concentrate authoritative decision-making in a handful of individuals in the executive, some of whom in a presidential system will be appointed not elected. The political decisions that the elected representatives of the majority can then take are usually restricted by constitutions. In democracies with some form of judicial review, a constitutional court can strike down laws passed by elected legislatures. This constitutional practice protects minorities, and the minorities protected include, via property rights, the rich.[45]

In the first instance, then, representative democracy appears principally prone to growing aristocratic excess through time. This can happen in several different ways. Executives can usurp power that previously belonged to, or was constrained by, legislatures. Both executives and legislatures can be captured by a dominant economic class. Constitutional courts can assert judicial authority over matters previously contested in democratic politics. Elections can become the means by which representatives are bought by those who finance their campaigns. Those who decide, influence, and advise can enrich themselves in exchange for providing access to power.

Nonetheless, representative democracies are not entirely lacking in democratic features, starting with equal voting rights. Accordingly, democratic excess can destabilize them over time too, creating demands to rebalance them in the opposite direction. Legislatures can make it impossible for executives to govern and the representatives of electoral majorities can appoint judges who interpret the law to partisan ends. Governments can appropriate property, default on debt, and suspend constitutional protections for minorities. In the search for votes, parties can make material promises they cannot possibly keep and appeal to vengeful passions. In the early twentieth century, the German political economist and sociologist Max Weber thought that representative democracy ensured permanent demagoguery. Every democracy once it moved to a wide franchise was, Weber argued, vulnerable to decay into the monarchy of Caesarism through the necessity of voters selecting leaders in elections.[46]

Historically, debt was perceived to be the primary cause of democratic excess leading through time towards democratic dissolution. In part, this judgement arose because debt itself is a temporal matter: interest is what is paid for having early access to future revenue. But by consuming an ever-growing proportion of present income, the burdens of excessive debt also increase through time. It was for this reason that some ancient societies prescribed debt forgiveness at regular intervals to prevent debt being passed down the generations, leading to land being concentrated in too few hands.[47] In ancient Athens, forced debt cancellation was taken to be an inexorable part of democracy. In the nineteenth century, it was precisely because the French and American revolutions produced debt defaults and paper currencies that democracy's critics equated democracy with demagoguery.[48] In Britain, extending the franchise in 1832 and 1867 broke the previously tight relationship between Parliament and creditors, whereby creditors could be trusted to vote for the taxes necessary to service the state's debt.[49] Recognizing the problem this severance posed for an emerging democracy, governments from the mid-nineteenth century endeavoured to spread the national debt among as many voters as possible via citizen saving accounts and citizen bond issues.[50] As Abraham Lincoln said, 'men readily perceive that they cannot be much oppressed by a debt which they owe to themselves'.[51] The citizen creditor was far from the only creditor used by representative governments in the second half of the nineteenth and early twentieth centuries; they also borrowed in international capital markets. But the citizen creditor put in place some safeguards against debt destabilizing representative democracies.

The conflicting propensities towards temporal decay encapsulated around debt make repairing and reforming democracies particularly hard. Machiavelli, who thought historically and systematically about the general problem of political time, started from the premise that states, including republics, had to change to sustain themselves against time. Quite often, he argued, external events imposed that change upon them, interrupting the internal temporal cycle. But change could also be brought about by 'renovation', where laws took states 'back to their origins' or a virtuous individual imposed himself.[52]

'Renovation' was always difficult, but, for Machiavelli, the attempts to reform a republic burdened by aristocratic excess were particularly tough, as the Roman Republic's fate proved. In the late second century bce, the Gracchi brothers served as tribunes of the plebeians—the non-patrician citizens—against a backdrop of acute class conflict where indebted plebeian soldiers lost their land to patricians in the Senate who stayed at home and did not fight to expand the Empire. The Gracchi tried to restore the Republic's earlier agrarian laws limiting how much land any citizen could hold. These reforms, Machiavelli suggested, were necessary. But, he argued, the senatorial opposition to land reform each time the issue arose ensured that 'the whole city was turned topsy-turvy' by the Gracchi's actions, producing 'armed conflict and bloodshed'.[53] Rather than stabilizing Rome, the reforming Gracchi sped up, Machiavelli insisted, the Republic's descent towards military dictatorship and eventually Caesarism.[54]

Excess in the American Republic

The Roman Republic's fate, whether understood in Machiavelli's terms or otherwise, cast a heavy shadow over early representative democracies, nowhere more so than in the United States. Like Rome, the early American republic engaged in territorial expansion, began with a slave population, and struggled with the class politics of debt. This history is revealing in itself about the conflicts democratic politics generate, their relationship to nationhood, and contests over reform to remedy problems understood in terms of aristocratic and democratic excess. But it also matters for the present democratic crisis in the American republic because some of the conflicts inherent to that crisis result from the original constitution.

In hard political terms around interests, the struggle over the American constitution was a political fight about debt and territorial expansion. The United States had won its independence from Britain as a security confederation. In 1787, that confederation, constructed under the Articles of Confederation, was unable to service its debt. Left uncreditworthy, it was in no position to finance an army, including one that could defeat the Native American resistance to westward expansion beyond the Appalachian Mountains, which many Americans saw as a principal reward of independence.[55]

Both the Confederation Congress, which was the site of such central authority as there was prior to the federal constitution, and the individual states had borrowed heavily from domestic and foreign creditors to finance the war against Britain. Under the Articles of Confederation, the thirteen individual states had the capacity to tax and so in principle could service their debt, although some state legislatures, facing debtor and tax rebellions, chose not to do so. In sharp contrast, the Confederation Congress had neither the authority to levy taxes directly nor the power to compel the states to deliver the revenues it requested from them. Those who drafted the American federal constitution in 1787 wanted to re-establish American credit-worthiness by removing what they saw as democratic excess in the states. Accordingly, they designed a constitution that took away most powers of taxation from the states, created a primary power of taxation for the federal government to service debt, and protected the Senate and the presidency against direct elections.

In the fight to ratify the constitution, the Federalists turned to past history to express their fear of democratic excess. For James Madison, the American Senate would be a safeguard against the kind of 'Popular Liberty' that left Athens under 'the indelible reproach of decreeing to the same citizens, the hemlock on one day, and statues on the next'.[56] For Alexander Hamilton, history taught 'that of those men who have overturned the liberties of republics the greatest number have begun their career by paying an obsequious court to the people, commencing Demagogues, and ending Tyrants'.[57] By contrast, the constitution's chief opponents saw the federal republic as an aristocratic construction that would become more aristocratic in time. Taking the Roman pseudonym Brutus, one influential anti-federalist argued that the constitution could lead only to the rule of the rich, and the rich would rule for themselves. Although the rhetoric around the constitution would, he argued, salute virtue, 'it [would] literally be a government in the hands of the few to plunder the many'.[58]

For those who feared aristocratic excess, the American republic very quickly descended into something all too familiar from Roman history. America's debt was once again the cause. In 1790 Hamilton, the first US treasury secretary, published a *Report on the Public Credit*. He proposed that the federal government should assume the debts of the states, pay interest on all debts at face value, and establish a Sinking

Fund to repay the debt over time. Immediately, Madison and his friend Thomas Jefferson denounced Hamilton's plan as unconstitutional. The plan, they insisted, would ensure oligarchic corruption, especially since Hamilton had, they charged, encouraged northern financiers to buy national and state securities speculatively at very cheap prices prior to the report's publication.[59] In this accusation, Hamilton saw only a path led by demagogues to the republic's end.

In part, politics in the American republic became repeated contests around these debt-driven dynamics and their relationship to class conflict and competing conceptions of American nationhood. From the Civil War onwards, industrialization and the rise of the railroads and Standard Oil, which through their credit requirements were inexorably tied to the New York banks, created new economic concentrations of aristocratic power. For the next few decades, this new economic aristocracy dominated the republic's politics through its ability to buy political influence and protect its sectoral monopoly power. This overt aristocratic excess then prompted a strong democratic reaction that appealed back to the republic's founding.

During the 1890s economic depression, the American People's Party mobilized a coalition of farmers and debtors to challenge the corruption and demand monetary reform and better access to credit. Its 1892 Omaha Platform, symbolically unveiled on the Fourth of July, proclaimed that the republic had fallen and that 'we meet in the midst of a nation brought to the verge of moral, political and material ruin' by credit. In demanding access to credit—as well as a directly elected Senate, term limits for presidents, unlimited silver coinage, an income tax, and shorter working hours—they saw themselves as reinstituting the original constitution and 'restor[ing] the government of the Republic to the hands of "plain people" with which class it originated'.[60]

Over the next years, the American Populists' attempts at democratic reform demonstrated several destabilizing tendencies that arise in such endeavours, especially in a long-standing constitutional republic.[61] In part, the Populists rhetorically stressed national unity and made the republic's salvation dependent on it. In the Omaha Platform, they declared that 'this republic can only endure as a free government while built upon the love of the whole people for each other and for the nation'. But their rhetoric showed the divisiveness that followed from appealing to the idea of the nation to win a specific group of citizens' votes. The Populists imagined the American republic in class terms, such that they pitted a democratic, 'American', and producer class of farmers and factory labourers against a non-productive, aristocratic, internationalist, and parasitic creditor class.[62] This language easily lent itself to antisemitism. When the populist William Jennings Bryan captured the 1896 Democratic presidential nomination, he tied the economic aristocracy to a disloyal cosmopolitanism in conflict with American nationhood. Gold, Bryan changed, belonged to Anglophile and Jewish financiers in Atlantic-oriented New York who let 'foreign potentates and powers' destroy American sovereignty.[63] In accepting the Democratic nomination, Bryan compared the burden of gold on American farmers to a 'crown of thorns' and the 'crucifixion of mankind'.[64] Silver, by contrast, was 'American money for Americans' where Americans meant the producer class.[65] The very notion of restoring the class balance of the original republic also implicitly cast out those whose ancestors as slaves had originally been excluded from any political balance, even though some of the early Southern Populists built a cross-racial class alliance and fought for African Americans' voting rights.

This restrictive idea of nationhood relating back to the republic's founding was far from confined to the Populists. In depending on a notion of a reconciliation between the racially segregated former Confederacy and the North, the language of post–Civil War American nationhood deployed by democratic politicians had a strong racial component, compounded by the premise, established in the 1790 Naturalization Act and recharged in the 1882 Chinese Exclusion Act, that Asian immigrants could not become citizens.[66] The Populists' distinctiveness was to tie nativist language around nationhood to class-saturated rhetoric around debt and the constitutional republic. This form of expression of political grievance would reoccur in democratic politics, and not just in the United States.

The political era that followed the Populist rebellion was partially one of democratic reform against aristocratic excess. Economically, the Progressives took aim at the railroad owners and Standard Oil's monopoly power, and secured a constitutional amendment allowing for a federal income tax. They also pushed for elections free from corruption and bribery. They introduced primaries, and in some states referenda and the right to petition to hold them, and secured the amendments to the constitution that provided for direct elections to the Senate and eventually votes for women.[67] When former president Theodore Roosevelt split the Republican Party to form the Progressive Party, he made what he called 'new nationalism'—where the 'national government' acted to achieve the common economic welfare against sectional corporate influence—the rhetorical centrepiece of his 1912 presidential campaign. But in turning to economic nationhood, the older Roosevelt's version of progressive politics again deployed an explicitly racial discourse that excluded African and Asian Americans.[68]

The Progressives also demonstrated that representative democracies could yield another version of aristocracy, namely technocracy where political privileges accrued to experts. Although they saw the plutocratic concentration of wealth and corruption as threats to the republic, some Progressives also thought that there was a growing administrative state that should produce its own aristocracy constituted by those possessing scientific and technical knowledge, and this elite would not be subject to corruption through time.[69]

During the early twentieth century, America's debt and finance conflicts were resolved in a way that conflated the old aristocratic concentration of power around New York finance with the new claims of technical expertise as a source of political authority. In the early American republic, the question of whether there should be a central bank was repeatedly answered and the answer then repudiated, as the one established yielded in time to aristocratic excess. In 1791, Hamilton initiated the first Bank of the United States against fierce opposition. In 1811, when the bank's charter was soon to expire, the Senate decided not to renew it on the vice president's casting vote. After the 1812 war against Britain left the federal government with heavy debt, Congress legislated in 1818 for the Second Bank of the United States on a twenty-year charter. Again, its charter was not renewed in 1836 after President Andrew Jackson charged the bank had become 'a government' that exercised power over the people.[70] It was not until seven decades later, in 1913, that the Federal Reserve Act created the Federal Reserve system.

The Fed's proponents presented an American central bank as a necessary progressive reform to prevent future bank panics, like the one in 1907, and allow the dollar to become an international currency.[71] But its creation could not escape the old class conflicts. A group of Wall Street bankers developed the initial proposals on a private island off the Georgia coast, and the bill's chief sponsor, Nelson Aldrich, had acquired a large fortune under suspicion he sold political influence.[72]

The Federal Reserve's internal structure encapsulated the tension between the political need to guard against both aristocratic excess—for which the president appointed a Board of Governors—and democratic excess—such that the twelve regional banks were owned by private banks. Although formally the Board of Governors decided monetary policy, in practice this was left to the Federal Reserve Bank of New York dominated by the House of Morgan. The First World War immediately amplified this fault line. Since—as discussed in chapter one—JP Morgan acted as Britain and France's creditor, and since the 1916 presidential election became a contest between a Morgan-backed pro-war candidate and the then anti-war President Wilson, the long-standing class conflict in the American republic around debt was from 1914 exacerbated by one about American geopolitical influence in Eurasia.

Between the Wars

The interwar years graphically demonstrated representative democracies' weaknesses, even before Nazi Germany invaded and ended several European democracies. In his forlorn insistence that Europe should be constituted by democracies according to the principle of national self-determination, Wilson articulated the common presumption that the end of the internal European empires meant an age of democratic nation states. But, again, nationhood was double-edged: its pursuit was often deeply destabilizing, especially when coercion was deployed against minority groups of citizens.

By the time the First World War ended, there were already more national identifications in Europe than its democracies could bear. The end of the multinational Austro-Hungarian and Ottoman Empires and Germany's territorial losses could never have yielded successor states corresponding with existing political claims to nationhood. Instead, in the successor states a predominant national community

had to coexist politically with minorities whose nationhood had already
been articulated against the old empires or who identified as German
outside Germany.

In a number of democracies, governments sought to return to
Bismarck's understanding that nationhood could at least in part be
constructed by extending material protection to citizens through a
welfare state. But these attempts ran into the constraints of bond
markets, the demands of bank creditors, and the need to maintain a
currency's position on the gold standard. At times of financial crisis,
this left governments choosing between a more full-blown economic
nationalism that threatened international trade, or curtailing expenditure on the welfare state.

If economic nationhood proved difficult, appeals to a restrictive
nationhood remained a readily available tool for politicians, particularly when it could be expressed as anti-Bolshevik. In Europe, some
governments withdrew full citizenship from minorities. In the United
States, amid the economic depression of the early 1920s. Congress
passed laws to curtail immigration from Southern and Eastern
Europe, including the countries from where the vast majority of
American Jews had come, and forbade immigration from Japan.[73]

But democratic politics' need for nationhood was also demonstrated during the interwar years, not least when it was nearly entirely
absent. In the first Austrian republic, two evenly balanced parties, the
Christian Socials (the Blacks) and the Social Democrats (Reds)—the
Blacks dominating the countryside and the Reds Vienna—engaged in
what now is termed a culture war centred around Catholicism and
anti-clericalism. Each party sought to remake the Austrian republic
according to the cultural and religious identity it cultivated, and each
availed itself of paramilitaries. In 1933, the Christian Social chancellor, Engelbert Dollfuss, established a dictatorship that banned all the
parties' opponents in the name of an Austrian unity that was strictly
Christian and Catholic. A year later, Austria descended into civil war.
After the catastrophes that followed were finally exhausted, veterans
of both sides of the Austrian culture war saw the only basis for post-
war Austrian democracy in the idea, as one Socialist put it, that 'we
are Austrians . . . and we want to remain an independent people'.[74]

Meanwhile, the questions of who should pay taxes when all citizens
could vote and how to finance war debts and welfare states under an

international monetary system generated intense democratic conflict. Full-franchise democracy invoked fear among the wealthy about taxation. Assuming, as Aristotle had supposed, that government of the many meant government for the poor, the rich frequently saw in democracy a path to their income and wealth being confiscated. Tax havens—jurisdictions where non-residents and corporations that do their business predominantly elsewhere can be taxed at a much lower rate—had first emerged in the late nineteenth century. As states that had been neutral during the war, Switzerland and the Netherlands became after the war places where wealthy Europeans moved sizeable amounts of money to avoid taxes voted for by democratic legislatures. So too did the British Crown dependencies.[75]

Most graphically, the French democratic state's ability to tax was eroded in the mid-1920s by these fears when, having been unable to restore the franc to the gold standard, the French government could scarcely borrow in capital markets. What, as governments came and went, appeared to be democratic chaos in France drove the rich to sell short-term financial assets and move capital abroad. Since this ensured that the franc kept losing external value, capital flight became a self-perpetuating phenomenon.[76]

Together, tax havens and the fear of capital flight meant that the tax systems that emerged under full-franchise democratic politics eventually generated as much a risk of aristocratic as democratic excess. By the mid-1920s governments were making fiscal decisions on the premise that the rich had the practical means to protect their wealth and income from taxation. Tax avoidance by the wealthiest Americans was so effective that Congress passed tax cuts in hope this would reduce avoidance, significantly diluting the intent behind the Sixteenth Amendment that the rich should pay a higher share of tax.[77] In 1928, the French government also introduced a large cut in income tax, after a report that went to the French prime minister concluded that for large taxpayers income tax 'tend[ed] increasingly to take the form of a voluntary contribution'.[78]

Nonetheless, the old notion that tied unsustainable debt to democracy hardened during the interwar years. Most infamously, the early Weimar Republic was cast as recklessly and disastrously irresponsible for printing money to cope with Germany's debt problems. As a story about German democracy, this narrative oversimplified.[79]

Weimar Germany began with extremely high levels of debt from the war and reparations. Moreover, Germany's central bank, the Reichsbank, which was legally independent from the Weimar governments, played its own part in the hyperinflation.[80] But the old problem—where states' ability to borrow money relied on creditor confidence that legislatures would authorize the taxes to service that debt—reappeared in Germany with some vengeance. Without confidence that the Reichstag would vote for new taxes to service German debt, creditors were not keen on lending new money or rolling over existing debt, which left the central bank to print money to cover the state's expenditure.[81]

As it would in the 1970s, peacetime inflation ignited fears of both aristocratic and democratic excess, and spawned new appeals to restrictive nationhood. In Germany, the material shock to savers from hyperinflation rendered many who might reasonably have been expected by their previous class position to support the Weimar Republic sufficiently materially anxious during its later crisis years to prefer anti-democratic forces.[82] But inflation created perceptions of aristocratic excess too. For those who wanted to end Weimar, inflation became another pretext for nativism, and in particular antisemitism. Most lethally, during the German hyperinflation, Hitler persistently attacked 'the Jewification of the economy', casting Jews as dual villains by making them both Marxists and profiteers.[83]

Before its termination, the interwar gold standard similarly destabilized democracies. By promising monetary stability, the gold standard could be perceived as a check against the fears of democratic excess. But by requiring governments to privilege financial stability over welfare states, it ensured a democratic rebellion against its foundational assumption that monetary policy did not belong in democratic politics. The post-1929 Depression strongly politicized central banks in Europe in ways that were familiar from the earlier American republic. Where, as in Britain and Sweden, governments took political control of monetary policy, and, as in the United States, a president confronted the banks, the gold standard was abandoned in the name of a national economic autonomy that democracy itself required. When Franklin Roosevelt took the dollar off gold in 1933, one banker damned the move as 'mob rule' and claimed that 'I think we may find that we've been in a revolution more drastic than the French Revolution.'[84]

The New Deal

This was partisan hyperbole. But Roosevelt's act did begin a qualitatively different way of conceiving democratic reform around economic nationhood that his Treasury officials later sought with Keynes to embed in the post-war international monetary system. For Roosevelt, the ability of banks and the rich to use an international economy where capital flowed freely to defend their material interests, not least with regard to taxation, was an aristocratic power, and one that in a democracy had to be curtailed.

Commanding a project to restore a lost class balance and the republic's foundational values, Roosevelt was heir to the American Populists.[85] His political coalition joined farmers and factory workers to the middle classes plunged into economic desperation. In his first inaugural speech, he declared that 'the money changers have fled from their high seats in the temple of our civilization'. With the money changers gone, he proclaimed, the temple could be 'restore[d] to the ancient truths'. That meant, he continued, addressing the 'overbalance of populations in our industrial centres at the expense of the land'. International trade, he said, was 'necessarily secondary to the establishment of a sound national economy'. The first sentence of that inaugural speech included the words 'our nation'.[86] The legislation that gave labour federal rights to form trade unions was the National Labor Relations Act. Together, labour and management became the economic nation. Their mutually dependent relationship was institutionalized in the National Industrial Recovery Act. In accepting the 1936 Democratic nomination in Philadelphia—the same city where 'political tyranny was wiped out' in 1776—Roosevelt said the 1932 election had been 'the people's mandate' to end the 'despotism' of the 'economic royalists', and that 'for too many of us the political equality we once had won was meaningless in the face of economic inequality'.[87]

Practically, the New Deal's reforms were financed by new taxes on the richest Americans. Most required establishing federal sites of authority and power. These regulated banks, lowered borrowing

costs for homeowners and farmers, increased agricultural prices, and
delivered electricity to agricultural areas that the large energy companies had ignored. To exercise these new federal powers, Roosevelt
claimed emergency powers for the executive as if the country were at
war. After the Supreme Court struck down more than half of the New
Deal laws passed by Congress, he tried, until stopped by the Senate, to
pack the Court with six new judges.

But the New Deal also demonstrated the tension between the idea
of nationhood as shared democratic economic fate and exclusionary
languages of nationhood. In promising a national economic rejuven-
ation, Roosevelt included in the Democratic political coalition Catholic and Jewish immigrants from Southern and Eastern Europe who
had been defined out of American nationhood by the restrictive
immigration laws passed in the 1920s. But Roosevelt also acquiesced
to what had become the prevalent political discourse of American
nationhood defined in terms of those who were ethnically white and
European in origin. In particular, his administrations used the array of
federal powers over housing and mortgage finance established by New
Deal legislation to support home ownership exclusively for white
Americans; consequently, the New Deal intensified racial segregation
in housing.[88] Politically, he had little alternative if he was to pursue
reform: without Southern Democratic support in Congress there
would have been no New Deal.[89] Yet—as will be shown in chapter
nine—the long-term consequences for the distribution of wealth in the
American republic still burden it today.

The politics of the New Deal was further tied to the American
republic's historical relationship to race via oil. Since an oil price
slump for domestic American producers had been central to the
American economic depression, oil was a fundamental part of the
New Deal, with Roosevelt legislating to ensure strict production limits
and allocating production quotas to push prices back up to profitable
levels. This had consequences for the territorial balance of power
within the American republic. The independent producers Roosevelt
sought to help primarily operated in Texas. In 1935, six oil-producing
states led by Texas formed the Interstate Oil Compact. In the name of
the old Southern rhetorical cause of states' rights—once used to
defend slavery—these states defeated the New Dealers' initial hopes
that there could be a nationally regulated oil industry.[90] Having won

this political battle, Texas was able to use its oil regulatory agency, the Texas Railroad Commission, to set the world's oil prices for the next forty years.[91] This economic power gave the Texan congressional delegation outsized political influence, exemplified in the leadership positions held by a succession of Texans from Sam Rayburn to Lyndon Johnson. In igniting old conflicts about federal versus state authority in the part of the Union where states' rights arguments were both historically resonant and still used to restrict voting rights, the politics of oil production placed direct pressure on deep fault lines in the American republic.

In this respect, as in others, the legacy of the interwar years was very different for American democracy than it was even for those European countries where democracy survived. From 1933, the American republic was economically reformed to rebalance the distribution of class influence, but it did not become a full-franchised democracy and, in an energy-producer country with a federal constitution, the states acquired some structural power in ways that qualified the idea of economic nationhood. If the New Deal became the economic and electoral basis of American politics for most of the next three decades, the New Deal republic could still be challenged in the name of democracy and eventually it would be at the same time as American energy power began to decline. By contrast, in Germany, Italy, and France, the interwar and wartime disasters had ensured that new democracies were founded, in Germany's case in a truncated territorial state, without any of this particular historical burden around the franchise. The New Deal was indeed the harbinger of a world of democratic nation states and less internationalized and less financialized economies. But it was in Europe where that future would more straightforwardly materialize.

8

The Rise and Decline of the Democratic Tax State

There were few issues capable of uniting Donald Trump and the European Commission. The digital retail behemoth Amazon was an exception. Throughout 2018, Trump took to Twitter to attack the company, tweeting on one occasion that Amazon's failure to pay tax was 'doing great damage to tax-paying retailers'.[1] More consequentially, the European Commission ordered Amazon in October 2017 to repay €250 million in what it deemed illegal state aid from Luxembourg gained as tax advantages as part of an agreement that allows Amazon to structure its business to pay little tax on its operations elsewhere in Europe. 'Paying taxes', the Commission insisted, 'is part of doing business in Europe.'

But it is not easy for the EU to act on this notion. When, in May 2020, Angela Merkel and Emmanuel Macron unveiled their proposal for an EU Recovery Fund based on funds the European Commission would borrow in the EU's name, they proposed no EU taxes to service the new EU debt, saying only that 'improving the framework for fair taxation in the EU' would 'remain a priority' and 'ideally' this would entail establishing a basis for common corporate taxation. The formal proposal that followed did propose an EU corporation tax tied to access to the single market and an EU digital tax on tech giants. But the actual agreement on the Recovery Fund, struck at the EU summit in July 2020, contained no EU tax on corporations and no commitment to harmonize national corporation tax rates. Instead, the EU would acquire the authority to tax non-recyclable plastic waste, and committed itself to future discussion on carbon and digital taxes, as well as a financial transactions tax that it had already been debating for a decade.

The EU's inability to agree on anything like a common approach to corporation tax is just the beginning of the political difficulties the EU faces around taxation. What was absent through the debate over the Recovery Fund was any suggestion that EU citizens should be taxed as *citizens* to support the new debt authority. Indeed, the French European Commissioner, Thierry Breton, boasted on Twitter after the summit that this is precisely what would not happen: 'For the first time, Europe borrows money for Europe and Europeans. And to finance this historic loan, no taxes for our fellow European citizens. It is only at the border of our internal market that we will put taxes.'[2]

Where the historical relationship between tax, debt, and democracy is concerned, the EU absents itself. What remains of the democratic tax state is to be found only at the national level. For the EU as a legal order, being a citizen has taken on a meaning entirely independent of debt or taxes. To understand how this disjuncture came about and its broader implications for democratic politics beyond the EU, we need to go back to the post-war representative democracies of Western Europe and the United States, and how some of their more democratic features around economic policy, including in relation to taxation, began to unravel in the 1970s.

Economic Nationhood

Where democracy was refounded after the Second World War, perceptions about where the decisive temporal risks lay varied with consequences that still matter for how the EU approaches debt. In France and Italy, where forceful Communist parties emerged from the war, the democratic impulse was strong. After a referendum, the Italian First Republic was established without a monarchy. The French Fourth Republic's constitution was agreed in a constituent assembly, legitimated in a referendum, and established a strong legislature. By contrast, the West German constitution, imposed on the country by the Allies, contained strong safeguards against democratic excess.[3] It did not allow for referendums except on a new constitution or redefining the constituent regional states of the West German Federal Republic—the *Länder*. It strongly protected individual rights and established a powerful constitutional court. No European democracy had ever given the judiciary the authority the German Federal

Constitutional Court possesses. It has the sole right to declare parties unconstitutional, and, in the 1950s, the Court banned both the Neo-Nazi Party and the Communist Party. A 1958 decision by the Court meant effectively that any legal or political decision could be subject to judicial review, and the *Bundesverfassungsgericht* justices have subsequently ruled upon many charged political issues from their home in Karlsruhe, including public debt and EU treaties.[4]

Beyond these constitutional questions, the post–Second World War geopolitical and economic world was much more conducive for the future of democracies than the post–First World War environment. Structurally, the Bretton Woods system offered support to post-war Western European democracies by facilitating the idea of economic nationhood. Certainly, the story of Bretton Woods as a political safeguard for Western Europe democracies can be overdone. The driving impulse for the post-war international monetary order was—as discussed in chapter two—Harry Dexter White's desire to create a dollar-based financial and trading order in which the United States could enjoy economic autonomy free from the risks of competitive devaluations and cross-border gold movements. He and his Treasury colleagues were primarily interested in American monetary power, American financial stability, and, in Dexter White's case, helping the Soviet Union.[5] The Bretton Woods system was then significantly compromised by the Truman administration's unwillingness to stop illegal capital flight and willingness to use the Marshall Plan to circumscribe Italian democratic politics by shutting out the Communists from power. By the time the European currencies were actually convertible for trade purposes, the Eurodollar markets had begun and Bretton Woods' eventual demise—as explained in chapter five—was set in motion.

Nonetheless, the Roosevelt administration's willingness to accept national capital controls, as well as the American commitment to provide external access to short-term credit, did have some crucial consequences for Europe's democracies. Financial nationalism allowed democratic governments to enjoy political autonomy on monetary policy. By reducing the opportunities for capital flight, it enabled the taxation of wealth and income to be politically contested. If post-war governments wished, as they did, to present national economies as shared communities of economic fate responsive to democratic politics, then, whatever its limitations, Bretton Woods was a necessary, although far from sufficient, condition for their endeavours.

In the name of the nation, the state assumed final responsibility for ensuring employment, controlling inflation, supporting national agriculture, and providing economic security against misfortune. Post-war West European politicians spoke to voters as citizens of a nation that gave them formal and informal economic rights, and they largely competed over how those rights could practically best be realized. Accordingly, governments and officials conceived of economies in national terms, with national accounts and nationally measured growth.[6] Of course, this did not mean that the benefits of economic nationhood were anything like evenly distributed, or that all classes shared equally in political influence. In Italy, the industrial working class was at least partially excluded from the economic nation. But what the state did economically provided a means for politicians in West European countries, as it had before the war in the United States, to talk as if the nation as a political community shared a common material fate.

In France under Charles de Gaulle this idea was particularly expansive. For him, economic nationhood necessarily meant the absence of foreign dependency. If nation states were defined as political entities independent from empires—and the United States was in de Gaulle's mind a military and financial empire—France had to be free from American capital as well as American nuclear weapons. But de Gaulle also never supposed that economic nationhood could be sufficient. For him, nationhood had to elevate, and that meant the national economy had to serve a more humanly encompassing idea of the French nation.

In Germany, economic nationhood took a less expansive shape, and paradoxically assumed more political importance. The West German economy's resounding success compared to almost any other country in the post-war world allowed a national story that effectively legitimated the post-war democratic constitution and the institutions it established, including a central bank, the Bundesbank, that was independent from democratic political control.[7] German democracy's legitimacy became near indistinguishable from national economic success, in particular national production and national price stability. Looking back at the end of the 1980s, the historian Charles

Maier suggested that 'for almost four decades, the Federal Republic has lived, so to speak, by bread alone'.[8]

In Britain, a strong language of economic nationhood replaced both the imperial trade and currency policies practised in the 1930s and the faith in free trade that had previously prevailed. Notably, after Britain had risked starvation in the two world wars from its dependence on foreign food imports, British governments pushed towards national self-sufficiency in food production, effectively reversing the decision to repeal the Corn Laws made in 1846.[9]

In Italy, establishing a relatively unifying economic nationhood proved harder. Despite a state-led attempt to reconstruct southern Italy economically, north Italy grew much more rapidly and an industrial–agrarian regional split persisted. Weak growth in the south produced high levels of migration to the north and to other European Economic Community states. Anti-Communism saturated the narrative of Italian nationhood and this spilled over into the economy: it was hard to include the trade unions in the kind of cooperative corporatist arrangements that prevailed in West Germany when until 1962 even the non-Communist left was excluded from any chance of joining the government.[10]

By contrast, in the United States, economic nationhood weakened in several ways when compared with the New Deal era, and its racial restrictiveness remained in place. National wage bargaining became diluted.[11] This divided workers into those bound into New Deal programmes; those who through union–firm level agreements for company benefits beyond wages became tied to what the historian Meg Jacobs has called a 'private welfare state'; and those excluded, including racially, from either.[12] Meanwhile, the South began another divergence. The huge expansion of the defence industry and low state taxes produced a movement of people and capital to the South.[13] This new Southern economy became increasingly less unionized than other parts of the country. This singularity in labour markets reinforced the impact of the Texan oil industry. During the Second World War, the Texas Railroad Commission had wielded less influence, as the federal government took considerable charge of the oil industry. But after the war ended, it re-established its grip over prices and supply.[14]

Nonetheless, the economic pressures that had quickly generated conditions of aristocratic excess, and then a political reaction to it, after the First World War were largely missing. For the best part of three decades, there were no economic depressions and the few recessions that there were lasted for less than a year, ensuring that unemployment only ever rose mildly and briefly. After the immediate post-war years, inflation was largely absent. Believing that inflation undermined democratic stability, governments, aided by low and steady oil prices, successfully deployed price controls. There were no banking crises and, after a series of European devaluations in 1949, few currency crises outside Britain, where governments sought to retain privileges for sterling, including to pay for oil. The financial crises that did change the course of any country's democratic politics arose when, as at Suez, an American president used access to dollars to reverse West European governments' decision-making.

Democracies also began the post-war years with little downward pressure on wages. The wartime economy protected lower wages more than higher salaried earnings.[15] In Germany, the war's end and its immediate aftermath saw a drop in income inequality.[16] In Britain and in the United States, the war had seen a renewed upsurge in unionization.[17] Corporatist arrangements in a number of West European countries allowed trade unions not only to protect their wage gains but to exercise some political influence without confrontational action through strikes.

Crucially, the European democracies were less prone to fiscal crises during the post-war era than they had been in the 1920s. Post-1945 governments were largely able to turn wartime high-tax regimes, including substantial taxes on the rich, into peacetime welfare states that lasted for several decades, not a few years.[18] In this, governments were aided by capital controls that made at least some tax avoidance and evasion more difficult. They also did not have to struggle to meet interest payments on past debt. This was partly a matter of American policy. The injection of American official capital through the Marshall Plan was soon accompanied by debt reduction, especially for West Germany. The 1953 London Debt Conference reduced by half West Germany's cumulative debt from the Weimar Republic, the first post-war years and Marshall aid, extended the time for repayment, and limited the country's debt obligations to the size of its trade surplus. Consequently, post–Second World War West German democracy was protected from external debt demands and class conflicts about how to manage debt. But, just as importantly, this freedom from debt politics was also a function of the fact that, for the most part, Western democracies did not run up new debt. Until the Americans turned to borrowing to finance the Vietnam War, post-war governments largely ran balanced budgets, ensuring that what democracies spent they raised in taxes from their own citizens and national businesses.

The Burdens of History

Yet the idea of the national economy bound to the citizen-taxpayer was not sufficient to put nationhood as a political problem to rest. Certainly, the dangers around nationhood were less destabilizing than during the interwar years. Indeed, they were diminished by the very catastrophes they had precipitated: the Holocaust tragically destroyed the Jewish population in Europe and the waves of brutal ethnic cleansing that occurred during the Second World War and its aftermath left fewer national minorities.[19] Meanwhile, the disaster of the *Anschluss* left pan-Germanism much weakened in Austria as a political force.[20]

But the tensions inherent in rendering any kind of national historical story that could unite a changing population of citizens did not go away, especially when, during the first decades of the post-war era, several West European states encouraged migration from their former colonies, or in the case of Germany 'guest-workers' from Turkey. In the French Fourth Republic, past divisions about French nationhood remained unresolved in the present. Fourth Republic governments pressed a version of the recent past that made French wartime resistance the French nation in action.[21] But the left-led Resistance in France itself had been only one of several French experiences during the war. To add to the tensions, the Fourth Republic began with an imperial notion of the French nation and was a singular political union that included French overseas departments and territories— most consequentially Algeria—with full citizenship rights across its component parts, despite growing nationalist resistance to French rule. This missing imperial consent over Algeria destroyed the Fourth Republic.[22]

The French Fifth Republic was imaginatively founded on de Gaulle's version of French nationhood. Although de Gaulle did not dispense with the idea that the French nation was embodied in the revolutionary republican ideal, he assimilated a longer story of historical continuity into French nationhood.[23] After Algerian independence was finally settled, the Fifth Republic became much more politically stable than its predecessor. But it still struggled with the legacy of empire. From the late 1950s to the late 1960s, North African migration to France significantly increased. The Third Republic had already opened up citizenship to Islamic migrants. But the post-imperial language of French nationhood proved harder to adapt to large-scale economic migration from those with little interest in French revolutionary history. While some earlier migrants became French citizens through military service in the First World War, the Fifth Republic was born from a war fought to protect an empire. High levels of migration also reactivated older divisions about French nationhood that went all the way back to the revolution, at the same time as it excited new ones. Increasingly, part of the right would insist that there could be no idea of the French nation without Christianity, some on the left that the secular nation was foundational to any French republic, and others—on both the right and the left—that French nationhood now had to accommodate a partially religious multiculturalism.[24]

For post-war West German democracy, economic nationhood, however successful, could not ultimately suffice in defining a German people. The German Federal Republic's first chancellor, Konrad Adenauer, always insisted the Federal Republic was the only representative of an enduring German historical nation that included East Germans. But this notion raised awkward questions about the Nazi period. In the 1980s, German historians would fiercely debate just what the Holocaust meant for German national identity. This scholarly dispute showed how hard it was for Germans to agree about what they could remember. But it also demonstrated on both sides that collective disregard for the pre-war past was neither possible nor desired. Either Germans could still remember who they were as a people before the Holocaust and recognize its sins as one part of an ongoing history, or they were a people because they had a moral obligation to consider Auschwitz as an end point to one national identity and the beginning of a quite different one.[25] Whichever way they went, Germans were a people by virtue of German history, rendering far from straightforward the assimilation of Turkish and North African guest-workers who stayed in the country into a story of German citizenship.

For different reasons, what could be collectively remembered about the past complicated British nationhood too. The Second World War made telling a historical story about British nationhood easier than it had ever been. During the war, the British democratic state mobilized its citizens to fight as citizen-soldiers, work as citizen-producers, and lend money as citizen creditors.[26] This demand for sacrifice was accompanied by a national and democratic story told by Winston Churchill in his wartime speeches. In this tale, the British people had under his leadership, with the Labour Party's support, dispensed with an establishment willing to surrender national independence in 1940 and decided to fight.[27] Yet this story of British nationhood, which as Churchill had articulated it was in good part a story of Empire, had to function in post-war British democracy as the Empire was coming to an end. Migration from countries still or previously subject to British imperial rule made the historical story about British nationhood Churchill had told restrictive, even as the wartime experience had made it meaningful for many.

Eventually, the end of the British Empire also opened up the question of whether British political identity was sufficiently strong to override the older claims to Scottish, Welsh, and English nationhood. By the late 1960s, some Scottish nationalists were arguing that the multinational UK state relied on the historical lure of imperial economic gain and that without it the Anglo-Scottish union was redundant.[28] By the early 1970s, the difficulties in a story of British nationhood that allowed the citizens of British democracy to see themselves as a collective people became evident. Northern Ireland, where the minority had never identified as British, descended into violence, and the British army, sent to restore order, only fuelled Catholic grievances about a system of rule that ensured Catholic marginalization. Meanwhile, the rise of the Scottish Nationalist Party and Plaid Cymru ensured that all British governments through the 1970s devoted serious political capital to finding a way to give more autonomy to Scotland and Wales without succeeding in doing so.

In the United States, as in Britain, the state mobilized many citizens as soldiers, producers, and creditors during the Second World War.

Americans bought what amounted to virtually a bond for every adult citizen and every group of Americans in every part of the country took part.[29] But the United States also fought the war with a very largely racially segregated military. Weber's assumption that those who fought for conscripted national armies could not thereafter be deprived of the vote proved erroneous, and racial disenfranchisement continued in the South. Only in the 1960s did the federal government manage to force democratic political change on the Southern states, establishing a full-franchise American democracy for the first time. Still, the ongoing problems posed for American nationhood by slavery's historical coexistence with the American republic, and a racial hierarchy's persistence after its abolition, endured.

In his crusade for African American civil rights, Martin Luther King Jr went back to the founding of the American republic. For him, an ideal of American nationhood that included African Americans had existed from the republic's beginning, and Lincoln had reaffirmed that faith. Looking back on the achievements of the sit-in protestors who had fought for civil rights in the early 1960s, he said they were 'carrying the whole nation back to those great wells of democracy which were dug deep by the Founding Fathers in the formulation of the Constitution and the Declaration of Independence'.[30] This American nation could not exist for King without the past. But others within the civil rights movement were more sceptical about redeeming American nationhood by restoring hitherto unfulfilled foundational ideals. Their insistence that the American republic was founded as a white republic and that the language of American nationhood was inherently tied to racial hierarchy led to black nationalism during the 1960s, including the hope of creating a new state within the territory of the existing American republic.[31]

Post-war Asian and Hispanic migration fuelled further the question of what endured from American history that could be compatible with an idea of nationhood for all American citizens. A 1952 law ended the ban on Asian migration and the restrictions on the naturalization of Asian Americans. Later, the 1965 Immigration and Nationality Act terminated the national origins quota regime that had been in place since the 1920s. This legislation led to a significant increase in migration from outside Europe, over time significantly altering the country's demographic composition. But in cancelling the guest worker programme for Mexicans that had facilitated considerable seasonal movement over the border, the 1965 legislation additionally led to unauthorized migration into the south-west. By the 1980s, there were several million people who had lived in the United States for years without a legal right to do so. In 1986, Congress passed a law offering an amnesty to many unauthorized migrants and mandated stronger border controls. But unregulated migration from Mexico continued, in part encouraged by businesses that welcomed the cheap labour it brought. Soon Spanish speaking increased. By the 1980s, this language issue, allied to a growing interest in multiculturalism as a way of understanding the American historical experience, became particularly politically divisive. In this respect, American democracy found itself confronted with an issue about the relationship between language and nationality that had been central and politically destabilizing to European states' nation-building in the nineteenth century.[32]

This shift to a more ethnically diverse democracy in which all citizens' voting rights were protected by the federal government occurred at the same time as a conscript army was fighting in Vietnam. Instead of conscription for a now racially integrated army providing a basis for a political renewal of nationhood, it produced racial and class conflict. Under the rules of the draft, significant numbers of affluent white men could use education to defer service. By contrast, African Americans were heavily overrepresented in troop deployments and casualties, especially in the war's early stages.

Conscription did not survive the Vietnam War. As the Jacobins' introduction of conscription had symbolized a decisive turn to political nationhood in legitimating state authority in Europe, so its effective end in the United States in 1973 proved symbolic for the American republic. Without any sense that the homeland was under military threat, the American federal government had used a conscript army to fight a war in Eurasia in a manner that selectively protected some citizens from the obligation to take up arms. The political fallout exposed all the other fragilities in the idea of American nationhood. But if terminating the draft was politically necessary, its absence would also leave few historically recognizable options for resurrecting American nationhood: the economic conditions that had underpinned the New Deal version were coming apart.[33]

The 1970s Juncture

During the 1970s, the American republic and the Western European democracies were plunged back into instability. Unprecedentedly, inflation accelerated without a prior war. Nearly everywhere, there was a palpable sense that politics could not be contained within the existing constitutional orders. Democracies were more violent and confrontational than they had been a decade earlier. There were secessionist movements in Northern Ireland and the Basque region in Spain. In West Germany and Italy, left-revolutionaries engaged in murderous campaigns against politicians and the business class. Some targeted Jews. Their violence was matched by that of neo-fascist paramilitary groups. In the United States, the violence had started earlier on the streets. It spilled into elections in 1968 and continued in domestic terror groups into the 1970s.

This instability led some to charge that democracies were in the grip of democratic excess that would destroy them.[34] Shortly before his resignation, the West German chancellor, Willy Brandt, expressed his fear that Western democracies were sufficiently far down the path of temporal decay that they had only two or three decades left before they would slide through chaos into dictatorships.[35] A belief that democratic nation states simply could not cope because they had become too democratic and too nationalistic was reflected in the *Crisis of Democracy* report published in 1975 by the Trilateral Commission, an influential forum established two years earlier to bring together politicians and business figures from North America, Europe, and Japan to contemplate the future. In his essay in the report, the American political scientist Samuel Huntington used the term 'an excess of democracy' to explain what he took to be the governability crisis unfolding.[36]

For all the report's authors, democracy's degeneration was inexorably tied to inflation. Indeed, Huntington described inflation as 'the economic disease of democracies' since 'it becomes difficult if not impossible for democratic governments to curtail spending, increase taxes, and control prices and wages'.[37] In the 1980s and 1990s, this argument was frequently deployed about monetary policy. Indeed, the whole intellectual foundation of the Eurozone articulated in the monetary–economic distinction laid out in the Maastricht Treaty was premised on the assumption that democratic control over monetary policy led to inflation.

But the perception that democratic excess expressed in inflation shaped the 1970s and a necessary reaction over the following two decades is a distortion of what happened. Economically, a change that fits the democratic excess thesis did occur in the 1970s. Wages as a proportion of national income increased in the 1970s, and corporate profits fell.[38] Some trade unions in Western Europe did make it difficult for their governments to bring down inflation. Fearing more strikes, British, French, and Italian governments all at various times accepted wage demands from workers regardless of their consequences. In Italy, the government introduced a wage index, named the *Scala Mobile*, that guaranteed to trade unions that wages would increase with inflation. Since the Communist Party, which was politically strongest among the unionized northern industrial working class, was excluded from the Italian government, it proved impossible for Italian governments to reform the *Scala Mobile* without inviting an industrial and political confrontation. In the United States, independent, non-unionized truckers rebelled against gasoline shortages with wildcat strikes and blockades of interstate highways and bridges, using Citizens' Band radios to coordinate their action. In 1974 the action turned violent and the highways became, in the words of historian Meg Jacobs, 'zones of armed combat'.[39]

But the idea that it was the majoritarian dynamics of democracies that generated or then sustained inflation is problematic. The price and wage controls governments used to try to reduce inflation enjoyed widespread support, particularly among the working class and lower middle classes. Indeed, Richard Nixon was never more popular in his first term than when he introduced a wage and price freeze in 1971.[40] It was big business, in the United States in particular, that had an interest in higher prices and pressed their case for them.[41] Under Margaret Thatcher's leadership, the Conservative Party in Britain easily won the 1979 general election by appealing to a backlash of working-class voters against the series of strikes that became known as the Winter of Discontent. The foreword to the Conservative manifesto that year cast the party's purposes, of which reducing inflation was primary, in the language of 'restor[ing] the balance of power in favour of the people'.[42]

The governments elected to office in the late 1970s and early 1980s that committed to restricting trade unions in the name of fighting inflation succeeded. Certainly, the changes in external economic conditions helped them, as did the immediate consequences of some of their own anti-inflationary policies. Much higher unemployment, largely afflicting industrial sectors that were already having to adjust to East Asian competition and some offshoring of production, made it harder for unions to press for wage hikes. Where service sectors eventually generated new employment, fewer workers were unionized. Even where they were, they did not possess the disruptive capacity that those once employed in indispensable industries like mining, steel production, and docking possessed. Nonetheless, far from rendering democracies ungovernable, these reforming governments, like Margaret Thatcher's, stayed in power. Strike-restricting legislation in most Western European democracies passed without causing anything like the political instability that should have been expected if, as the Trilateral Commission suggested, 'the demands on democratic government' were growing 'while the capacity of democratic government stagnates'.[43] Under these policies and conditions, union membership in quite a number of European democracies, but certainly not all, fell, sometimes sharply. Even where union membership held up better, as in Germany and Sweden, national wage bargaining weakened.[44]

Oil, too, complicates any narrative where inflation is cast as a democratic disease overcome by capital-friendly politics in the 1980s and 1990s. In part this is because oil was an important cause of the 1970s inflation, and the fall in oil prices after the early 1980s generated by new supply had a significant role in bringing inflation down— as discussed in chapter four. But it is also because oil firms led those businesses that pushed for higher prices.

In the United States, which had a long-established domestic oil industry that had often invited charges of aristocratic excess, oil, more generally, had complex effects on the country's democratic politics. For the four decades after the New Deal, there had been relatively little overt conflict in the American republic over oil, although the oil producers had continued to exercise considerable political influence, not least over how they were taxed. When, after American production peaked in 1970, prices started to rise and the first shortages appeared, democratic conflicts around oil reappeared, in a manner with some strong echoes of the first American Populists. The Democratic senator Henry Jackson led a political charge for more regulation to protect those he presented as the people. George McGovern, the 1972 Democratic presidential candidate, at times adopted similar rhetoric, declaring on one occasion that 'Big Oil won out over the people.'[45] Some within the party presented the oil shortages as a conspiracy. Lee Aspin, a Democratic representative from Wisconsin said: 'There is little doubt that the so-called gasoline shortage in the Midwest is just a big, lousy gimmick foisted on consumers.'[46] But the crucial change for American democratic politics in the 1970s was that the country became dependent on foreign oil and the Texas Railroad Commission lost the ability to set prices.

By telling some truths to both voters and American producers about the energy crisis, including that the American economy required OPEC imports to function, Jimmy Carter probably destroyed his presidency. When he tried to make conservation part of his move to restore energy independence, his critics, in his energy secretary's words, 'responded that conservation is not the American way; production is the American way'.[47]

This approach was Ronald Reagan's solution to the energy crisis. He initially allowed higher prices to increase overall supply. This short-term response was paradoxically geared both to winning votes against Carter's requests for sacrifice and to pleasing domestic producers who wanted energy inflation. For the medium term, by intensifying foreign energy dependency, it shunted oil out of the sphere of democratic political conflict into the geopolitical sphere, not least towards more American engagement in the Middle East. Notably, when the Reagan administration was caught having illegally sold arms to the Iranian government and diverting the profits to the Nicaraguan Contra rebels, Reagan reverted to the geopolitical argument that Iran's oil and geographical situation on the Persian Gulf meant there was a 'national interest' in improving relations with the country.[48]

The response to the loss of relative energy self-sufficiency also had implications for nationhood. Nixon and Carter wished to make the energy issue a national project. In a televised address in 1973, Nixon declared that 'we, as a Nation, must now set upon a new course . . . which will give us the capacity to meet our needs without relying on any foreign nation'.[49] He compared this task to the United States' founding as an independent state two centuries earlier. In what became known as his 'malaise' speech, Carter pronounced that the energy crisis 'strikes at the very heart and soul and spirit of our national will. We can see this crisis in the growing doubt about the meaning of our own lives and in the loss of a unity of purpose for our nation.' He insisted that 'the confidence that we have always had as a people is not simply some romantic dream or a proverb in a dusty book that we read just on the Fourth of July'. Rather it was 'the idea which founded our nation and has guided our development as a people' and which now had to be repaired through shared sacrifice to overcome the energy crisis and restore the American nation.[50]

But the energy crisis could not unite American citizens when the conflict between American producers and consumers within different geographical parts of the republic had become strongly zero-sum. The New Deal had protected oil producers without inflicting prices that provoked a political reaction from consumers. In the 1950s and 1960s, the Texas Railroad Commission had kept prices from going too high and too low. But when American supply had peaked and OPEC's influence on prices was accelerating, there was no political equilibrium obtainable. In trying to manage the conflict, the federal government directly involved itself in the allocation of energy in ways that invariably fuelled sectional grievances. Under legislation Congress passed in December 1973, federal agencies controlled what was refined for gasoline and for heating oil, and to what industries and states the oil companies distributed supply for what use. The oil-producing states wanted to produce more at market prices. The non-oil-producing states, especially in New England where winter is cold, wanted prices controlled and more fuel allocated for heating. The Democratic Party divided on energy across these regional lines, and then again over oil's environmental impact. Carter, who wanted higher prices to serve both reduced consumption and energy independence, was eventually abandoned by both sides.[51]

Although Reagan's abolition of all remaining federal energy controls in 1981 ended the pressures energy allocation had heaped on the Union, these oil-generated divisions left a centrifugal legacy. This was temporarily disguised by Reagan's landslide victory in 1984 on the back of the partial economy recovery that occurred after oil prices finally came down. But when, in the 2000s, it became clear that neither energy independence nor Middle Eastern foreign policy could solve the energy problem, those sectional fault lines would reassert themselves in new forms.

Aristocratic Excess Renewed

For all the furore about democratic excess in the 1970s, it was the risks of aristocratic excess in democracies that turned out never to have gone away. The post-war international institutions fashioned the conditions for a much larger international political class than the pre-war central bankers and financiers who had run the gold standard and the Bank for International Settlements. The original Bretton Woods settlement was also significantly diluted in ways that allowed more space for international finance than Dexter White and Keynes had envisaged. The Eurodollar markets facilitated the growth of a dollar-based international banking system operating beyond the control of governments and central banks. These markets offered opportunities for democratic governments to fund political parties and conduct foreign policy beyond any scrutiny by legislatures or voters and, on occasion, for politicians to enrich themselves and their business associates in patronage networks. The French oil company Elf, created by de Gaulle out of the French state-oil agencies, used the Eurodollar markets to run a massive private banking operation, through which it provided funds to the primary French political parties and to bribe foreign governments and firms.[52] In Germany, from at least the 1970s, both the Christian Democratic and Social Democratic parties used the offshore Eurodollar markets to protect donors from taxes, distribute slush funds, and evade party funding laws.[53]

The conjunction of the Cold War and decolonization, meanwhile, ensured that the relationship between elected governments on one side and militaries and intelligence agencies on the other generated threats to democratic government. In 1958, de Gaulle came to power through a disguised coup in which it was clear that the next French government had to be acceptable to the French army. After the French referendum on Algerian independence in 1961, de Gaulle would himself have fallen to a coup if he had not been saved by the refusal of conscript soldiers to follow orders. The following year, he survived a serious assassination attempt organized by renegade French military officers. In Italy in December 1970, retired army personnel and Mafia members joined together in an attempted coup.

In the United States, the Cold War produced what President Eisenhower described in his farewell address as a 'military-industrial complex' conjoining 'an immense military establishment [to] a large arms industry', which created 'the potential for the disastrous rise of misplaced power'. Although less commented upon, Eisenhower also warned that the 'technological revolution' behind the 'military-industrial complex' risked the 'danger that public policy could itself become the captive of a scientific-technological elite'. What was needed, Eisenhower suggested, was for American citizens to recognize the problem of political time. American democracy, two centuries old as it was, constituted 'a political and spiritual heritage' now at risk from 'plundering for our own ease and convenience the precious resources of tomorrow'.[54] The Cold War also fuelled what came to be called an imperial presidency in the United States. From Harry Truman through to Richard Nixon, presidents took decisions to use American military power with minimal if any congressional involvement, even though it was Congress that had the constitutional authority to declare war. Lyndon Johnson used a legislative resolution passed after a dubiously reported incident in the Gulf of Tonkin as the basis to send American troops to Vietnam. Nixon fought a war in Cambodia and Laos for two years without Congress even being notified of the action. Meanwhile, successive presidents used the Central Intelligence Agency to conduct interventions, including paramilitary operations, in foreign states. In this sense, a good proportion of the exercise of American geopolitical power after 1945 became detached both from its citizens in a genuinely national army and from citizens' representatives.[55]

In Europe, the EEC, established in 1957, had weak democratic foundations. There was no initial democratic legitimation to authorize the EEC's creation beyond parliamentary votes, even though both France and Italy had held referendums on their post-war constitutions. Those who identified as European federalists and cultivated a trans-European political network to push the EEC towards ever closer union often saw constitutional and cosmopolitan authority as a counter to democratic, national authority.[56] The Habsburg Empire's enduring influence on the Central European political imagination left its mark.[57] Some on the right, like the Austrian-born Friedrich Hayek, who supported a federal Europe did so because they thought that it would strengthen international liberalism at the expense of democracy. For Hayek, negating any idea of a national people in a cosmopolitan economic union would make big welfare states politically impossible, protectionist trade policies much more difficult, and all together produce a less interventionist state.[58] In France, there was relatively little support among French political parties for any site of supranational European authority, but French bureaucrats pushed that agenda anyway, ultimately successfully.[59]

Nor in practice did the EEC become more democratic. None of the EEC's institutions was directly elected. The unelected European Commission had the sole authority to initiate legislation. The 1960 Dehousse Plan for direct elections to the European Parliament was rejected, as was de Gaulle's counterproposal for member states to hold concurrent national referendums to legitimate EEC decision-making.[60] In two decisions in 1963 and 1964, the European Court of Justice asserted that the EEC constituted a legal order that imposed obligations on national governments and citizens, and that Community law was supreme over national law by direct result of the treaty establishing the Community. The eventual common market created a legal order that made government intervention in a good number of economic sectors illegal.[61] In the end, the EEC proved to be a rather limited supranational entity. Indeed, for the governments who created it, the attraction was in part that it strengthened the nation state's capacity to act economically, including in regard to energy.[62] Nonetheless it diluted democracy in its member states by insulating executives from democratic demands expressed in national legislatures without providing an alternative supranational outlet for democratic discontent.

* * *

Against this backdrop, it is unsurprising that by the mid-1980s, when labour's bargaining power was decisively weakened, it was the risk of aristocratic not democratic excess that threatened individual democracies' future. Economically, it could scarcely be otherwise. There never was a possibility that a return to open international capital flows would not significantly magnify democracies' aristocratic features.

Certainly, this return to borrowing in international capital markets had its advantages in assembling majority electoral coalitions. As unemployment rose, governments could maintain welfare states without sharp tax increases. They could also use debt to adjust to higher oil prices and run trade deficits that allowed domestic consumer demand to rise.[63] But, beyond the United States, protected as it was by the dollar's position as the world's pre-eminent currency, the bigger budget and trade deficits became, the more governments' macroeconomic decision-making was at the mercy of foreign exchange markets. Once a currency came under severe downward pressure, a government could only stabilize it by taking action that either depressed growth and often employment or restricted public expenditure. That did not prevent some governments, especially the Italian, running sizeable budget deficits for a lengthy period of time, and it did not lead to a general retrenchment of welfare states in Europe.[64] But, as President Mitterrand painfully discovered in March 1983, European governments in the ERM needed anti-inflationary credibility. Indeed—as discussed in chapter four—maintaining exchange rate stability, and with it interest rate levels that made debt manageable and growth possible, required as many instruments of economic policy as politically feasible to be used for anti-inflationary purposes.

Meanwhile, from the 1980s, open international capital flows, including via the still-growing Eurodollar markets, would eventually make taxing the wealthy and internationalized corporations harder. Starting with the Reagan administration, many governments in the 1980s changed the rates of taxation and allowances. This did not necessarily lead to states collecting less overall tax from their citizens and national corporations. However, the composition of the taxes levied was refashioned. Where taxes on income and corporations were concerned, rates came down and allowances were restricted. Some of these changes were not particularly motivated by international financial conditions: promises of cuts on the lowest rates of income tax could help win elections, and once they came down any suggestion of raising them became a severe electoral liability. But from the 1980s, governments competed to attract investment from multinational corporations via benign corporate tax regimes.[65] While few large states wished to take corporation tax as low as a state like Luxembourg, they were, nonetheless, pushed by the smaller states into lower corporation tax rates than democratic politics incentivized.[66] This international corporation tax competition then had knock-on consequences domestically. Large gaps often opened up between top rates of income tax and corporation tax, affecting governments' ability to tax the income of those who could take their income as company dividends.[67]

In time, in this international financial environment, it became significantly easier to tax those citizens on middle to high incomes where tax was deducted at source than the very rich and those with the discretion to organize their earnings, including in relation to capital gains, and move money abroad. As the Swiss historian Jacob Burkhardt wrote of third-century imperial Rome, something of an 'aristocracy of freedom from taxation' emerged.[68] This shift in the balance of political influence within democracies around taxation became structurally entrenched. Offshore tax havens flourished.[69] Since these were often bound up with offshore banking operating through the Eurodollar system, governments in challenging them, even cooperatively, would have to contemplate serious disruption to the international dollar credit environment.[70] Consequently, accepting the tax loss, regardless of the democratic cost, became the path of least resistance, especially when the offshore banking system yielded clear political benefits for some in power.

Beyond the effects of the Eurodollar system on tax politics, the growth of financial sectors from the 1970s also accelerated the descent towards aristocratic excess. More finance-centric economies advanced the political influence of those who owned financial assets at the same time as organized labour's wage bargaining power diminished. As well as offering very high salaries with income gains concentrated at the top, financial sectors created whole new financial assets with high returns.[71] This had a significant impact on wealth and income inequality in those countries with international financial centres. In the United States, in particular, the top 1 per cent dramatically increased its share of income from the 1970s to the mid-2000s; the top 0.1 per cent gained even more.[72] Those who owned these assets then sought political protection for them. Funds from the financial sector became from the 1970s indispensable to American politicians seeking to raise large sums of money to run for elected office. In the meantime, large businesses led by financial firms also augmented their permanent lobbying presence in Washington.[73]

Yet through all these changes reinforcing the dangers of aristocratic excess, the lesson taken from the 1970s and 1980s by European politicians in both centre-left and centre-right parties was that, in macro-economic matters anyway, it was democratic excess manifested in inflation that was the permanent hazard. This risk, many governments concluded, had to be guarded against by taking monetary policy out of democratic politics and making central banks independent, as was already the case in West Germany and more complicatedly in the United States. In the EU, central bank independence was made a necessary condition of participating in monetary union. Rather than inflation becoming a matter of democratic contest as debt grew and political strategies to manage that debt were required, its eradication became a near moral economic principle to be constitutionalized out of democratic politics in the name of preventing democratic excess.

The cumulative effect of more internationalized and financialized economies from the 1970s terminated economic nationhood. As the external environment that had underpinned it evaporated, the notion that there was a national political community with a shared economic fate for which the state could successfully take responsibility shattered. Citizens' interests became too fiercely and too obviously divided. Inflation sharpened the conflicts of interests between consumers, generations, non-unionized workers, and those workers who initially could protect their wages via strikes and sector agreements.[74] National corporatism—which in a number of European countries, including West Germany, had produced national collective wage bargaining—broke down, and under conditions of open capital flows and increasingly internationalized production it could not be restored.[75] High unemployment, manufacturing decline, and the growth of financial sectors then strongly divided what had been largely national economies on a regional basis. In the United States, the inflation and regional divisions came together, with the non-unionized manufacturing economy in the South weathering the economic fallout of the strong dollar and high interest rate policies of the early 1980s better than the Midwest's Rust Belt.

Predictably, debt played a crucial role in this unravelling of economic nationhood. When governments turned back to borrowing in international capital markets, the practice of using citizens as savers and taxpayers to finance the state and contain the risks to democratic politics from creditor–debtor conflicts ended.[76] Democratic states became much more dependent on international financial markets to finance their expenditure and much less so on their citizens as savers and taxpayers. Henceforth, the interest costs of financing budget deficits fell on citizens via their taxes without any accompanying material return via their savings at the same time as democratic states' dependency on international financial markets constrained which citizens they could tax at what rate.[77]

Beyond sovereign debt, the sharp rise in private debt also fuelled new domestic creditor–debtor conflicts, especially when, after oil prices slumped from the mid-1980s, there were fewer inflationary pressures anywhere, except for a while in Britain, to reduce its real value.[78] Wage stagnation was masked by this rising household debt, a significant proportion of which was acquired on high-interest-rate credit cards issued by banks that were now subject to fewer restrictions on their lending practices.[79]

The accumulating pressures towards aristocratic excess and economic nationhood's fall were largely two sides of the same phenomenon. There was a democratic argument to be made against the idea of the national economy protected by capital controls. If democracies' long-term stability depended upon relatively high levels of material well-being, then nationally oriented economies appeared to subordinate universal aggregate gain to minority producer interests and allowed those with power to allocate capital for partisan purposes. But this argument treated economic nationhood as only an economic matter when, so far as it had worked, it had served as a political safeguard for democracies against aristocratic excess and, in principle, provided a low-danger means of defining national citizenship. If changing economic conditions rendered it impossible to sustain, then politically it still needed to be replaced without opening up potentially more destabilizing conceptions of nationhood.

* * *

For some in the 1980s, the European Community was a partial remedy to this problem. If European democracies could not be rebalanced within nation states, a theoretical answer lay in refounding democratic political authority at the European level.

Certainly, the enlargement of the EC in 1973 enhanced the prospects for greater democratic legitimation at the national level. The French government held a referendum on ratifying the treaty for Britain, Denmark, Ireland, and Norway's accession. Three of these four states then held referendums on completing membership. In rejecting entry, the Norwegian electorate showed that democratic consent to the EC was far from a given. In the 1980s, the Danish and Irish governments also adopted a more cautious approach to constitutional change than the original six states, with both holding referendums on the Single European Act. Greenland, which had joined the EC as part of Denmark in 1973 and acquired home rule in 1979, voted in a 1982 referendum to leave.

By contrast, British accession revealed just what difficulties moving the EC towards democratic legitimation could bring when the member state remained the lodestar of democratic authority. The Conservatives under Edward Heath made a commitment to negotiate for accession in their 1970 manifesto. Since the Labour and Liberal parties had also promised to begin negotiations, there was no electoral outlet for those who were opposed to membership to express dissent. Having negotiated a treaty, Heath pushed the accession legislation through the House of Commons on a strongly whipped vote.[80] Labour's commitment in the February 1974 general election to holding a retrospective referendum after renegotiating the terms of membership then exposed just what conflicts asking citizens to decide directly on EC matters could ignite in national democratic politics. Those who supported membership objected that referendums were demagogic and a tool of executive dictators like Louis Napoleon, as well as in the British case a constitutional anomaly.[81] The first line of argument ignored what had happened in Denmark, Ireland, and Norway. The second line wished away the fact that referendums were the most coherent way the British constitutional system, which largely allows Parliament legally to legislate as it chooses, could deal with the future primary of EC law in a democratic manner.[82] That there was so little agreement about how the issue should be settled as a matter of national democracy—by Parliament or a referendum—was a portent of how an EC that in time would become more supranational posed a new set of issues around consent, including ultimately losers' consent.

Within the EC, the commitment in the 1986 Single European Act to complete the single market by 1992 also in practice decreased the chances of renewing democratic political authority at the European level. The single market effectively ended national labour markets and further weakened what remained of national corporatism without creating a structure for European-level wage bargaining.[83] It fortified de facto economic rights to sell goods and services, work, and move capital within the EC without any concurrent democratic political rights for citizens that let them collectively choose representatives who would be responsible for what would become a single regulatory area or any obligations to pay tax. Indeed, rather than providing a balance against aristocratic excess in national democracies, the single market established a transnational site for lobbying almost entirely dominated by business representation where the dominant political discourse was technocratic.[84] It also established the basis for significant class divides between citizens within member states. Those who benefited most directly from the economic rights the single market constitutionalized were generally an affluent minority, whose interests would henceforth at least in part be better served by EC-level politics than the political struggles within democratic nation states that might jeopardize those rights.[85]

Monetary union only intensified the EC's aristocratic features. There was no possibility that the German government would agree to subordinate the European Central Bank (ECB) to a site of democratic political authority where the ends of monetary policy could be politically contested. The EC's monetary union then removed what was still the democratic component in the Bundesbank's political position from the European version of Germany's monetary approach. While the Bundesbank at least existed in relation to the German state, the ECB's authority was independent of any state. Rather, it possessed a constitutional mandate that had been agreed on a confederal basis and then legitimated by a divergent range of national democratic methods. Once a democratic state ratified the treaty creating the ECB, its elected representatives could not change their minds in response to democratic pressures about the

ECB's authority to decide monetary policy without leaving the monetary union.[86]

*   *   *

As economic nationhood hollowed out, democracies were left with the particular notions of 'the people' that were acquired during their earlier historical experience, with all the attendant complications in relation to migration, and in the United States, to the ongoing legacy of slavery. In good part, losers' consent still prevailed, helped by the fact that election results were often decisive, not least in the United States. Although nationalist movements in Western Europe's three multinational states—the UK, Spain, and Belgium—grew, they did not come close to dissolving any existing unions in the 1980s. By the 1980s' end, however irreversible the path towards aristocratic excess, the majority of citizens' living standards were still rising and the corporations that a few decades later would permeate everyday life while paying minimal taxes did not exist.

Nonetheless, nationhood had not disappeared from democratic politics as either a presence or a danger. What remained was largely an imaginative story about a shared past. Virtually everywhere, especially in the United States, these historical stories resonated with many citizens while they were challenged by many others who believed they were too archaic and too burdened with imperialism and racism to unify. In the EC, some citizens of national democracies wanted to replace a political identification around nation states with one around a European political community. But the EC could not act like its member states did, not least because it had no capacity to tax and borrow, and democratically legitimating the authority it did have could incite sharp democratic contest within its member states. These conflicts left democracies with deep long-term problems. Parasitic as they were on what remained of nationhood, Western democracies would become more turbulent as, in the twenty-first century, the conflict over the legitimacy of nationhood spilled directly back into the economic sphere, not least via greater migration.

9

Whither Reform

Reflecting in 2015 on the state of American politics, former president Jimmy Carter said that America had been 'a great country' because of its political system, but 'now it's just an oligarchy' that functions with 'unlimited political bribery'.[1] The following year's presidential election partially played out around the question of whether the American republic had indeed become an oligarchy. The initial frontrunners for each nomination suggested a dynastic contest between Hillary Clinton and Jeb Bush. Of the two, only Clinton proved able to defeat an unexpected, insurgent challenger. On the Democratic side, Bernie Sanders made restoring American democracy his central campaign message. In a speech in 2014, Sanders contended that 'the great political struggle we now face is whether the United States retains its democratic heritage or whether we move towards an oligarchic form of society where the real political power rests with a handful of billionaires, not ordinary Americans'.[2] In his declaration speech, he said that by prohibiting restrictions on corporations and other associations' expenditure on election communications, the Supreme Court had 'totally corrupted' the 'American political system', and rendered the country's democracy an 'oligarchy'.[3] In seeking the nomination, Sanders eschewed all the usual vehicles by which corporations give money to candidates, and relied on small donations from individual citizens. On the Republican side, Trump presented himself as a whistle-blower on an oligarchic class to which, as a big donor, he himself belonged. In one debate he blurted out:

> Before this, before two months ago, I was a businessman. I give to everybody. When they call, I give. And you know what? When I need something from them, two years later, three years later, I call them. They are there for me.[4]

Just as starkly, the 2016 election dramatized the long-standing conflicts around American nationhood and citizenship. Sanders made unauthorized migration and corporate support for it a class issue: 'What right-wing people in this country would love is an open-border policy. Bring in all kinds of people, work for $2 or $3 an hour, that would be great for them. I don't believe in that. I think we have to raise wages in this country.'[5] Again, Trump disingenuously portrayed himself as a truth-teller, saying in one Republican debate: 'I know the H1B [a visa for temporary foreign workers] very well. And it's something that I frankly use and I shouldn't be allowed to use it. We shouldn't have it. Very very bad for workers.'[6] However, unlike Sanders, Trump's outbursts on migration went well beyond class: Trump's regular attacks on unauthorized migration doubled as nativist assaults on any notion of multicultural or multi-ethnic American identity. In promising to build a wall to shut the Mexican border, he also constructed a brutal one through American nationhood that shut out millions of American citizens from their rights and identity.

The movement of people across state borders in search, for whatever reason, of new lives played just as crucial a part in the European electoral upheavals over the 2010s.[7] In Germany, it was Angela Merkel's response to the 2015 refugee and migrant crisis that turned the initially anti-euro *Alternative für Deutschland* (AfD) into an electoral force that would make it harder for German political parties to form governing coalitions. In Italy, the *Lega* party, led by Matteo Salvini, used the burdens placed on the country in patrolling the EU's borders to propel an 'Italy for the Italians' rhetoric. In Britain, constitutionally guarded freedom of movement helped Leave win the 2016 referendum on EU membership.[8]

But the EU's single market and common border policies made the political context in which migration electorally played out in Europe rather different than in the United States. In the case of Brexit, the fact that the British government had no authority to restrict migration from other EU states forced a reckoning around a question that had been suppressed since the introduction of the Maastricht Treaty: were the British electorate content to locate British democracy in a broader European legal and constitutional order whereby certain matters, like intra-European migration, were removed from national democratic politics? The result of that referendum then delivered another reckoning stemming from the same treaty: since Maastricht, the citizens of the EU's member states were also citizens of a Union that brought them economic rights, but that Union could not ultimately guarantee those rights without the consent of national citizens and their representatives.

When the Covid-19 crisis struck, the Eurozone was confronted with a different version of the EU's sovereignty–democracy misalignment. For those states inside the single currency, there is no monetary sovereignty. In a world in which monetary policy overwhelmingly provides the space for fiscal decision-making, it would be the supra-national ECB that decided whether to support national borrowing. Three months into the Covid-19 crisis, the German Constitutional Court offered its ruling on the ECB's first programme of QE. The question at stake went to the political heart of the tension between European-level authority and national democratic legitimation. In ruling that the ECB had acted outside its competences, the German Constitutional Court insisted that the sovereignty of the German people could not be transferred to the EU and that any decisions that 'determine the overall financial burden imposed on citizens' in Germany had to be a matter for the Bundestag.[9]

The German court had first seriously pressed the argument that democracy could only be located in the nation state in ruling on the Maastricht Treaty. Then, it had not prevented monetary union. In 2020, its decision had near immediate repercussions, forcing German politicians to make more strategic choices about the euro's future than they had been accustomed to. The result—as discussed in chapter six—was new authority for the European Commission to borrow for the EU as a political entity and with it more pressure on the EU as a multi-currency union.

This is nothing like what happened in the United States during the spring and summer of 2020. Although the post-1945 stories of the American republic and the West European democracies ran along broadly parallel lines up to the 1980s, during the 1990s they diverged more sharply. In part, this is because of the politics of race and citizenship in the American republic. It is also because with the Maastricht Treaty, the EU acquired a specific set of democratic difficulties that are absent in the American context. Both have been central to the last decade of democratic disruption, including that around losers' consent. But what has happened in Europe and in the United States are not the same story and they need to be told separately.

Maastricht and Monetary Union

It is the path the Maastricht Treaty established towards a not-quite common currency that has driven much of what has happened to European democracies for the past three decades. As a presage of the long-term problems it would cause, the treaty proved hard to legitimate. The 1992–93 ERM crisis—as discussed in chapter four—ensured that the referendums in Ireland, Denmark, and France occurred against a backdrop of currency crises. In Denmark, the referendum was lost, and the Danish government proceeded to negotiate various opt-outs, including from monetary union. In France, it was won by a tiny margin dependent on a large 'yes' vote in Paris. In substance, the treaty proved the beginning of a story where monetary union hollowed out the old party systems of several of its participants, nowhere more so than in France.

Monetary union began as a French reform project and became at Maastricht a French failure. It rested on a firm separation between economic policy, which could be democratically contested, and monetary policy, which the treaty deemed unpolitical. Few, if any, French politicians accepted the distinction. One of François Mitterrand's regular ministers, Jean-Pierre Chevènement, campaigned against ratification, charging monetary union meant the 'dismantlement of the republican state'.[10] The principal centre-right party, then named the *Rassemblement pour la République*, divided during the referendum. Future-president Jacques Chirac supported ratification. But the other leading party personality, Philippe Séguin, cast monetary union as a betrayal of de Gaulle's vision of the French state, and led a majority of centre-right voters into the 'no' bloc.[11]

Despite Maastricht's ratification, the second round of the 1995 presidential election pitched two candidates—Chirac and the Socialist Lionel Jospin—against each other who entertained serious doubts about France joining the single currency. During his first months in office, Chirac contemplated a change of course, only to be persuaded to proceed by pressure on the franc and considerable harrying from the West German chancellor, Helmut Kohl.[12] Chirac's subsequent attempt to force the French budget deficit below 3 per cent to allow France to join the euro precipitated a general strike. When, in 1997, Chirac called early parliamentary elections in the hope of mobilizing support for pension reforms, the Socialists and their allies won a majority. With even less enthusiasm for monetary union than he had previously shown, Jospin became prime minister and insisted France could not accept the fiscal rules laid out in the Stability and Growth Pact. But, again, pressure on the franc drove a French prime minister and president to acquiesce to German preferences.

With neither main French party able to act upon its leaders' reservations about monetary union, support for each began to erode. By the end of the 1990s, the far-right *Front National* party was becoming the one vehicle for opposition to the euro, even though disquiet among voters and the political class went well beyond its supporters.[13] In the 2002 presidential election for the first time the Socialist Party candidate—again Jospin—did not make it into second round while the *Front National* candidate, Jean-Marie Le Pen, did. Jospin lost because of a proliferation of candidates to his left, including the anti-euro Chevènement, who won significantly more votes than the margin between Jospin and Le Pen.[14]

For Germany, legitimating the Maastricht Treaty generated a qualitatively different problem. Ratification became a judicial rather than a democratic contest. The Constitutional Court upheld the treaty's legality. Nonetheless, it insisted that any act outside the transfer of sovereignty laid out in that treaty would not be valid in Germany, and that any further treaty change around monetary union would have to be compatible with German Basic Law. For the Court, the authority of the EU in any particular matter only had 'binding effects within the German sovereign sphere by virtue of the German instruction that its law be applied'.[15] The Court also marked out some democratic parameters for the EU. Allowing for the EU's legal order, 'the [member] States need', the Court ruled, 'sufficiently important spheres of activity of their own in which the people of each can develop and articulate itself in a process of political will-formation which it legitimates and controls, in order thus to give legal expression to what binds the people together (to a greater or lesser degree of homogeneity) spiritually, socially and politically'. Accordingly, there were, the Court insisted, 'limits . . . set by virtue of the democratic principle to the extension of the European Communities' functions and powers'.[16] This was not the first time the Court had ventured into waters suggesting German constitutionality needed to be an enduring component of the EU's legal order. But this decision had much more long-term significance, pointing to an EU where the German constitutional order would serve as a serious constraint on both the substance and speed of reform.

In agreeing the Maastricht Treaty, the German government had laid out formidable safeguards against Italy's accession to the euro becoming a live question. But for Italian democracy, the criteria for qualification for the euro generated an immediate political crisis, the resolution of which opened a path to the country joining the Eurozone. Within months of the Maastricht Treaty being agreed, the Italian First Republic collapsed under the weight of a massive judiciary-led investigation into the corruption that ran through the Christian Democrat and Socialist parties. In part, the structural cause of the First Republic's fall was the Cold War's end, with the Italian Communist Party's demise eliminating the justifying pretext for the corruption.[17] But the prospect of Italy's exclusion from monetary union played a crucial role too. Since the patronage networks inside the party system were financed by government borrowing, the First Republic's political dynamics were brutally incompatible with Italy joining the euro. In retrospect, Italy's finance minister during the Maastricht negotiations, Guido Carli, recalled: 'The Italian *classe politica* did not realize that by agreeing to the Treaty, it put itself in the position of already accepting a change of such magnitude that it [*sic*] would hardly leave it unscathed.'[18]

The technocrats who headed Italy's Maastricht negotiating team were under paltry ministerial direction. Effectively, they made the choices that privileged euro membership over maintaining the First Republic.[19] The senior official was Mario Draghi, then general director of the Italian Treasury, followed by Carlo Azeglio Ciampi, the governor of the Bank of Italy. For Draghi and Ciampi, what euro qualification required became a means of replacing the First Republic caste of party politicians with technocratic monetary experts who, bound by external fiscal demands, could reform Italian democracy.[20]

The First Republic reached its symbolic end in April 1993. After the Italian president refused to accept a decree from the Socialist

Party premier de facto legalizing illegal party financing, the old Christian Democratic–Socialist regime fell. The president asked Ciampi to form a technocratic Cabinet. This began a pattern in which the Italian president would terminate governments, as Giorgio Napolitano did in dismissing Silvio Berlusconi's in 2011. Ciampi's government was later followed by a second technocratic ministry led by another former *Banca d'Italia* official, Lamberto Dini. In 1996, Romano Prodi's Olive Tree centre-left coalition came to power after an election, but Prodi appointed Ciampi to be his finance minister. Since under the Second Republic executive decision-making was, consequently, relatively unhampered by electoral considerations, Italy could reduce its budget deficit to something approaching monetary union's requirements.

During the 1990s, this propensity towards euro-justified technocracy was not particularly politically destabilizing. Most voters wanted Italy to join the euro and were willing to make sacrifices to ensure it: Prodi's government was able to brand a time-limited tax increase on personal incomes 'a tax for Europe'. Indeed, the technocratic bias that allowed Italy to qualify diminished a secessionist challenge from the *Lega Nord*—*Lega*'s predecessor—which under Umberto Bossi's leadership argued that if Italy failed to enter the euro, the North's 'nation of producers' should secede.[21]

Nonetheless, the political demands of joining monetary union left a legacy. The huge fiscal retrenchment weakened the Italian economy. By 1997, unemployment was above 11 per cent and growth was poor. In avoiding a secessionary crisis, the discontent reappeared on the other side, with the South suffering persistently high unemployment. Moreover, being subject to the Stability and Growth Pact, Italian governments had fewer economic instruments to pursue interventionist policies towards the region.[22] Inside the euro, the debt the Second Republic inherited from the First could be serviced significantly more cheaply. But this necessarily circumscribed the space for Italian democratic politics, particularly for the centre-right. While under Berlusconi's leadership it played little part in executive government during the 1990s—Berlusconi served a seven-month term as prime minister in 1994–95—it was far from a spent political force. Berlusconi's commitment to euro membership was variable at best and near non-existent around the Stability and Growth Pact, especially since his whole personal operation was bound to the First Republic patronage networks. When he became prime minister again in 2001, just as the growth benefits generated by euro membership were disappearing, he began to lash out at monetary union, claiming in 2005 that 'Prodi's Euro has screwed everybody.'[23]

The French 'No'

Constitutionally, the enlarged EU of the post–Cold War world could not be the same as the Cold War EC. Facilitating the 2004 accession of the ten new states necessitated revisiting the rules for majorities in those legislative votes where each member state did not have a veto. The first attempt to deal with these issues was the 2001 Nice Treaty. This new treaty caused a legitimation issue in Ireland where a majority voted in a referendum against ratification. It also quickly became discredited.[24] Despite the fact that Germany had a significantly bigger populace than any other country and the new system in principle allocated votes to states according to population size, Chirac had successfully insisted that the Franco-German parity be retained. By giving Spain and, on accession, Poland nearly the same voting rights as Germany, despite them having half the population, majorities could not easily be mobilized.[25] Needing a way out, the EU declared at Laeken that it now sought a constitution to bring it 'closer to its citizens', less than a year after the Nice Treaty had been agreed and before a second a referendum had taken place in Ireland.[26]

Unlike Maastricht, the eventual Constitutional Treaty proved impossible to ratify. Ever since then, the fallout from that legitimation crisis has been a source of disruption within the EU.[27] In Britain, the argument pressed in 1972 and 1975 that membership did not have constitutional implications fell flat over an explicitly named Constitutional Treaty. For months, the British prime minister, Tony Blair, resisted demands for a referendum, only, in April 2004, finally to concede. Blair's decision prompted a succession of other governments in states that had never previously held a referendum on a treaty, as well as some of the new states, to follow suit.

For the French government, Blair's move was particularly problematic. Rejecting the referendum option had always been a risk for President Chirac. It had been a long-standing Gaullist position that constitutional change should only occur in France after a referendum. Indeed, this proposition was central to the way de Gaulle had conceived the Fifth Republic, and he fell from power after losing one in 1969. But until Blair U-turned, Chirac, fearing a French 'no' quite probable, held out.[28]

When asked their opinion, French voters did indeed decline to ratify the treaty, as a few days later did the Dutch. In both cases, the EU's enlargement eastwards and the prospect of Turkish accession played a part in the rejection.[29] But the two referendums also revealed a growing perception that the EU shut down democratic political contest over economic policy. In much the same way that the Gaullists had split over the Maastricht referendum, the French Socialists fell apart over the Constitutional Treaty.[30] When the vote came, more than half the Socialist Party's supporters voted against the treaty, as in the Netherlands did more than half of Dutch Labour Party voters, and within the centre-left electoral coalitions, these dissenters were largely working-class voters.[31]

The French 'no' doomed the Constitutional Treaty. But the EU's decision-making structure could not be left as it was without retaining the voting rules agreed at Nice. In response, the EU governments repackaged the Constitutional Treaty as the Lisbon Treaty and encouraged each other to eschew referendums. Former French president Giscard D'Estaing, who had presided over the convention that preceded the Constitutional Treaty, privately explained this strategy in blunt terms when he said that 'public opinion will be led—without knowing it—to adopt the policies we would never dare present to them directly. All the earlier proposals will be in the new text but will be hidden or disguised in some way.'[32] When the Irish government, constrained as it was by the Irish constitution, did hold a referendum and elicited another rejection, the other states offered a few concessions before Irish voters were asked to reconsider.

* * *

It was in Germany, France, and Britain where the longer-term fault lines around democratic legitimation from the Lisbon Treaty played out most emphatically. In Germany, the Constitutional Court's ruling over the Maastricht Treaty cast a long shadow. After the legislature voted to ratify Lisbon in June 2008, the German president, at the Court's request, declined to sign the law until the Court had ruled on a challenge to the treaty's constitutionality brought by a group of complainants that included the left-wing party, *Die Linke*. When, a year later, the Court did hand out its judgment, it raised the bar protecting the German constitution even higher than it had done over Maastricht. On the immediate legal issues, it declared that the manner in which the Lisbon Treaty had been ratified violated the German legislature's rights. Any attempt to move the EU from its present political existence as a 'union of rule founded on international law' to a federal state would, it insisted, require a new German constitution.[33] Without that constitutional change, it continued, 'the system of democratic rule in Germany' would be undermined. Accordingly, national parliaments had to have sufficient 'space' to deliberate on the 'economic, cultural, and social circumstances of life', not least in 'political decisions' that 'particularly depend on previous understanding as regards culture, history, and language'.[34] Within the EU itself, there could legally be no claim to policy competence that violated a member state's 'constitutional identity'.[35] For the Lisbon Treaty, the Bundestag and the Bundesrat could meet the Court's requirements by holding a further vote. But one month after German ratification was completed, the Greek euro crisis began, ensuring that the German government would soon have tacitly to decide whether, to save the euro, the ECB should start to act well beyond the powers conferred upon it.

For the French and British governments, the Lisbon Treaty posed a rather similar problem, although the fallout from the decisions made about legitimation played out with very different consequences. For French politicians, the question of what to do after the 2005 referendum defeat was urgent. Before any discussions about a replacement treaty could begin, France held a presidential election in 2007 and the two second-round candidates had to take a position on what should come next. The centre-right candidate, Nicolas Sarkozy, proposed a 'mini' treaty based on what he claimed were the uncontroversial parts of the Constitutional Treaty and opposed another referendum; the Socialist candidate, Ségolène Royal, advocated a comprehensive new treaty that would include changes to the ECB and then holding another referendum.

Sarkozy won. But what ensued at Lisbon was a treaty strikingly similar to the one French voters had previously rejected. Judging that another referendum would yield another 'no', Sarkozy decided to avoid one, saying that 'a referendum now would bring Europe into danger. There will be no Treaty if we had a referendum in France, which would again be followed by a referendum in the UK.'[36] Parliamentary ratification heaped pressure on the French Socialists. Despite Royal's election pledges, most Socialists in the National Assembly voted for the treaty. Again, a French party split over EU legitimation. This time it was Jean Luc Mélenchon, a minister under Jospin, who founded a breakaway party, the *Parti di Gauche*. In the first round of the 2017 election, Mélenchon under a different banner would take 13 per cent more of the vote than the Socialist Party candidate.

The two referendums France held in 1992 and 2005 and the one it did not in 2008 did heavy accumulative damage to the principal French parties. This left the French political class reluctant to contemplate more treaty change. Indeed, in his first major speech on European matters as president, Emmanuel Macron expounded on these dynamics. 'There was a time', he said, 'we twisted people's arms and said, "careful, we'll no longer be making proposals and we'll no longer be coming to ask your opinions". And we entered that "glacial period" when France, like many others, was afraid to make proposals because it was afraid of something taboo, something dreadful: a treaty change.'[37] The irony was though that Macron's bid for the presidency using a personal movement had only been possible because the fallout from EU constitutional reform so impaired the French party system.

* * *

For British prime minister Gordon Brown, the Lisbon Treaty was likewise a democratic burden. Had he put it to a referendum, 'no' would almost certainly have won. Faced with this reality, Brown repudiated Labour's 2005 manifesto promise to hold a referendum over the Constitutional Treaty, again with the spurious argument that Lisbon was qualitatively different from its predecessor.[38]

What was different in Britain and France was how the opposition party approached the issue of consent. The British Conservatives were opposed to both the treaty itself and parliamentary ratification. Under

David Cameron's leadership, the Conservatives offered a 'cast-iron' guarantee that if ratification had not occurred by the time a Conservative government took office there would be a referendum, and said that the party would campaign against the treaty.[39] Consequently, as one of Sarkozy's former EU advisers observed, the Lisbon Treaty's fate became 'a race between the second Irish referendum and the death throes of Gordon Brown's government'.[40]

Yet Lisbon's eventual parliamentary ratification proved insufficient to suppress the consent issue in British democratic politics. The Conservatives had also promised that if the treaty were ratified by the time they entered office, they 'would not let matters rest there' since 'the treaty would lack democratic legitimacy in this country'.[41] In the 2010 British general election, the Conservatives included manifesto commitments to legislate for an obligatory referendum on EU treaties and to negotiate to repatriate powers to Westminster. Against this backdrop, the British Parliament passed legislation in 2011 that necessitated a referendum on any treaty conferring new powers on the EU. If, as former Commission President Jean-Claude Juncker would later say, 'there can be no democratic choice against the European treaties', then the British response became that new treaties had to be authorized by more than transient parliamentary majorities.[42]

Yet the 2011 EU Act proved insufficient to repair democratic consent in Britain. Cameron's coalition government could reclaim powers back from the EU only in the context of a new treaty where the British government could table demands as the price of its support. But, even leaving aside French reluctance to contemplate any such thing, the very fact that Britain would now have to hold a referendum on another treaty rendered the other EU members less likely to embark on one. After his failure in December 2011—recounted in chapter six—Cameron had then to ask for singular negotiations for Britain. In deciding to gamble on putting their outcome to a subsequent referendum, Cameron put Britain's EU membership to a democratic probe it would not survive. Democratic consent to the EU in Britain, he said, in his 2013 Bloomberg speech, was 'wafer thin'. The referendum outcome would vindicate that judgement.[43]

That a referendum was supposed to settle the issue of Britain's membership of the EU raised profound problems around losers' consent. In part this was because it deepened the pressure on the

UK as a multinational state: in two parts of the UK—Scotland and Northern Ireland—the majority voted for Remain. But the weak losers' consent after the referendum showed how far EU membership itself could destabilize democratic politics. Some Remain proponents argued that a referendum could not legitimately end the legal rights attached to EU citizenship. This charge effectively cast the referendum as democratic excess, risking in its implementation executive dictatorship.[44] Indeed, some Remainers who wanted to contest the government's decision to pursue withdrawal via Article 50 of the Lisbon Treaty on the basis of the plebiscitary vote appealed to the courts in the name of constitutional rights. Predictably, these moves invited a counter charge of aristocratic excess. Seen from this viewpoint, those able to take cases to the courts were seeking to thwart the majority will legitimately expressed in an election. In this respect, Brexit showed that EU citizenship had created constitutional economic and residential rights that, being subject to the contingent outcomes of national democratic politics, were in the final instance unprotected. For those non-nationals without a vote in a referendum in which those rights were at stake, losing them was hard to accept. For those who valued their Union-level rights and could participate in the referendum, their very electoral defeat showed why they might be more invested in the heavily constitutionalized EU order than the democratic national order that left them on the losing side.

Since Maastricht, the EU has acted as a divisive force upon democratic politics in its member states. It has made democratic consent tougher to obtain and factionalized citizens around where democratic politics should take precedence over constitutional rules. Seen this way, the German Constitutional Court was both right and wrong in its assertions about democracy. Within the EU, the act of democratic authorization did remain solely with the nation state. But this was not because there was sufficient homogeneity within member states to talk meaningfully about a people who were socially, economically, culturally, or spiritually sufficiently bound together to have agreed in perpetuity to be part of a shared democratic political space. Indeed, in offering an alternative conception of a European political community to national citizens, the EU itself played a part in ensuring the increasing absence of any such unity.

Eurozone Creditor–Debtor Politics

For the democracies inside monetary union, the Eurozone crisis let loose a set of difficult dynamics around debt. Certainly, the Eurozone democracies were far from alone in experiencing class fury at the public expenditure cuts and tax increases, quickly labelled austerity, inflicted to reduce budget deficits so soon after banks received bailouts.[45] Debtor and taxpayer anger was manifested in the Occupy movement that spread from the United States to Europe. Independently of the Eurozone crisis, these protests played a part in the rise of insurgent political parties across Europe.[46] But in the Eurozone, creditor–debtor conflicts also involved inter-state relations. Northern banks had lent large sums to Southern European governments, corporations, and banks that from late 2009 could not be cheaply refinanced. When Southern Eurozone members were shut out of international capital markets, the subsequent bailouts primarily allowed debtor states to pay their Northern creditors, who then did not need bailing out at the national level. Meanwhile, since the Eastern Eurozone governments had pursued domestic debt reduction and their banks were not exposed, they contributed to bailouts for debtor states and creditor banks from which they took no benefit.[47] Politically, containing these conflicts required a Eurozone with harder relations between the member states, suppressing democratic conflicts inside the weaker states.[48]

Predictably, it was in Southern Europe where debt politics led to the loudest calls for democratic reforms and the most overt language of aristocratic excess. In 2011, maybe a sixth of the Spanish population participated in the 15-M movement. The protestors explicitly directed their anger at what they saw as a corrupt and dynastic oligarchy tied to finance that had corrupted Spain's democracy, presenting themselves as grassroots networked citizens claiming democracy back for those to whom it belonged.[49] Out of 15-M emerged a new political party, Podemos, that positioned itself as the agent of bottom-up democratic renewal. It used digital technology to allow thousands of citizens to take part in party decision-making. It also advocated debt reform to favour debtor over creditor interests and proposed what it called a citizens' basic income.[50]

This creditor–debtor politics erupted into Spain's territorial politics. In part, this was a matter of timing. In the Eurozone crisis' early months, the Spanish Constitutional Court struck down parts of the 2006 Statute of Autonomy approved by Catalan voters in a 2006 referendum, including a provision that recognized Catalan nationality. Under these already charged political conditions, the Spanish and Catalan governments came into conflict over the policy changes that might keep capital markets open for Spain while complying with Eurozone fiscal rules. While historically Catalan nationalism had been left-wing, austerity imposed from Madrid, allied to the fact that financial markets shut out the Catalan government from borrowing in 2012, generated separatist sentiment on the centre-right. In the November 2012 Catalan Parliament election, the centre-right party campaigned for independence for the first time and the left-wing secessionist party made significant gains.[51] The secessionist coalition that assumed power after the election held a non-binding referendum on independence in 2014, and then, after more parliamentary elections in 2015, another referendum in October 2017. After a 'yes' on a low turnout, the Catalan Parliament formally declared independence. However, the Spanish government refused to recognize the vote, beginning legal proceedings against members of the Catalan government and imposing direct rule that lasted until June 2018.

If Spain survived its secessionist crisis in 2017–18 by applying coercion to the problem, the rise of centre-right Catalan nationalism at the same time as Podemos, nonetheless, has made forming durable governments more difficult for Spanish politicians. There were two general elections in quick succession in December 2015 and June 2016 before a government could be assembled. At the second of two more elections in 2019, the Socialists took the largest number of seats but fell far short of a legislative majority. In January 2020, the Socialists finally formed a minority government in coalition with Podemos, by using abstentions from Catalan nationalist parties to reach a parliamentary majority.

* * *

In Germany, creditor–debtor issues were both judicialized and became a cause of fragmentation in the party system. Once the Greek crisis began, the German government sought to prevent a banking collapse. For Merkel, another round of expensive German bank bailouts after 2008 would have been politically risky.

Yet financing a bailout for Greece and later other Eurozone members also carried a domestic price.[52] In selling the bailouts as necessary for Southern European states while keeping German banks, including their dollar borrowings, out of the national political debate, Merkel obfuscated the actual creditor–debtor dynamics at work. To make these bailouts domestically palatable, she also had to ask for fiscal concessions from other member states, including the Fiscal Compact's new constitutional rules on borrowing.[53]

In the Eurozone crisis' early months, the Karlsruhe judges appeared to offer the German government breathing space over letting the ECB take more of the strain. In an important non-euro case, they set the bar much higher than over Maastricht and Lisbon for the claim that an EU institution had acted beyond its authority. When, later, they provisionally ruled that Draghi's Outright Monetary Transactions was legally and constitutionally problematic, they eschewed a confrontation by asking the European Court of Justice to pass judgment first.[54] In first looking at the QE case, they again appeared reluctant to instigate a crisis, even as they said there were 'grave reasons' for concern, and once more referred the case to the Luxembourg court.[55]

Nonetheless, the fact that the ECB had acquired powers that no one could reasonably argue were ordained by the Maastricht Treaty had significant repercussions for German democratic politics, especially when aligned to Merkel's decision to Europeanize bank bailouts. Opposition to the bailouts led a group of economists, lawyers, and businesspersons to form the AfD. The party's 2017 election manifesto declared that 'the principles of the original German consent to the Maastricht Treaty, which led to the introduction of the Euro, have been nullified'.[56] Although the AfD received insufficient votes to enter the Bundestag in the 2013 general election, that same autumn it did win representation in several *Länder* parliaments. Undoubtedly, fear that the AfD could emerge as a party to the Christian Democrats' right played a part in German finance minister Wolfgang Schäuble's efforts in 2015 to expel Greece from the Eurozone and his willingness to criticize QE. Indeed, at one moment in 2016, Schäuble lashed out at Draghi as responsible for the AfD's rise.[57] It was also AfD members, including one of its original pre-2015 founders, who were the petitioners in the QE case to the German Constitutional Court. When the Bundestag voted in July 2020 retrospectively to legitimate what the ECB had done, the AfD voted against the motion.[58]

How disruptive the AfD would have proved in the German Parliament without the 2015 refugee crisis is very much open to question. Certainly, the party began to win more votes once thereafter, and under different leadership, it embraced an anti-immigration stance and an anti-Islamic rhetoric around German national identity. But the AfD, along with *Die Linke,* also provided outlets for expressing discontent about the gap between Maastricht and the reality of monetary union, a discontent that was shared well beyond those who voted for either party.[59]

The toll imposed by the insurgent parties on German democracy was evident in the 2017 general election and its aftermath. The Christian Democrat and Christian Social Union bloc and the Social Democrats received only 53 per cent of the vote, compared to 67 per cent in the previous election in 2013, with the AfD and *Die Linke,* as well as the Free Democrats and the Greens, benefiting. This fragmentation in the party system made coalition formation more difficult than in the past. Since neither the AfD nor *Die Linke* were acceptable national coalition partners for the Christian Democrats and the Social Democrats would then accept *Die Linke* only in *Länder* governments, there were few viable options available beyond some form of grand coalition across the centre left and centre right.

But sustaining these grand coalitions also became a source of democratic disruption. The Christian Democratic–Social Democratic coalition eventually agreed almost six months after the 2017 general election took place left the AfD as the formal opposition. Thereafter, both coalition parties faced major difficulties. Concern that the Greens had become the second party in German politics led Social Democrat party members, in November 2019, to elect two insurgent joint candidates to the party leadership who campaigned against the prevailing grand coalition agreement. After Merkel resigned the Christian Democratic Party leadership, her chosen successor, Annegret Kramp-Karrenbauer, was brought down by a regional crisis about coalition formation. In the Thuringian state election in October 2019, *Die Linke* and the AfD polled more than half of the vote. To prevent another election after Merkel had declaimed that the formation of a government reliant on AfD votes was morally unacceptable, the Thuringian Christian Democrats had to vote for a minority government that included *Die Linke*.[60]

In the 2021 general election, grand coalition politics appeared to have reached its limits, with the two principal parties falling below 50 per cent of the vote, even as the Social Democrats secured significantly more seats than in 2017. Contrary though to what had happened in Thuringia prior to the pandemic, neither the AfD nor *Die Linke* were the beneficiaries. Indeed, the idea that *Die Linke* might enter government in a coalition with the Social Democrats and Greens appears to have pushed some Christian Democratic voters to stick with the party, despite the deep unpopularity of Armin Laschet, its candidate for chancellor. Instead, Germany was left with negotiations to form its first three-party government. Which three-party coalition, excluding the AfD and *Die Linke*, that would be was driven by negotiations between two parties—the Free Democrats and the Greens—that between them won less than 30 per cent of the seats and that took sharply polarised positions on German's debt brake and Eurozone debt.

* * *

For the French Fifth Republic, the Eurozone's creditor–debtor politics ultimately reasserted the older problems about the EU treaties and democratic change.[61] In winning the 2012 presidential election, François Hollande overtly attacked aristocratic excess, saying at one point that 'my enemy is the world of finance' and promising to impose a 75 per cent tax rate on those earning above one million euros.[62] He rejected the new constitutional fiscal restrictions monetary union imposed via the yet unratified Fiscal Compact treaty. He also attacked the de facto German veto on the instruments the ECB could use to drive down borrowing costs, saying that 'it's not for Germany to decide for the rest of Europe'.[63] Hollande's willingness to campaign against an EU treaty—albeit one constructed on an intergovernmental basis and formally outside EU law—exposed once again the tension between possible national democratic change and the EU's treaty-based constitutional order. Faced with the prospect of a French election derailing the treaty, Merkel intervened, declaring her support for Sarkozy in a joint interview with him on French and German television.[64]

Hollande's defiance quickly floundered under the weight of French borrowing costs, capital flight, and rising unemployment. Like Mitterrand, Chirac, and Jospin before him, Hollande turned back towards his predecessor's commitments. Although he obtained a large parliamentary majority for the Fiscal Compact, ratification caused some consternation within the Socialist Party, allowing the *Parti de Gauche* to seize on the issue. Like his retreating forerunners, Hollande then found the accompanying domestic reforms extremely difficult. Notably, his economy minister, Emmanuel Macron, resorted to pushing through labour market reforms, against a backdrop of violent protests, without holding a parliamentary vote.[65]

Hollande's presidency eventually produced a definitive crisis for the French party system. By his last year in office, Hollande was extraordinarily unpopular. His failure effectively destroyed the Socialist Party and, allied to corruption issues around the centre-right, produced a presidential election in 2017 short of a Socialist or centre-right party candidate in the second round. Without Macron's decision to launch a personal movement, *En Marche*, the French party system might have survived longer. But the decline of the duopoly at its centre was structural rather than accidental. Both parties had been weakened by Eurosceptic defections. In their inability in office to redeem the promise that monetary union was a move to a more French and less German Europe, they predictably lost votes to outright Eurosceptic parties, whether the *Front National*—from 2018 rebranded as *Rassemblement National*—or the more movement-style *La France Insoumise* (Indomitable France) party that Mélenchon formed prior to the 2017 presidential election.

Yet neither of the two principal parties could turn itself into a Eurosceptic party since, given the volume of French debt, exiting the euro would be too costly and call into question just why endeavouring to reform it on French terms had proved such a forlorn exercise. In this respect, Macron's decision to dispense with the party system to win the presidency had a logic beyond his own personal ambition: the main parties could not be vehicles for the political action necessary to make France a rule-abiding euro member.

But Macron's attempt at individual, charismatic rule beyond the parties to achieve an old ambition whereby French nationhood is realized through Franco-German leadership in the EU could not succeed either. Internally, this still required achieving economic reforms where his predecessors had failed in the face of protests and strikes. If he did not prevail, opposition would near inevitably continue either to drift towards *Front National* and *La France Insoumise* electorally or to intensify on the streets. For if *En Marche* represented a vehicle for citizens wanting democratic renewal of the party system, the *Gilets Jaunes* marked another for its effective destruction, with what started off as protests against green taxes moving into demands for democratic reform, including citizen-initiative referendums. Externally, Macron had to assume, against all past experience, that German democratic politics was biddable to French influence.[66] Although, after the 2017 election, Macron was spared a German government that included the liberal Free Democrats who were opposed to debt-sharing, the new Social Democrat finance minister in the grand coalition did not back his Eurozone demands. When Macron then had to make fiscal concessions to the *Gilets Jaunes* in late 2018, both sides of the French impasse came together. Any chance there was of making the Eurozone more susceptible to democratic political control relied on Macron being the president who in observing the Eurozone's constitutionalized fiscal rules could finally persuade a German government to change them. Instead, Macron became the president who excited exceptionally lengthy protests.

Macron's presidency became another example of how difficult the euro can make democratic politics when the distribution of taxation is at the same time circumscribed by international capital markets and offshore banking. Adapting the euro to changing economic conditions is limited by German electoral and judicial politics. The more governments, accordingly, pursue domestic reforms that hurt those materially dependent on state expenditure and who pay new taxes, the more they create domestic grievances that the principal parties— which must remain committed to monetary union—cannot absorb. Faced with the *Gilets Jaunes'* demands for more democracy and fewer taxes, Macron eventually sought to co-opt them into his own endeavour to govern France without parties. In early 2019, he began a two-month 'great national debate' with citizens around the country. But this local deliberation had to be on questions set out by Macron that ruled out higher taxes on the rich. When it was over, Macron gave a national televised speech explaining how the government would respond. He promised income tax cuts for the middle class and more provision for referendums. But courting more direct democracy cannot be an exercise in democratic repair when a significant amount of economic policy is either constitutionalized within the Eurozone, or constrained by the need for ECB monetary support to borrow cheaply in international capital markets. In this respect, the euro ensures that some forms of aristocratic excess, whether around taxes or monetary technocracy, are very difficult politically to touch.

*   *   *

Unsurprisingly, it was in Italy where the consequences of the Eurozone crisis for democratic politics proved most severe. That an Italian president would replace Berlusconi with Monti's technocratic Cabinet—as discussed in chapters four and six—was not an aberration, even if neither the ECB nor the German chancellor had intervened in government formation in Italy previously. As the external support the ECB offered via an asset-purchase programme deepened, so the space for democratic politics over economic policy narrowed further: as a condition of access the new government had to achieve labour market reforms on top of fiscal discipline.[67]

Unsurprisingly, Berlusconi's removal disrupted the Italian party system, producing another ascendant party that, as with Podemos in Spain, rejected representative democracy's parameters. The *Movimento 5 Stello* (Five Star) movement was founded in 2009 by comedian Beppe Grillo and an internet entrepreneur. It began by attacking the Second Republic as corrupt, dismissing its political class as the '*casta*', and arguing that what Italy needed was more participatory democracy in which citizens could be heard.[68] In the 2013 general election, the first it contested, Five Star won the largest single party share of the vote in the lower house Chamber of Deputies. Since it ruled out governing with other parties, its success required the centre-left and centre-right groupings, plus the centrist party formed by Monti, to form a government.

In winning enough votes to make the technocratic option more difficult, Five Star generated grand coalition politics. By the European Parliament elections in 2014, Five Star had also become a decidedly Eurosceptic party, arguing for a referendum on euro membership, and attacking monetary union as 'tailored to Germany and the financial oligarchies'.[69] Allied to a resurgence of *Lega Nord* as a pan-Italian Eurosceptic party—now just called *Lega*—Five Star made the euro a contested political issue in the Second Republic, even though there was no evidence that it, or *Lega*, had a coherent plan for withdrawal.

This rising Euroscepticism further deepened the tensions between Italian democracy and the Eurozone. After the 2013 election, the grand coalition government sought to navigate between the external need for ECB support and the domestic political need to put up some resistance to fiscal surveillance by the Eurozone institutions.[70] This dynamic led Berlusconi to withdraw his party's ministers from the coalition to reform his old party *Forza Italia*. After considerable internal turbulence within the centre-left Democrats, the young mayor of Florence, Matteo Renzi, emerged in February 2014 at the head of a narrower grand coalition government that did not include *Forza Italia*. On the other side of the pincer, this government was plunged into crisis when, in the summer of 2014, the Italian economy slid back into recession with no latitude for a fiscal response. At that point, the ECB had nothing to offer unless Italy applied for a bailout, but the unpopularity of the accompanying conditionality would have destroyed any government that asked for one. For there to be any chance of the ECB resuming asset purchasing, Renzi had to promise labour market reforms tougher than anything Monti had contemplated.[71] To all intents and purposes, this Italian policy shift became the necessary political condition for the ECB's move to QE in 2015.[72]

Of course, in offering the Italian government unprecedented support, the ECB deepened the structural tensions at work. Renzi's labour market legislation was met by large demonstrations and a general strike. While Renzi's coalition was dependent on the ECB to buy Italy's debt, with Berlusconi's party, Five Star, and *Lega* all outside the government, it still needed to attack the fiscal rules. In a confrontation in autumn 2016 over Italy's upcoming budget deficit, Renzi raged: 'What will Brussels say no to? Money for Amatrice [a town in the Lazio region hit by an earthquake in August 2016]. Money for schools? Two billion more for healthcare. They should tell us.'[73] Having sacrificed considerable popularity to the labour market reforms, in December 2016, Renzi then lost a constitutional referendum he pushed on reforming the Italian Parliament. His departure made the underlying stress all too visible. Only a government that the ECB, and indirectly Germany, could tolerate could receive QE. Consequently, some kind of grand coalition that excluded Five Star and *Lega* had to be propped up for as long as possible by the ECB. Indeed, any prospects that QE could end by 2017, as before Renzi's referendum defeat had seemed quite possible, disappeared.[74]

In the end, under the constitution, elections had to come. When they did in April 2018, the only plausible government was one constituted by the Eurosceptic Five Star and *Lega*. But to make this externally acceptable, the party leaders accepted that neither would become prime minister, a position that went to a non-elected law professor, Giuseppe Conte, and that a technocrat would be appointed finance minister. QE's end in December 2018 loosened the constraints on the composition of the government at the risk of escalating borrowing costs, only for deteriorating economic conditions in 2019 across the Eurozone to reignite the original problem. In August 2019, *Lega*'s Matteo Salvini ended the Five Star–*Lega* coalition and sought elections. He was thwarted when Five Star defected to the grand coalition, producing a Democrat–Five Star government still headed by a technocratic prime minister. One month later, the ECB announced it would begin another QE programme in November. Probably, Salvini's departure made QE's return palatable. But the return of QE without *Lega* also appeared to ensure that if the next Italian election put the party into government again, the Italian republic's debt-bearing capacity would be called into question, not least from the impact Salvini, or the far-right *Fratelli d'Italia* as a possible coalition partner for *Lega*, would have on German politics.

* * *

Achieved via a treaty that could not readily be reformed, monetary union placed immense strains on EU democracies. Some of the destabilizing dynamics were in place from the start. There was a radically insufficient political consensus to support its essentially German terms being constitutionalized across member states, not least given the general issues caused by the awkward relationship between national elections and EU treaties. Elections, especially in France, produced demands for change that could not be met. In Italy, the euro acted as a safeguard against a democratic contest about debt that if it had taken place would have risked a financial crisis. But although monetary union made Italy's debt serviceable, it also imposed a non-democratic straitjacket around who could exercise power and narrowed party competition between those who did. The ins and outs of a territorially incomplete monetary union pushed the constitutionalized single market into British democratic politics. As Hollande campaigned in 2012 against a treaty he was in no position to reject, so Cameron had campaigned in 2010 for an immigration target he was in no position to implement.

By reopening German politics to questions about the euro, the post-2008 monetary environment and the need to transform the ECB without the possibility of treaty change added more disruptive capacity to these foundational dynamics. The 2015 border crisis complicated further the politics generated by Germany's position inside the EU and the Eurozone. It turned the AfD into the party standing outside constitutional norms and post-war German nationhood on migration while laying claim to be the party of strict constitutional propriety where the euro was concerned.

In Britain, democratically expressed discontent prevailed only to produce more instability in the UK's multinational union. Elsewhere, democratic discontent with very different aspects of the euro had to be suppressed. In Germany, and especially Italy, this contributed to the move to grand coalition politics.[75] In France, this was not an option because the euro and EU treaties had so weakened the main parties. There, street protest politics grew, eliciting an at times brutally coercive response from the French state. In Spain, the Catalan question seems to preclude grand coalitions; even more than in France, it has produced considerable coercion.

Within the Eurozone itself, the structural pressure has moved towards a possible democratic contest over a new treaty that could accommodate the post-2010 ECB and the prospect of permanent EU-issued debt. Yet the very political difficulties treaties cause for EU democracies, the severity of the contest that would ensue, and the fact that the EU and the Eurozone are not aligned ensure that such a treaty would become the source of another serious disruption for the EU.

The American Repair That Wasn't

The strains on the American republic that would become overtly manifest in the 2016 presidential election were rather different. Democratic contest was circumscribed less obviously by the formal constitutional order, which was increasingly contested, than the oligarchic influence of money upon elections. The crucial question would become not what had to remain the same regardless of elections, but whether election results were accepted as legitimate, especially for the presidency. One frame for understanding this is how the difficulties around American nationhood intensified from the 1990s onwards and how they interacted with the problems of aristocratic excess generated by the post-1970s world economy.

Beginning with Bill Clinton's presidency, there was a serious attempt to repair American nationhood. Both Clinton and George Bush Jr's administrations sought to address the inequity of racialized home ownership that had been entrenched during the New Deal. In 1994, the year Clinton announced a plan to drive up ownership among minority groups, 70 per cent of white Americans owned their home while only just over 40 per cent of Hispanics and African Americans did.[76] Under the old New Deal framework, reform might have been achieved by direct federal action. Instead, Clinton encouraged private mortgage creditors to lend to households hitherto excluded from loans by securitizing the debt and mandated the two congressionally chartered but privately owned mortgage corporations, Fannie Mae and Freddie Mac, to buy mortgage-backed securities containing those loans, as well as purchase more mortgages given to low-income earners.

One outcome of this approach to the home ownership problem was to amplify the growing aristocratic excess in the American republic. Mortgage securitization encouraged financial corporations to borrow vast sums of dollars to purchase mortgage-backed securities that deepened their dependency on short-term funding markets, shaping the context of the 2008 bank bailouts. Setting ambitious targets for Fannie Mae and Freddie Mac encouraged a culture of accounting irregularities that yielded huge personal rewards for top executives. The two corporations then defended these practices to Congress, many of whose members' electoral campaigns were financed by individuals working for Fannie Mae and Freddie Mac and their lobbyists.[77]

The Clinton and Bush administrations' willingness to sacrifice American manufacturing jobs to integrating China into the world economy—as discussed in chapter five—reinforced the same plutocratic trends. In 1992, Bill Clinton campaigned on a 'get tough on China' stance, promising to oppose renewing China's then bilateral trading status, which had to be authorized on an annual basis. Under pressure from huge business lobbying, often supported directly by the Chinese government, he gravitated in office towards an entirely different policy.[78] After the 1996 election, evidence mounted that Chinese government agents had donated to Clinton's re-election campaign and Democratic candidates in congressional elections.[79] Unsurprisingly, as American manufacturing jobs disappeared, the federal government's China policy became perceived by many working-class voters in class terms as one where geopolitical cooperation, corporate profits, and campaign funds were prioritized over their interests.[80]

Meanwhile, the Clinton administration tried and failed to diffuse the political conflicts around migration and citizenship that emerged after 1965. Legislation Congress passed in 1994 and 1996 allowed for much-increased policing along the Mexican border. But this succeeded only in pushing migrants to cross into the country at more dangerous parts of the border. The non-citizen resident population continued to grow.[81] In 1990 there were 3.5 million unauthorized migrants in the United States. By 2007, there were 12.2 million.[82] Successive administrations' inability to control the border, despite electoral promises to do so, provoked anger, especially when some large businesses lobbied for more migration.[83] But on the opposite side, democratic pressure also grew to align the actually existing American population with citizenship. A political impasse ensued, exemplified in failed congressional attempts to reform immigration law: there was insufficient support for extending citizenship and insufficient practical capacity to tighten a more than 3,000-kilometre border. In the ensuing political space, federal–state conflicts materialized about where the responsibility for funding federally mandated entitlements for unauthorized migrants lay.[84]

If economic nationhood could not be resurrected to include more citizens or the citizenship issue settled, the need for losers' consent was amplified by the Cold War's end and demographic change. Absent the Republicans starting with their Cold War advantage on foreign policy issues and with the Democrats' post-1964 weakness in its previous stronghold in the South continuing, both parties struggled to command popular electoral majorities. In 1992, Bill Clinton won the presidency with 43 per cent of the popular vote. In winning in 2000, George Bush Jr accumulated around half a million fewer votes than his defeated opponent, Al Gore. In 2004, Bush did just reach 50 per cent, but a small change in the votes cast in Ohio would have swung the election to John Kerry.

The other federal institutions of the republic heightened the pressure on losers' consent. The bitter contests around Supreme Court rulings since the 1960s made each presidential election in part a contest about the Court's future political direction, undermining the idea that the Court's role was to uphold an agreed constitution. Redistricting in the House of Representatives—where congressional districts are refashioned decennially after each census—became embroiled in racial politics.[85] Meanwhile, the differences in population size between the fifty states were growing, accentuating the Senate's anti-majoritarian structure, where each state regardless of the number of voters has two senators. In 1995, the long-standing senator for New York, Daniel Patrick Moynihan, pronounced that 'sometime in the next century the United States is going to have to address the question of apportionment in the Senate'.[86]

These dynamics began to heap pressure on the legitimacy of the electoral college, where the democratic and federal principles of the constitution exist in hybrid form. The 2000 presidential election ended up in the Supreme Court. On this occasion, losers' consent held. But the fact that five justices appointed by Republican presidents used some awkward constitutional reasoning to stop recounts in Florida and hand the election to Bush could only deepen the conflicts over the Court's political direction and underlying legitimacy. These close elections further aggravated the tensions brought about by a labour force where some did not possess political rights. While unauthorized migration did not straightforwardly divide the parties from each other, it did divide the class coalitions within them, a reality reflected in the use both Trump and Sanders made of the issue as insurgent candidates against their nominal parties in 2016.

The 2008 election offered the impression of a respite. The victory of a candidate of mixed race promising democratic reform appeared to bury the ethnically restrictive version of American nationhood and ignited hopes that elections could bring a meaningful change in economic direction. Obama's sizeable electoral college victory, with a higher percentage of the popular vote than any president since 1988, also suggested that presidential elections could still produce decisive results.

But these hopes proved illusory. The 2008 result rested just as much on the relative turnouts of antagonistic demographical coalitions as those in 2000 and 2004.[87] Obama was more a symbol of the aspiration for political change than the agent of it. His biography could indeed be projected into a repurposed American nationhood, and his rhetoric sought to reclaim the republic's foundations for an inclusive American people.[88] In declaring his candidacy, he made democratic renewal his rallying call, appealing to those like him who believed that 'we can be one people' and articulating a faith in democratic repair made possible because the 'genius of our founders... designed a system of government that can be changed'.[89] But there was little if anything in his economic policy that distinguished him from his primary Democratic opponents. In office, his presence in the White House did serve as a transcendent symbol, but one that also appeared to make some white voters more responsive to contrary appeals to race and ethnicity.[90] If no leader in a democracy can personally be a vehicle of national unity without delegitimating democratic political conflict, the messianic hopes not infrequently projected onto Obama amplified this problem by tacitly denying it.

Even without the fallout of the 2008 crash, the conditions for a class politics driven by anger at aristocratic excess remained in place throughout the two Obama presidencies. In 2008, Obama raised massive sums of money from Wall Street.[91] In breaking away from the public financing system that placed limits on election expenditure, Obama ensured a subsequent money-raising arms race. The Supreme Court then accelerated this competition by its insistence in 2010 in the Citizens United case that corporations have a constitutional right to spend as much money as they like during elections.

During the Obama presidency, large corporations continued to employ those who had previously worked in the executive. Non-profit organizations and foundations set up by former politicians, like Bill Clinton, still financed charity work through donations from the same people who amply funded political candidates, as well as foreign governments. Large corporations that operated off Pentagon contracts and furnished a regular line of party donors still often failed to supply the military wherewithal for which they bid.[92] If the point of vast military expenditure was to win wars, the reality, by 2016, appeared to be a continuous supply of tax revenue to a small number of firms while American military forces struggled at best to impasse and at worse to disaster in the Middle East and Afghanistan.

Oil's Return

After disappearing as a potent domestic issue during the 1990s, oil complicated how the American republic could contain these destructive forces. Oil's overt reappearance began with George Bush Jr's bid for the presidency. Bush raised large sums of money from the oil and gas industry, and was repeatedly attacked as the energy sector's candidate.[93] He then made Dick Cheney—the CEO of Haliburton, a large oil field services corporation—his vice-presidential nominee, and a perception that business energy interests dominated the administration intensified through the build-up to the Iraq war.[94] The war's failure to reactivate Iraqi production decisively reopened the 1970s divide between energy-producing states, consuming states, and environmental groups. From 2005, the administration had to prioritize what had always been the domestic side of its energy agenda, namely increased national oil production. In his 2007 State of the Union address, Bush ventriloquized Nixon and Carter: 'For too long our nation has been dependent on foreign oil. And this dependence leaves us more vulnerable to hostile regimes and terrorists who could cause huge disruptions of oil shipments and raise the price of oil and do great harm to our economy.'[95] In 2005 and 2007, Congress passed two pieces of legislation—the second of which was named the 'Energy Independence and Security Act'—to remove some of the regulations on production and to provide considerable subsidies to oil and gas firms.

Before oil prices slumped and Lehman Brothers' bankruptcy, the 2008 presidential election was dominated by the energy issue. With oil prices reaching their near $150 nominal peak that July, Bush lifted the executive ban on offshore drilling. Although many congressional

Democrats would have preferred to prioritize the environment, they joined with Republicans to allow limited exploration.[96] For the Republican candidate, John McCain, the Congressional Democrats' partial opposition to more drilling and Obama's to suspending gasoline taxes appeared a potential election winner. A July poll showed that more than three-quarters of the electorate agreed that gasoline prices would be extremely or very important in how they voted. Another showed a large majority in favour of drilling on federally protected land.[97] At the Republican National Convention, 'Drill baby drill' became a Republican campaign cry, even though McCain himself was opposed to drilling in the Arctic wilderness.

The allure of energy independence facilitated by the shale boom made democratic politics in the United States oil-centric after the crash too. Well aware that many voters wanted lower prices, less corporate profit-making, and more action on climate change, Obama tried to face all ways in office. In March 2010, his administration announced it would allow new offshore drilling. But after the Deepwater Horizon oil spill in the Gulf of Mexico the following month, it reversed this decision. Caught between the price and environmental imperatives, Obama delayed for six years making a decision on whether the fourth stage of the Keystone XL pipeline— commissioned in 2010 to carry tar sands oil from Alberta in Canada to the Gulf of Mexico—could go ahead. During the 2014 mid-term elections, the Republicans used the issue as part of their successful effort to win back the Senate. But, holding a vote even before the new Congress sat, the Republican majority leader fell one vote short of the sixty required to force approval. In 2015, without any further elections to worry about, Obama finally announced he would not approve the pipeline. In his statement rejecting the pipeline, Obama suggested oil had become a symbolic issue divorced from its actual content on both sides, where the only frames for discourse were either the evil of the oil companies, or ill-informed passion blocking what economic growth and jobs made necessary. But he also introduced his own levels of disingenuousness by conflating the very different questions of 'clean' energy and 'home-grown' energy for both of which he wished to claim political credit.[98]

On the Republican side, oil played a significant part in the 2016 election, as it had done in 2000. It provided the central context for

Jeb Bush's party establishment bid for the Republican nomination. Following a similar path to his brother, Bush attacked environmental regulations and the export ban, saying he would increase state over federal authority on drilling and immediately approve Keystone. The oil and gas industry donated more funds to Bush's campaign than to all the other Republican candidates put together.[99] This vast sum of money and his dynastic name made Bush the poster boy for aristocratic excess in 2016, even as Bush presented himself as defender of the majority interest, protecting consumers from high prices and excessive environmental concern.[100] Bush's candidacy ended ignominiously. But making cheap prices and abundant supply the democratic cause was an obvious move that Trump would later exploit: even as a growing number of voters attached importance to climate change, there was no evidence that most citizens wished to pay more for their energy consumption or reduce it.

American Creditor–Debtor Politics

The immediate practical necessity of shale production and its dependence on vast credit helped shape a relatively broad political consensus in the United States around zero interest rates that was absent in the German-dominated Eurozone. Nonetheless, after the crash there was severe political conflict about whose debt the federal government and central bank's resources should support.

The Bush administration's bailouts for financial corporations, the Troubled Asset Relief Programme (TARP), produced immediate democratic discontent. At the first time of asking, the House of Representatives voted TARP down. On the right, the anger drove an anti-bailout and anti-borrowing Tea Party movement, which quickly challenged the Republican Party leadership.[101] Insurgent candidates won some Republican primaries in the 2010 mid-term elections and played a significant part in the party retaking control of the House of Representatives. For Tea Party activists, the Republican leadership had failed to protect citizens as taxpayers against both the banks' demands for bailouts and the federal government's own borrowing, which they charged was used to support non-citizens. Utilizing old American Populist rhetoric, the Tea Party often depicted unauthorized migrants as outsiders to productive citizenry and charged that the left wanted to extend the franchise to non-citizens to make their conservative votes matter less.[102]

In seeking both to change the Republican Party's direction and contest elections under the party's name, the Tea Party was quickly trapped in the American party system's aristocratic features. The billionaire Koch brothers, with family oil and pipeline interests, soon emerged as major funders.[103] Some Republican candidates for Congress, like 2016 Republican presidential contender Marco Rubio, mobilized activist support to run on the Tea Party label before moving once in Washington to follow the policy prescriptions of their corporate donors, not least on unauthorized migration.[104]

If TARP ignited clamour for the federal government to borrow less, the mortgage foreclosure crisis drove the dispossessed to demand the federal government bail out their debt as generously as it had that of the banks. But, unlike in the 1930s, neither political party offered a reform programme designed to protect mortgage debtors. The ensuing debtor discontent was manifested most obviously in the Occupy movement in 2011, with its quite literal attack on aristocratic excess in the slogan 'we are the 99 per cent'. These protests helped produce a younger generation of activists within the Democratic Party determined to move the party to the left, away from its entire economic trajectory since Bill Clinton's turn towards liberalizing trade with China.

Across left and right, a common belief that the American republic was neither politically nor morally equipped to respond to economic grievance was now palpable. This would have been a heavy democratic burden in its own right even without the racial fallout of the foreclosures crisis. The debtors who lost their property, including to systematic fraud, were disproportionately African American and Hispanic.[105] Consequently, what had been long-standing racial inequalities in wealth sharply increased after 2007.[106] In the five decades after the civil rights reforms that restored citizenship to African Americans in the South, American politicians had proved unable to extend the same economic benefits in federal support for home ownership to African American and Hispanic citizens that their predecessors once had to white citizens. Indeed, in attempting to remedy the problem by using internationalized banking to provide the money, American politicians had only made it worse.

Against this backdrop, African American voting rights also became severely politicized. A number of Republican-controlled legislatures, including in the South, pushed changes to state electoral law that were prohibited under the 1965 Voting Rights Act. But, in 2013, the Supreme Court ruled that two provisions of the Voting Rights Act restricting six Southern states' authority to make electoral law changes without federal approval were unconstitutional. Thereafter, some Republican state congresses, not only in the South, made new electoral rules to enforce voter ID requirements, cut early voting, and close down local polling stations, the effect of which was often to reduce African American and Hispanic turnout.[107]

As the contest over which citizens could in practice exercise their constitutional right to vote increased within states, the federal contest over whether the millions of resident non-citizens should be made citizens and what to do about the Mexican border continued. Another reform bill that included a path to citizenship for unauthorized migrants failed to pass Congress in 2013. After Republicans took control of the Senate and increased their House majority in the 2014 mid-term elections—in part by using the border issue—Obama issued executive orders to grant legal reprieves for some long-standing residents and extend visa programmes in a number of economic sectors. This move took the conflict ever more into the judicial sphere. The Texas state government and twenty-four other states pursued a case against Obama's executive orders. After a lower federal court ruled the orders unconstitutional, the Supreme Court, with only eight judges sitting due to Justice Antonin Scalia's death, tied 4–4 on the case in June 2016, leaving the lower court ruling standing. As on other some other matters, the American republic appeared trapped: it could neither resolve the citizenship issue nor control the border, and any attempt to do either only reminded its citizens how little they agreed about what it meant to share a democracy with each other.

Trump's Insurgency

Without the political potency of the citizenship and border issues, there would probably not have been a path for Donald Trump to the Republican presidential nomination in 2016. In utilizing the issue,

Trump drew from the deep wells of restrictive American nationhood. His language, whether it was his promise to build a wall on the Mexican border or his claim that a judge of Hispanic descent presiding in a fraud lawsuit against Trump University could not be impartial, all appealed to the ethnic version of American citizenship that had been approved judicially until 1952. This rhetoric necessarily delegitimated millions of American citizens and utterly dismayed many others.

But Trump's effective hijacking of the Republican nomination from extremely well-funded party insiders and his victory against Hillary Clinton also brought out other fault lines running through the republic. As well as blatantly appealing to nativism, Trump mobilized class discontent against aristocratic excess. He used China-trade policy, the bank bailouts, the Fed's QE programmes, business lobbying over unauthorized migration, and the Middle Eastern wars to present the American republic as oligarchic in form and outcome. That he openly partook in the aristocratic excess himself was in political rather than moral terms beside the point. Indeed, it made him like the Populares in the ancient Roman republic, who, while belonging to the senatorial class, used the plebeians' class grievances to compete with fellow class members for power.

Whatever the domestic implications of the geopolitical reorientation away from China, Trump's presidency was never going to be an exercise in democratic repair. The republic's oligarchic features offered him the opportunity to use the presidency to advance his business interests and bestow patronage on his family. During the general election campaign, he took significant sums of money from billionaire and corporate Republican Party donors, dismantling immediately his primary season argument that his wealth meant he could not be politically bought. To staff his administration, he turned in his early senior appointments to military generals. To pass legislation, he needed support from Republican members of Congress, whose agenda was not the large-scale infrastructure expenditure on which Trump had campaigned but the standard party fare of tax cuts and authorizing Keystone.

Indeed, Trump's relationship to oil politics encapsulated the distance between the part of his rhetoric slyly framed around democratic reform and the reality of governing in the American republic.

During the primaries he lashed out against his rival Ted Cruz as 'totally controlled by the oil companies'.[108] Unlike other Republicans who treated Keystone authorization as an article of faith, he said he would allow it in return 'for a big piece of the profits for the American people'.[109] On at least one occasion, he suggested that local communities should have the right to vote on whether to ban shale drilling.[110] Even during the general election, Trump, unlike Clinton, received very little money from the oil and gas industry.[111] But, in office, Trump's attitude predictably radically changed. At the suggestion of Condoleezza Rice, former national security adviser to George W. Bush, Trump made Rex Tillerson, the CEO of ExxonMobil—one of the world's largest oil companies—his first secretary of state. In his first days in office, he issued an executive order to begin Keystone's approval without any mention of the federal government acquiring a share of the profits. Any scepticism about shale vanished too. Indeed, like Obama before him, he wanted the credit for what he called American 'energy dominance' and a 'golden era of American energy'.[112]

Here, Trump was little different from any insider politician who might have occupied the White House during the shale era. Pre-Covid, he was well aware that his re-election prospects were at the mercy of decisions made in Riyadh and Moscow, since this era of supposed 'energy dominance' did not mean American shale companies determined prices if the other two large producers co-operated. Anyone else would not have demanded the Saudis increase production over Twitter. But affordable oil prices are what any incumbent American president facing election would wish for, as Joe Biden has already demonstrated, even as American politicians are able to insulate a good number of other policy areas from majority sentiments.

What made Trump's presidency singular was not so much what he did but his rhetorical and presentational relationship to the office: for many citizens his very presence in the White House was always democratically illegitimate and he regularly acted to aggravate that perception as much as possible. The fact that Trump did not win the popular vote, and that this was the second presidential election in sixteen years where the republic's federal features had prevailed over its democratic, immediately weakened losers' consent. Long before his extraordinarily reckless and shameful conduct after the 2020 election, those never able to accept Trump's presidency saw his inflammatory nativist rhetoric and administrative incompetence as evidence of how democracy decays into chaos without enforced constitutional constraints and norms.[113] For Trump's defenders before the 2020 election, some of their fellow citizens' unwillingness to accept defeat in 2016 was an attack on democracy motivated by class interests.[114]

Underneath weak losers' consent lies the problem of American nationhood and its relationship to federalism. Issues about American historical memory, and the founding of the American republic in particular, ignite disintegrative political passions. Accepting the confederacy's history as part of the collective American historical experience was part of the post–Civil War compromise. But, in a Union where former slaves became citizens, that left the language of American nationhood viciously restrictive. The republic has not yet found a story about the past that can imaginatively ground the idea of an American people that includes all American citizens. The one that once politically prevailed—where the republic's foundations were upheld as an ideal to be fulfilled in time—now appears insufficient. That notion was always at odds with the changes that time would bring in the demographics of who enjoys citizenship, as well as the sheer difficulty of economic reform in a republic so dominated by moneyed interests. But for many, any idea that the beginning of the American republic is irredeemable and cannot inspire democratic regeneration appears an attack on their understanding of what it means to be an American citizen. This clash of judgements is compounded by the fact that population changes mean that the Senate's anti-majoritarian structure weighs ever more heavily on political outcomes. Under these political conditions, not only do elections risk democratic crisis, but the constitution itself, including the rules of statehood, has become increasingly democratically contested.

Pandemic Democracies

As it did geopolitically and economically, the pandemic shone a harsh light on the long-term fault lines running through democracies. Again, the American experience was distinctive, and again what happened in the large European democracies, outside Britain, was inexorably tied to the EU and the Eurozone.

That governments had to take extraordinary decisions urgently made the early politics of the pandemic a matter of who had the authority to decide what. Executives, not legislatures or judiciaries, became pivotal. This exposed those democracies where the legitimacy of the authority at the centre was eroded. While, in the United States, the federal government might have been expected to use its powers to lead an emergency response, Trump was either unwilling or unable to mobilize the administrative state to devise one.[115] Left largely to their own devices, state governors asserted their states' autonomy. In the crisis' early weeks, California's governor, Gavin Newson, ordered a lockdown in the name of a Californian 'nation state' and bought medical equipment from China, despite Trump's efforts to intensify decoupling from Beijing.[116] When Trump threated to use federal emergency powers to impose a quarantine on New York and New Jersey that would have stopped transit in and out of those states, the New York state governor, Andrew Cuomo, said such an action would be 'a federal declaration of war' and Trump backed down.[117]

With the African American George Floyd's death at the hands of a white Minneapolis police officer in May 2020, all of the American republic's legitimacy difficulties were laid bare. In the first instance, this was obviously a matter of the legacy of slavery and the racial hierarchy that persisted long after its abolition. The protests, the police brutality, and the riots that followed, then, became inseparable from the contested legitimacy of Trump's presidency and Trump's cultivation of the emotion raged against him. For many American citizens during these months, whether there was a constitutional and moral right to protest during a health emergency was a function of neither state law nor the health risks but the political cause professed. Little sense that citizens shared the same constitutional rights was evident. Indeed, what those protesting the lockdowns or racial injustice perceived as legitimate about their own cause and its relationship to the emergency, they often denied for others.

In this political atmosphere, a presidential election took place where it was clear before a single vote had been cast both that the sitting president did not accept as a self-evident truth the democratic necessity for him to leave office if defeated and that his re-election would produce a political crisis. When Trump lost, he endeavoured to drag the republic's highest court and its legislature into his disastrous attempt to hang onto office. After some Trump supporters attacked the Capitol, Joe Biden was inaugurated as president in a Washington DC that looked more like an occupied military zone than the physical centre of the American republic.

In Europe, national governments were able to implement national lockdowns in the spring of 2020 almost entirely by consent. In the case of the German Federal Republic, where the *Länder* possessed the authority to decide on measures, the federal government still coordinated that lockdown. But the fractures in the multinational states were also very evident. In Britain, the emergency premium on executives over legislatures soon showed how flimsy the UK constitutional order was: asymmetrical devolution had empowered executives in Scotland, Wales, and Northern Ireland but left England without one. Once decisions about lifting lockdowns were required, the Scottish, Welsh, and Northern Irish governments' willingness to use their devolved powers on health and education to proceed differently from the UK government turned the UK government into a de facto English executive. Yet there was no constitutional authority for this outcome, nor in some ways any democratic legitimacy for it. As an effective competition of executives grew and the line between governing the UK and governing England blurred, in early 2021 support for Scottish independence reached its highest ever level.

When it came to economic recovery, the problem was conceptually the opposite for the weaker Eurozone states: like England, the Eurozone lacked a formal, sovereign executive, but in this case there was no possibility that one would arise without a new EU treaty or Eurozone agreement. For Macron, the emergency appeared an opportunity for reform. In demanding in the spring of 2020 that the German government agree to a common Eurozone debt instrument, Macron gambled, as Hollande had done in 2012, on putting France at the head of a Southern European alliance. But when he was rebuffed by Merkel, Macron retreated into the familiar path: he went back to Berlin to find what less ambitious measures might be agreed. Whatever the puffery that greeted the Franco-German proposal for the Recovery Fund, and the version of it the EU states agreed in July 2020 to implement, the EU has still not moved towards taxing its citizens to support debt.

Consequently, the political impasse around the Eurozone remains in place. Taxes have always required some underlying consent in a democracy. Historically, this first came—as discussed in chapter seven—from tying voting rights to paying taxes and encouraging all citizens to be creditors as well as taxpayers. By the 1920s, attempts to make the rich pay more tax helped destabilize European democracies. That under conditions of open international capital flows capital flight and the problems of financing debt reappeared was indirectly a crucial context for the euro's creation. But, lacking an accompanying political union, this transnational monetary union also still lacks a sufficient sense of shared political community to sustain common taxes.[118] Instead, Eurozone politicians reach for ideas about taxing corporate profits that internationalized and heavily financialized economies make extremely difficult to realize.

In this respect, the general economic obstacles to democratic repair evident before the pandemic still take a particularly acute shape for the Eurozone. Democratic politics has been divorced from monetary decision-making for some time, and in Germany's case even longer. Indeed, as a result of the Eurozone crisis, the relationship between the monetary sphere and political authority via elections became directly opposite to the usual requirements of democratic politics: only governments tolerable to the ECB could plausibly govern. After all the political disruption that followed from it, the monetary–economic distinction entrenched in the Maastricht Treaty, where the monetary realm is supranational and technocratic and the rest of economic policy is national and democratic, has near entirely broken down.

The EU Recovery Fund has acted as another catalyst in propelling these dynamics. The fiscal discretion the promised revenue bestowed on Italy led to the fall of the Conte-led grand coalition in January 2021 at the hands of a party that had not even existed at the time of the previous general election. Alarmed by Conte's plans for using the Recovery Fund, former prime minister Matteo Renzi demanded other ministers in the governing coalition be given more control over it. Renzi appeared to understand that the perception in Germany of how any EU fiscal support structure for Italy is being used is crucial to its survival, as it is to any chance that shared debt will become permanent. The end result of Renzi's moves was another technocratic government, with Mario Draghi as prime minister and non-elected ministers in all the large-spending departments. In good part, Draghi's appointment took the second Italian Republic to its logical conclusion: if only governments headed by a prime minister the ECB trusts can govern, then the best candidate is an Italian former president of the ECB.

But the accompanying political logic of grand coalition between the pro-euro parties did not go away with Draghi's appointment. The parliamentary majority supporting Draghi's government, as well as some of its ministers, came from widening the grand coalition to include *Lega*. This produced a government supported by parties that took 86 per cent of the vote in the 2018 election, leaving the opposition as the most Eurosceptic and anti-migrant party in the Italian Parliament, *Fratelli d'Italia*, which reached only 4 per cent in that same election. If for *Lega* this was a significant U-turn, Salvini's willingness to join the grand coalition at least temporarily showed how the EU's support structure for Italy can entice as well as circumscribe.

Once again, Italy's democratic politics was shown to be inseparable from change in the EU. Only opening up the EU's future to a democratic political contest over another treaty can undo this dynamic where what in the short term stabilizes Italian democratic politics risks destabilizing German politics. But constitutionally revisiting the legal order around the euro risks showing how weak the support is for a European political community based on some common taxation.

The now three-decade propensity in the second Italian republic towards technocratic prime ministers and finance ministers is unlikely to be democracy's general future. Nonetheless, Italy is revealing of the difficulties that European democracies now find in structuring political conflict around competing political parties except for ministries inside executives.[119] In Italy, as in other countries where there has been a move to grand coalition politics, citizens as voters cannot reliably choose who will make decisions. Although electoral systems based on proportional representation have long diluted this property of democracies, this occurrence is now not infrequent. In the case of France, with its presidential system, the same general problem manifests rather differently in the absence of the conventional two parties of the centre-right and centre-left. Under Macron at least, French democracy looks more like what Charles de Gaulle described as republican monarchy in which the conflicts within the people represented by the French state are not politically articulated within the institutional structures of the republic. This problem is exacerbated because distributional conflicts are intensifying not diminishing—as will be discussed in the conclusion. Unburdened by the demands of a supranational monetary union, democratic political competition in the United States and Britain still accommodates sharper conflicts. But this is in good part because the constitutional shape these democracies take is being quite bitterly contested. In both instances, albeit in different forms, this makes losers' consent precarious and the stakes of elections higher than democracies can easily bear.

Conclusion

The More Things Change

The dramatic nature of political events in 2016 from the Brexit referendum to Donald Trump's election encouraged much short-sighted political analysis. Each of these junctures marked a significant turning point, without which the present, geopolitical, economic, and democratic political world would be recognizably different. But they were part of stories that have been playing out over decades, and the disruptive fault lines from which they emerged were overt in their effects as early as the middle of the 2000s.

In several respects, it was 2005 that was the year that the world in which we now live first took shape. In neither Washington nor Beijing did the US–China economic relationship appear as a simple political given. By 2005, as for the last time American carbon emissions outstripped China's, both Democrats and Republicans were already charging that Beijing's trade and currency practices cost American manufacturing jobs. Protectionist pressure in Congress forced China formally to reconfigure its exchange rate policy. The Chinese leadership might have still judged the cross-Pacific relationship a net asset, but it was also already entertaining what would later become Xi Jinping's more conspicuous Eurasian ambitions. If energy security in a world militarily dominated by American naval power has been the primary logic of Xi's Belt and Road project, it was the second Iraq War that first focused minds in Beijing on China's vulnerability in the Strait of Malacca. Having persuaded Russia to build an Asian oil pipeline in the same month that George Bush Jr prematurely declared the Iraq War over, China, two years later, held its first ever joint military exercises with Russia.

In the Middle East, the American attempt to impose a new order was in disarray, yet there was no path away from the region that any American president was likely to take. In 2005, the Sunni insurgency in Iraq accelerated, ending Bush's plan to withdraw from the country and ensuring that the 2008 American presidential election would become the first of a series focused in significant part on the United States' 'forever wars'. This American failure in Iraq was one of the reasons that crude oil production stagnated in 2005, just at a moment when China's demand for oil was accelerating. As Mervyn King warned when, that year, he pronounced the NICE era to be over, the ensuing oil price shock led to serious economic trouble. It also represented another geopolitical boon for Russia.

Meanwhile, in Europe, the world made by the Cold War's end, German reunification, and the run of EU treaties from Maastricht had begun to unravel. It was in 2005 that the Dutch and French electorates voted against ratifying the EU Constitutional Treaty. Just to ask what would have happened if French voters had narrowly voted 'yes' in 2005 and Tony Blair had lost the referendum he had promised to hold shows how David Cameron's decision-making, far from being an aberrant beginning, was the end of a story about weakening British democratic consent to the EU. Would there have been a replay of the Lisbon story in France with all the consequences that has had for the French party system? Would the EU have been stuck with the Nice Treaty, as the German and French governments accepted that consent issues might play out differently in a member state without euro-denominated debt? Or had Britain voted no in that hypothetical referendum in 2005 would that lost referendum have become a problem solely for the British government—just as acting as an employer of last resort to a monetary union to which it did not belong would later become—and played out to an earlier Brexit?

By 2005, Germany had reached several turning points. Economically, the re-emergence of a long-term preference for export-led growth and a large trade surplus left the Eurozone structurally divided, with the deficit states stripped of the safeguard of devaluation the ERM had once provided. Democratically, the 2005 German election began the era of grand coalition politics: between 1949 and 2004, a grand coalition had governed in Germany for less than three years; after the 2005 general election, a grand coalition had, by the start of 2021, governed Germany for all but four years. Geopolitically, a reunified Germany was beginning to reshape Europe's energy geography. In 2005, Gerhard Schroeder's government signed the agreement with Russia to construct the first Nord Stream pipeline, threatening Ukraine's future as an energy transit state for Europe and diminishing Turkey's utility as one. In the same year, Viktor Yushchenko became president of Ukraine and set about trying to achieve EU and NATO membership while Turkey began EU accession talks.

As these plates spun, the financial markets appeared detached from the emerging geopolitical and economic risks. Monetary tightening might have ended NICE, but it would have next-to-no short-term effect on credit conditions for financial corporations. The Eurodollar markets had become their own world, detached not, since they offered various opportunities to politicians, from politics, but from the ability of central bankers to manage an economic cycle and disincentivize excessive risk taking. Only on 9 August 2007 did the mechanisms of the entire complex funding system on which banks depended dramatically break down. From that day, the international monetary and financial system ceased to function without systematic support from the American central bank.

That so many of the causes of the disruptions of the 2010s were in place before the 2007–8 crash reflects the fact that so many of their deeper origins lie in the 1970s. That was the decade when American oil self-sufficiency ended, the oil price shocks and the age of fiat money began, a revolutionary regime seized power on the eastern side of the Persian Gulf, and Germany became decisively dependent on Soviet energy. It was the decade in which Deng Xiaoping turned China towards international trading markets. In the United States, it was in the 1970s that the end of conscription marked a symbolic end of one form of American nationhood, as well as revealing how politically difficult it was for the world's dominant power to win land wars in Eurasia. In Europe, it was in the 1970s that the first attempt at monetary cooperation was undone by German economic strength, that the Italian First Republic started to rack up the debt that now so weighs down the Second Republic, and that national referendums first became the means used to legitimate the EU as a constitutionalized order. It was also in the 1970s that Eurodollar markets began to drive large-scale dollar credit.

That the latter parts of the 1980s and the 1990s were in good part intermissions from the intensity of these geopolitical and economic problems was largely the function of an energy interlude. Low oil prices, aided by the last years of China's energy self-sufficiency, yielded low inflation and reasonably high growth. Soviet and then Russian weakness, as well as Washington's ability to use first Iraq to contain Iran and then air power to police Iraq, allowed the United States to exercise power in the Middle East while fighting only one brief land war to free Kuwait. Separately, relative German economic weakness in the late 1990s and early 2000s meant that the euro's early years were fairly conflict-free.

Of course, these largely benign conditions did not eliminate the disruptive capacity of some of the forces that began to move before the 1980s. The immediate turbulence generated by the Maastricht Treaty and the 1992–93 ERM crises bequeathed systemic problems: at the turn of the millennium, the EU was a multi-currency union that contained a Eurozone larger than Germany had ever intended with an offshore financial centre located in the wider Union. Quite clearly, the EU also had a long-term predicament centred around the relationship between Union-level treaties and national elections. In the United States, the fact that the 1992 presidential election was won on the lowest percentage of the popular vote since 1912 and the prolonged attempt by congressional Republicans to remove Bill Clinton from office by impeachment were early indications of the path the American republic was on towards weak losers' consent.

By 2005, the interlude had passed. Into the array of fractures then evident came the 2007–8 crash and the Syrian War. The crash was in part a moment of domestic revelation. To take historian Adam Tooze's visceral language, the crisis showed 'an unpalatable and explosive truth that democratic politics on both sides of the Atlantic has choked on'.[1] It also proved another turning point in the emerging penetration of the world economy by geopolitics. The post-2008 world economy was more dependent on Chinese credit driving growth and Europe on Chinese trade and investment. If Xi saw this as an opportunity, the monetary environment also left the Chinese economy much more constrained by the Fed. The place of coal in China's huge fiscal response to the crash also decisively changed the international politics of climate change, simultaneously increasing the incentive for Sino-American cooperation and beginning a whole new round of geopolitical competition over energy, as pollution at home pushed China to aim for greener development.

By transforming the monetary environment around debt and financial markets, the Fed inadvertently both provided a remedy for the oil problem and deepened the economic and geopolitical disruption caused by it. Initially, many in financial markets assumed the result of quantitative easing (QE) would be the return of something else from the 1970s, namely inflation. But beyond asset prices, this is not what happened, rendering central banks' attempt to mitigate the debt burden with modest inflation a failure.

The absence of inflation, in part another by-product of the shale boom, did as much as anything else to upend the Eurozone from its original conception. If the short-term fallout of the crash broke the Eurozone as a unified credit market, the fact that an inflationary dread was written into the Maastricht Treaty at German insistence made repairing monetary union a lengthy, destructive, and incomplete exercise. It also helped ensure that Germany's already large trade surplus became larger still. For the wider EU, the Eurozone's rigidity directed the disruption towards Britain, standing as it did inside the single market and outside the euro while possessing the single currency's financial centre.

The humanitarian tragedy in Syria, meanwhile, was even more disruptive than the Iraq War. It yielded a caliphate that took the United States and some European NATO states into another Middle Eastern war. For the first time since the 1970s, it brought Russia militarily back into the centre of the Middle East. It encouraged Erdogan's neo-Ottoman ambitions. Once it became clear that Assad would survive, it pushed Ankara to reach an accommodation with Russia and bitterly divided the United States and Turkey. It left Turkey hosting several million refugees whom Erdogan turned into a weapon against the EU. Disappointment at the United States' retreats in 2013 and 2019, as well as fury at Turkish intervention, turned France against NATO. These events have bequeathed a new Turkish–French rivalry in the eastern Mediterranean, which now bisects an EU already riven with geopolitical divisions around Russia and China.

What happened after the crash and in Syria did much geopolitically and economically to bring together the separate sources of disruptive capacity already in existence. Where energy is concerned, this was predictable. The shale oil boom was dependent on the monetary environment, constituted a geopolitical shock, and restored to American democratic politics a contest between domestic energy producers and those prioritizing environmental imperatives. In causing oil prices to crash in 2014 and pushing the dollar upwards, it triggered currency problems for economies pegged to the dollar, including China's, even before the Fed's attempts in 2015 to re-establish some semblance of monetary normalcy.

Here, shale oil reinforced the complex impact of the post-2007 dollar-credit environment in which China's eventual vulnerability to a dollar shortage dented growth prospects for the world economy. This access to dollars for non-American banks and corporations also became more sharply a geopolitical matter. In making dollar shortage a problem that could only effectively be dealt with by dollar swaps, the post-crash monetary environment left Ukraine and Turkey—so critically entwined with the EU's geopolitical difficulties—outside the Fed's support structure and very vulnerable to a financial crisis.

In any circumstances, such interactive energy, dollar, and security dynamics would have been disruptive. But they also became tied to the changes around American and Chinese power. American military power in the Middle East weakened beyond the Persian Gulf, while its energy and financial power grew. China's power as a creditor diminished while its foreign oil dependency and carbon emissions replaced those of the United States in significance. As American power changed in both directions, American presidents could no longer simply maintain the status quo, as evidenced by Obama's attempted Pivot to Asia and retreat from Syria. The repercussions left the American political class divided about what geopolitically to prioritize. In partisan terms, these conflicts were most sharply structured around Iran and climate. But Xi's turn to technological and green energy competition in mid-2015 just as the presidential candidates were declaring themselves created the space for China policy to feature strongly in the election for the Oval Office the following year. Even if Hillary Clinton had beaten Trump in 2016, there was a structural logic pushing Washington towards a more confrontational China policy and one that complicated the deep disagreement between Democrats and Republicans over the Paris Accord.

In Europe, Germany was pivotal to the political turbulence of the 2010s. The monetary fault lines running through and around Germany that were evident by 2005 worked as conduits to spread disruption from the 2007–8 crash through the Eurozone crisis around the EU. After the crash, German power was strengthened by the economy's still widening structural trade surplus and dominance of manufacturing supply chains within the single market, as well as Berlin's capacity to act as a creditor and a tacit arbitrator of what the ECB could do. This rise in German influence inside the EU proved the proximate external origins of Brexit.

Since Berlin succeeded in forcing on the rest of the Eurozone its own near-constitutionalized approach to debt, German economic strength came to burden other Eurozone members' democratic politics. The French party system disintegrated in part because democratically expressed discontent about economic policy could change little. Offering himself as somebody beyond the party failures and seeking to legitimate an idea of the EU that his French heroism would restore, Macron could only reinforce the dynamics he purported to escape. Meanwhile, the long-term reality that the Italian Second Republic's debt is sustained by the euro began, with the ECB's asset purchases, to require overt German consent: hence, Merkel's intervention in Italian democratic politics in 2011 and the later convergence of technocratic and grand coalition politics in Draghi's premiership.

But German monetary power was also diminished by the transformation of the ECB, the debt-centric monetary environment, and the absence prior to 2021 of general inflation. Given what German citizens gave up in conceding monetary union, the loss of German control over debt, which had seemed constitutionally guaranteed by the Maastricht Treaty, necessarily spilled over into German democratic politics. Since saving rates were higher and household debt relatively low compared to other democracies, Germany's net savers were in a strong position in relation to net debtors. The German Constitutional Court provided an outlet for these interests to be forcibly articulated.

Within the EU, Germany also bore the brunt of the consequences of the American shale gas boom and Xi's strategic economic turn in 2015. In the misaligned EU–NATO relationship, Germany was the biggest contributor to Washington's resentment of European freeriding and had the deepest structural energy relationship of any European state with Russia. Having an export-centric economy, for all its strength in the single market, strongly oriented towards China and the United States, it was hardest hit by the deterioration of the Sino-American trade relationship, Made in China 25, and weaker Chinese growth.

Geopolitically, the German position became structurally exposed. It was unable to stop China picking off EU members for deeper economic associations. Yet its own singular trade and investment relationship with China and the place of Germany in China's land trade routes into Europe very much contributed to making China a growing source of EU division. It became reliant in dealing with Russia on a security alliance that in its European formation was no longer a priority in Washington and which German decision-making over energy pressurized, not least in relation to the East European states NATO is supposed to protect. Without significant military capacity, Germany's land and sea links to Eurasian markets must be made physically secure by one or both of the United States or China.

Germany also became the arbiter of the EU's policy towards Ankara at a time when Turkey proved a conduit for disruption moving from the Middle East into Europe. Without events around the 2015 refugee crisis, the problem of Britain's EU membership might well have been suppressed for longer, or indeed worked out to a different conclusion. The post-2016 geopolitical conflicts involving Turkey in North Africa, the Middle East, and the eastern Mediterranean—all of which were connected to Turkey's foreign energy dependency—made the EU's response to this large state on its borders a matter of increasingly fierce contest, not least between Berlin and Paris.

The Covid-19 emergency accelerated much of the disruption flowing from all these fault lines. Much more QE was needed to stabilize financial markets, compensate for the absence of corporate cash reserves, and support a massive expansion of government debt. What was the shale-driven accommodation between oil rivals Saudi Arabia and Russia first imploded and then, in a world where every oil-producing economy is vulnerable to low prices, had to be put back together again from Washington. Turkey's exclusion from the list of additional states the Fed took into its embrace during the dramatic dollar shortage crisis in March 2020 pushed it back into an acute financial crisis. It was in this economic context that Erdogan took his watershed step in the summer of 2020 over Hagia Sophia, adding a cultural dimension to deteriorating Franco-Turkish relations in the eastern Mediterranean.

Beyond the Fed's willingness to open a direct line of dollar credit, what trust remained in the Sino-American relationship shattered, and Britain's decoupling from China sharpened. Already fragmenting in the hyper-geopolitically charged world economy ushered in by Made in China 25 and the Trump administration's response, global manufacturing supply chains were overwhelmed by governments' desperate desire for greater security of production. With the pandemic, politicians in Western democracies added vaccines and medical equipment to their emerging industrial strategies centred on green energy and high-tech manufacturing. As Sino-American rivalry escalated, Germany's waning capacity to shape the EU around its economic interests was exposed further. Although, with the help of the Commission, Merkel forced through the EU–China investment agreement in December 2020, it took only a few months for its weak foundations to unravel.

Almost certainly, the pandemic was decisive in ending Trump's presidency. It also deepened the tension around whether the United States could hold a peaceful election. After the attack on Congress, Biden's inauguration simultaneously appeared a respite for the republic and, in its military backdrop, a shocking indictment of the state of American democratic politics. At home, the Biden administration took advantage of the monetary space created by QE Infinity to pass legislation authorizing massive amounts of federal expenditure.

Nonetheless, in the first year of Biden's presidency, there was no evidence of a geopolitical reset on China. That the EU responded to Biden's imminent arrival by signing an investment deal with China suggested that Merkel, at least, saw the change in power in Washington as, in the final instance, incidental. That the Biden administration could infuriate the French over the Australia-UK-US security pact agreed in September 2021 at least as much as any single act of its predecessor had done led to much the same judgement being made in Paris.

The question of how far American naval power in the Persian Gulf must still be matched by some minimal deployment of land and air power in Iraq is also likely to prove just as difficult to resolve for the Biden administration as its two predecessors, even as Biden promised in July 2021 to end US combat operations by the end of that year. Any subsequent descent of Iraq into instability will force decisions about whether to use the advisory troops that remain and strain relations with Paris, which remains firmly wedded to a military fight against ISIS in the country. It will do so as the debacle of the final American withdrawal from Afghanistan has reinforced the perception in some European capitals that the United States is extremely cavalier about its decision-making over Europe's neighbourhoods.

On climate, Biden immediately signalled his desire for change by returning the United States to the Paris Accord, revoking the Keystone pipeline's permit, and making green energy jobs central to the large infrastructure spending bill he sent to Congress. But this energy policy change was also born of the geopolitical fear that, as he told a group of senators, 'if we don't get moving, they [the Chinese] are going to eat our lunch'.[2]

Across the Atlantic, the move to the Recovery Fund and the decision by the German Constitutional Court that pushed the German government to propose it have intensified the pressures that arise inside the EU and Eurozone. They have also escalated the move away from party-structured democratic political conflict in Italy. Absent an actual collapse, the Eurozone states have gone too far monetarily to return to debt denominated in national currencies. Logically, this should propel the Eurozone towards fiscal union with accompanying democratic political institutions to make decisions about debt and taxes. Yet the conflicts around the Recovery Fund suggest that a politics that would drive such a change is still absent. What politically remains of nationhood in European democracies may well be insufficient to support a tax state, and the national-citizen creditor cannot be recovered. But there is no evidence of a belief in, or acquiescence to, an idea of a people that could legitimate Eurozone-level taxes on citizens and no institutions representing a democratic people that could authorize them. To be an EU citizen is to be free of tax obligations; that cannot change without either tangling up the Eurozone further with the wider EU, or radically reforming the EU's constitutional order and seeking troublesome national democratic legitimation for that change, nowhere more so than in Germany.

Hitting after Britain's formal departure from the EU but before the transition period that kept the country inside the single market had ended, the pandemic briefly appeared capable of reopening the terms of Brexit. But under new leadership, the Labour opposition withdrew from acting as a fulcrum for those in Parliament who want to keep Britain more closely aligned with the EU. This broader consensus over Brexit has not stabilized British politics. The relatively free internal hand Boris Johnson's government had to pursue a minimalist trade agreement with the EU only heaped pressure on the Union in relation to Northern Ireland at the same time as the pandemic was exposing just how deep the constitutional difficulties around the Union run and, temporarily at least, increased support in Scotland for independence. If the comparative British vaccine success in early 2021 makes it harder for those who want to realign Britain to the EU, the fault lines in the UK Union and Britain's future relationship with the EU are inseparable, especially in regard to Northern Ireland. Indeed, under the Biden presidency, the form Brexit has taken makes Northern Ireland a broader geopolitical burden for Britain in a world in which almost all geopolitical predicaments connect.

* * *

The pandemic has been both a catalyst for substantial change and part of a continuum of the older disruption. This is perhaps particularly true around energy, where several Western governments had sought in 2019 to accelerate energy change and the Biden administration, propelled into office by the pandemic and events during it, then joined them. Green ambitions in Western countries appear simultaneously directed at the climate crisis, Made in China 25, weak growth, and democratic stability.

Geopolitically, an energy change will necessarily result in upheaval. If Britain was the power that climbed to dominance during the age of coal and the United States the power that ascended during the age of oil and coal, the spectre haunting Washington is that without a decisive American strategic turn to renewables and electrification, the new energy age that depends on metals and minerals will belong to China. For the EU, there is the hope that green energy will prove an escape from the world of oil and gas that through the twentieth century did so much to weaken the European powers.

Economically, large-scale green investment justifies a turn towards big fiscal stimuluses, after a decade in which relying on monetary policy to boost financial markets, lower government borrowing costs, and alleviate the oil crisis could not restore higher growth. In recreating manufacturing jobs and swelling the construction sector, green-driven growth, in principle, offers the prospect of a higher return to labour. Even if a considerable volume of the investment required in technologies like carbon capture is commercially unviable, this need not matter if it is part state-funded and the necessary government borrowing is supported by central banks.

Democratically, the possible political pay-offs include a new version of economic nationhood. Joe Biden began his presidency talking about green energy as a national project in the same way that Nixon and Carter framed energy independence in the 1970s. The president he obviously wanted to emulate was Franklin Roosevelt. In Britain, one apparent objective of Boris Johnson's frequently expressed ambition to turn Britain into the 'Saudi Arabia' of offshore wind power is to reintegrate the east coast Scotland with the east coast of England: it was, of course, North Sea oil that fuelled the rise of Scottish nationalism. For the EU, the energy union in place since 2015 is supposed to serve as a collective project of economic modernization, starting from the premise that for energy there can be a singular European economy.[3]

It is the present monetary environment that has established the conditions for the attempted energy revolution. Compared to the aftermaths of both the 2007–8 crash and the 2015 Paris Climate Accord, Western governments—most consequentially those in Washington and Berlin—are much more confident than they were about the latitude for sovereign borrowing, albeit the politicians in the two capitals are operating on rather different fiscal scales. The Fed's de facto return to QE in September 2019 proved a decisive turning point for the whole world economy; that repudiation of any path back to monetary normalcy was buttressed six months later by QE Infinity. Meanwhile, the German Constitutional Court's attempt in May 2020 to constrain the ECB's return to QE shifted the German government's perspective to allow the EU, albeit modestly and without a tax base, to act as a sovereign debtor. Strikingly, the terms enshrined in the EU Recovery Fund tied a quarter of all the money available to member states to green transition projects.

Nonetheless, the predicaments that shaped the first two decades of the twenty-first century remain in all respects extant. The very geo-political motivation for accelerating green energy investment will intensify the Sino-American rivalry. Most obviously, the more the United States succeeds in breaking its dependency on Chinese manu-facturing supply chains, the more it will elicit a reaction from Beijing. As China expands its domestic markets to compensate, there will be little left of the world economy that is not permeated by the Sino-American geopolitical rivalry. All states caught in it will have to treat maritime transportation as a matter of economic security. In Eurasia, this will politicize further the rail routes China has pursued as part of its transcontinental land Belt. Around climate, China's implicit weapon in this emerging world will be its capacity to burn coal, despite the huge domestic incentives it has created around pollution alone to move away from doing so.

The geopolitical dynamics that green energy creates will coexist with those long generated by oil and gas. Since China will continue to be reliant on oil from the Middle East, and since the Pakistani part of China's Eurasian Belt can be only a partial hedge against China's vulnerability in the Strait of Malacca, China still has energy reasons to fear American military and financial power. China's Middle Eastern dependency also will make it hard for the United States to withdraw from the Persian Gulf. The geopolitical ramifications of this old energy reality could not have been made clearer when, in March 2021, China and Iran struck a twenty-five-year economic partnership, including a Chinese commitment to large-scale investment in Iran's oil and gas sectors. Just as Iran was pivotal to Britain's ability to win the European imperial competition over the Middle East, so it will still continue to be of crucial importance as governments face up to the difficulties of relying on oil and gas while trying to leave them behind.

For the EU, expediting green energy is unlikely to be unifying. As three decades of ongoing conflict over gas supply and transportation have demonstrated, the EU's authority in energy policy is weak and the member states are unlikely to make common judgement about where national interests lie. Again, German politics, this time around nuclear power, makes unity difficult.[4] Given its anti-nuclear position alone, Germany cannot unwind its gas dependency on Russia with any alacrity. The Russian–German gas relationship ensures that the long-standing energy incoherencies around NATO will persist: they will do so as Russia continues its bid to cut Ukraine loose from its gas transit system. In suddenly moving in May 2021 to rescind sanctions on Nord Stream 2, Biden decided to accept German defiance on Russian gas as a means of leveraging concessions about China, at the cost of deeply angering NATO's Eastern European members. But Germany's trade and investment relationship with China and de facto participation in China's land Belt now runs too deep to be readily reversed, even if there were a German government willing to depart from its predecessors' insistence that German energy and commercial interests come before geopolitical alignments. This German commitment is a significant constraint on France's capacity to pursue a strategic role in the Indo-Pacific, a reality indirectly made clear by France's humiliation over the Australia-UK-US defence alliance.

Where Turkey is concerned, there are no available options that will not aggravate at least some of the multiple problems the EU and NATO face. Turkey's economic development through the 2010s was coal-centric. It has not ratified the Paris Climate Accord and did not join the flurry of governments making a commitment to carbon neutrality during 2019 or 2020. In reorienting Turkey back towards the country's geopolitical foundations in the Lausanne Treaty, Erdogan has increasingly deployed extraordinarily aggressive revanchist language about oil and gas.[5]

The dysfunctional dynamics generated by the geographical and financial conditions around oil production cannot be undone. Where supply is concerned, shale oil was always only a medium-term remedy to the stagnation in conventional output. If investment in the oil sector in pursuit of higher-cost supply is not resurrected, the world economy will, for the next few decades, be as dependent on expensive oil from the Middle East and Russia as it became in the 2000s. The return of high prices will in principle incentivize investment, but only if there is also a less critical attitude from investors to fossil fuels. Higher prices will, meanwhile, seriously constrain economic growth and once again destroy demand, causing instability in oil–producing countries, not least Iraq. The old problems that reliance on OPEC Plus will reinvigorate will play out at the same time as the cartel's members need to adjust to the huge medium- to long-term changes that competition for oil from electricity in the transportation sector will bring.

Economically, overall energy costs will rise and, once again, act as an inflationary pressure. Gas prices in Europe are particularly vulnerable to issues with Russian supply and transit, whether technical or generated by Putin's willingness to use gas as a blunt strategic instrument. Without major breakthroughs on battery storage, there is no guarantee that electricity powered by renewables can escape an inflationary dynamic. Whatever the low unit costs of producing solar- or wind-powered electricity, at the system level—especially in those places, like Germany, where renewables are a significant proportion of the sector but the weather is unpropitious—the inefficiencies of intermittent renewable capacity have thus far often yielded higher electricity prices for consumers.

It is likely that this energy-driven inflation will eventually unsettle the bond markets and make borrowing more expensive for governments. Already in February 2021, investors sold off US Treasury bonds on the expectation of an inflation spike as the American economy reopened. Investor doubts were nowhere near sizeable enough to change the super-benign monetary and financial environment that makes massive government borrowing possible. Nonetheless, the fact that the Biden administration's $2 trillion infrastructure bill published a month later included substantial tax increases suggests that even in Washington a belief prevails that sovereign borrowing still requires some kind of tax base. Whether the 2020 financial crash will be a warning that there are still limits in the world of QE-backed bond markets, or suggests that central banks still have considerable policy arsenal left before a debt reckoning arrives, remains to be seen.

Politically, energy consumption will invariably cause fierce new distributional conflicts that will reinforce the old ones. This is in part an issue of how the shift to green energy and electrification will be financed and incentivized: in France, the *Gilets Jaunes'* response to the diesel tax showed dramatically that the problem of losers' consent is not confined to elections. It is also a matter of the substantive shape of the energy future. As electricity is decarbonized and the energy presently provided directly by oil and gas is replaced with electricity, there is no a priori reason to think that energy can be consumed at the same aggregate rate. As Angela Merkel acknowledged in a speech in January 2020, energy change 'means turning our backs on our entire way of doing business and our entire way of life'.[6]

Personal transportation, in particular, will become a site of political conflict. Electric vehicles are some distance away from being the equivalent of Henry Ford's Model T. The future could well entail a return to the pre-Fordist world where car ownership was a luxury good and a source of class resentment.[7] At some point, the difficulties around oil and the difficulties of electrifying the transportation sector will meet. As the distributional implications for personal energy consumption become clearer, how carbon neutrality should be achieved—not least how much carbon can be offset rather than eliminated—will move beyond governments announcing targets into the realm of electoral contest. In those Eurozone democracies that struggle to structure much economic conflict in the electoral contests between parties, there will be pressures that pull in the opposite direction from the need to minimize macro-economic dissensus.

Here, there is considerable potential for geopolitics to continue to fuel democratic disruption. Since winning a competition with China over electric vehicles has become a matter of technological prowess, governments and investors appear to be pushing the sector regardless of the democratic political risks attached to minority car ownership. Economically, green energy and electrification also are not panaceas that will curtail the wider predicaments of the last few decades. Where they are pursued as growth strategies in economies in which manufacturing has been particularly hollowed out, as in Britain, or in democracies, as in the United States, riddled with aristocratic excess from the relationship between politicians and corporate lobbying and campaign donations, they may well reinforce old problems. If past national economic weaknesses mean foreign companies dominate markets, it is far from clear how many domestic jobs will be generated: in Scotland, where, thanks to the volume of wind, the proportion of electricity generated by renewables is extremely high, many fewer jobs have been created by the transition than was hoped.[8] Meanwhile, large-scale infrastructure projects are open invitations to cronyism when contracts are awarded: the Obama administration's provision of funds to a huge construction project to give California a high-speed railway produced not a new public transport system for the state but a bonanza for consulting firms.[9]

In approaching the energy revolution, politicians in Western democracies, and the investors who started in 2019 to abandon fossil fuels, have made a wager that yet to be invented technology will allow much about present material conditions to be replicated with different energy sources. To succeed, this technology will have to facilitate an energy revolution, leaving nuclear power aside, in which lower-density primary energy supplants higher-density energy.[10] Thus far, renewable energy has increased overall energy consumption rather than replacing fossil fuel energy consumption. Indeed, since 1995—the year of the first United Nations climate summit—primary coal consumption has risen by more than two-thirds, oil consumption by more than a third, and gas by more than four-fifths.[11] While most Western countries have seen falls in oil consumption and some also large drops in coal consumption, this is in part the consequence of offshoring significant amounts of industrial production to Asia. For the moment at least, the attempted energy revolution is also entirely reliant on the fossil fuel energy inputs it seeks to replace, as well as potentially scarce materials like rare earth metals. It is more likely that there will be a long energy transition than a rapid one. In one sense perhaps, this outlook is nothing new: uncertainty, hoping for the best, and investing with a 'can-do' mindset have always been the basis of capitalist economies. But, since energy is the foundation of all economic activity, including the production of food, and is subject to the laws of physics, needing technological innovation in energy is quite a different requirement. There is already a considerable history going back to the 2000s of governments and corporations unveiling plans for fossil fuel–free energy that have proved near entirely fanciful.[12]

To mitigate against the possibly destructive nature of the politics to come, collective understanding needs to catch up with what the conjunction of physical realities about energy and the realities of climate change entails. Careening between the ideas of technologically driven salvation and an inescapable *Götterdämmerung* is a hopeless response. To contain the specific predicaments that the energy revolution will both generate and reinforce, governments will have to decide on what concurrent risks must be taken in relation to different time scales. Those decisions will invite geopolitical conflict, including over the territory where critical resources are located. In Western democracies, politicians will need to make palatable the likely sacrifices demanded of citizens, without entrenching further aristocratic excess. Both the biosphere and the application of energy impose limits, even as human beings must push against them. In a nonphysical form, they also exist for democracies, as for any other site of political order. How, within those limits, democracies can be sustained as the likely contests over climate change and energy consumption destabilize them will become the central political question of the coming decade.

Afterword 2022

War

In the early hours of 24 February 2022, Russian troops entered Ukraine. Later that day, the Russian navy captured Snake Island in Ukraine's Black Sea waters. When the news broke, oil and European gas prices soared.

This was the world of war in Europe. In Germany, where European peace had been the historical condition of reunification, it had already been a desperate few weeks. Although American intelligence had warned, since the previous autumn, that a Russian attack was coming, the German government had clung to the hope that diplomacy could prevail. On 7 February, Olaf Scholz, who had become chancellor just eight weeks before, was in Washington, DC. There, he heard Joe Biden declare that if Russia invaded, 'we will bring an end to [Nord Stream 2]'.[1] A week later, Scholz travelled to Kyiv, where he pressurized the Ukrainian president, Volodymyr Zelenskyy, to accept the unimplemented Minsk 2 peace accords, agreed in 2015, for the two separatist regions of Donetsk and Luhansk. The following day, Scholz met Vladimir Putin, tweeting afterwards: 'working for peace is our goddam duty' and 'lasting security cannot be achieved without Russia'.[2] Undeterred, Putin recognized Donetsk and Luhansk as independent states. Reportedly furious at the Kremlin's move, Scholz requested a reassessment of whether Nord Stream 2's operation was compatible with German gas security.[3]

On the invasion, the stakes for Germany moved from one unopened pipeline to its fifty-year commitment to *rapprochement* with Moscow. Within seventy-two hours, Scholz promised to send German weapons to Ukraine, establish a €100 billion fund to increase military expenditure, and end energy dependency on Russia by opening the country to sea-borne gas. Since Putin had, Scholz told the German parliament, 'demolish[ed] the European security order that had prevailed for almost half a century since the Helsinki Final Act' in 1975, everything had changed. 'We are', Scholz said, 'living through a watershed era (*eine Zeitenwende*), . . . mean[ing] that the world afterwards will no longer be the same as the world before'.[4]

In part the German chancellor was right. But Scholz' version of why European history fractured in February 2022 also distorts. Self-evidently, the European security order before Russia's war was nothing like the one that prevailed in the mid-1970s: six new European states stood where once was the western Soviet Union. Having no prior history of peacetime independence, Ukraine's emergence in 1991 as Europe's largest territorial state had constituted an extraordinary change. The new Ukrainian nation-state had always been geopolitically precarious.[5] Since at least 2009, Putin had openly denied the legitimacy of its existence. In the treaties Ukraine signed with Moscow during the 1990s, it had ceded Russian military rights in Crimea. Then, in 2014, it lost the Crimean peninsula and entered a war against Russian-backed separatist rebels in the southeast of the country. If Russia's invasion severed the present from the past, the shock was the scale of suffering Putin was willing to inflict to destroy Ukraine's viability as an independent state, amplified by the chasm between the size of his ambition to seize power in Kyiv and a military mobilization entirely inadequate to the task.

As for Germany, its energy trade with Russia had long embroiled Berlin in Ukraine's struggle for national sovereignty. Since 2005, successive German governments had invested considerable political capital in trying to escape the energy-security problems the Russia-Ukraine conflict caused. In treating Ukraine as an unreliable transit state and an unwelcome member of NATO, they had sided with Russia. But from 2009, they had also tried, largely in vain, to entice Ukraine to modernize the country's pipelines via associated EU membership. After the Crimean crisis and the Donbas war began, Germany's problem was that in prioritizing energy security over Ukraine's independence it was bound to antagonize Washington while, despite investing time in Minsk 2, it could not pacify Russia-Ukraine relations. When Biden lifted American sanctions on Nord Stream 2 in May 2021, Angela Merkel appeared to have prevailed in her insistence on Germany's right to decide for itself on its national energy security. But when a serious Russian military build-up on the

Ukraine border began four months later, Biden was able to extract a promise from Scholz—as the likely incoming chancellor after the September 2021 general election—to end Nord Stream 2 on any Russian invasion.[6] Shortly thereafter, the German energy regulator temporarily stopped the certification process for the project. Rather than belonging to a new Europe, Scholz' pre-invasion death rite for Nord Stream 2 reflected the reality that this second pipeline under the Baltic Sea was built on borrowed time in a world where either further Russian aggression or an attempt by Ukraine to retake the territory it had lost in 2014 was a quite probable possibility.

Yet whatever the fault lines around Ukraine writ large in the post-1991 European order, the *Zeitenwende* narrative does have some resonance. Expansionist wars necessarily create profound ruptures, and this one was no exception. It entailed a nuclear power conquering territory immediately beyond its borders where the world's dominant power was already providing considerable military aid to the state defending its independence. Consequently, every day of the conflict has risked escalation into a bigger war.

The non-military means of warfare were also transformative. The financial sanctions Washington and others deployed against Russia amputated it from the principal international payment system and isolated its central bank. While Russia might have been expected to terminate gas supplies to countries supporting Ukraine—as Saudi Arabia had embargoed oil sales to Israel's allies during the Yom Kippur war—the sanctions net-energy-importing states imposed on the world's principal energy exporter in 2022 were unprecedented.

The sabotage of both of the Nord Stream pipelines in September 2022 constitutes another point of departure. If, as first and perhaps erroneously presumed, the explosions had been an act of Russian aggression against its own infrastructure, the intent would have been so nihilistic it would suggest that Putin had abandoned any conception of Russian national interest in projecting Russian power. If, perhaps, the Biden administration allowed, or brought about, the destruction of the pipelines, it showed a new American willingness to move forcibly to separate Washington's European NATO allies strategically from Russia. Consequently, for Berlin, the detonation of Nord Stream 1 was a symbolically humiliating final end to the post-Suez era whereby it managed its foreign energy dependency by exchanging capital and technology for Russian resources and then sought to defend the infrastructure of that trade from Washington's censure. If there were a juncture marking the changing times in 2022, this moment of the material destruction of a pipeline that, when constructed, had brought little trans-Atlantic criticism was perhaps it.

Europe's Tempest

The Nord Stream explosions were part of what, from the point of Russia's invasion, had been a bloodless but destructive energy war. Here, European governments found that political imperatives instantly clashed with what was materially possible in a supply-constrained energy world. Twelve days after the invasion, the European Commission unveiled proposals to reduce dependence on Russian gas by two-thirds before the year ended and to terminate all fossil-fuel energy trade with Russia 'well before 2030'.[7] But the EU did not impose any sanctions on any Russian energy exports until the following month and then only on coal. For the first months of the war, Germany continued to receive pipelined Russian gas, including through Nord Stream 1. It was Gazprom, which was benefitting from higher revenues in the present but facing losses in the future, that made the first big move in the immediate gas war by radically reducing the flow under the Baltic Sea to Germany and some other European countries in June 2022. In the emergency, the only possible short-term return move became to reduce energy consumption. But in deciding, in July 2022, to cut gas usage by 15 per cent over the next nine months, the EU agreed to a collective sacrifice that took little account of the fact that Germany's vulnerability was not shared by all other member states. Although it did not veto the collective plan, the Hungarian government negotiated a new supply deal with Gazprom soon afterwards while Viktor Orbán told the Commission that it was not acceptable to redistribute gas from states with sufficient reserves to those without them.[8]

The urgent search for sea-borne, non-Russian supply reconfigured the European geopolitical landscape. In the absence of gas flowing Westwards into Europe from Siberia, the countries with Atlantic-facing liquid natural gas (LNG) ports—Britain, France, Spain, and Portugal—became re-exporters to their Eastern neighbours. Gas arriving in the Iberian peninsula raised new pipeline questions too, revealing serious differences over the continent's medium-term energy future. Against French opposition, Germany, Spain, and Portugal advocated reviving a previous project to take gas through the Pyrenees. Under this pressure, Emmanuel Macron agreed, in October 2022, to pursue plans for an alternative undersea pipeline between Barcelona and Marseille with the capacity to transfer both gas and hydrogen. But the French and Spanish governments soon dropped gas from the project because its inclusion precluded EU funding. More immediately, new supplies from Algeria came with their own geopolitical tensions. After Washington had recognized Moroccan sovereignty over western Sahara in 2020, diplomatic relations between Algeria and Morocco had broken down. In November 2021, Algeria had stopped sending gas to Spain through the pipeline running through Moroccan territory. When Spain then sided with Morocco a month after Russia's invasion, Algeria shut down imports to Spain through the undersea pipeline. By contrast, in its bid to replace Russian supply, the Italian government successfully prioritized securing Algerian flows.

Nonetheless, supply constraints ensured energy trade with Russia continued even after the Nord Stream explosions. The EU did not sanction Russian uranium nor did Moscow embargo its export. Meanwhile, shipped Russian oil still arrived in Europe as refined petroleum products from India.[9] Driven by French and Spanish demand, Russian LNG exports to Europe were more than 40 per cent higher during the first nine months of the year compared with the same period in 2021.[10] Some came from a new Russian LNG port on the Baltic Sea coast close to the entry point of Nord Stream.

If the wreckage of the Nord Stream pipelines closed the post-Suez energy era, the geopolitical shadow of Suez still loomed. Then, west European leaders had seen the Soviet Union and Algeria as alternative sources of oil to Middle Eastern imports, and they had hoped that an energy revolution via nuclear power could eventually eliminate foreign oil dependency altogether. Although the Soviet energy relationship succeeded, albeit without removing the need for Middle Eastern oil, the other two ambitions crashed in the face of Algerian independence, oil nationalism, and the costs and limits of nuclear power, including the need to procure uranium from abroad.

Now, European governments seek short-term hydrocarbon alternatives to their one post-1956 success while they pursue another vision of regional or national energy self-sufficiency. In each case, access to African resources is pivotal. But since African governments themselves desperately want to increase domestic energy consumption and European states must compete with China for a metal resource base in Africa, the offer of capital and technology is unlikely decisively to entice this time, as it had done for the Soviet Union.

The hierarchy of power within NATO exposed in the Suez crisis also remains a geopolitical nightmare for Europe. From the moment of Russia's invasion, it was Washington's reaction that set the parameters for the European states' response. Although initially pessimistic about Ukraine's prospects, the Biden administration appeared to recalibrate with Russia's failure to establish air superiority. Discerning, from late March 2022, a chance to inflict a strategic blow upon Russia, it ordered arms transfers and economic aid on a much larger scale. This American move had a particularly forceful impact on Germany. Having decided to arm Ukraine when Washington assumed the war would be over swiftly, Scholz faced repeated calls once the war became protracted to deliver more assistance while having no influence over Kyiv's war aims.

The terms on which the war finally ends around the Black Sea matter greatly for Europe's geopolitical future. If Washington were ever willing to back Ukraine in fighting for full sovereignty over Crimea, the stakes would become whether Russia retains Sevastopol, the port which has hosted Russia's Black Sea navy almost continuously since the 1780s. More generally, the Black Sea status quo on navigation rights has held since the 1936 Montreux Convention. It gives Turkey sole rights to control access to the Dardanelles and Bosphorus Straits during any war and to decide what indeed constitutes war. While this long-standing international law constrains Russia in the Middle East, a reality—as described in Chapter 2—that explains Turkey's membership of NATO, it also shields Russia against a maritime attack from the south, as shown during the Second World War and the Cold War. Now, by constraining the long-term defence of Ukraine, protecting the Convention, especially Turkey's right to decide on what constitutes war, has become a vital Russian interest.

Further north, the geopolitical disturbance let loose by Moscow's war is already evident. Alarmed by Russia's territorial revanchism, Sweden and Finland applied to join NATO in May 2022, with Finland's accession completed eleven months later. On Swedish membership, all the Baltic States except Russia will be inside the military alliance. This enlargement of NATO also has the potential to weaken German power within the EU by creating a north European alliance led by Poland—a state now committed to establishing the largest land NATO army in Europe by 2030—with an acute security interest in cultivating deeper relations with post-Brexit Britain.

This final Swedish-Finnish retreat from neutrality also intensifies growing geopolitical tensions in the Arctic. While the polar region has long been known to be rich in oil, gas, and minerals, extracting these resources proved a formidable challenge until temperatures started rising. During the 2010s, Russia, NATO, and China all increased their military activity in the Arctic, sparking friction around the demilitarized Svalbard archipelago. Under a treaty signed in 1920, Norway has sovereignty over these islands while fifty other states have the legal right to explore them for resources. In the weeks before Russia's invasion of Ukraine, a cable connecting the world's largest satellite ground station on Svalbard to the Norwegian mainland was sabotaged, apparently by Moscow. After the invasion, the non-Russian members suspended the Arctic Council, the intergovernmental body set up by the eight states with sovereign territory in the Arctic Circle in the early post-Cold War years, leaving Russia politically isolated as an Arctic power.

Yet Russia remains a pivotal economic power in the Arctic. The war incentivized Moscow to double-down on its commercial use of the Arctic seas. The Northern Sea Route from northeast Europe and Russia to Pacific Asia is less than half the length of transit through the Suez Canal, and the warming Arctic makes passage with icebreakers possible during the winter months. Even before the war, the Northern Sea Route was a site of dispute. Since the journey passes through an exclusively Russian economic zone, Russia claims the right to control foreign navigation. After the invasion, non-Russian transit crashed while Russia's grew, including by LNG vessels bound to southern and western European ports. With the war placing a new premium on Russia's Asian export markets, the Russian energy company Rosneft began work on a large Arctic oil terminal. If the Northern Sea Route becomes the principal route for Russian oil to reach China in a world in which more of China's oil comes from Russia, this will be a major geopolitical change. It would diminish China's 'Malacca Dilemma' and introduce a Bering Strait predicament, whereby China's trade could be choked in the narrow body of water that separates eastern Russia from the United States. If the outcome of the war is not Russian decline in the Black Sea but Russian ascendancy, it would mean that Russia has emerged as a significant commercial maritime power with every reason to use its navy to defend its new trade routes while, separately but simultaneously, China has acquired stakes in most of Europe's major ports on the North Sea and the Mediterranean/Aegean. In this sense, the age in which the American navy has largely acted alone as guarantor of open seas for trade may well be ending.

In both the southeastern and northeastern European geopolitical spheres, Russia's war deepens the fault lines around Europe's Turkey question. Turkey has proved crucial to Ukraine's defence, sending life-saving drones to Kyiv, and brokering two agreements with Moscow to allow Ukraine to export food from Odessa. Having been a strategic and tactical headache over Syria, Turkey has proved indispensable to NATO in a war around the Black Sea. Yet since it refused to use sanctions against Russia, Turkey has also showed its proclivity to act as a rogue NATO state. It also continues to face both ways as an energy hub. When, in July 2022, the EU agreed with Azerbaijan to double the volume of gas sent through the Trans-Anatolian pipeline, Turkey's significance to the transit of non-Russian gas was again augmented. But after the Nord Stream explosions, Erdogan joined Putin in saying that the Turkstream pipeline under the Black Sea should become the pivotal entry point for Russian gas coming into Europe.[11] Erdogan also created a serious road block to Sweden's accession to NATO.

Predictably, open conflict in the Black Sea further exacerbated the geopolitical fault line running through NATO over the east Mediterranean. Apparently emboldened by Turkey's usefulness to NATO, Erdogan repeatedly threatened to punish Greece for militarizing the Greek islands that lie close to the Turkish coast, declaring that 'we can come down suddenly one night when the time comes'.[12] In September

2022, Greece sent a letter to NATO saying that Europe was at risk of another war on the continent. Since the Greek government believes the Montreux Convention supports its position over Turkey's in relation to the islands, this Turkish–Greek altercation firmly ties events in the east Mediterranean to the balance of power in the Black Sea. Any scenario where the war yields, as either an endpoint or a stasis, ongoing Russian control of most of Ukraine's northern Black Sea coastal territory would move Russia closer to the gas-rich east Mediterranean. Perhaps cognizant of the dangers of Turkey exploiting Russia's position in the Black Sea for its own ends, the Greek prime minister, in January 2023, refused to send Leopard tanks to Ukraine, despite possessing more of them than any other European country, saying they were essential for Greece's own defence.

The EU must confront the new Turkey question, having committed itself in June 2022 to another eastern enlargement centred on the Black Sea. Ukraine's candidate status alone raises serious questions for the EU. Economically reconstructing Ukraine, a country where prior to the war living standards had already been far below the European average, will require enormous sums of money. For any state with land and sea borders with Russia, let alone disputed ones, EU membership would also appear to require NATO accession. Yet it is far from clear whether all the EU states would support this move or that Turkey would in practice acquiesce.

Regardless of Ukraine's prospects for entering the EU or NATO, Ukraine's national resilience against Russia has itself charged Europe geopolitically. In a 1984 essay, the Czech novelist Milan Kundera wrote that the Ukrainian nation, 'one of the great European nations, . . . is slowly disappearing. And this enormous, almost unbelievable event is occurring without the world realizing it'.[13] Ukraine's independence seven years afterwards only partly introduced western Europeans to Ukrainian history.[14] But, by trying to eliminate Ukrainian nationhood, Putin has instead ensured that it has become a permanent feature of Europe with which the EU must grapple. The post-Cold War EU relied on a measure of German-Russian reconciliation to allow for German reunification even as the eastern European states had only just successfully asserted their nationhood against the Soviet version of the imperial Russian empire. Thereafter, the Holocaust, as an end point for German nationalism and the catastrophic culmination of decades of ethnic division in eastern Europe, became pivotal to the imaginative construction of the idea of European unity.[15] By contrast, in 2022, a state subject to the simultaneous experience of the Holocaust and Soviet mid-20th-century terror became an official candidate for EU membership by fighting a defensive war for its territorial national sovereignty. In doing so, it claimed the right to nation-build, including by suppressing minority languages in the public sphere. No aspect of this experience sits easily with the notion of the post-Maastricht EU as a post-national and peace-oriented construction. An EU that admits Ukraine as a war-formed nation-state would necessarily become a different kind of entity, one that could not be rhetorically legitimated without a new narrative about its historical purpose partially grounded in Russia's existence as a geopolitical opponent. In Berlin and Paris, an EU with such a relationship to Europe's resource-rich, continental-size neighbour would indeed belong to a *Zeitenwende*.

The World Economy at War

Inevitably, the energy upheavals generated by a war started by the world's energy-exporting superpower delivered a succession of economic shocks. But while exclusively blaming the war for these energy troubles proved politically convenient, this impulse ignored the price-centred energy crisis already in play by the start of 2022. In reality, Western politicians had been searching for energy remedies since the previous summer.[16] A month before the invasion, oil prices stood at their highest level since late 2014. During 2021, European countries had also experienced a gas price shock comparable in its severity to any historical oil blow: with Chinese demand for LNG imports growing by 15 per cent, EU natural gas futures were eighteen times higher in December 2021 than their pre-pandemic level.[17]

Quite simply, the war exposed pre-existing supply constraints before it began to disrupt the geographical patterns of energy trade flows. The 2021 gas shock that hit Europe reflected an emerging Eurasian-wide competition for LNG. Consequently, in 2022, for all the difficulties they caused, exorbitant prices were the necessary condition for Western countries winning the wartime contest for sea-borne gas.[18]

In oil markets, the structural problems were those long generated by the stagnation of conventional supply from 2005 and the fall in investment from 2014. In 2021, shale oil's diminishing compensatory capacity was very apparent: for the year, world consumption was 1.5 million barrels per day (bpd) more than world production.[19] Even at the year's end, American crude output was still more than 1 million bpd lower than two years earlier.[20] After failing in his first months in office to move Iran towards a new nuclear deal that would have relieved sanctions on Iran's oil exports, Biden tried to persuade OPEC Plus to increase production quotas. Failing there too, his administration moved to co-ordinate strategic reserve releases with China that autumn. By driving up oil prices yet again, the war only increased the prior pressure on Biden to push OPEC Plus to adjust its output. Where in 2021 Biden had leaned on OPEC Plus while deploying critical rhetoric against Saudi Arabia, in July 2022 he headed to Riyadh to meet Mohammed Bin Salman. But shale-era American influence over its erstwhile principal Arab ally remained minimal. While the divergence between Saudi and Russian responses to the emergency of the pandemic had allowed Trump to force a production cut in April 2020, the energy war, in encouraging the G7 and the EU to adopt price caps on Russian oil products, only re-inforced Riyadh's underlying shared interests with Moscow.

Three months after Biden's visit, OPEC Plus announced an imminent cut of 2 million bpd from its production targets, provoking fury in Washington. But since several OPEC Plus members were missing their existing quotas, the effective cut was rather less than proclaimed. This reality reflected the ongoing stagnation in conventional oil output. In order to function in 2022 even with prices deemed politically intolerable in 2021, the world economy had to rely on Biden ordering large withdrawals from the US Strategic Petroleum Reserve. Weak Chinese demand, driven by Beijing's zero-Covid policies, lessened the burden. Where in the 2010s, with shale output accelerating, world economic growth had depended on China's economic growth, in 2022 avoiding a full-scale oil crisis relied on the absence of such growth.

Yet without the cheap Chinese exports of the mid-2000s, there was no counter-point to the inflationary effects of what from autumn 2021 to mid-2022 amounted to the third oil price shock of the century.

If the absence of NICE was now more conspicuous than when Mervyn King had delivered his 2005 speech, central banks were still much slower to act than in 2004–6, or in the ECB's case in 2011. Only in March 2022, when inflation was already at nearly 8 per cent, did the Fed tighten monetary policy while the ECB waited another four months.

In the post-2008, highly leveraged international financial system, monetary tightening at any time threatened financial instability, with episodes of significant market stress becoming more frequent through the 2010s and early 2020s. But the economic response to the pandemic had allowed for more inflationary conditions again, especially in the United States, ensuring that in time the pressure on central bankers to increase interest rates would build. Consequently, there was little room for monetary manoeuvre in 2021: early interest rate hikes would have delivered a hard blow to consumer confidence when the pandemic was not yet over, on top of exposing banks to the kind of crisis that in 2023 would engulf Silicon Valley Bank as the paper value of its holdings of Treasury bonds fell on rising rates.

Outside the United States, however, inaction could only encourage exchange rate pressures at a time when the dollar was rising steadily. A monetary world where the ECB and the national central banks were then confronted with a rate-raising Fed reintroduced the Volcker-era trade-off between asserting monetary autonomy and accepting an inflationary currency depreciation at a time of high energy prices. Having eliminated the possibility of internal exchange rate instability between its members, the Eurozone offered some protection from the problem that had so bedeviled Francois Mitterrand's experiment. But the ECB still risked a return to an interest rate spread between Germany and Italy whether it acted or did not act.

The political trepidation generated by high energy prices on a soaring dollar in the second and third quarters of the year only magnified the monetary predicament. Virtually all European governments turned to additional borrowing to cushion households and firms from the shock. Those that judged they had the market latitude to borrow the most, like Germany and Britain, offered massive fiscal support. For Britain's shortest lived prime minister, Liz Truss, adding tax cuts to the new fiscal-monetary mix proved disastrous, leading to a collapse in liquidity in UK bond markets, a sterling crisis, and her exit from office in October 2022. Hoping to reduce the pressure on the

Bank of England to raise rates to shore up sterling, her successor, Rishi Sunak, dismantled not just her tax cuts but much of the energy support package.

If China's poor growth in 2022 was a saving contingency in a macro-economic environment structurally conducive to stagflation, Russia's war still aggravated the post-2005 China-US fault lines destabilizing the world economy. Prior to 24 February 2022, the accelerating Sino-American trade and technology conflict was offset by the Fed's backstop for China as an insurance against acute dollar shortage. Thereafter, Washington's financial sanctions against Russia could only encourage the Chinese leadership to rethink China's integration into the dollar-based international credit system. But, given the size of Beijing's dollar exposure, exit remained a tricky option. While China did reduce its US Treasury holdings by nearly a fifth between February and the end of 2022, it also increased its Fannie Mae and Freddie Mac assets by a proportionate amount, repeating the move it had made prior to its complete loss of confidence in the two mortgage corporations' debt in 2008.[21]

As Beijing grappled with its dollar problem, the risk of a US-China military conflict, in which its reserves outside China could be confiscated, escalated. In meeting Xi Jinping three weeks before the Ukraine invasion, Putin sought to make China a fellow traveller in his territorial revisionism. While Ukraine, he suggested, was Russian so Taiwan was Chinese. Whether in response or not, Biden moved Washington to a much more explicit commitment than ever before to defend Taiwan. At the same time, by imposing a ban on the sale of semi-conductors to China in October 2022, Biden intensified the American bid to curtail China's technological ambitions. The result was high-stakes Sino-American tension in a world in which 90 per cent of advanced micro-chip production takes place in Taiwan. Whereas during Russia's war the United States could release reserve oil to increase supply, it would be unable to offset materially what would be lost in a war over the northwest Pacific island.

In framing Russia's war as 'democracy versus autocracy', the Biden administration also harried European governments over China at a time when the gas crisis was already weakening European firms in cross-Atlantic industrial competition.[22] Driven by this energy problem, the German company BASF—the world's largest chemical producer—announced in October 2022 that it was 'permanently' downsizing in Europe 'as quickly as possible'.[23] But in planning an alternative plant in China on the scale of its main German operation, BASF can only test the degree of autonomy from Washington both German corporations and the German government can salvage on commerce with China. Unless Sino-American relations improve, China's awareness of this vulnerability can only then incentivize Beijing to try to draw the EU away from the United States.

Here, the bid to revolutionize energy again complicates the European predicament. In August 2022, the US Congress passed the Inflation Reduction Act. This climate-framed legislation incentivizes capital investment in low-carbon technology and production. In part, it does so by rewarding companies that source production from American firms and those in countries with whom the United States has a free-trade agreement. If the explicitly stated aim is to divert present supply chains away from China, this approach also shuts out European firms from future ones since neither the EU nor any European state outside the EU has a free-trade agreement with Washington. In a letter to the US Treasury, the European Commission warned that the legislation 'threatens the multilateral trading system at a time when its value is more important than ever for both American and European businesses'.[24] Yet this argument presumes a uniformity of interests across the Atlantic that scarcely exists. Instead, the deep economic divergence of the United States from Europe that began with the shale boom is accelerating. After the World Trade Organization ruled against Washington in December 2022 in a steel-tariffs case, the Biden administration pronounced the world's multilateral trade institution irrelevant to the new security-ridden geopolitical times.[25] By contrast, European states' interests are closer to China's. For each, multilateral trade still protects energy security by facilitating the export earnings needed to pay, and at times compete, for fossil-fuel energy imports, an imperative perpetually more difficult to meet at times of dollar strength.

Energy, War, and Aristocratic Excess

In a war jeopardizing immediate energy security, European governments resuscitated the narrative of energy sacrifice deployed by

Jimmy Carter. In spring 2022, the Italian prime minister, Mario Draghi, asked: 'do we want to have peace or do you want to have the air conditioning on?'[26] But the ghost of Carter's political failure lingered, including in the United States. Palpably fearing a democratic rebellion on energy, Western politicians did not ask citizens to endure too much economic pain in the name of any claim to political community—whether that community be the nation, Europe, or a democratic West. Justifying his use of the Strategic Petroleum Reserve, Biden promised 'to do everything' he could 'to minimise Putin's price hike here at home'.[27] Throwing fiscal caution to the wind, European governments subsidized household fuel bills and some, notably the British and French, still faced a wave of strikes. None appeared to show qualms about European companies buying spot-market LNG already contracted to Pakistan.[28] In Italy, Draghi's government fell in July 2022 after Five-Star withdrew its support, charging that the former ECB president was prioritizing Ukraine over reducing energy prices. Tellingly, when the subsequent general election once again saw the party uncompromised by technocratic and grand coalition politics win the largest number of seats, this time the Brothers of Italy, its leader, Giorgia Meloni, was allowed to become prime minister.

By contrast, reducing energy consumption in the name of lowering carbon emissions remained off-limits. Instead, in making a new case for the energy transition, the war emergency encouraged further the idea that economic transformation could recreate the cross-class interest in national manufacturing production lost from the 1970s. With the Inflation Reduction Act, American climate policy near explicitly became a political bulwark against another 2016-style shock where Trump or a Trump-style candidate again wins by appealing to the losers of American deindustrialization. In contrast to its New Deal predecessor, this federal intervention is explicitly racially inclusive in its conception of nationhood. Indeed, for the Biden administration, it is an act of reparation for the restrictive American nationhood of the past as well as an attempt at restoring the New-Deal-originating idea of economic nationhood. Whether by reshoring manufacturing production it can succeed in its own terms is open to question. But the fact the United States under Democratic party rule in 2022 entered the same political space European governments sought to occupy in 2019 with their Net Zero 2050 commitments constrains European ambitions. The American move establishes a competitive geopolitical contest between Western countries around using energy change to address issues of aristocratic excess in which European states and the EU are disadvantaged by higher fossil-fuel energy costs and American financial power. Already the failure of Boris Johnson's government, which bet its post-Brexit 'levelling-up agenda' on investment in low-carbon sectors, testifies to the problem. With the Inflation Reduction Act, the stakes for Britain in securing a post-Brexit free-trade agreement with the United States are now quite possibly high enough to force a future choice between British companies' presence in US-centred low-carbon supply chains and the domestic burden of accepting Washington's trade terms.

Even in the United States, reconfiguring energy production towards national self-sufficiency cannot happen quickly enough to be democratically transformative. As a response to Trump's 2016 insurgency candidacy, this project leaves the border and citizenship issues untouched. In betting on rapidly building a low-carbon America, the Biden administration has also left itself open to the charge that it is subordinating present energy needs to an unrealizable future-oriented project to the benefit of those corporations that procure the available subsidies.

Here, the fundamental problem of energy time has not shifted. Of the transformative forces unleashed by Russia's war, game-changing technological break-throughs of the kind necessary for a low-carbon energy future was not one. Following hard on the 2021 China gas shock, the energy trade disruption caused by Russia's war, meanwhile, intensified the separate problem of the energy present. The 2022 crisis demonstrated just how politically hard it is for European politicians to reduce the expectations for consumption formed in a prior geopolitical era, or ask their citizens to engage with the energy poverty of people in many non-Western parts of the world. If Russia's war has changed the prior democratic predicaments around energy, it is by spreading energy consciousness, including letting loose the spectre of future energy scarcity in polities premised on energy abundance. Where, in the West, energy consciousness was acute for those exercising power but often weak among citizens, the war means these citizens now better understand their material aspirations and fears as energy demands and anxieties. They do so at a time when Western democracies generally have still not recovered from the blows delivered by the 2008 crash—even without a new round of bank interventions in March 2023—and when in France violent street protest has become a persistent feature of expressed discontent. In principle, greater energy consciousness could loosen the technocratic logic behind the original European formulation of realizing an energy revolution by 2050. But it is more likely to trap Western democracies deeper in aristocratic excess by exposing the chasm between the interests everyone shares in facing climate change and the inequalities that will come from electrifying personal transport and that are always generated by high fossil-fuel prices. In this future, energy will not be a subterranean source of political disorder, as in the first two decades of the 21st century, but the principal currency of it.

Notes

Introduction

1. Quoted in Joshua Posaner, 'Merkel Blasts "Unforgivable" Thuringia Election', *Politico*, 6 February 2020, https://www.politico.eu/article/angela-merkel-blasts-unforgivable-thuringia-election-far-right-afd/

2. *The Economist*, 'Transcript, Emmanuel Macron in His Own Words (English)', Transcript 7 November 2019, https://www.economist.com/eur ope/2019/11/07/emmanuel-macron-in-his-own-words-english

3. Quoted in Victor Mallet, Michael Peel, and Tobias Buck, 'Merkel Rejects Macron Warning Over NATO "Brain Death"', *Financial Times*, 7 November 2019, https://www.ft.com/content/2ee4c21a-015f-11ea-be59-e49b2a136b8d

4. Joint statement from President Macron, Chancellor Merkel, and Prime Minister Johnson on the Situation in Iraq, 6 January 2020, https://www.gov.uk/government/news/joint-statement-from-president-macron-chancellor-merkel-and-prime-minister-johnson-on-the-situation-in-iraq

5. Quoted in 'Clinton Accuses Trump of Being Putin's "Puppet"', *Reuters*, 20 October 2016, https://www.reuters.com/article/us-usa-election-debate-russia-idUSKCN12K0E7

6. For examples of arguments that treat populism as an authoritarian or anti-pluralist phenomenon see Yascha Mounk, *The People Versus Democracy: Why Our Freedom is in Danger and How to Save it* (Cambridge, MA: Harvard University Press, 2018); Jan-Werner Müller, *What is Populism?* (Philadelphia: University of Pennsylvania Press, 2016); Pippa Norris and Ronald Inglehart, *Cultural Backlash: Trump, Brexit, and Authoritarian Populism* (Cambridge: Cambridge University Press, 2019). For arguments that present populism as a more structural feature of democracy see Roger Eatwell and Matthew Goodwin, *National Populism: The Revolt Against Liberal Democracy* (London: Pelican, 2018); Barry Eichengreen, *The Populist Temptation: Economic Grievance and Political Reaction in the Modern Era* (New York: Oxford University Press, 2018). For the argument that populism is one side of a more complicated phenomenon best understood as technopopulism see Christopher J. Bickerton and Carlo Invernizzi Accetti, *Technopopulism: The New Logic of Democratic Politics* (Oxford: Oxford University Press, 2021). For the debate between economic and cultural factors in populism see Noam Gidron and Peter A. Hall, 'The Politics of Social Status: Economic and Cultural Roots of the Populist Right', *British Journal of Sociology 68*, no. S1 (2017): pp. S57–S84; Ronald Inglehart and Pippa Norris, 'Trump and the Xenophobic Populist Parties: The Silent Revolution in Reverse', *Perspectives*

on Politics 15, no. 2 (2017): pp. 443–54. Mark Blyth, 'After The Brits Have Gone and the Trumpets Have Sounded: Turning a Drama into a Crisis that Will Not Go To Waste', *Intereconomics 51*, no. 6 (2016): pp. 324–31; Jonathan Hopkin and Mark Blyth, 'The Global Economics of European Populism: Growth Regimes and Party System Change in Europe' (The Government and Opposition/Leonard Schapiro Lecture 2017), *Government and Opposition 54*, no. 2 (2019): pp. 193–225; Jonathan Hopkin, *Anti-System Politics: The Crisis of Market Liberalism in Rich Democracies* (Oxford: Oxford University Press, 2020). For arguments that democracy is in crisis see Steven Levitsky and Daniel Ziblatt, *How Democracies Die: What History Reveals About Our Future* (London: Viking, 2018); David Runciman, *How Democracies End* (London: Profile, 2018). For the argument that it is nationalism that has returned see John B. Judis, *The Nationalist Revival: Trade, Immigration and the Revolt Against Globalization* (New York: Columbia Global Report, 2018). For recent defences of nationalism and national identity from different starting positions see Yael Tamir, *Why Nationalism* (Princeton: Princeton University Press, 2019); Francis Fukuyama, *Identity: The Demand for Dignity and the Politics of Resentment* (New York: Macmillan, 2018); Jill Lepore, 'A New Americanism: Why a Nation Needs a National Story', *Foreign Affairs 98*, no. 2 (March/April 2019): pp. 10–19; Yoram Hazony, *The Virtue of Nationalism* (New York: Basic Books, 2018). For laments for a lost liberal international order see Bill Emmott, *The Fate of the West: The Battle to Save the World's Most Successful Political Idea* (London: Economist Books, 2017); Edward Luce, *The Retreat of Western Liberalism* (London: Little Brown, 2017); Thomas J. Wright, *All Measures Short of War: The Contest for the Twenty-First Century and the Future of American Power* (New Haven: Yale University Press, 2017). For critiques of this liberal lament see John J. Mearsheimer, *The Great Delusion: Liberal Dreams and International Realities* (New Haven: Yale University Press, 2018); Stephen M. Walt, *The Hell of Good Intentions: America's Foreign Policy Elite and the Decline of U.S. Primacy* (New York: Farrar, Straus and Giroux, 2018).

7. See, for example, Max Weber, 'Suffrage and Democracy in Germany' in *Max Weber: Political Writings*, edited by Peter Lassman and trans. Ronald Spiers (Cambridge: Cambridge University Press, 1994).

8. The concept of geopolitics has a long and fraught history. In this book, I take it to be a sphere where geography, the power of states, and the transnational purposes of non-state actors interact to structure economic and political choices. For a perspective on geopolitics more focused on the everyday and multiple non-state agents see Klaus Dodds, *Geopolitics: A Very Short Introduction*, third edition (Oxford: Oxford University Press, 2019).

9. I occasionally through the book use 'Western' as a shorthand for North American and European, but I am not attributing any deeper meaning to a Western cohesion.

10. The book's story of geopolitical change is incomplete. It only peripherally engages with the parallels between European foreign energy dependency and Japan's. In charting the geopolitical shifts since the 1990s, it conspiculously neglects India's industrial development and the competition for resources in Africa. In telling a story about the disruptive impact of events in the Middle East, it does not engage with the specific impact of Egypt on the region's internal instability from 2011 or much with Turkey's influence in the Middle East. Its economic history ignores some intrinsically significant developments like demographic changes in the working age population, issues around technological innovation in the productive economy, and the rise of surveillance capitalism. On the first and second see Robert J. Gordon, *The Rise and Fall of American Growth: The US Standard of Living Since the Civil War* (Princeton: Princeton University Press, 2016). On the third see Shoshana Zuboff, *The Age of Surveillance Capitalism: The Fight for a Human Future at the New Frontier of Power* (London: Profile, 2019). Although Japan was the first large economy to experience QE, Japan's monetary story does not appear.

11. John Gray tells part of story about the ongoing presence of religion in European and American politics with great erudition in two books, *Black Mass: Apocalyptic Religion and the Death of Utopia* (London: Penguin, 2007) and *Seven Types of Atheism* (London: Allen Lane, 2018). For the long-term impact of Christianity on Western history see Tom Holland, *Dominion: The Making of the Western Mind* (London: Little Brown, 2019). A tenson between material and religious questions inevitably remains in this book. That comes out most obviously around Turkey's relationship to the EU: one reason why the EU has struggled for decades about what to do about Turkey arises from a conflict between treating Turkey's EU relations as a matter of religion and as a matter of energy and military security, and sometimes what is motive and what pretext and rationalization is far from easy to discern.

12. Geoffrey West, *Scale: The Universal Laws of Life and Death in Organisms, Cities, and Companies* (London: Weidenfeld and Nicolson, 2017), p. 233.

13. On energy's primary importance to human life via the fundamental limits energy flows impose on material human action and material possibilities see Vaclav Smil, *Energy and Civilization: A History* (Cambridge, MA: MIT Press, 2017). Many economists and political economy scholars ignore energy despite the fact that, as Smil has correctly pointed out, 'all economic activities are, in fundamental physical (thermodynamic) terms, simple or sequential energy conversions aimed at producing specific products or services'. Vaclav Smil, *Growth: From Microorganisms to Megacities* (Cambridge, MA: MIT Press, 2020), p. 376.

14. This is shown clearly by the spectacular rise in China's GDP over the past two decades: between 2000, after when China's growth began to accelerate, and 2019, China's primary energy consumption increased by more

than 330 per cent. Our World in Data, Energy, China Country Profile, https://ourworldindata.org/energy/country/china?country=~CHN

15. For optimism on how this can be achieved see Namit Sharma, Bram Smeets, and Christer Tryggestad, 'The Decoupling of GDP and Energy Growth: A CEO Guide', *McKinsey Quarterly*, 24 April 2019, https://www. mckinsey.com/industries/electric-power-and-natural-gas/our-insights/ the-decoupling-of-gdp-and-energy-growth-a-ceo-guide

16. West, *Scale*, pp. 234–8.

Chapter 1

1. Full Transcript of Trump's Speech on the Iran Nuclear Deal, 8 May 2018, *New York Times*, https://www.nytimes.com/2018/05/08/us/politics/trump-speech-iran-deal.html

2. 'Six Charts that Show How Hard US Sanctions have Hit Iran', *BBC News*, 9 December 2019, https://www.bbc.co.uk/news/world-middle-east-48119109

3. Reuters staff, 'France: More Countries Back European-Led Naval Mission in Hormuz', *Reuters*, 20 January 2020, https://www.reuters.com/ar ticle/uk-mideast-iran-france/france-more-countries-back-european-led-naval-mission-in-hormuz-idUKKBN1ZJ1AI?edition-redirect=uk

4. Kenneth Pomeranz, *The Great Divergence: China, Europe, and the Making of the World Economy* (Princeton: Princeton University Press, 2001), p. 16.

5. John Darwin, *After Tamerlane: The Rise and Fall of Global Empires, 1400–2000* (London: Penguin, 2007), p. 19. On the development of Eurasia as a landscape and the historical rise of civilizations in Eurasia to the fourteenth century see Barry Cunliffe, *By Steppe, Desert, and Ocean: The Birth of Eurasia* (Oxford: Oxford University Press, 2015). On the historical rise of US power see Victoria de Grazia, *Irresistible Empire: America's Advance Through Twentieth Century Europe* (Cambridge, MA: Harvard University Press, 2006); Giovanni Arrighi, *The Long Twentieth Century: Money, Power and the Origins of Our Times*, new edition (London: Verso, 2009); Neil Smith, *American Empire: Roosevelt's Geographer and the Prelude to Globalization* (Berkeley: University of California Press, 2004).

6. By contrast, as Russia expanded across a continent to the Pacific over several centuries, it never escaped border conflicts to its west and south.

7. On the importance of oil to American power over the twentieth century see David S. Painter, 'Oil and the American Century', *Journal of American History 99*, no. 1 (2012): pp. 24–39.

8. Vaclav Smil, *Energy and Civilization: A History* (Cambridge, MA: MIT Press, 2018), p. 408.

9. H.D. Lloyd, 'The Story of a Great Monopoly', *Atlantic*, March 1891, https://www.theatlantic.com/magazine/archive/1881/03/the-story-of-a-great-monopoly/306019/

10. On the rise of Russian oil see Daniel Yergin, *The Prize: The Epic Quest for Oil, Money, and Power* (New York: Simon & Schuster, 1993), pp. 57–63, 71–2.

11. Yergin, *The Prize*, pp. 61–72.

12. On the commercial rivalry and attempts at cooperation of Standard Oil and the Russian companies see Yergin, *The Prize*, pp. 63–72. On Austria-Hungary's later resistance to Standard Oil see Alison Frank, 'The Petroleum War of 1910: Standard Oil, Austria, and the Limits of the Multi-National Corporation', *The American Historical Review 114*, no. 1 (2009): pp. 16–41.

13. Bülent Gökay, 'The Battle for Baku (May 1918–September 1918): A Peculiar Episode in the History of the Caucasus', *Middle Eastern Studies 34*, no. 1 (1998): p. 30.

14. Yergin, *The Prize*, pp. 131–3.

15. Ever since the United States' industrial ascendancy began from the 1870s, the European states had looked to annex territory in Africa as a resource-rich economic hinterland that would allow them to compete with the continental industrial behemoth across the Atlantic. For the impact of the American continental expansion and rapid industrialization on Europe before and after the First World War see Sven Beckert, 'American Danger: United States Empire, Eurafrica, and the Territorialization of Industrial Capitalism, 1870–1950', *American Historical Review 122*, no. 4 (2017): pp. 1137–70.

16. The Ottoman Grand Vizier granted the concession on oil in Mesopotamia to the Turkish Petroleum Company the day Archduke Francis Ferdinand was assassinated. Edward Mead Earle, 'The Turkish Petroleum Company—A Study in Oleaginous Diplomacy', *Political Science Quarterly 39*, no. 2 (1922): p. 266.

17. On pre-war Anglo-American rivalry over oil-based navies see John A. DeNovo, 'Petroleum and the United States Navy before World War I', *The Mississippi Valley Historical Review 41*, no. 4 (1955): pp. 641–56.

18. Some of the oil used in the British experiments with new ships was shale oil extracted in Scotland. On the history of the British Navy's early moves to oil see Warwick Michael Brown, 'The Royal Navy's Fuel Supplies, 1898 to 1939; The Transition from Coal to Oil', PhD dissertation submitted to King's College London, University of London, 2003.

19. Quoted in Timothy C. Winegard, *The First World Oil War* (Toronto: University of Toronto Press, 2016), p. 57.

20. Yergin, *The Prize*, p. 160; Winegard, *The First World Oil War*, p. 59.

21. On the importance of oil in both world wars see W. G. Jensen, 'The Importance of Energy in the First and Second World Wars', *Historical Journal 11*, no. 3 (1968): pp. 538–54. On the impact of the First World War on oil as an energy source see Dan Tamir, 'Something New Under the Fog of War', in *Environmental Histories of the First World War*, edited by Richard Tucker, Tait Keller, J. R. McNeill, and Martin Schmid (Cambridge University Press, 2018), pp. 117–35.

22. Tamir, 'Something New Under the Fog of War', p. 118.

23. Winegard, *The First World Oil War*, p. 93.

24. Alison Fleig Frank, *Oil Empire: Visions of Prosperity in Austrian Galicia* (Cambridge, MA: Harvard University Press, 2007), pp. 21, 251.

25. On the battle for Baku see Bülent Gökay, 'The Battle for Baku', pp. 30–50.

26. Quoted in Yergin, *The Prize*, p. 183; Yergin, *The Prize*, p. 178.

27. Priscilla Roberts, 'Benjamin Strong, the Federal Reserve and the Limits to Interwar American Nationalism', *Economic Quarterly Federal Reserve Bank of Richmond 86* (2000): p. 65. On the impact of the First World War in creating an Atlantic orientation to American foreign policy through creditor power see Priscilla Roberts, 'The First World War and the Emergence of American Atlanticism 1914–20', *Diplomacy and Statecraft 5*, no. 3 (1994): pp. 569–619; Harold James, 'Cosmos, Chaos: Finance, Power, and Conflict', *International Affairs 90*, no. 1 (2014): pp. 46–7.

28. Barry Eichengreen and Marc Flandreau, 'The Rise and Fall of the Dollar, or When Did the Dollar Replace Sterling as the Leading International Currency?' NBER Working Paper Series 14154, July 2008, p. 3, https://www.nber.org/papers/w14154

29. Quoted in Roberta Allbert Dayer, 'The British War Debts to the United States and the Anglo-Japanese Alliance, 1920–1923', *Pacific Historical Review 45*, no. 4 (1976): p. 577.

30. Liaquat Ahamed, *Lords of Finance: 1929, the Great Depression, and the Bankers Who Broke the World* (London: Windmill Books, 2009), p. 144.

31. American industrial prowess during the 1920s continued to invoke a desire for emulation. On the German and Soviet attempts to copy and surpass American Fordism see Stefan J. Link, *Forging Global Fordism: Nazi Germany, Soviet Russia, and the Contest over the Industrial Order* (Princeton: Princeton University Press, 2020). On Hitler's obsession with the Model T car see Wolfgang König, 'Adolf Hitler vs. Henry Ford: The Volkswagen, the Role of America as a Model, and the Failure of a Nazi Consumer Society', *German Studies Review 27*, no. 2 (2004): pp. 249–68.

32. On where the Ottoman Middle East as a site of a geopolitical conflict won by the British and French sat within the wider geopolitical Eurasian and African landscape see Anthony D'Agostino, *The Rise of Global Powers: International Politics in the Era of the World Wars* (Cambridge: Cambridge University Press, 2012), ch. 4.

33. Sean McMeekin, *The Ottoman Endgame: War, Revolution, and the Making of the Modern Middle East 1908–1923* (London: Penguin Random House), p. 404. In 1923, an American rear-admiral, Colby Mitchell Chester, appeared to have secured a concession from the new Turkish state to build railways from the Black Sea into Anatolia and down into Basra (British controlled but Turkey still then hoped to retain), and, as with the Berlin–Baghdad rail agreement, explore for oil. But once the Turkish government had agreed the Lausanne Treaty, the concession fell away.

34. Quoted in McMeekin, *The Ottoman Endgame*, pp. 421–2.

35. See Sean McMeekin, *The Berlin-Baghdad Express: The Ottoman Empire and Germany's Bid for World Power, 1898–1918* (London: Penguin, 2010).

36. Darwin, *After Tamerlane*, p. 378.

37. See John Darwin, *The Empire Project: The Rise and Fall of the British World System 1830–1970* (Cambridge: Cambridge University Press, 2009), pp. 375–85.

38. Gregory Nowell argues that the United States 'Open-Door' policy in the 1920s 'was the American diplomatic thrust of Standard Oil's worldwide campaign against exclusion from foreign oil resources, especially the Anglo-French oil alliance of 1920'. Gregory Nowell, *Mercantile States and the World Oil Cartel 1900–1939* (Ithaca: Cornell University Press, 1994), p. 185.

39. Quoted in Yergin, *The Prize*, p. 195.

40. Yergin, *The Prize*, p. 189; Anand Toprani, 'An Anglo-American "Petroleum Entente"? The First Attempt to Reach an Anglo-American Oil Agreement, 1921', *The Historian 79*, no. 1 (2017): p. 64.

41. John A. DeNovo, 'The Movement for an Aggressive American Oil Policy Abroad, 1918–1920', *American Historical Review 61*, no. 4 (July 1956), p. 865.

42. Yergin, *The Prize*, p. 201.

43. Yergin, *The Prize*, pp. 289–92.

44. See Melvyn P. Leffler, *Safeguarding Democratic Capitalism: US Foreign Policy and National Security, 1920–2015* (Princeton: Princeton University Press, 2017), ch. 3; Mervyn Leffler, 'American Policy Making and European Stability', *Pacific Historical Review 46*, no. 2 (1977): pp. 207–28.

45. Ron Chernow, *The House of Morgan: An American Banking Dynasty and the Rise of Modern Finance* (New York: Grove Press, 2010), p. 203.

46. Quoted in Adam Tooze, *The Deluge: The Great War, America, and the Remaking of the Global Order, 1916–1931* (London: Penguin, 2015), p. 65.

47. Leffler, 'American Policy Making and European Stability', p. 215; Chernow, *House of Morgan*, pp. 181–2.

48. Roberts, 'Benjamin Strong, the Federal Reserve and the Limits to Interwar American Nationalism', p. 74.

49. Ahmed, *The Lords of Finance*, p. 140.

50. On the place of the different debts in British–American relations see Robert Self, 'Perception and Posture in Anglo-American Relations: The War Debt Controversy in the "Official Mind", 1919–1940', *The International History Review 29*, no. 2 (2007): pp. 282–312.

51. Adam Tooze, *The Wages of Destruction: The Making and Breaking of the Nazi Economy* (London: Penguin, 2007), p. 6.

52. Frank Costigliola, 'The United States and the Reconstruction of Germany in the 1920s', *The Business History Review 50*, no. 4 (1976): pp. 498–502.

53. Ahmed, *The Lords of Finance*, p. 395; Tooze, *The Wages of Destruction*, pp. 7, 13, 657.

54. Tooze, *The Wages of Destruction*, p. 28.
55. Ahmed, *The Lords of Finance*, p. 462.
56. Quoted in Ahmed, *The Lords of Finance*, p. 470.
57. For the influential argument that the depression's primary cause was the United States' inability as the theoretical hegemon of the international monetary system to act as a stabilizer see Charles Kindleberger, *The World in Depression 1929–1939*, 40th anniversary edition (Berkeley: California University Press, 2013).
58. Yergin, *The Prize*, p. 329.
59. Thomas Parke Hughes, 'Technological Momentum in History: Hydrogenation in Germany 1898–1933', *Past and Present 44*, no. 1 (1969): p. 123.
60. Raymond Stokes, 'The Oil Industry in Nazi Germany, 1936–1945', *Business History Review 59*, no. 2 (1985): p. 257.
61. Tooze, *The Wages of Destruction*, pp. 116–18, 226–7. On the Nazi regime's oil policies and their ultimate failure see Anand Toprani, *Oil and the Great Powers: Britain and Germany 1914–1945* (Oxford: Oxford University Press, 2019), chs. 6–8. On the failure, by contrast, of Japan's attempt to build a synthetic fuel industry see Anthony N. Stranges, 'Synthetic Fuel Production in Prewar and World War II Japan: A Case Study in Technological Failure', *Annals of Science 50*, no. 3 (1993): pp. 229–65.
62. On Hitler's oil motives for Operation Barbarossa see Tooze, *The Wages of Destruction*, pp. 423–5, 455–60; Joel Hayward, 'Hitler's Quest for Oil: The Impact of Economic Considerations on Military Strategy, 1941–1942', *Journal of Strategic Studies 18*, no. 4 (1995): pp. 94–135; Anand Toprani, 'The First War for Oil: The Caucasus, German Strategy, and the Turning Point of the War on the Eastern Front, 1942', *Journal of Military History 80*, no. 3 (2016): pp. 815–54. On the Nazi creation in 1940–41 of an oil company—The Continental Oil Company (Konti)—to rival the Anglo-American companies and the place of this in Nazi Germany's ambition to make Germany a world power see Anand Toprani, 'Germany's Answer to Standard Oil: The Continental Oil Company and Nazi Grand Strategy, 1940–1942', *Journal of Strategic Studies 37*, no. 6–7 (2014): pp. 949–73.
63. Yergin, *The Prize*, pp. 339–43.
64. Quoted in B.S. McBeth, *British Oil Policy 1919–1939* (London: Cass, 1985), pp. 34–5.
65. Yergin, *Prize*, p. 332.
66. On the failure of Britain's interwar bid to end American oil dependency see Toprani, *Oil and the Great Powers*, chs. 3–4; McBeth, *British Oil Policy 1919–1939*.
67. Hans Heymann Jr, 'Oil in Soviet-Western Relations in the Interwar Years', *The American Slavic and Eastern European Review 7*, no. 4 (1948): pp. 303–16.
68. Anand Toprani, 'The French Connection: A New Perspective on the End of the Red Line Agreement, 1945–1948', *Diplomatic History 36*, no. 2 (2012): p. 263 fn.7.

69. For an analysis of French oil policy through the lens of transnational commercial competition and the weakness of the French state in relation to that competition through the first third of the twentieth century see Nowell, *Mercantile States and the World Oil Cartel.*

70. Michael B. Stoff, 'The Anglo-American Oil Agreement and the Wartime Search for Foreign Oil Policy', *Business History Review 55*, no. 1 (1981): p. 63.

71. On French resistance to the end of the Red Line Agreement and how Washington used French financial dependency to break it see Toprani, 'The French Connection'.

72. Yergin, *The Prize*, p. 425.

73. James Barr, *Lords of the Desert: Britain's Struggle with America to Dominate the Middle East* (London: Simon & Schuster 2018), pp. 61–7.

74. Painter, 'Oil and the American Century', p. 29.

75. On Germany's problems in this respect see McMeekin, *The Berlin-Baghdad Express*, epilogue.

76. Rapid Soviet industrialization under Stalin was in part made possible by the hard currency Soviet oil exports produced. Yergin, *The Prize*, p. 266.

77. Quoted in D'Agostino, *The Rise of the Global Powers*, p. 43.

78. H.J. Mackinder, 'The Geographical Pivot of History', *The Geographical Journal 23*, no. 4 (1904): p. 436.

79. The initial plan devised by the Roosevelt administration for post-war Germany—the Morgenthau Plan—would have solved the problem by deindustrializing Germany. Now, when the issue is as much gas and the transit of that gas as oil, the Nord Stream pipelines can be seen, as Anthony D'Agostino has described them, 'as a kind of economic Rapallo'. D'Agostino, *The Rise of Global Powers*, p. 477.

Chapter 2

1. US Energy Information Administration, International Data, Petroleum and Other Liquids, https://www.eia.gov/international/data/world Data from the US Energy Information Administration is subject to revision. These numbers were those provided by EIA in September 2021.

2. US Energy Information Administration, US Imports from OPEC Countries of Crude Oil and Petroleum Products, https://www.eia.gov/dnav/pet/hist/LeafHandler.ashx?n=pet&s=mttimxx1&f=a

3. US Energy Information Administration, US Exports of Crude Oil and Petroleum Products, https://www.eia.gov/dnav/pet/hist/LeafHandler.ashx?n=PET&s=MTTEXUS2&f=A

4. Quoted in Helen Thompson, *Oil and the Western Economic Crisis* (London: Palgrave, 2017), p. 80.

5. Quoted in Ivana Kottasová, 'Saudi Arabia Tries to Break "Dangerous" Addiction to Oil', *CNN Business*, 25 April 2016, https://money.cnn.com/2016/04/25/news/economy/saudi-arabia-oil-addiction-economy-plan/index.html

6. Timothy Gardner, Steve Holland, Dmitry Zhdannikov, and Rania El Gamal, 'Special Report—Trump Told Saudis: Cut Oil Supply or Lose US Military Support', *Reuters*, 30 April 2020, https://www.reuters.com/article/us-global-oil-trump-saudi-specialreport/special-report-trump-told-saudi-cut-oil-supply-or-lose-u-s-military-support-sources-idUKKBN22C1V4

7. Benn Steil, *The Battle of Bretton Woods: John Maynard Keynes, Harry Dexter White, and the Making of a New World Order* (Princeton: Princeton University Press, 2013), p. 155.

8. Steil, *The Battle of Bretton Woods*, p. 135.

9. Steil, *The Battle of Bretton Woods*, p. 301.

10. Lawrence A. Kaplan, 'The United States and the Origins of NATO 1946–49', *The Review of Politics 31*, no. 2 (1969): p. 213.

11. Steil, *The Battle of Bretton Woods*, pp. 290–1; Benn Steil, *The Marshall Plan: Dawn of the Cold War* (Oxford: Oxford University Press, 2018), p. xii. On Dexter White's espionage and Soviet sympathies see Steil, *The Battle of Bretton Woods*, pp. 35–46, 318–26.

12. On the role of Iran in the origins of the Cold War see Gary Hess, 'The Iranian Crisis of 1945–46 and the Cold War', *Political Science Quarterly 89*, no. 1 (1974): pp. 117–46; Louise Fawcett, *Iran and the Cold War: The Azerbaijan Crisis of 1946* (Cambridge: Cambridge University Press, 2009).

13. Steil, *The Marshall Plan*, pp. 362–3. On the centrality of West Germany to the Marshall Plan see Helge Berger and Albrecht Ritschl, 'Germany and the Political Economy of the Marshall Plan, 1947–1952: a re-revisionist view', in *Europe's Post-War Recovery*, edited by Barry Eichengreen (Cambridge: Cambridge University Press 1995).

14. Stanley Hoffman, 'Obstinate or Obsolete? The Fate of the Nation-State and the Case of Western Europe', *Daedelus 95*, no. 3 (1966): p. 908. Armin Rappaport, 'The United States and European Integration: The First Phase', *Diplomatic History 5*, no. 2 (1981): pp. 121–2. On the initial American push for West European integration see Geir Lundestad, *Empire by Integration: The United States and European Integration, 1945–1997* (New York: Oxford University Press, 1998), ch. 4.

15. Hoffman, 'Obstinate or Obsolete?', p. 907.

16. On NATO's creation see Lawrence S. Kaplan, *NATO 1948: The Birth of the Transatlantic Alliance* (Lanham, MD: Rowan & Littlefield, 2007).

17. Charles Maier, *Among Empires: American Ascendancy and its Predecessors* (Cambridge, MA: Harvard University Press), p. 175.

18. On the American push for the European Defence Community see Brian R. Duchin, 'The "Agonizing Re-appraisal": Eisenhower, Dulles and the European Defense Community', *Diplomatic History 16*, no. 2 (1992): pp. 201–21.

19. Our World in Data, Energy, Global Primary Energy: How has the Mix Changed Over Centuries?, https://ourworldindata.org/energy-mix

20. US Energy Information Administration, US Energy Facts Explained, https://www.eia.gov/energyexplained/us-energy-facts/

21. Our World in Data, Energy, France CO2 Country Profile: Energy Consumption by Source, https://ourworldindata.org/co2/country/france?country=~FRA Our World in Data, Energy, Italy CO2 Country Profile: Energy Consumption by Source, https://ourworldindata.org/energy/country/italy?country=~ITA

22. Vaclal Smil, *Energy and Civilization: A History* (Cambridge, MA: The MIT Press, 2017), p. 327.

23. Bruce W. Jentleson, 'Khrushchev's Oil and Brezhnev's Natural Gas Pipelines: The Causes and Consequence of the Decline in American Leverage Over Western Europe' in *Will Europe Fight for Oil? Energy Relations in the Atlantic Area*, edited by Robert J. Lieber (New York: Praeger, 1983), pp. 35–8.

24. Ethan B. Kapstein, *The Insecure Alliance: Energy Crises and Western Politics Since 1944* (Oxford: Oxford University Press, 1990), p. 69.

25. Kapstein, *The Insecure Alliance*, p. 95.

26. Steven G. Galpern, *Money, Oil and Empire in The Middle East: Sterling and Post-War Imperialism, 1944–1971* (Cambridge: Cambridge University Press, 2013), pp. 7–8; James Barr, *Lords of the Desert: Britain's Struggle with America to Dominate the Middle East* (London: Simon & Schuster, 2018), pp. 116, 120.

27. Daniel Yergin, *The Prize: The Epic Quest for Oil, Money, and Power* (New York: Simon & Schuster, 1993), p. 424; David S. Painter, 'The Marshall Plan and Oil', *Cold War History 9*, no. 2 (2009): pp. 159–75.

28. Jeffrey R. Macris, *The Politics and Security of the Gulf: Anglo-American Hegemony and the Shaping of a Region* (London: Routledge, 2010), p. 82; Kapstein, *The Insecure Alliance*, p. 203.

29. Michael J. Cohen 'From "Cold" to "Hot" War: Allied Strategic and Military Interests in the Middle East after the Second World War', *Middle Eastern Studies 43*, no. 5 (2007): pp. 727–31.

30. See Laila Amin Morsy, 'The Role of the United States in the Anglo-Egyptian Agreement of 1954', *Middle Eastern Studies 29*, no. 3 (1993): pp. 526–58; Douglas Little, 'His Finest Hour? Eisenhower, Lebanon and the 1958 Middle Eastern Crisis', *Diplomatic History 20*, no. 1 (1996): pp. 27–54.

31. Quoted in Steil, *The Marshall Plan*, p. 44.

32. Tyler Priest, 'The Dilemmas of Oil Empire', *Journal of American History 99*, no. 1 (2012): pp. 236–51.

33. For an insider American perspective on Turkey's accession to NATO see George C. McGhee, *The US-Turkey-NATO-Middle East Connection* (New York: Macmillan, 1990). For a Turkish perspective see Paul Kubicek, 'Turkey's Inclusion in the Atlantic Community: Looking Back, Looking Forward', *Turkish Studies 9*, no. 1 (2008): pp. 21–35.

34. Barr, *Lords of the Desert*, pp. 102–3.

35. On the CIA–MI6 coup see Barr, *Lords of the Desert*, ch. 14.

36. Barr, *Lords of the Desert*, p. 174; Yergin, *The Prize*, pp. 470–8.

37. For analysis of the Suez crisis as a systemic crisis see Ralph Dietl, 'Suez 1956: A European Intervention', *Journal of Contemporary History 43*, no. 2 (2008): 259–78; Hans J. Morgenthau, 'Sources of Tension Between Western Europe and the United States', in *Annals of the American Academy of Political and Social Science 312* (1957): pp. 22–8.

38. US Department of State, Office of the Historian, Foreign Relations of the United States, 1955–57, Suez Crisis, July 26–December 31 1956, vol XVI, Message from Prime Minister Eden to President Eisenhower, London, 27 July, 1956, https://history.state.gov/historicaldocuments/frus1955-57v16/d5

39. US Department of State, Office of the Historian, Foreign Relations of the United States, 1955–57, Suez Crisis, July 26–December 31 1956, vol XVI, Letter from President Eisenhower to Prime Minister Eden, Washington, DC, 31 July, 1956, https://history.state.gov/historicaldocuments/frus1955-57v16/d35

40. Yergin, *The Prize*, p. 491; Barr, *Lords of the Desert*, p. 245; David S. Painter, 'Oil and the American Century', *Journal of American History 99*, no. 1 (2012): p. 31.

41. Quoted in Yergin, *The Prize*, p. 491.

42. Steil, *The Battle of Bretton Woods*, p. 332.

43. Gregory Brew, '"Our Most Dependable Allies": Iraq, Saudi Arabia, and the Eisenhower Doctrine, 1956–58', *Mediterranean Quarterly 26*, no. 4 (2015): pp. 89–109.

44. Jeffrey R. Macris, *The Politics and Security of the Gulf: Anglo-American Hegemony and the Shaping of a Region* (London: Routledge, 2010), p. 113; Yergin, *The Prize*, p. 498.

45. See Douglas Little, 'His Finest Hour? Eisenhower, Lebanon and the 1958 Middle Eastern Crisis', *Diplomatic History 20*, no. 1 (1996): pp. 27–54.

46. Quoted in Dietl, 'Suez 1956', p. 261.

47. Quoted in Stefan Jonsson, 'Clashing Internationalisms: East European Narratives of West European Integration' in *Europe faces Europe: Narratives from its Eastern Half*, edited by Johan Fornäs (Bristol: Intellect, 2017), p. 70.

48. Hoffman, 'Obstinate or Obsolete?' p. 894.

49. Wolfram Kaiser, *Using Europe, Abusing the Europeans: Britain and European Integration 1945–63* (Basingstoke: Palgrave Macmillan, 1996), pp. 151–4.

50. See Kaiser, *Using Europe, Abusing the Europeans*, chs. 5 and 6.

51. On the impact of de Gaulle see Hoffman, 'Obstinate or Obsolete?', pp. 872–4, 893–903.

52. On the relationship between oil, French rule in Algeria, and France's support for the EEC see Robert Cantoni, *Oil Exploration, Diplomacy, and Security in the Early Cold War: The Enemy Underground* (Abingdon: Routledge, 2017), chs. 2–3.

53. Megan Brown, 'Drawing Algeria into Europe: Shifting French Policy and the Treaty of Rome', *Modern and Contemporary France 25*, no. 2 (2017): p. 195–6. On the long history of the push for European unity and

colonialism in Africa see Peo Hansen and Stefan Jonsson, *Eurafrica: The Untold History of European Integration and Colonialism* (London: Bloomsbury Academic, 2014).

54. Yergin, *The Prize*, p. 569.

55. Barr, *Lords of the Desert*, p. 274.

56. Kevin Boyle, 'The Price of Peace: Vietnam, the Pound, and the Crisis of the American Empire', *Diplomatic History 27*, no. 1 (2003): p. 43.

57. On the ENI–Soviet relationship see Cantoni, *Oil Exploration, Diplomacy, and Security*, chs. 1 and 5.

58. Kapstein, *The Insecure Alliance*, p. 137.

59. Quoted in Bruce W. Jentleson, 'From Consensus to Conflict: The Domestic Political Economy of East-West Energy Trade Policy', *International Organization 38*, no. 4 (1984): p. 640.

60. Jentleson, 'From Consensus to Conflict', pp. 643–4.

61. Bruce W. Jentleson, 'Khrushchev's Oil and Brezhnev's Natural Gas Pipelines: The Causes and Consequence of the Decline in American Leverage over Western Europe' in *Will Europe Fight for Oil? Energy Relations in the Atlantic Area*, edited by Robert J. Lieber (New York: Praeger, 1983) pp. 46–7.

62. Jentleson, 'Khrushchev's Oil and Brezhnev's Natural Gas Pipelines', p. 47.

63. Kapstein, *The Insecure Alliance*, p. 138; Jentleson, 'Khrushchev's Oil and Brezhnev's Natural Gas Pipelines', p. 49.

64. Jentleson, 'From Consensus to Conflict', p. 641; Yergin, *The Prize*, pp. 516–20.

65. Yergin, *The Prize*, p 523; Jentleson, 'From Consensus to Conflict', p. 641.

66. On French oil policy and the Arab states see Robert J. Lieber, *The Oil Decade: Conflict and Co-operation in the West* (New York: Praeger, 1983), ch. 5.

67. Kapstein, *The Insecure Alliance*, p. 144; Galpern, *Money, Oil and Empire in the Middle East*, p. 368.

68. On the fallout of the British exit from the Persian Gulf see Jeffrey R. Macris, *The Politics and Security of the Gulf*, ch. 5.

69. Boyle, 'The Price of Peace', p. 45.

70. Quoted in Galpern, *Money, Oil and Empire in the Middle East*, p. 278. On US–Iranian relations during the Johnson and Nixon years see Roham Alvandi 'Nixon, Kissinger, and the Shah: The Origins of Iranian Primacy in the Persian Gulf', *Diplomatic History 36*, no. 2 (2012): pp. 337–72.

71. Yergin, *The Prize*, pp. 532–5, 637–8.

72. See Eugenie M. Blang, 'A Reappraisal of Germany's Vietnam Policy, 1963–1966: Ludwig Erhard's Response to America's War in Vietnam', *German Studies Review 27*, no. 2 (2004): pp. 341–60. On previous German Cold War policy see Ronald J. Granieri, *The Ambivalent Alliance, Konrad Adenauer: The CDU/CSU, and the West, 1949–1966* (New York: Berghahn Books, 2003). On the Nixon Administration's reaction to Ostpolitik see Jean-François Juneau, 'The Limits of Linkage: The Nixon Administration and Willy Brandt's Ostpolitik, 1969–72', *International History Review 33*, no. 2 (2011): pp. 277–97.

73. Quoted in Robert M. Collins, 'The Economic Crisis of 1968 and the Waning of the "American Century"', *American Historical Review 101*, no. 2 (1996): p. 416.

74. Thompson, *Oil and the Western Economic Crisis*, p. 94.

75. Thompson, *Oil and the Western Economic Crisis*, p. 94.

76. On the centrality of Central and Western European exports to Soviet development of the west Siberian gas fields and its implications for the Soviet–German relationship see Thane Gustafson, *The Bridge: Natural Gas in a Redivided Europe* (Cambridge, MA: Harvard University Press, 2020), ch. 2. On the German green movement and nuclear power see Stephen Milder, *Greening Democracy: The Anti-Nuclear Movement and Political Environmentalism in West Germany and Beyond, 1968–1983* (Cambridge: Cambridge University Press, 2017).

77. Jentleson, 'From Consensus to Conflict', pp. 645–6; Jentleson, 'Khrushchev's Oil and Brezhnev's Natural Gas Pipelines', p. 49.

78. US Department of State, The Washington Summit: General Secretary Brezhnev's Visit to the United States June 18–25, 1973, p. 51, http://insidethecoldwar.org/sites/default/files/documents/The%20Washington%20Summit%2C%20June%2018-25%2C%201973.pdf

79. Jentleson, 'From Consensus to Conflict', p. 648.

80. On US–Soviet relations during the Yom Kippur War see John L. Scherer, 'Soviet and American Behaviour During the Yom Kippur War', *World Affairs 141*, no. 1 (1978): pp. 3–23.

81. Yergin, *The Prize*, p. 595.

82. Thomas Robb, 'The Power of Oil: Edward Heath, The "Year of Europe" and the Special Relationship', *Contemporary British History 26*, no. 1 (2012): p. 79.

83. Kapstein, *The Insecure Alliance*, p. 166.

84. Macris, *The Politics and Security of the Gulf*, pp. 202–4.

85. Quoted in Kapstein, *The Insecure Alliance*, p. 165.

86. Quoted in Robb, 'The Power of Oil', p. 80.

87. Kapstein, *The Insecure Alliance*, p. 174.

88. Yergin, *The Prize*, pp. 643–4.

89. Richard Nixon, Address to the nation about national energy policy, 7 November 1973, https://www.presidency.ucsb.edu/documents/address-the-nation-about-national-energy-policy

90. See Shahram Chubin, 'The Soviet Union and Iran', *Foreign Affairs 61*, no. 2 (1983): pp. 921–49.

91. Jimmy Carter, Address to the nation: energy and the national goals, 15 July 1979, https://www.jimmycarterlibrary.gov/assets/documents/speeches/energy-crisis.phtml

92. Quoted in Melvyn Leffler, 'From the Truman Doctrine to the Carter Doctrine: lessons and dilemmas of the Cold War', *Diplomatic History 7*, no. 4 (1983): p. 246.

93. Quoted in Leffler, 'From the Truman Doctrine to the Carter Doctrine', p. 261.

94. There was a clear parallel between the Carter Doctrine and Britain's 'Persian Gulf Declaration' in May 1903: 'We should regard the establishment of a naval base, or of a fortified port, in the Persian Gulf by any other Power as a very grave menace to British interests, and we should certainly resist it with all the means at our disposal.' Quoted in Pascal Venier, 'The Geographical Pivot of History and Early Twentieth Century Geopolitical Culture', *The Geographical Journal 170*, no. 4 (2004): p. 332.

95. Victor McFarland, 'The United States and the Oil Price Collapse of the 1980s' in *Counter-shock: The Oil Counter-Revolution of the 1980s*, edited by Duccio Basosi, Giuliano Garavini, and Massimiliano Trentin (London: I.B. Taurus, 2020), p. 273.

96. Kapstein, *The Insecure Alliance*, p. 195; Walter J. Levy, 'Oil and the Decline of the West', *Foreign Affairs 58* (Summer 1980): p. 1011.

97. Robert J. Lieber 'Will Europe Fight for Oil?: Energy and Atlantic Security' in Lieber, ed. *Will Europe Fight for Oil?* p. 4; Lieber, *The Oil Decade*, p. 62.

98. Leffler, 'From the Truman Doctrine to the Carter Doctrine', p. 259.

99. Quoted Steven Rattner, 'Britain Defying US Restriction in Soviet Project', *New York Times*, 3 August 1982.

100. Lieber, *The Oil Decade*, p. 9.

101. Yergin, *The Prize*, p. 743.

102. See, for example, Peter Schweizer, *Victory: The Reagan Administration's Secret Strategy that Hastened the Collapse of the Soviet Union* (New York: Grove Press, 1994).

103. Painter, 'Oil and the American Century', p. 36. For discussion of the evidence see David Painter, 'From Linkage to Economic Warfare: Energy, Soviet-American Relations and the End of the Cold War' in *Cold War Energy: A Transnational History of Soviet Oil and Gas*, edited by Jeronim Perović (London: Palgrave Macmillan, 2017); Majid Al-Moneef, 'Saudi Arabia and the Counter-shock of 1986' in *Counter-shock*, pp. 112–13; Yergin, *The Prize*, pp. 756–8; Victor McFarland, 'The United States and the Oil Price Collapse of the 1980s' in *Counter-shock*, pp. 262–9.

104. Quoted in Meg Jacobs, *Panic at the Pump: The Energy Crisis and the Transformation of American Politics in the 1970s* (New York: Hill and Wang, 2016), p. 289.

105. On the economic consequences of the reverse oil price shock for the American oil industry and the economy more generally see McFarland, 'The United States and the Oil Price Collapse of the 1980s'.

106. Jacobs, *Panic at the Pump*, p. 284.

107. James Schlesinger, 'Will War Yield Oil Security?' *Challenge 34*, no. 2 (1991): p. 27.

108. On the importance of oil to the Soviet collapse see Yegor Gaidar, *Collapse of an Empire: Lessons for Modern Russia* (Washington, DC: Brookings Institution Press, 2008), pp. 100–9.

Chapter 3

1. US Department of State, 'Background Briefing on Secretary Kerry's Meeting with Russian Foreign Minister Sergey Lavrov', Press Release, 27 September 2015, https://2009–2017.state.gov/r/pa/prs/ps/2015/09/247376.htm

2. Full Transcript, Second 2016 Presidential Debate, *Politico*, 10 October 2016, https://www.politico.com/story/2016/10/2016-presidential-debate-transcript-229519

3. Full Transcript, First 2016 Presidential Debate, *Politico*, 27 September 2016, https://www.politico.com/story/2016/09/full-transcript-first-2016-presidential-debate-228761

4. Zbigniew Brzezinski, *The Grand Chessboard: American Primacy and its Geostrategic Imperatives*, Basic Books, Kindle edition, ch. 3.

5. On the immediate development of European defence policy after the St Malo Declaration see Anand Menon, 'Playing With Fire: The EU's Defence Policy', *Politique Européenne 4*, no. 8 (2002): pp. 32–45.

6. Benn Steil, *The Marshall Plan: Dawn of the Cold War* (New York: Simon & Schuster, 2018), p. 395. For optimism as late as 2010 about NATO's capacity to generate democracy see Charles Kupchan, 'NATO's Final Frontier: Why Russia Should Join the Atlantic Alliance', *Foreign Affairs 89*, no. 3 (May/June 2010). For much earlier scepticism see Dan Reiter, 'Why NATO Enlargement Does Not Spread Democracy', *International Security 25*, no. 4 (2001): pp. 41–67.

7. On whether NATO's expansion was inevitable see Kimberly Marten, 'Reconsidering NATO Expansion: A Counterfactual Analysis of Russia and the West in the 1990s', *European Journal of International Security 3*, no. 2 (2018): pp. 135–61.

8. Quoted in Craig C. Smith, 'Chirac Upsets East Europe by Telling it to "Shut Up" on Iraq', *New York Times*, 18 February 2003, https://www.nytimes.com/2003/02/18/international/europe/chirac-upsets-east-europe-by-telling-it-to-shut-up-on.html

9. Anand Menon, 'From Crisis to Catharsis: ESDP After Iraq', *International Affairs 80*, no. 4 (2004): p. 639.

10. Steil, *The Marshall Plan*, p. 389.

11. In Zbigniew Brzezinski's book, *The Grand Chessboard*, Ukraine is the 'geopolitical pivot' of the post–Cold War world.

12. See Andrew Wilson, *Ukraine's Orange Revolution* (New Haven: Yale University Press, 2005).

13. Quoted in Mathias Roth, 'EU-Ukraine Relations After the Orange Revolution: The Role of the New Member States', *Perspectives on European Politics and Society 8*, no. 4 (2007): p. 509.

14. Helen Thompson, *Oil and the Western Economic Crisis* (London: Palgrave, 2017), pp. 16–17.

15. On the politics of the Nabucco pipeline see Pavel K. Baev and Indra Øverland, 'The South Stream Versus Nabucco Pipeline Race: Geopolitical and Economic (Ir)rationales and Political Stakes in Mega-Projects', *International Affairs 86*, no. 5 (2010): pp. 1075–190.

16. Thompson, *Oil and the Western Economic Crisis*, p. 17.

17. Saban Kardas, 'Geo-strategic Position as Leverage in EU Accession: The Case of Turkish-EU Negotiations on the Nabucco Pipeline', *Southeast European and Black Sea Studies 11*, no. 1 (2011): p. 38.

18. Quoted in Meltem Müftüler-Bac, 'The Never-Ending Story: Turkey and the European Union', *Middle Eastern Studies 34*, no. 4 (1998): p. 240.

19. Müftüler-Bac 'The Never-Ending Story', p. 240.

20. Quoted in Ekavi Athanassopoulou, 'American-Turkish Relations Since the End of the Cold War', *Middle East Policy 8*, no. 3 (2001): p. 146.

21. For the American perspective see Kemal Kirisci, *Turkey and the West: Faultlines in a Troubled Alliance* (Washington, DC: Brookings Institution Press, 2018), ch. 2.

22. Peter W. Rodman, 'Middle East Diplomacy After the Gulf War', *Foreign Affairs 70*, no. 2 (Spring 1991): pp. 2–3.

23. James Schlesinger, 'Will War Yield Oil Security?' *Challenge 34*, no. 2 (1991): p. 30.

24. US Energy Information Administration, International Data, Petroleum and Other Liquids, https://www.eia.gov/international/data/world

25. For a critique of the war's energy logic see Christopher Layne, 'America's Middle East Grand Strategy After Iraq: The Moment for Offshore Balancing has Arrived', *Review of International Studies 35*, no. 1 (2009): pp. 5–25.

26. Alan Greenspan, the former chairman of the Federal Reserves, in his memoirs wrote: 'I am saddened that it is politically inconvenient to acknowledge what everyone knows: the Iraq war is largely about oil.' Alan Greenspan, *The Age of Turbulence* (London: Allen Lane, 2007), p. 463. For a critique of neo-conservative hopes in Iraq from a realist perspective see John J. Mearsheimer, 'Hans Morgenthau and the Iraq War: Realism Versus Neo-Conservatism', *Open Democracy*, 18 May 2005, https://www.opendemocracy.net/en/morgenthau_2522jsp/ For the argument that the Iraq War was motivated by realist thinking see Daniel Deudney and G. John Ikenberry, 'Realism, Liberalism, and the Iraq War', *Survival 59*, no. 4 (2017): pp. 7–26.

27. Andrew Bacevich, 'Ending Endless War: A Pragmatic Military Strategy', *Foreign Affairs 95*, no. 5 (September/October 2016): p. 39.

28. On the failure of American planning for post-war Iraq see Aaron Rapport, *Waging War, Planning Peace: US Noncombat Operations and Major Wars* (Ithaca: Cornell University Press, 2015), ch. 3.

29. Hans Kundnani, 'Germany as a Geo-Economic Power', *The Washington Quarterly 34*, no. 3 (2011): p. 35.

30. Quoted in R. Nicholas Burns, 'NATO Has Adapted: An Alliance With a New Mission', *New York Times*, 24 May 2003, https://www.nytimes.com/2003/05/24/opinion/IHT-nato-has-adapted-an-alliance-with-a-new-mission.html On the war's consequences for the US–German relationship see Stephen F. Szabo, *Parting Ways: The Crisis in German-American Relations* (Washington, DC: Brookings Institution Press, 2004).

31. Quoted in John Hooper and Ian Black, 'Anger at Rumsfeld Attack on "Old Europe"', *Guardian*, 24 January 2003, https://www.theguardian.com/world/2003/jan/24/germany.france

32. Daniel Yergin, *The New Map: Energy, Climate, and the Clash of Nations* (London: Allen Lane, 2020), p. 157.

33. See Marc Lanteigne, 'China's Maritime Security and the "Malacca Dilemma"', *Asian Security 4*, no. 2 (2008): pp. 143–61.

34. Erica Downs, 'Sino-Russian Energy Relations: An Uncertain Courtship' in *The Future of China-Russia Relations*, edited by James Bellacqua (Lexington, KY: University of Kentucky Press, 2010), p. 148.

35. Thane Gustafson, *The Bridge: Natural Gas in a Redivided Europe* (Cambridge, MA: Harvard University Press, 2020), p. 319.

36. On the implications of gas dependency for Europe see Agnia Grigas, *The New Geopolitics of Natural Gas* (Cambridge, MA: Harvard University Press, 2017), ch. 4.

37. Euractiv, 'Nord Stream "a Waste of Money" Says Poland', 11 January 2010, https://www.euractiv.com/section/central-europe/news/nord-stream-a-waste-of-money-says-poland/

38. On the importance of Italian, German, and French firms in determining the Italian, German, and French governments' energy policies towards Russia see Rawi Abdelal, 'The Profits of Power: Commerce and Realpolitik in Eurasia', *Review of International Political Economy 20*, no. 3 (2013): pp. 421–56.

39. For the argument from within the State Department for NATO enlargement to the Black Sea and the Caucasus see Ronald Asmus, 'Europe's Eastern Promise: Rethinking NATO and EU Enlargement', *Foreign Affairs 87*, no. 1 (January/February 2008): pp. 95–106.

40. Adam Tooze, *Crashed: How a Decade of Financial Crises Changed the World* (London: Penguin, 2018), pp. 136–7.

41. See Jolyon Howorth, '"Stability on the Borders"; The Ukrainian Crisis and the EU's Constrained Policy Towards the Eastern Neighbourhood', *Journal of Common Market Studies 55*, no. 1 (2017): pp. 121–36.

42. European Commission, Communication from the Commission to the European Parliament and Council, European Energy security strategy,

28 May 2014, p. 2, https://eur-lex.europa.eu/legal-content/EN/ALL/?uri=CELEXper cent3A52014DC0330

43. José Manuel Durão Barroso, President of the European Commission Signature of the Nabucco Intergovernmental Agreement, Ankara, 13 July 2009.

44. European Commission, Communication from the Commission to the European Parliament and Council, European Energy Security Strategy, 28 May 2014, p. 2. Saban Kardas, 'Geo-strategic Position as Leverage in EU Accession: The Case of Turkish-EU Negotiations on the Nabucco Pipeline', *Southeast European and Black Sea Studies 11*, no. 1 (2011): p. 43.

45. Erhan İçener, 'Privileged Partnership: An Alternative Final Destination for Turkey's Integration with the European Union?' *Perspectives on European Politics and Society 8*, no. 4 (2007): pp. 421–5.

46. Quoted in Kardas, 'Geo-strategic Position as Leverage in EU Accession', p. 35.

47. Kardas, 'Geo-strategic Position as Leverage in EU Accession', p. 46.

48. Henry Kissinger, *World Order: Reflections on the Character of Nations and the Course of History* (London: Penguin, 2015), pp. 323–4.

49. On the post-2003 American decision-making on Iraq see Michael R. Gordon and Bernard E. Trainer, *The Endgame: The Inside Story of the Struggle for Iraq, from George W. Bush to Barack Obama* (New York: Atlantic Books, 2012).

50. On the importance of the Iraq War to the 2008 presidential election see Gary C. Jacobson, 'George W. Bush, the Iraq War, and the Election of Barack Obama', *Presidential Studies Quarterly 40*, no. 2 (2010): pp. 207–24.

51. On the Obama administration's internal trajectory to the Pivot to Asia see Nicholas D. Anderson and Victor D. Cha, 'The Case of the Pivot to Asia: System Effects and the Origins of Strategy', *Political Science Quarterly 132*, no. 4 (2017): pp. 595–617.

52. BBC News, 'Obama: The United States is a Pacific Power Here to Stay', 17 November 2011, https://www.bbc.co.uk/news/av/world-asia-15768505

53. Our World in Data, Energy, China: Country Energy Profile, https://ourworldindata.org/energy/country/china?country=~CHN

54. Charles A. Kupchan, *No-one's World: The West, the Rising Rest, and the Coming Global Turn* (New York: Oxford University Press, 2013), p. 101. For the importance of maritime geography to China see Bernard Cole, *China's Quest for Great Power: Ships, Oil and Foreign Policy* (Annapolis, MD: Naval Institute Press, 2016), ch. 1.

55. Quoted in Yergin, *The New Map*, p. 182.

56. Min Ye, *The Belt Road and Beyond: State-Mobilised Globalisation in China 1998–2018* (Cambridge: Cambridge University Press, 2020).

57. On the importance of Gwadar to China see Syed Fazl-e-Haider, 'A Strategic Seaport: Is Pakistan Key to China's Energy Supremacy?', *Foreign Affairs*, 5 March 2015, https://www.foreignaffairs.com/articles/china/2015-03-05/strategic-seaport

58. Quoted in Cole, *China's Quest for Great Power*, pp. 51, 128.

59. Economist, 'America Wants a Bigger Navy of Smaller Ships to Compete with China's Fleet', 21 September 2020, https://www.economist.com/united-states/2020/09/21/america-wants-a-bigger-navy-of-smaller-ships-to-compete-with-chinas-fleet

60. Quoted in Megan Ingram, 'With American Natural Gas, Russia is Losing European Energy Chokehold', *The Hill*, 3 July 2017, https://thehill.com/blogs/pundits-blog/energy-environment/340502-with-american-natural-gas-russia-is-losing-european

61. Gustafson, *The Bridge*, pp. 356, 413.

62. On the financial reasons why Nabucco failed see Morena Skalamera, 'Revisiting the Nabucco Debacle: Myths and Realities', *Problems of Post-Communism 65*, no. 1 (2018): pp. 18–36.

63. For some sharp remarks on Bulgaria's geopolitical difficulties given its border with Turkey and closeness to Russia see Robert D. Kaplan, *The Return of Marco Polo's World: War, Strategy, and American Interests in the Twenty-First Century* (New York: Random House, 2019), pp. 36–8.

64. Anca Gurzu and Joseph J. Schatz, 'Great Northern Gas War', *Politico*, 10 February 2016, https://www.politico.eu/article/the-great-northern-gas-war-nordstream-pipeline-gazprom-putin-ukraine-russia/

65. Younkyoo Kim and Stephen Blank, 'The New Great Game of Caspian Energy in 2013–14: "Turk Stream", Russia and Turkey', *Journal of Balkan and Near Eastern Studies 18*, no. 1 (2016): p. 37.

66. Quoted in Gustafson, *The Bridge*, p. 380.

67. Jeffrey Goldberg, 'The Obama Doctrine', *Atlantic* (April 2016), https://www.theatlantic.com/magazine/archive/2016/04/the-obama-doctrine/471525/

68. Goldberg, 'The Obama Doctrine'; 'Emmanuel Macron in his Own Words (English)', *Economist*, 7 November 2019. https://www.economist.com/europe/2019/11/07/emmanuel-macron-in-his-own-words-english

69. Goldberg, 'The Obama Doctrine'.

70. Quoted in Dan Roberts and Spencer Ackerman, 'Barack Obama Authorises Airstrikes Against ISIS Militants in Syria', *Guardian*, 11 September 2014, https://www.theguardian.com/world/2014/sep/10/obama-speech-authorise-air-strikes-against-isis-syria

71. Quoted in Zeke J. Miller and Michael Sherer, 'President Obama Attacks Republicans for Paris Response', *Time*, 18 November 2015, https://time.com/4117688/barack-obama-paris-attacks-republican/

72. On the relationship between dollar finance and the American use of extraterritorial sanctions see Daniel W. Drezner, 'Targeted Sanctions in a World of Global Finance', *International Interactions 41*, no. 4 (2015): pp. 755–64.

73. European Commission, Communication from the Commission to the European Parliament and Council, pp. 16 and 2.

74. Reuters staff, 'Obama Thanks Putin for Role in Iran Deal', *Reuters*, 15 July 2015, https://www.reuters.com/article/us-iran-nuclear-russia-call-idUSKCN0PP2RI20150715

75. On the problem of using American military power to compel in the Middle East see Christopher Layne, 'Impotent Power? Re-Examining the Nature of America's Hegemonic Power', *The National Interest 85* (September/October 2006): pp. 41–7.

76. Quoted in Quint Forgey, 'Trump Levels New Sanctions Against Iran', *Politico*, 24 June 2019, https://www.politico.com/story/2019/06/24/donald-trump-iran-strait-of-hormuz-1377826

77. US Energy Information Administration, US Petroleum Imports: Total, and from OPEC, Persian Gulf, and Canada, 1960–2019, https://www.eia.gov/energyexplained/oil-and-petroleum-products/imports-and-exports.php

78. For the argument that the United States should minimize its commitments in the Middle East but can't escape the Persian Gulf see Mara Karlin and Tamara Cofman Wittes, 'America's Middle East Purgatory', *Foreign Affairs 98*, no. 1 (January/February 2019): pp. 88–100. For a set of arguments that the change in the United States' energy position does allow for a reappraisal of the military commitment to the Persian Gulf see Charles Glaser and Rosemary A. Kelanic, eds., *Crude Strategy: Rethinking the US Commitment to Defend Persian Gulf Oil* (Washington, DC: Georgetown University Press, 2016).

79. Stephen F. Szabo, *Germany, Russia and the Rise of Geo-economics* (London: Bloomsbury Academic, 2014), p. 3.

80. US Energy Information Administration, Today in Energy, 1 December 2020, https://www.eia.gov/todayinenergy/detail.php?id=46076

81. US Energy Information Administration, Natural Gas Data, Liquid US Natural Gas Exports by Vessel and Truck, https://www.eia.gov/dnav/ng/hist/ngm:epg0_evt_nus-z00_mmcfM.htm

82. Sarah White and Scott DiSavino, 'France Halts Engie's US LNG Deal Amid Trade, Environment Disputes', *Reuters*, 23 October 2020, https://www.reuters.com/article/engie-lng-france-unitedstates/france-halts-engies-us-lng-deal-amid-trade-environment-disputes-idUSKBN27808G

83. Reuters staff, 'In Shift, Merkel Backs an End to EU-Turkey Membership Talks', *Reuters*, 3 September 2017, https://cn.reuters.com/article/instant-article/idUSKCN1BE15B

84. House of Commons, Foreign Affairs Committee, UK-Turkey Relations and Turkey's Regional Role, Twelfth Report of Session 2010–2012, 4 April 2012, paras, 135, 143.

85. Quoted in House of Commons, Foreign Affairs Committee, UK-Turkey Relations and Turkey's Regional Role, para 167.

86. House of Commons, Foreign Affairs Committee, UK-Turkey Relations and Turkey's Regional Role, p. 174.

87. Quoted in George Parker, 'Turkey Unlikely to Join EU "Until the Year 3000", Says Cameron', *Financial Times*, 22 May 2016, https://www.ft.com/content/de1efd42-2001-11e6-aa98-db1e01fabc0c

88. Michael Peel and Richard Milne, 'Macron Warns Turkey Not to Undermine NATO Allies' Solidarity', *Financial Times*, 28 November 2019, https://www.ft.com/content/7177e13e-1203-11ea-a225-db2f231cfeae

89. Quoted in Reuters staff, 'Turkey's Erdogan Says Talks with EU May End over Cyprus Sanctions', *Reuters*, 12 November 2019, https://www.reuters.com/article/us-cyprus-turkey-eu-idUSKBN1XM19C

90. Economist, 'Emmanuel Macron in His Own Words'.

91. Economist, 'Why Germany's Army is in a Bad State', *Economist*, 9 August 2018, https://www.economist.com/the-economist-explains/2018/08/09/why-germanys-army-is-in-a-bad-state

92. Quoted in Justin Huggler, 'Nato "More Important Now than in the Cold War", Angela Merkel Says in Rebuke of Emmanuel Macron', *Daily Telegraph*, 27 November 2019, https://www.telegraph.co.uk/news/2019/11/27/nato-important-now-cold-war-angela-merkel-says-rebuke-emmanuel/; quoted in Reuters staff, 'Merkel Ally Calls for Better Franco-German Ties After NATO Row', *Reuters*, 24 November 2019, https://www.reuters.com/article/us-germany-france-idUSKBN1XY0I6

93. Quoted in Guy Chazan, 'US Envoy Defends Nord Stream 2 Sanctions as 'Pro-European', *Financial Times*, 22 December 2019, https://www.ft.com/content/21535ebe-23dc-11ea-9a4f-963f0ec7e134

94. Guy Chazan, 'Merkel Faces Calls to Scrap Nord Stream 2 After Navalny Poisoning', *Financial Times*, 3 September 2020, https://www.ft.com/content/81e7d355-e478-49fc-ba75-49f43cbfc74f

95. On Turkish moves in the Eastern Mediterranean see Economist, 'A Row Between Greece and Turkey Over Gas is Raising Tension in the Eastern Mediterranean', *Economist*, 22 August 2020, https://www.economist.com/international/2020/08/20/a-row-between-turkey-and-greece-over-gas-is-raising-tension-in-the-eastern-mediterranean

96. Quoted in Laura Pitel and David Sheppard, 'Turkey Fuels Regional Power Game over Mediterranean Gas Reserves', *Financial Times*, 19 July 2020, https://www.ft.com/content/69a222d4-b37c-4e7e-86dc-4f96b226416d

97. Michaël Tanchum, 'The Logic Beyond Lausanne: A Geopolitical Perspective on the Congruence Between Turkey's New Hard Power and its Strategic Re-Orientation', *Insight Turkey* 22, no. 3 (2020): p. 51, https://www.insightturkey.com/commentaries/the-logic-beyond-lausanne-a-geopolitical-perspective-on-the-congruence-between-turkeys-new-hard-power-and-its-strategic-reorientation

Chapter 4

1. Corriere della Serra, Economia, 'Trichet e Draghi: Un'Azione Pressante Per Ristabilire La Fiducia Degli Investitori', https://www.corriere.it/economia/11_settembre_29/trichet_draghi_inglese_304a5f1e-ea59-11e0-ae06-4da866778017.shtml

2. Alan Crawford and Tony Czuczka, *Angela Merkel: A Chancellorship Forged in Crisis* (Chichester: Wiley Bloomberg Press, 2013), p. 14.

3. Marcus Walker, Charles Forelle, and Stacy Meichtry, 'Deepening Crisis Over Europe Pits Leader Against Leader', *Wall Street Journal*, 30 December 2011, https://www.wsj.com/articles/SB10001424052970 2033911045771244800046463576

4. Quoted in Silvia Ognibene, 'Italy's Northern League Chief Attacks Euro, Says Preparing for Exit', *Reuters*, 7 February 2018, https://www.reuters.com/article/instant-article/idUKKBN1FR30Z

5. Quoted in Adam Tooze, *Crashed: How a Decade of Financial Crises Changed the World* (London: Penguin, 2018), p. 438.

6. Peter Spiegel, *How the Euro Was Saved*, Kindle edition (London: Financial Times, 2014), ch. 3.

7. Helen Thompson, *Might, Right, Prosperity and Consent: Representative Democracy and the International Economy 1919–2001* (Manchester: Manchester University Press, 2008), pp. 78–9.

8. Benn Steil, *The Battle of Bretton Woods: John Maynard Keynes, Harry Dexter White, and the Making of a New World Order* (Princeton: Princeton University Press, 2013), pp. 331–5. One part of this problem was made famous by the American economist Robert Triffin. Triffin insisted that Bretton Woods imposed an impossible burden on the United States since in requiring an American balance of payments deficit to provide a flow of dollars for international trade to grow, it would also require the Federal Reserve to use its monetary policy to defend the dollar's value, and recession would ensue. Robert Triffin, *Gold and the Dollar Crisis: The Future of Convertibility* (Oxford: Oxford University Press, 1960). But Triffin did not provide a persuasive explanation of why Bretton Woods broke down on two scores. First, even before Triffin articulated his paradox, the system had already generated a counter-action to the gold–dollar problem in the Eurodollar markets which was what put huge strain on Bretton Woods well before its end. Second, after 1965, American policymakers did not orient American fiscal and monetary policy towards maintaining dollar–gold convertibility. Michael D. Bordo and Robert N. McCauley, 'Triffin: Dilemma or Myth?', BIS Working Papers, no. 684, 19 December 2017, https://www.bis.org/publ/work684.htm

9. Bordo and McCauley, 'Triffin: Dilemma or Myth?', p. 5.

10. For a history of the Eurodollar markets see Gary Burn, *The Re-Emergence of Global Finance* (Basingstoke: Palgrave Macmillan, 2006); Catherine R. Schenk, 'The Origins of the Eurodollar Market in London: 1955–1963', *Explorations in Economic History 35*, no. 2 (1998): pp. 221–38.

11. On the crucial importance of London to the early Eurodollar markets and its long-term significance see Jeremy Green, *The Political Economy of the Special Relationship: Anglo-American Development from the Gold Standard to the Financial Crisis* (Princeton: Princeton University Press, 2020); Gary Burn, 'The State, the City, and the Euromarkets', *Review of International Political Economy 6*, no. 2 (1999): pp. 225–61.

12. Milton Friedman, 'The Euro-Dollar Market: Some First Principles', Federal Reserve Bank of St Louis, July 1971, pp. 16, 21, https://files. stlouisfed.org/files/htdocs/publications/review/71/07/Principles_ Jul1971.pdf

13. Federal Reserve Board, Federal Open Market Committee, Memoranda of Discussion, 17 December 1968, pp. 20–22, https://www.federalreserve. gov/monetarypolicy/files/fomcmod19681217.pdf

14. Jeffry Frieden, *Banking on the World: The Politics of American International Finance* (New York: Routledge Revivals, 2016), p. 81.

15. Quoted in Francis Gavin, *Gold, Dollars and Power: The Politics of International Monetary Relations, 1958–1971* (Chapel Hill, NC: University of North Carolina Press, 2004), p. 121.

16. Michael J. Graetz and Olivia Briffault, 'A "Barbarous Relic": The French, Gold, and the Demise of Bretton Woods', Yale Law & Economics Research Paper No. 558; Columbia Law & Economics Working Paper No. 560 (2016), p. 13. For the French view of Bretton Woods and the case for a return to a gold standard from a leading adviser to de Gaulle see Jacques Rueff, *The Monetary Sin of the West* (New York: Macmillan, 1972).

17. Helen Thompson, *Oil and the Western Economic Crisis* (London: Palgrave, 2017), p. 94.

18. For the argument against the inevitability of the end of Bretton Woods see Harold James, 'The Multiple Contexts of Bretton Woods', *Oxford Review of Economics Policy 28*, no. 3 (2012): pp. 420–3.

19. Steil, *The Battle of Bretton Woods*, p. 25.

20. James, 'The Multiple Contexts of Bretton Woods', p. 424.

21. On the growth of the Eurodollar markets in the 1970 see Carlo Edoardo Altamura, *European Banks and the Rise of International Finance: The Post Bretton-Woods Era* (London: Routledge, 2017).

22. Thompson, *Oil and the Western Economic Crisis*, p. 96.

23. David Spiro, *The Hidden Hand of American Hegemony: Petrodollar Recycling and International Markets* (Ithaca: Cornell University Press, 1999), pp. 107–20; Andrea Wong, 'US Discloses Saudi Holdings of US Treasuries for First Time', *Bloomberg*, 16 May 2016, https://www.bloomberg.com/news/art icles/2016-05-16/u-s-discloses-saudi-arabia-s-treasuries-holdings-for-first-time

24. Spiro, *The Hidden Hand*, pp. 122–4, 148.

25. Samba Mbaye, New Data on Global Debt, IMF Blog, https://blogs.imf. org/2019/01/02/new-data-on-global-debt/

26. For some considered arguments that frame economic life since the 1970s around neoliberalism see David Harvey, *A Brief History of Neo-Liberalism* (Oxford: Oxford University Press, 2007); Andrew Gamble, *Crisis Without End?: The Unravelling of Western Prosperity* (London: Palgrave, 2014); Daniel Stedman Jones, *Masters of the Universe: Hayek, Friedman, and the Birth of Neoliberal Politics*, updated edition (Princeton: Princeton University Press, 2014).

27. On the intellectual origins of neoliberalism in the aftermath of the Habsburg Empire's fall sce Quinn Slobodian, *Globalists: The End of Empire and the Birth of Neo-Liberalism* (Cambridge, MA: Harvard University Press, 2018).

28. For a cogent argument that the 1970s represented the end of a century of material, technological and demographic conditions that drove a growth in American productivity that won't return see Robert J. Gordon, *The Rise and Fall of American Growth: the U.S. Standard of Living since the Civil War.* (Princeton: Princeton University Press, 2016).

29. For a similar concern for the material causes of the 1970 crisis see Adam Tooze, 'Neo-liberalism's World Order', *Dissent* (Summer 2018), https://www.dissentmagazine.org/article/neoliberalism-world-order-review-quinn-slobodian-globalists. For discussion of the centrality of energy to the deregulation political agenda in the United States in the 1970s and early 1980s see Meg Jacobs, *Panic at the Pump: The Energy Crisis and the Transformation of American Politics in the 1970s* (New York: Hill and Wang, 2016). For a discussion of the relationship of dollar issues to liberalizing economic rhetoric see David E. Spiro, 'The Role of the Dollar and the Justificatory Discourse of Neoliberalism' in *Counter-Shock: The Oil Counter-Revolution of the 1980s*, edited by Duccio Basosi, Giuliano Garavini, and Massimiliano Trentin (London: I.B. Taurus, 2020), pp. 36, 49, 51.

30. Jacobs, *Panic at the Pump*, chs. 3–4.

31. Quoted in Jacobs, *Panic at the Pump*, p. 271.

32. Jacobs, *Panic at the Pump*, p. 109.

33. Perry Mehrling, 'An Interview with Paul A. Volcker', *Macroeconomic Dynamics 5*, no. 3 (2001): p. 443.

34. Graetz and Briffault, 'A "Barbarous Relic"', p. 17.

35. Barry Eichengreen, *Exorbitant Privilege: The Rise and Fall of the Dollar and the Future of the International Monetary System* (Oxford: Oxford University Press, 2011), p. 75.

36. Geoffrey Bell, 'The May 1971 International Monetary Crisis: Implications and Lessons', *Financial Analysts Journal 27*, no. 4 (1971): p. 88.

37. Quoted in James, *Making the European Monetary Union*, p. 87.

38. Quoted in EC: Heath-Brandt Meeting—Resumed (Possible Joint EC Float), 1 March 1973, UK National Archive. Available via the Margaret Thatcher Foundation: Britain & the Origin of the EMS.

39. Quoted in Callaghan Note of EMS Discussion (At Copenhagen European Council Dinner, 7 April 1978), UK National Archive. Available via the Margaret Thatcher Foundation: Britain & the Origin of the EMS, https://www.margaretthatcher.org/archive/EMS_1978

40. Quoted in Transcript of Meeting of the Bundesbank Council, 30 November 1978; The National Archive, Schmidt Note of Remarks on EMS. UK National Archive. Available via the Margaret Thatcher Foundation: Britain & the Origin of the EMS.

41. Charles P. Kindleberger, 'The Dollar Yesterday, Today and Tomorrow', *Banca Nazionale Del Lavoro Quarterly Review 155* (December 1985): p. 306.

42. Kiyoshi Hirowatari, *Britain and European Monetary Cooperation 1964–1979* (London: Palgrave Macmillan, 2015), p. 50.

43. Quoted in Catherine Schenk, 'Sterling, International Monetary Reform, and Britain's Applications to Join the European Economic Community in the 1960s', *Contemporary European History 11*, no. 3 (2002): p. 367.

44. Schenk, 'Sterling, International Monetary Reform', p. 369.

45. Hirowatari, *Britain and European Monetary Cooperation 1964–1979*, pp. 48–9.

46. Harold James argues that it was only possible to get some EC monetary cooperation if Britain stayed out and left it to France and West Germany. James, 'The Multiple Contexts', p. 421.

47. For his own account of the Volcker shock see Paul A. Volcker with Christine Harper, *Keeping at It: The Quest for Sound Money and Good Government* (New York: Public Affairs, 2018).

48. Alexandre Reichart, 'French Monetary Policy (1981–1985): A Constrained Policy, Between Volcker Shock, the EMS, and Macroeconomic Imbalances', *Journal of European Economic History 44*, no. 1 (2015): p. 15.

49. Jeremy Leaman, *The Political Economy of Germany Under Chancellors Kohl and Schröder: Decline of the German Model?* (New York: Berghahn Books, 2009), pp. 26–30.

50. See Helen Thompson, *The British Conservative Government and the European Exchange Rate Mechanism 1979–1994* (London: Pinter, 1996), chs. 2–5.

51. James, 'Bretton Woods and its Multiple Contexts', pp. 427–8.

52. On Plaza and Louvre and the failed attempt at mid-1980s exchange rate cooperation see C. Randall Henning, *Currencies and Politics in the United States, Germany, and Japan* (Washington, DC: Peterson Institution of International Economics, 1994); Yoichi Funabashi, *Managing the Dollar from the Plaza to the Louvre*, second edition (Washington, DC: Peterson Institute for International Economics, 1989).

53. Spiro, 'The Role of the Dollar and the Justificatory Discourse of Neoliberalism', p. 41.

54. On how the French government reached the monetary union decision in 1988 see David J. Howarth, *The French Road to European Monetary Union* (London: Palgrave Macmillan, 2001).

55. The fact that some, including Jacques Delors at the Commission, hoped that in time a European currency could offer an alternative to the dollar have led some—for example Barry Eichengreen, *Exorbitant Privilege*, p. 86—to stress dollar motives in the move. But it was the Deutsche Mark constraint and not the dollar constraint that was to the fore in 1987–88, and the French move immediately followed the Franco-German Council's early demise.

56. There remains a persistent line of argument that monetary union emerged as a response to German unification, but the EC had already

agreed to implement the Delors Report on monetary union in June 1989. For a demolition of these claims see Andrew Moravcsik, *The Choice for Europe: Social Purpose and State Power from Messina to Maastricht* (London: UCL Press,1999), pp. 396–401.

57. On the Bundesbank's claim to represent the German people in a different way than the German state and the mythical stories about German economic history used to legitimate that claim see Hjalte Lokdam, 'Banking on Sovereignty: A Genealogy of the European Central Bank's Independence', PhD dissertation submitted to the London School of Economics, 2019, ch. 2.

58. See Chiara Zilioli and Martin Selmayr, 'The Constitutional Status of the European Central Bank', *Common Market Law Review 44*, no. 2 (2007): pp. 355–99.

59. On the move to monetary union and the terms agreed in the Maastricht Treaty see James, *Making the European Monetary Union*, chs. 6–8; David Marsh, *The Euro: The Battle for the New Global Currency* (New Haven: Yale University Press, 2009), chs. 3–6.

60. Nonetheless, the Italian government was the French government's initial strongest supporter in asking for monetary union.

61. Moravcsik, *The Choice for Europe*, p. 404.

62. Moravcsik, *The Choice for Europe*, p. 443.

63. James Sloam, *The European Policy of the German Social Democrats: Interpreting a Changing World* (London: Palgrave Macmillan, 2004), pp. 138–40.

64. Alan Cowell, 'Kohl Casts Europe's Economic Union as War and Peace Issue', *New York Times*, 7 October 1995, https://www.nytimes.com/1995/10/17/world/kohl-casts-europe-s-economic-union-as-war-and-peace-issue.html

65. Cowell, 'Kohl Casts Europe's Economic Union as War and Peace Issue'.

66. David Howarth, 'The French State in the Euro-Zone: "Modernization" and Legitimatizing Dirigisme' in *European States and the Euro: Europeanization, Variation, and Convergence*, edited by Kenneth Dyson (Oxford: Oxford University Press, 2002), p. 167.

67. Moravcsik, *The Choice for Europe*, p. 446.

68. Maria Demertzis, Konstantinos Efstathiou, and Fabio Matera, 'The Italian Lira: The Exchange Rate and Employment in the ERM', *Bruegel Blog*, 13 January 2017, https://www.bruegel.org/2017/01/the-italian-lira-the-exchange-rate-and-employment-in-the-erm/

69. Quoted in Katherine Butler and Yvette Cooper, 'Lira Up as Italy's Tax for Europe Gets Go-Ahead', *Independent*, 22 February 1997, https://www.independent.co.uk/news/business/lira-up-as-italy-s-tax-for-europe-gets-goahead-1279992.html

70. Quoted in Butler and Cooper, 'Lira Up as Italy's Tax for Europe Gets Go-Ahead'.

71. Thompson, *The British Conservative Government and the European Exchange Rate Mechanism*, pp. 203–7.

72. For the argument that it was calculations about the financial sector that drove British governments' decision to stay outside see Ophelia Eglene, *Banking on Sterling: Britain's Independence from the Euro Zone* (Lanham, MD: Lexington Books, 2010).

Chapter 5

1. Janet Yellen, 'The Outlook for the Economy', Remarks at the Providence Chamber of Commerce, Providence, Rhode Island, 22 May 2015, https://fraser.stlouisfed.org/title/statements-speeches-janet-l-yellen-930/outlook-economy-521732

2. Yellen, 'The Outlook for the Economy'.

3. The renminbi is China's official currency and used to describe the currency as a medium of exchange. The yuan is the unit of account for measuring prices.

4. Federal Open Market Committee, Press Conference, 17 September 2015, https://www.federalreserve.gov/monetarypolicy/fomcpresconf20150917.htm

5. G20 Finance Ministers and Central Bank Governors' Meeting, Shanghai, 27 February 2016, Communiqué, http://www.g20.utoronto.ca/2016/160227-finance-en.html

6. National Security Strategy of the United States of America, https://trumpwhitehouse.archives.gov/wp-content/uploads/2017/12/NSS-Final-12-18-2017-0905.pdf, pp. 27, 3, 18.

7. Remarks By Vice President Pence on the Administration's Policy Towards China, Hudson Institute, Washington, DC, 4 October 2018, https://www.hudson.org/events/1610-vice-president-mike-pence-s-remarks-on-the-administration-s-policy-towards-china102018

8. Quoted in Richard N. Haass, 'The Crisis in US-China Relations: The Trump Administration has Staked Out an Aggressive Position, But its Critique of Chinese Behaviour Is Widely Shared and Points to the Need for a New American Strategy', *Wall Street Journal*, 19 October 2018, https://www.wsj.com/articles/the-crisis-in-u-s-china-relations-1539963174. Former Australian prime minister Kevin Rudd gave a speech in October 2018 on the Trump administration's China approach in 2018 as a watershed for the world. 'The United States and China and the avoidable war', Speech at the United States Naval Academy, 10 October 2018, https://asiasociety.org/policy-institute/united-states-and-china-avoidable-war

9. Quoted in Jim Brunsden, 'EU Warns of $300 billion Hit to US Over Car Import Tariffs', *Financial Times*, 1 July 2018.

10. US Census, Foreign Trade, Trade in Goods with China, https://www.census.gov/foreign-trade/balance/c5700.html

11. On the French employment shock see Clément Malgouyres, 'The Impact of Chinese Import Competition on the Local Structure of Employment

and Wages: Evidence from France', Banque de France, Document du Travail, No. 603. In Germany, but not elsewhere, there was a large counter-movement of exports, including cars and machinery, into China. Wolfgang Dauth, Sebastian Findeisen, and Jens Suedekum 'The Rise of the East and the Far East: German Labour Markets and Trade Integration', *Journal of the European Economic Association 12*, no. 6 (2014): pp. 1643–75.

12. The case for a large shock has been made in several studies by the economists David Autor, David Dorn, and Gordon Hanson. See, for example, David H. Autor, David Dorn, and Gordon H. Hanson, 'The China Shock: Learning from Labour Market Adjustment to Large Changes in Trade', NBER Working Paper Series, 21906. See also Justin R. Pierce and Peter K. Schott, 'The Surprisingly Swift Decline of US Manufacturing Employment', *American Economic Review 106*, no. 7 (2016): pp. 1632–62; Daron Acemoglu, David Autor, David Dorn, Gordon Hanson, and Brendan Price, 'Import Competition and the Great U. S. Employment Sag of the 2000s', *Journal of Labor Economics 34*, no. 1 (2016): pp. S141–198. For criticisms of Autor, Dorn, and Hanson's arguments see Jonathan T. Rothwell, 'Cutting the Losses: Reassessing the Costs of Import Competition to Workers and Communities' (19 October 2017), https://papers.ssrn.com/sol3/papers.cfm?abstract_id= 2920188. For an argument stressing the benefits see Kyle Handley and Nuno Limão, 'Policy Uncertainty, Trade, and Welfare: Theory and Evidence for China and the United States', *American Economic Review 107*, no. 9 (2017): pp. 2731–83.

13. Federal Reserve of St Louis Data, Current Employment Statistics, All Employees, Manufacturing, https://fred.stlouisfed.org/series/MANEMP

14. For example, the early period from 2000 to 2002 coincided with a period of dollar strength. On how to read this variable in relation to the China shock see Brad Setser, 'China's WTO Entry, 15 Years On', Council on Foreign Relations Blog, https://www.cfr.org/blog/chinas-wto-entry-15-years

15. Quoted in Robert E. Lighthizer, Testimony Before the US-China Economic and Security Review Commission: Evaluating China's Role in the World Trade Organization Over the Last Decade, 9 June 2010, p. 10, https://www.uscc.gov/sites/default/files/6.9.10Lighthizer.pdf

16. Quoted in Helen Thompson, *China and the Mortgaging of America: Domestic Politics and Economic Interdependence* (London: Palgrave, 2010), p. 38.

17. There were substantial reasons for thinking that China's currency was a primary reason for China's trade surplus. See Brad Setser, Testimony before the Senate Committee on Small Business and Entrepreneurship, Hearing on Made in China and the Future of US Industry, 27 February 2019, https:// www.sbc.senate.gov/public/_cache/files/3/b/3bd85987-d8b4-48b3-a53e- 8b49d2060821/4E39BD152B9F358A5E4254D80A512D8B.setser- testimony.pdf. For the argument that the problem was not China but US

macro-economic policy see Ronald McKinnon, *The Unloved Dollar Standard: From Bretton Woods to the Rise of China* (Oxford: Oxford University Press, 2013), ch. 13.

18. See Henry M. Paulson, Jr, 'A Strategic Economic Engagement: Strengthening US-China Ties', *Foreign Affairs 87*, no. 5 (September/October 2008): pp. 59–77.

19. Sean Starrs, 'American Economic Power Hasn't Declined—It Globalised! Summoning the Data and Taking Globalization Seriously', *International Studies Quarterly 57*, no. 4 (2013): pp. 818–20.

20. Quoted in Charles Duhigg and Keith Bradsher, 'How the US Lost out on iPhone Work', *New York Times*, 21 January 2012, https://www.nytimes.com/2012/01/22/business/apple-america-and-a-squeezed-middle-class.html

21. Quoted in Duhigg and Bradsher, 'How the US Lost out on iPhone Work'.

22. Greg Linden, Kenneth L. Kraemer, and Jason Dedrick., 'Who Captures Value in a Global Innovation System? The Case of Apple's iPod', UC Irvine Personal Computing Industry Center, The Paul Merage School of Business, University of California, Irvine, June 2007, https://citeseerx.ist.psu.edu/viewdoc/download?doi=10.1.1.419.2289&rep=rep1&type=pdf

23. Matthew Klein and Michael Pettis have suggested that trade wars are ultimately class wars. In regard to US–China trade, and indeed US–German trade, they argue that 'the world's rich were able to benefit at the expense of the world's workers and retirees because the interests of American financiers were complementary to the interests of Chinese and German industrialists'. Matthew C. Klein and Michael Pettis, *Trade Wars are Class Wars: How Rising Inequality Distorts the Global Economy and Threatens International Peace* (New Haven: Yale University Press), p. 224.

24. US Energy Information Administration, international statistics. On rising demand see Thompson, *Oil and the Western Economic Crisis*, pp. 10–12.

25. On the supply problems see Thompson, *Oil and the Western Economic Crisis*, pp. 12–24.

26. Macro-trends, Crude Oil Prices—70 Year Historical Chart, https://www.macrotrends.net/1369/crude-oil-price-history-chart

27. Carlo Edoardo Altamura, *European Banks and the Rise of International Finance* (London: Routledge, 2017), ch. 3. On consortium banking in the Eurodollar markets see Richard Roberts (with C. Arnander), *Take Your Partners: Orion, the Consortium Banks and the Transformation of the Euromarkets* (London: Palgrave Macmillan, 2001).

28. On the emergence of an international banking sector up to the late 1970s see Helmut W. Mayer, 'Credit and Liquidity Creation in the International Banking Sector', BIS Economic Papers, no. 1, 1 November 1979, https://www.bis.org/publ/econ1.htm On the shift in the US to a more finance-centric economy see Judith Stein, *Pivotal Decade: How the*

United States Traded Factories for Finance in the Seventies (New Haven: Yale University Press, 2011).

29. See Carlo Edoardo Altamura, *European Banks and the Rise of International Finance*, ch 3. There was again some debate after the second oil price shock including draft proposals by central banks to force banks to publish consolidated balance sheets that would include their Eurodollar activities, but nothing eventually materialized. Izabella Kaminska, 'A Global Reserve Requirement for All Those Eurodollars', *Financial Times Alphaville*, 15 April 2016, https://www.ft.com/content/226e90ec-ead3-311d-9361-b0f2c2bfd9e3. On the importance of European states to international approaches to open capital flows see Rawi Abdelal, *Capital Rules: The Construction of Global Finance* (Cambridge, MA, Harvard University Press, 2007). On the importance of central banks to the development of the post–Bretton Woods version of the Eurodollar system see Benjamin Braun, Arie Kramp, and Steffen Murau, 'Financial Globalization as Positive Integration: Monetary Technocrats and the Eurodollar Market in the 1970s', *Review of International Political Economy*. Published online 22 March 2020, DOI: 10.1080/09692290.2020.1740291; Rawi Abdelal, 'Writing the Rules of Global Finance: France, Europe, and Capital Liberalization', *Review of International Political Economy 13*, no. 1 (2006): pp. 1–27.

30. Charles Goodhart, *The Basel Committee on Banking Supervision* (Cambridge: Cambridge University Press, 2011), p. 41.

31. Alan Greenspan, 'The Challenge of Central Banking in a Democratic Society', Remarks, 5 December 1996, https://fraser.stlouisfed.org/ti tle/statements-speeches-alan-greenspan-452/challenge-central-banking-a-democratic-society-8581

32. Greenspan, 'The Challenge of Central Banking in a Democratic Society'.

33. Greenspan, 'The Challenge of Central Banking in a Democratic Society'.

34. Claudio Borio and William White, 'Whither Monetary and Financial Stability? The Implications of Evolving Policy Regimes', BIS Working Papers, no. 147, 2004, p. 5, https://www.bis.org/publ/work147.pdf

35. At his most optimistic Greenspan argued that the large increase in the size of what he called 'cross-border finance' made it easier for the world economy to absorb shocks. Alan Greenspan, 'World Finance and Risk Management', Remarks at Lancaster House, London, 25 September 2002, https://www.federalreserve.gov/boarddocs/speeches/2002/200209253/default.htm. After the crash, Greenspan accepted some criticisms of his tenure but held to his view that monetary policy could not be directed pre-emptively at asset bubbles. See Alan Greenspan, 'The Crisis', Brookings Papers on Economic Activity (Spring 2010), pp. 201–46, https://www.brookings.edu/bpea-articles/the-crisis/. For the view expressed before the 2007–8 crash that the supposed Great Moderation necessarily contained the conditions for financial instability see Borio and White, 'Whither Monetary and Financial Stability?'.

36. On internationalized banking from the late 1990s see Iain Hardie and David Howarth, eds, *Market-Based Banking and the International Financial Crisis* (Oxford: Oxford University Press). For Germany's lead role see Helen Thompson, 'Enduring Capital Flow Constraints and the 2007-8 Financial and Euro-zone Crises', *British Journal of Politics and International Relations 8*, no. 1 (2016): pp. 216–33; Iain Hardie and David Howarth, 'Die Krise and Nòt la Crise? The Financial Crisis and the Transformation of German and French Banking Systems', *Journal of Common Market Studies 47*, no. 5 (2009): pp. 1017–39.

37. On the impact of internationalized banking on the sharp rise in international capital flows between 2002 and 2007 see: Philip R. Lane, *Capital Flows in the Euro Area*. European Commission, Economic Papers 497, April 2013, https://ec.europa.eu/economy_finance/publications/economic_paper/2013/pdf/ecp497_en.pdf; Philip. R. Lane, 'Financial Globalisation and the Crisis', BIS Working Papers, no. 39, December 2012, https://www.bis.org/publ/work397.htm; Philip R. Lane and Gian Maria Milesi-Ferretti, 'The Drivers of Financial Globalisation', *American Economic Review 98*, no. 2 (2008): pp. 327–32; Gian Maria, Milesi-Ferretti, Francesco Strobbe, and Natalia Tamirisa, 'Bilateral Financial Linkages and Global Imbalances: A View on the Eve of the Financial Crisis', IMF Working Paper, WP/10/257, 1 November 2010, https://www.imf.org/en/Publications/WP/Issues/2016/12/31/Bilateral-Financial-Linkages-and-Global-Imbalances-a-View-on-The-Eve-of-the-Financial-Crisis-24350

38. BIS Committee on the Global Financial System, *The Functioning and Resilience of Cross-Border Funding Markets*, CGFS Paper no. 37, March 2010, p. 10, https://www.bis.org/publ/cgfs37.htm; Patrick McGuire and Goetz von Peter, The US Dollar Shortage in Global Banking, *BIS Quarterly Review* (March 2009): p. 48, https://www.bis.org/publ/qtrpdf/r_qt0903f.pdf?noframes=1

39. Ben S. Bernanke, 'The Great Moderation', Speech at the Eastern Economic Association, Washington, DC, 20 February 2004, https://www.federalreserve.gov/boarddocs/speeches/2004/20040220/

40. Bernanke, 'The Great Moderation'.

41. Charles Bean, 'The Great Moderation, the Great Panic, and the Great Contraction', *BIS Review 101* (2009): pp. 4–7, https://www.bis.org/review/r090902d.pdf

42. See Sandra Eickmeier and Markus Kühnlenz, 'China's Role in Global Inflation Dynamics', *Macroeconomic Dynamics 22*, no. 2 (2016): pp. 225–54.

43. Charles Bean, Christian Broda, Takatoshi Ito, and Randall Kroszner, 'Low for Long? Causes and Consequences of Persistently Low Interest Rates', Geneva Reports on the World Economy 17, International Center for Monetary and Banking Studies (ICMB) and Center for Economic Policy Research (CEPR), Geneva and London, October 2015, pp. 1, 3, 14, https://voxeu.org/sites/default/files/file/Geneva17_28sept.pdf

44. Bean, Broda, Ito, and Kroszner, 'Low for Long?', p. 10.

45. Bean, Broda, Ito, and Kroszner, 'Low for Long?', pp. 28–32.
46. Ben S. Bernanke, 'The Global Saving Glut and the U.S. Current Account Deficit', Remarks at the Sandridge Lecture, Virginia Association of Economists, 14 April 2005, https://www.federalreserve.gov/boarddocs/speeches/2005/200503102/
47. Brad W. Sester and Arpana Pandey, 'China's $1.5 Trillion Bet: Understanding China's External Portfolio', Council for Foreign Relations, Working Paper, 13 May 2009, p. 1, https://www.cfr.org/report/chinas-15-trillion-bet
48. Michael P. Dooley, David Folkerts-Landau, and Peter Garber, 'The Revived Bretton Woods System', *International Journal of Finance and Economics 9*, no. 4 (2004): pp. 307–13.
49. Niall Ferguson and Moritz Schularick, 'Chimerica and the Global Asset Boom', *International Finance 10*, no. 3 (2007): pp. 215–39.
50. Lawrence H. Summers, 'The US Current Account Deficit and the Global Economy', Lecture at the Per Jacobsson Foundation, 3 October 2004, pp. 13, 8, https://www.imf.org/en/Publications/Other-Periodicals/Issues/2016/12/31/The-U-S-17872
51. On the general effect of oil prices on monetary decision-making for the Fed, ECB, and the Bank of England between 2004 and 2008 see Thompson, *Oil and the Western Economic Crisis*, pp. 26–34.
52. Alan Greenspan, *The Age of Turbulence* (London: Allen Lane, 2007), p. 463.
53. Quoted in 'Greenspan Clarifies Iraq War Comment', *Irish Times*, 17 September 2007, https://www.irishtimes.com/news/greenspan-clarifies-iraq-war-comment-1.812331
54. Mervyn King, Speech Given at CBI North East Annual Dinner, Gateshead, 11 October 2005, https://www.bankofengland.co.uk/speech/2005/cbi-north-east-annual-dinner
55. European Central Bank, Introductory Statement with Q&A, Jean-Claude Trichet and Lucas Papademos, Frankfurt am Main, 3 July 2008, https://www.ecb.europa.eu/press/pressconf/2008/html/is080703.en.html
56. Quoted in Tao Wu, 'The Long-Term Interest Rate Conundrum: Not Unravelled Yet?', *Federal Reserve Bank of San Francisco, Economic Letter*, 29 April 2005, https://www.frbsf.org/economic-research/publications/economic-letter/2005/april/the-long-term-interest-rate-conundrum-not-unraveled-yet/
57. On the dynamic of European banks recycling dollar credit back into the United States see Claudio Bordo, Harold James, and Hyun Song Shin, 'The International Monetary and Financial System: A Capital Account Historical Perspective', BIS Working Papers, no. 457, August 2014, pp. 15–19, https://www.bis.org/publ/work457.htm
58. For the analysis that showed how European banks stood at the financial crisis epicentre see: Robert N. McCauley, 'The 2008 Crisis: Transatlantic or Transpacific?', *BIS Quarterly Review* (December 2018): pp. 39–58, https://www.bis.org/publ/qtrpdf/r_qt1812f.htm; Claudio Bordo, Harold James, and Hyun Song Shin, 'The International Monetary and

Financial System'; Hyun Song Shin, 'Global Banking Glut and Loan Risk Premium', *IMF Economic Review 60*, no. 2 (2012): pp. 155–92; Naohiko Baba, Robert N. McCauley, and Srichander Ramaswamy, 'US Dollar Money Market Funds and Non-US Banks', *BIS Quarterly Review* (March 2009): pp. 65–81; Patrick McGuire and Goetz von Peter, 'The US Dollar Shortage in Global Banking', *BIS Quarterly Review* (March 2009): pp. 47–63; Claudio Borio and Piti Disyatat, 'Global Imbalances and the Financial Crisis: Link Or No Link?', BIS Working Papers, no. 346, May 2011, https://www.bis.org/publ/work346.pdf. For a magisterial analysis of the European banking crisis and how it was miscast as an Asian savings glut and American subprime crisis see Adam Tooze, *Crashed: How a Decade of Financial Crises Changed the World*, chs. 1–3.

59. For Bernanke's post-crisis savings glut analysis see Ben S. Bernanke, Carol Bertaut, Laurie Pounder DeMarco, and Steven Kamin, 'International Capital Flows and the Return to Safe Assets in the United States, 2003–07', Board of Governors of the Federal Reserve System International Finance Discussion Papers, 1014, February 2011, https://www.federalreserve.gov/pubs/ifdp/2011/1014/ifdp1014.htm. The 'banking glut' term comes from Shin, 'Global Banking Glut and Loan Risk Premium'.

60. Federal Reserve Bank of St Louis, House Price Indexes, https://fred.stlouisfed.org/categories/32261

61. On the American housing boom and subprime lending see Herman M. Schwartz, *Subprime Nation: American Power, Global Capital and the Housing Bubble* (Ithaca: Cornell University Press, 2009); Robert J. Schiller, *The Sub-Prime Solution: How Today's Global Financial Crisis Happened and What to Do About it* (Princeton: Princeton University Press, 2008), chs. 2–4.

62. William R. Emmons, 'The End is in Sight for the US Foreclosure Crisis', Federal Reserve Bank of St Louis, 2 December 2016, https://www.stlouisfed.org/on-the-economy/2016/december/end-sight-us-foreclosure-crisis

63. Thompson, *Oil and the Western Economic Crisis*, pp. 30–2.

64. Thompson, *Oil and the Western Economic Crisis*, pp. 35–7; James D. Hamilton, 'Causes and Consequences of the Oil Shock of 2007–08', *Brookings Papers on Economic Activity* (Spring 2009): pp. 215–61.

65. Thompson, *Oil and the Western Economic Crisis*, p. 34.

66. Thompson, *Oil and the Western Economic Crisis*, pp. 33–4.

67. Statement by Ben Bernanke before the Financial Crisis Inquiry Commission, Washington, DC, 2 September 2010, https://www.federalreserve.gov/newsevents/testimony/bernanke20100902a.pdf. The Commission in its final report took little notice of what Bernanke told it and made subprime lending central to its account of the crisis. The one common difficulty for the worst-afflicted banks in 2007–8 was a short-term funding dependency. See Andrea Beltratti and René M. Stulz, 'The Credit Crisis Around the Globe: Why Did Some Banks Perform Better?' *Journal of Financial Economics 105*, no. 1 (2012): pp. 1–17.

68. Iain Hardie and Helen Thompson, 'Taking Europe Seriously: European Financialization and US Monetary Power', *Review of International Political Economy 28*, no. 4 (2021) p. 4.

69. Izabella Kaminska, 'All about the Eurodollars', *Financial Times Alphaville*, 5 September 2014, https://www.ft.com/content/033a7ad2-9762-35c9-a0e5-f59ea2968757

70. Quoted in Baba, McCauley, and Ramaswamy, 'US Dollar Money Market Funds and Non-US Banks', p. 76. For a narrative account of how the Fed, the ECB, and the Bank of England managed the crisis from August 2007 see Neil Irwin, *The Alchemists: Three Central Banks and a World on Fire* (London: Penguin, 2014).

71. Federal Reserve Economic Data, Labour Participation Rate, https://fred.stlouisfed.org/series/CIVPART

72. Mark Carney, 'The Growing Challenges for Monetary Policy in the Current International Monetary and Financial System', Speech at the Jackson Hole Symposium, 23 August 2019, https://www.bis.org/review/r190827b.htm

73. Carney, 'The Growing Challenges for Monetary Policy'.

74. Carney, 'The Growing Challenges for Monetary Policy'.

Chapter 6

1. Michael Santoli, 'Breaking Down This Sell Off, Among the Most Extreme and Rare Wall Street has Ever Seen', *CNBC*, 22 March 2021, https://www.cnbc.com/2020/03/22/breaking-down-this-sell-off-among-the-most-extreme-and-rare-wall-street-has-ever-seen.html

2. Trading Economics, Markets, United States Government Bond 10Y, https://tradingeconomics.com/united-states/government-bond-yield

3. Quoted in Martin Arnold and Tommy Stubbington, 'Lagarde Triggers Investor Jitters As ECB Launches Virus Response', *Financial Times*, 12 March 2020, https://www.ft.com/content/11ab8f84-6452-11ea-b3f3-fe4680ea68b5

4. For a gripping account of the economic crisis of the early pandemic see Adam Tooze, *Shutdown: How Covid Shook the World's Economy* (London: Allen Lane, 2021).

5. Global Banking Directory, Banksdaily.com, https://banksdaily.com/top-banks/World/2007.html

6. Global Banking Directory, Banksdaily.com, https://banksdaily.com/topbanks/World/total-assets-2020.html

7. Derek Wallbank and Iain Marlow, 'Trump Calls Hong Kong Protests "Riots," Adopting China's Rhetoric', *Bloomberg*, 2 August 2019, https://www.bloomberg.com/news/articles/2019-08-02/trump-calls-hong-kong-protests-riots-adopting-china-rhetoric

8. For the argument that central banks both made the post-crash world and could not fix its economic and political problems see Mohamed A. El-Erian, *The Only Game in Town: Central Banks, Instability, and Avoiding the Next Collapse* (New York: Random House, 2016).

9. For narrative accounts of the Fed's policy actions see David Wessel, *In FED We Trust: Ben Bernanke's War on the Great Panic* (New York: Random House, 2010), chs. 10–14. Adam Tooze, *Crashed: How a Decade of Financial Crises Changed the World* (London: Penguin, 2018), chs. 7–8. On the Fed's emergence as an international lender of last resort see Christophe Destais, 'Central Bank Currency Swaps and the International Monetary System', *Emerging Markets Finance and Trade 52*, no. 10 (2016): pp. 2253–66; Daniel McDowell, 'The US as Sovereign International Last Resort Lender: The Fed's Currency Swap Programme During the Great Panic of 2007–9', *New Political Economy 17*, no. 2 (2012): pp. 157–78; Iain Hardie and Sylvia Maxfield, 'Atlas Constrained: The US External Balance Sheet and International Monetary Power', *Review of International Political Economy 23*, no. 4 (2016): pp. 583–613; Perry Mehrling, 'Elasticity and Discipline in the Global Swap Network', *International Journal of Political Economy 44*, no. 4 (2015): pp. 311–24.

10. On the politics of which emerging market states received dollar swaps see Aditi Sahasrabuddhe, 'Drawing the Line: The Politics of Federal Currency Swaps in the Global Financial Crisis', *Review of International Political Economy 26*, no. 3 (2019): pp. 461–89; Benn Steil, 'Taper Trouble: The International Consequences of Fed Policy', *Foreign Affairs 93*, no. 4 (July/August 2014): pp. 54–61.

11. Jeffrey Snider at Alhambra Investment Partners has written and spoken extensively on why the Eurodollar credit markets have never been restored to their pre-August 2007 functionality. See, for example, Jeffrey Snider 'Why Quantitative Easing Can Never Work', Alhambra Investment Partners, June 2016, https://alhambrapartners.com/wp-content/uploads/2016/06/Why-QE-Will-Never-Work.pdf

12. Robert N. McCauley, Agustín S. Bénétrix, Patrick M. McGuire, and Goetz von Peter, 'Financial De-globalization in Banking?' BIS Working Papers, no. 650, June 2017, https://www.bis.org/publ/work650.pdf; Jaime Caruana, 'Have We Passed Peak Finance?' Lecture for the International Centre for Monetary and Banking Studies, Geneva, 28 February 2017, https://www.bis.org/speeches/sp170228.htm; Gian Maria Milesi-Ferretti, 'Global Capital Flows and External Financial Positions Since the Global Financial Crisis', paper presented at the Irving Fischer Committee Satellite meeting at the ISI World Statistics Congress, Rio de Janeiro, Brazil, 24 July 2015, https://www.bis.org/ifc/publ/ifcb42_keynotespeech.pdf; Kristin Forbes, 'Financial "Deglobalization"?: Capital Flows, Banks, and the Beatles', speech at Queen Mary University, London, 18 November 2014, https://www.bankofengland.co.uk/speech/2014/financial-deglobalization-capital-flows-banks-and-the-beatles

13. Although the Fed's turn to QE and zero interest rates marked a massive disjuncture, the Bank of Japan was the first central bank to practise this unconventional monetary policy, first turning to a zero interest rate policy

in February 1999 and to QE in March 2001. See Kazumasa Iwata and Shinji Takenaka, 'Central Bank Balance Sheet Expansion: Japan's Experience' in 'Are Central Bank Balance Sheets in Asia Too Large?', BIS Working Papers, Bank for International Settlements, no. 66, June, p. 134, https://ideas.repec.org/b/bis/bisbps/66.html

14. On QE in relation to mortgage markets see Herman M. Schwartz, 'Banking on the FED; QE1-2-3 and the Rebalancing of the Global Economy', *New Political Economy 21*, no. 1 (2016): pp. 26–48.

15. Federal Housing Finance Agency, Office of Inspector General, Impact of the Federal Reserve's Quantitative Easing programmes on Fannie Mae and Freddie Mac, 23 October 2014, p. 13, https://www.fhfaoig.gov/sites/default/files/EVL-2015-002_1.pdf; Marco Di Maggio Amir Kermani Christopher Palmer, 'How Quantitative Easing Works: Evidence on the Refinancing Channel', NBER Working Paper 22638, p. 10, https://www.nber.org/papers/w22638

16. International Monetary Fund, 'Global Financial Stability Report: Lower for Longer', October 2019, p. 28, https://www.imf.org/en/Publica tions/GFSR/Issues/2019/10/01/global-financial-stability-report-octo ber-2019

17. See Bank of England, 'The Distributional Effects of Asset Purchases', *Quarterly Bulletin* (Q3: 2012): pp. 254–66, https://www.bankofengland.co. uk/-/media/boe/files/news/2012/july/the-distributional-effects-of-asset-purchases-paper

18. The Bank of England's research suggest that while a monetary policy mix that included QE disproportionately benefited older generations on asset prices, it disproportionately benefited the incomes of younger generations. Philip Bunn, Alice Pugh, and Chris Yeates, 'The Distributional Impact of Monetary Policy Easing in the UK between 2008 and 2014', Bank of England, Staff Working Paper no. 720, March 2018, https:// www.bankofengland.co.uk/working-paper/2018/the-distributional-impact-of-monetary-policy-easing-in-the-uk-between-2008-and-2014

19. In some countries, the rates of home ownership started slipping before the 2007–8 crash. In Britain, for example, the number of loans for first-time house purchases began a sharp fall in 2003.

20. See Schwartz, 'Banking on the FED'.

21. See Joseph Gagnon, Matthew Rasking, Julie Remache, and Brian Sack, 'The Financial Market Effects of the Federal Reserve's Large-Scale Asset Purchases', *International Journal of Central Banking 7*, no. 1 (2011): pp. 3–43.

22. Dietrich Domanski, Jonathan Kearns, Marco Lombardi, and Hyun Song Shin, 'Oil and Debt', *BIS Quarterly Review* (March 2015), pp. 55–65.

23. James Schlesinger, 'Will War Yield Oil Security?', *Challenge 34*, no. 2 (1991): p. 28.

24. Aasim M. Husain, Rabah Arezki, Peter Breuer, Vikram Haksar, Thomas Helbling, Paulo A. Medas, and Martin Sommer, 'Global Implications of Lower Oil Prices', IMF Staff Discussion Note, 14 July 2015, SDN.15/15,

https://www.imf.org/en/Publications/Staff-Discussion-Notes/Issues/
2016/12/31/Global-Implications-of-Lower-Oil-Prices-43052. For the
consequences of the oil price slump from November 2014 to early 2016
see Helen Thompson, *Oil and the Western Economic Crisis* (London: Palgrave, 2017), pp. 74–80.

25. On the financial crisis part of the Ukrainian crisis see Steil, 'Taper
Trouble'.

26. On the ECB before the Eurozone crisis see David Howarth and Peter
Loedel, *The European Central Bank: The New European Leviathan?* (London:
Palgrave Macmillan, 2003).

27. On the Eurozone crisis as a banking crisis see Mark Blyth, *Austerity: The
History of a Dangerous Idea* (New York: Oxford University Press, 2013), ch. 3.

28. Helen Thompson, 'Enduring Capital Flow Constraints and the
2007–2008 Financial and Euro Zone Crises', *The British Journal of Politics
and International Relations 18*, no. 1 (2016): pp. 216–33.

29. Quoted in Wolfgang Proissl, 'Why Germany Fell out of Love with
Europe', Bruegel Essay and Lecture Series, Brussels, 30 June 2010, p. 10.

30. Blyth, *Austerity*, ch. 3; Alison Johnston and Aidan Regan, 'European
Monetary Integration and the Incompatibility of National Varieties of
Capitalism', *Journal of Common Market Studies 54*, no. 2 (2016), pp. 318–36;
Heiner Flassbeck, 'Wage Divergence in Euroland: Explosive in the Mak-
ing' in *Europe and the World Economy: Global Player or Global Drag?*, edited by
Jürg Bibow and Andrea Terzi (Basingstoke: Palgrave Macmillan, 2007),
pp. 43–52.

31. See Paul De Grauwe, 'The European Central Bank as a Lender of Last
Resort', Vox, 18 August 2011, https://voxeu.org/article/european-
central-bank-lender-last-resort

32. See Blyth, *Austerity*, ch. 3.

33. On the problem of the ECB's legal authority after its crisis actions see
Nicole Scicluna, 'Integration through the Disintegration of Law?: The
ECB and EU Constitutionalism in the Crisis', *Journal of European Public
Policy 25*, no. 12 (2018): pp. 1874–91; Christian Kreuder-Sonnen,
'Beyond Integration Theory: The (Anti)-Constitutional Dimension of
European Crisis Governance', *Journal of Common Market Studies 54*, no. 6
(2016): pp. 1350–66.

34. Christoph Trebesch and Jeromin Zettelmeyer, 'ECB Interventions in
Distressed Sovereign Debt Markets: The Case of Greek Bonds', *IMF
Economic Review 66*, no. 2 (2018): pp. 287–322.

35. Thompson, *Oil and the Western Economic Crisis*, pp. 62–3.

36. See Martin Heipertz and Amy Verdun, *Ruling Europe: The Politics of the
Stability and Growth Pact* (Cambridge: Cambridge University Press, 2010),
part 2; Ben Clift, 'The New Political Economy of Dirigisme: French
Macro-Economic Policy, Unrepentant Sinning and the Stability and
Growth Pact', *British Journal of Politics and International Relations 8*, no. 3
(2006): pp. 351–67.

37. On the Italian debt crisis see Erik Jones, 'Italy's Sovereign Debt Crisis', *Survival 54* no. 1 (2012): pp. 83–110.

38. Timothy Geithner, *Stress Test: Reflections on Financial Crises* (New York: Crown Publishing Group), p. 476.

39. For a detailed account of this episode see Angel Pascual-Ramsay, 'The Management of the Economic Crisis in Spain by the PSOE Government: A Domestic Political Perspective', PhD Dissertation submitted to Cambridge University, 20 May 2017, ch. 6.

40. Economist, 'Spanish Practices', *Economist*, 18 February 2012. https://www.economist.com/europe/2012/02/18/spanish-practices

41. For analysis of Eurozone decision-making as 'emergency' politics see Kenneth Dyson, 'Sworn to Grim Necessity? Imperfections of European Economic Governance, Normative Political Theory, and Supreme Emergency', *Journal of European Integration 35*, no. 3 (2013): pp. 207–22; Claire Kilpatrick, 'On the Rule of, 2014 Law and Economic Emergency: The Degradation of Basic Legal Values in Europe's Bailouts', *Oxford Journal of Legal Studies 35*, no. 2 (2015): pp. 325–53; Jonathan White, 'Emergency Europe', *Political Studies 63*, no. 2 (2015), pp. 300–18; Wolfgang Streeck, 'Heller, Schmitt and the Euro', *European Law Journal 21*, no. 3 (2015): pp. 361–70; Jonathan White, *Politics of Last Resort: Governing by Emergency in the European Union* (Oxford: Oxford University Press, 2019).

42. Jean-Claude Trichet Speech: 'Lessons from the Crisis: Challenges for the Advanced Economies and for the European Monetary Union', Eleventh annual Stavros Niarchos lecture, 17 May 2012, https://piie.com/publications/papers/transcript-20120518niarchos-trichet.pdf

43. Speech by Mario Draghi, President of the European Central Bank at the Global Investment Conference in London, 26 July 2012, https://www.bis.org/list/speeches/author_mario+draghi/page_11.htm

44. Quoted in K. Gebert, 'A Place at the Top Table?: Poland and the Euro Crisis', European Council on Foreign Relations, February 2012, https://ecfr.eu/wp-content/uploads/Poland_final.pdf

45. Trebesch and Zettelmeyer, 'ECB Interventions in Distressed Sovereign Debt Markets', p. 295.

46. Peter Spiegel, *How the Euro Was Saved*, Kindle edition (London: Financial Times, 2014), ch. 1.

47. Spiegel, *How the Euro Was Saved*, ch. 1.

48. Guardian, 'Eurozone Crisis Live: Row after Merkel "Suggests Greece Hold Euro Referendum"', 18 May 2012, https://www.theguardian.com/business/2012/may/18/eurozone-crisis-stock-markets-greece-spain

49. Spiegel, *How the Euro Was Saved*, chs. 1–2.

50. On the consequences of the bailouts' conditionality on Greece's growth see Independent Evaluation Office of the International Monetary Fund, *The IMF and the Crises in Greece, Ireland and Portugal* (Washington DC: IMF, 2016).

51. Spiegel International staff, 'Interview with ECB President, Mario Draghi', Spiegel International staff, 29 October 2012, http://www.spiegel.

de/international/europe/spiegel-interview-with-ecb-president-mario-draghi-a-863971.html

52. The hitherto unused OMT looked a hollow tool to deal with the impending crisis as it required states to be in a sovereign bailout programme and neither Italy nor Spain was. It was also subject to an ongoing legal challenge in Germany. In February 2014, the German Constitutional Court had given a preliminary decision that OMT could well exceed the ECB's authority as well as impair the Bundestag's constitutional budgetary responsibility and asked the European Court of Justice (ECJ) to make a judgment. Ten days before the Greek election, the ECJ's advocate general said that with certain conditions OMT was in accordance with EU treaty law, and that without OMT the markets would continue to countenance the erroneous belief that the euro was reversible. On the German Court's decision see Niels Petersen, 'Karlsruhe Not Only Barks, But Finally Bites—Some Remarks on the OMT Decision of the German Constitutional Court', *German Law Journal 15*, no. 2 (2014): pp. 321–7. For the incoherencies in the ECJ argument see Michael A. Wilkinson, 'The Euro Is Irreversible!... or is it?: On OMT, Austerity and the Threat of "Grexit"', *German Law Journal 16*, no. 4 (2015): pp. 1049–72.

53. Mario Draghi, Introductory Statement to the Press Conference (with Q&A), EC, 22 January 2015, https://www.ecb.europa.eu/press/pressconf/2015/html/is150122.en.html

54. For narrative accounts of the effort to expel Greece see Spiegel International staff, 'A Government Divided: Schäuble's Push for Grexit Puts Merkel on the Defensive', *Spiegel International*, 17 July 2015 https://www.spiegel.de/international/germany/schaeuble-pushed-for-a-grexit-and-backed-merkel-into-a-corner-a-1044259.html; Ian Traynor, 'Three Days that Saved the Euro', *Guardian*, 22 October 2015. https://www.theguardian.com/world/2015/oct/22/three-days-to-save-the-euro-greece

55. Mario Draghi, Introductory Statement to the Press Conference (with Q&A), ECB, 26 July 2018, https://www.ecb.europa.eu/press/pressconf/2018/html/ecb.is180726.en.html

56. For a longer discussion around this point see Helen Thompson, 'How the City of London Lost at Brexit: A Historical Perspective', *Economy and Society 46*, no. 2 (2017): pp. 211–28.

57. The Czech Republic did not oppose the Fiscal Compact at the December 2011 EU summit, but, in January 2012, it indicated it would not be joining. In 2019 it did join.

58. Cameron's tactics depended on a dubious assumption that he could win a party argument on this question.

59. Blocking the other EU states using the Union institutions for a treaty outside the EU legal framework was the only leverage at Cameron's disposal. No doubt aware that any such move would have appeared hugely disproportionate for a member state outside the euro, Cameron

buckled to Merkel's insistence that the Eurozone required stronger fiscal rules.

60. For a longer version of this argument see Helen Thompson, 'Inevitability and Contingency: The Political Economy of Brexit', *British Journal of Politics and International Relations 19*, no.3 (2017): pp. 434–49. For a not dissimilar argument from Britain's former ambassador to the EU see Ivan Rogers, 'Cameron's Brexit referendum', Lecture at Hertford College, Oxford, 24 November 2017. Published by Politico at https://www.politico.eu/article/ivan-rogers-david-cameron-speech-transcript-brexit-referendum/ On the role of the freedom of movement issue in the referendum result see Matthew Goodwin and Caitlin Milazzo, 'Taking Back Control?' Investigating the Role of Immigration in the 2016 Vote for Brexit', *British Journal of Politics and International Relations 19*, no. 3 (2017): pp. 450–64.

61. On the hard authority of the single market for Britain see Matthias Matthijs, Craig Parsons, and Christina Toenshoff, 'Ever Tighter Union? Brexit, Grexit, and Frustrated Differentiation in the Single Market and Eurozone', *Comparative European Politics 17*, no. 2 (2019): pp. 209–30.

62. Jean-Claude Juncker, State of the Union Address 2017, 13 September 2017, https://ec.europa.eu/commission/presscorner/detail/en/SPEECH_17_3165

63. On initial French optimism about Eurozone reform see Charles Grant, 'Macron's Plans for the Euro', Centre for European Reform Insight, 23 February 2018, https://www.cer.eu/insights/macrons-plans-euro

64. Emmanuel Macron, 'Initiative on Europe', speech at the Sorbonne, 26 September 2017, http://international.blogs.ouest-france.fr/archive/2017/09/29/macron-sorbonne-verbatim-europe-18583.html

65. On the New Hanseatic League's emergence see 'Gang of Eight: Eurozone Reforms', *Economist*, 8 December 2018; Christian Reiermann and Peter Müller, 'The Sputtering German-French Motor', *Spiegel International*, 11 December 2018.

66. See Adam Tooze, '"Coronabonds" and Europe's North-South Divide', Social Europe, 13 April 2020, https://www.socialeurope.eu/corona-bonds-and-europes-north-south-divide

67. For a narrative account of her decision see Victor Mallet, Guy Chazan, and Sam Fleming, 'The Chain of Events that Led to Germany's Change Over Europe's Recovery Fund', *Financial Times*, 22 May 2020, https://www.ft.com/content/1d8853f4-726d-4c06-a905-ed2f37d25eee

68. 'German ECB Ruling Should "Spur" More Eurozone Integration: Merkel', *Euractiv*, 14 May 2020, https://www.euractiv.com/section/future-eu/news/german-ecb-ruling-should-spur-more-eurozone-integration-merkel/

69. As an example of the 'Hamiltonian moment' claims see Anatole Kaletsky, 'Europe's Hamiltonian Moment', *Project Syndicate*, 21 May 2020, https://www.project-syndicate.org/commentary/french-german-european-recovery-plan-proposal-by-anatole-kaletsky-2020–05?barrier=accesspaylog. For my

critique of this claim see Helen Thompson, 'Pandemic Borrowing', *International Politik Quarterly*, 27 November 2020, https://ip-quarterly.com/en/pandemic-borrowing

70. 'Germany Gains Most from Relaxed State Aid Rules', *Euractiv*, 4 May 2020, https://www.euractiv.com/section/competition/news/germany-gains-most-from-relaxed-eu-state-aid-rules/

71. Wolfgang Munchau articulates this frustration in 'How to Face Down Orban', *Eurointelligence*, 21 November 2020, https://www.eurointelligence.com/column/enhanced-cooperation

72. See Eric Helleiner and Hongying Wang, 'The Richness of Financial Nationalism—The Case of China', *Pacific Affairs 92*, no. 2 (2019): pp. 211–34; Benjamin Cohen, 'Renminbi Internationalization, a Conflict of Statecrafts', Chatham House Research Paper, March 2017, https://www.chathamhouse.org/sites/default/files/publications/research/2017-03-20-renminbi-internationalization-statecraft-cohen.pdf. On the Chinese leadership's views on geopolitical power and currencies see Eric Helleiner and Jonathan Kirshner, 'The Politics of China's International Monetary Relations' in *The Great Wall of Money: Power Politics and China's International Monetary Relations*, edited by Eric Helleiner and Jonathan Kirshner (Ithaca: Cornell University Press, 2014), pp. 1–22. On the geopolitics of currencies see Benjamin J. Cohen, *Currency Statecraft: Monetary Rivalry and Geopolitical Ambition* (Chicago: University of Chicago Press, 2018).

73. Zhou Xiaochuan, 'Reform the International Monetary System', *BIS Review 41* (2009), p. 1, https://www.bis.org/review/r090402c.pdf

74. For reasons why the dollar pre-eminence was always well founded and not vulnerable to a Chinese challenge see Benjamin J. Cohen, *Currency Power: Understanding Monetary Rivalry* (Princeton: Princeton University Press, 2015). Eric Helleiner, *The Status Quo Crisis: Global Financial Governance After the 2008 Meltdown* (Oxford: Oxford University Press, 2014); Harold James, 'The Enduring International Pre-Eminence of the Dollar' in *The Future of the Dollar*, edited by Eric Helleiner and Jonathan Kirshner (Ithaca: Cornell University Press, 2009), pp. 24–44. For arguments that there was scope for a serious challenge to American power after the crash see Jonathan Kirshner, *American Power After the Financial Crisis* (Ithaca: Cornell University Press, 2014); Barry Eichengreen, *Exorbitant Privilege: The Rise and Fall of the Dollar and the Future of the International Monetary System* (New York: Oxford University Press, 2011).

75. For some time prior to the crash, the Chinese leadership had toyed with such a move, but demurred from it. Helleiner and Wang, 'The Richness of Financial Nationalism', p. 223.

76. Benjamin J. Cohen, 'Renminbi Internationalization, a Conflict of Statecrafts', Chatham House Research Paper, March 2017, p. 1.

77. Cohen, 'Renminbi Internationalization, a Conflict of Statecraft', p. 5.

78. See Yu-wai Vic Li, 'Hong Kong in China's Financial Globalization: Market Power and Political Leverage', *Asian Survey 58*, no. 3 (2018):

pp. 439–63. On Hong Kong's internationalized economy prior to 1997 see Michael Taylor, 'Hong Kong's Economy and its Global Connections: Prospects for 1997 and Beyond' in *Hong Kong's Transitions, 1842–1997*, edited by Rosemary Foot and Judith M. Brown (Basingstoke: Palgrave, 1996), pp. 166–91.

79. David C. Donald, *A Financial Centre for Two Empires: Hong Kong's Corporate, Securities and Tax Laws in its Transition from Britain to China* (Cambridge: Cambridge University Press, 2014), p. 2.

80. On why renminbi internationalization could not succeed in relation to a dollar trap see Eswar S. Prasad, *The Dollar Trap: How the US Dollar Tightened its Grip on Global Finance* (Princeton: Princeton University Press, 2015).

81. Mark Carney, 'The Growing Challenges for Monetary Policy in the Current International Monetary and Financial System', speech at the Jackson Hole Symposium, 23 August 2019.

82. Trading Economics, China's Gross External Debt, https://tradingeconomics.com/china/external-debt

83. Colby Smith, 'China's Currency Will Not Replace the US Dollar', *Financial Times*, 19 September 2018. On the Chinese 2015–16 financial crisis see Tooze, *Crashed*, ch. 25.

84. Quoted in He Wei, 'How China's Mystery Author Called its Economic Slowdown', FT Confidential Research, *Financial Times*, 25 October 2018, https://www.ft.com/content/69002a74-c52a-435a-b381-07cb5feae0d5

85. IMF World Economic Outlook Update, 22 January 2018, p. 2. https://www.imf.org/en/Publications/WEO/Issues/2018/01/11/world-economic-outlook-update-january-2018

86. IMF World Economic Outlook, October 2019: Global Manufacturing Downturn, Rising Trade Barriers, p. xiv. https://www.imf.org/en/Publications/WEO/Issues/2019/10/01/world-economic-outlook-october-2019

87. Daniel Shane, 'Alibaba's Debut in Hong Kong Signals Change in Beijing's Mindset', *Financial Times*, 4 December 2019, https://www.ft.com/content/5257d548-1686-11ea-8d73-6303645ac406

88. See Brad Setser, 'Testimony Before the Senate Committee on Small Business and Entrepreneurship, Hearing on Made in China 2025 and the Future of American Industry', 27 February 2019, https://www.govinfo.gov/content/pkg/CHRG-116shrg35699/html/CHRG-116shrg35699.htm; James McBride and Andrew Chatzky, 'Is "Made in China 2025" a Threat to Global Trade?' Council on Foreign Relations Backgrounder, 13 May 2019, https://www.cfr.org/backgrounder/made-china-2025-threat-global-trade

89. Sophie Meunier, 'Beggars Can't Be Choosers: The European Crisis and Chinese Direct Investment in the European Union', *Journal of European Integration 36*, no. 3 (2014): pp. 284–91.

90. Thilo Hanemann, Mikko Huotari, and Agatha Kratz, 'Chinese FDI in Europe: 2018 Trends and Impact on New Screening Policies', Mercator

Institute for Chinese Studies, 6 March 2019, p. 8. https://merics.org/en/report/chinese-fdi-europe-2018-trends-and-impact-new-screening-policies

91. Heather A. Conley and Jonathan E. Hillman, 'The Western Balkans with Chinese Characteristics', Centre for Strategic International Studies, *Commentary*, 30 July 2019. https://www.csis.org/analysis/western-balkans-chinese-characteristics

92. Facts about German Foreign Trade, Federal Ministry for Economic Affairs and Energy. September 2019, p. 5, https://www.bmwi.de/Redaktion/EN/Publikationen/facts-about-german-foreign-trade.html

93. On the parallels between the issues created by the German and Chinese trade surpluses and how it was the German surplus issues that proved more persistent after 2008 see Guonan Ma and Robert N. McCauley, 'Global and Euro Imbalances: China and Germany', BIS Working Papers no. 424, 5 September 2013, https://www.bis.org/publ/work424.htm In a 2013 report, the US Treasury argued that the German trade surplus was a deflationary threat to the world economy: US Treasury Department, *Report to Congress on International Economic and Exchange Rate Policies*, Washington, DC: US Department of the Treasury, 30 October 2013, p. 3.

94. Laurens Cerulus, 'How US Restrictions Drove Deutsche Telecom and Huawei Closer Together', *Politico*, 8 July 2020, https://www.politico.eu/article/deutsche-telekom-huawei-us-security-measures/

95. Hanemann, Huotari, and Kratz, 'Chinese FDI in Europe', p. 12.

96. On the British government and the City of London's strategic efforts to make London the centre of offshore renminbi activity see Jeremy Green, 'The Offshore City, Chinese Finance, and British Capitalism: Geo-Economic Rebalancing under the Coalition Government', *British Journal of Politics and International Relations 20*, no. 2 (2018): pp. 285–302; Jeremy Green and Julian Gruin, 'RMB Transnationalization and the Infrastructural Power of International Financial Centres', *Review of International Political Economy*, published online 13 April 2020, https://www.tandfonline.com/doi/full/10.1080/09692290.2020.1748682

97. David Cameron, 'My Visit Can Begin a Relationship to Benefit China, Britain and the World', *Guardian*, 2 December 2013, https://www.theguardian.com/commentisfree/2013/dec/02/david-cameron-my-visit-to-china

98. James Kynge, 'China Poised to Issue Sovereign Debt in Renminbi in London', *Financial Times*, 13 October 2015. https://www.ft.com/content/5ef6329c-71c9-11e5-9b9e-690fdae72044 *BBC News*, 'George Osborne on UK's "Golden Era" as China's "Best Partner in the West"', 23 October 2015, https://www.bbc.co.uk/news/av/uk-34621254

99. Reuters Staff, 'Don't Sacrifice Hong Kong for a Banker's Bonus, UK Tells HSBC', *Reuters*, 1 July 2020, https://www.reuters.com/article/us-hongkong-protests-britain-banks-idUSKBN2425WI

100. Guy Chazan, 'Merkel Comes Under Fire at Home for China Stance', *Financial Times*, 7 July 2020, https://www.ft.com/content/bf1adef9-a681-48c0-99b8-f551e7a5b66d

101. Jakob Hanke Vele, Giorgio Leali, and Barbara Moens, 'Germany's Drive for EU-China Deal Draws Criticism from Other EU Countries', *Politico*, 1 January 2021, https://www.politico.eu/article/germanys-drive-for-eu-china-deal-draws-criticism-from-other-eu-countries/

102. Quoted in David Dayen, 'Corporate Rescue: How The Fed Bailed Out the Investor Class Without Spending a Cent', *The Intercept*, 27 May 2020, https://theintercept.com/2020/05/27/federal-reserve-corporate-debt-coronavirus/

103. David Dayen, 'Corporate Rescue'.

104. On the present geopolitical shock from China as part of a series that have shaped the EU's development see Scott Lavery and David Schmid, 'European Integration and the New Global Disorder', *Journal of Common Market Studies*, published online 12 February 2021, https://doi.org/10.1111/jcms.13184

Chapter 7

1. Michael Gove, 'The Privilege of Public Service', Ditchley Annual Lecture, 1 July 2020, https://www.gov.uk/government/speeches/the-privilege-of-public-service-given-as-the-ditchley-annual-lecture

2. On Roosevelt's New Deal as an archetype for democratic reform see Ira Katznelson, *Fear Itself: The New Deal and the Origins of Our Times* (New York: Liveright, 2013), pp. 4–7, 476–7. On the pessimism about democracy in the 1930s and 1940s including after the war's end see Katznelson, *Fear Itself*, chs. 1 and 3.

3. See John Dunn, *Breaking Democracy's Spell* (New Haven: Yale University Press, 2014).

4. Benedict Anderson, *Imagined Communities: Reflections on the Origin and Spread of Nationalism* (London: Verso, 1983).

5. There is a huge literature on the emergence of nationhood and nationalism and considerable scholarly disagreement about the historical origins of nationhood and in particular whether there were nations before the modern era. For a good review of different interpretations see Anthony Smith, *Nationalism and Modernism* (London: Routledge, 1998).

6. Michael Howard, 'War and the Nation-State', *Daedalus 108*, no. 4 (1979): p. 109.

7. Helmut Kohl's Ten-Point Plan for German Unity, 28 November 1989, http://ghdi.ghi-dc.org/sub_document.cfm?document_id=223

8. On the relationship between democracy and nationhood see Margaret Canovan, 'Democracy and Nationalism' in *Democratic Theory Today*, edited by April Carter and Geoffrey Stokes (Cambridge: Polity, 2000),

pp. 149–70; Bernard Yack, 'Popular Sovereignty and Nationalism', *Political Theory 29*, no. 4 (2001): pp. 517–36. For a more philosophical argument see David Miller, 'Bounded Citizenship' in *Cosmopolitan Citizenship*, edited by Kimberly Hutchings and Roland Dannreuther (London: Macmillan, 1990), pp. 60–80. For John Stuart Mill's argument that democracy was only possible in nation states see *Considerations on Representative Government* (Cambridge: Cambridge University Press, 2011), ch. 16. (First published in 1861.)

9. Howard, 'War and the Nation-state', p. 102.
10. On this point see Margaret Canovan, *The People* (Cambridge: Polity Press, 2005), pp. 57–63.
11. Canovan, *The People*, p. 31.
12. The argument that constitutions based on class distinctions were incompatible with nationhood was made forcefully by the Hungarian politician and writer, József Eötvös. For a summary of Eötvös' arguments on this point see D. Mervyn Jones, 'The Political Ideas of Baron József Eötvös', *Slavonic and East European Review 48*, no. 113 (1970): pp. 582–97.
13. Istvan Hont, *Jealousy of Trade: International Competition and the Nation-State in Historical Perspective* (Cambridge, MA: Harvard University Press, 2010), ch. 7.
14. For the argument that nationhood cannot be created without war, see Howard, 'War and the Nation-state', pp. 101–10.
15. Max Weber, 'Suffrage and Democracy' in Max Weber, *Political Writings*, edited by Peter Lassman and Ronald Speirs (Cambridge: Cambridge University Press, 1994), pp. 80–129.
16. Walter Scheidel, *The Great Leveller: Violence and the History of Inequality from the Stone Age to the Twenty-First Century* (Princeton: Princeton University Press, 2018), pp. 168–9.
17. William Saffran, 'State, Nation, National Identity, and Citizenship: France as a Test Case', *International Political Science Review 12*, no. 3 (1991): p. 222.
18. Yack, 'Popular Sovereignty and Nationalism', p. 520.
19. See Alexandre Grandazzi, *The Foundation of Rome: Myth and History* (Ithaca: Cornell University Press, 2000).
20. Quoted in Robert Tombs, *France 1814–1914* (London: Longman, 1996), p. 370. On European states using foreign policy and empire for nation-building see Helen Thompson, *Might, Right, Prosperity and Consent: Representative Democracy and the International Economy, 1919–2001* (Manchester: Manchester University Press), pp. 32–6.
21. On French nation-building during the Third Republic via language and national education see Eugene Weber, *Peasants into Frenchmen: The Modernisation of Rural France, 1870–1914* (Stanford: Stanford University Press, 1976).
22. On the relationship between socialism in Germany and France and nationhood see Sheri Berman, *The Primacy of Politics: Social Democracy and*

the Making of Europe's Twentieth Century (Cambridge: Cambridge University Press, 2006).

23. Saul Dubow and Gary Gerstle, 'Race, Ethnicity and Nationalism' in *A Cultural History of Democracy in the Modern Age*, edited by Eugenio Biagini and Gary Gerstle (London: Bloomsbury, 2021), p. 151.

24. Will Kymlicka, 'Modernity and Minority Nationalism: Commentary on Thomas Franck', *Ethics and International Affairs 11* (March 1997): pp. 171–6.

25. Michael Mann has argued that there is a strong historical relationship between democracy and ethnic cleansing. *The Dark Side of Democracy: Explaining Ethnic Cleansing* (Cambridge: Cambridge University Press, 2004).

26. On Lincoln's imaginative refounding of the American nation in the Gettysburg Address see Garry Wills, *Lincoln at Gettysburg: The Words that Remade America* (New York: Simon & Schuster, 1992). For the ways in which the Civil War more generally recast American nationhood see James M. McPherson, *The War that Forged a Nation: Why the Civil War Still Matters* (New York: Oxford University Press, 2015).

27. Yack, 'Popular Sovereignty and Nationalism', p. 521.

28. On the politics of exclusion for subversion in the United States see Gary Gerstle, *American Crucible: Race and Nation in the Twentieth Century*, revised edition (Princeton: Princeton University Press, 2017), ch. 3.

29. See John Boyer, *Political Radicalism in Late Imperial Vienna: Origins of the Christian Social Movement, 1848–1897* (Chicago: University of Chicago Press, 1981); John Boyer, *Cultural and Political Crisis in Vienna: Christian Socialism in Power, 1897–1918* (Chicago: University of Chicago Press, 1995).

30. J.G.A. Pocock, *The Machiavellian Moment: Florentine Political Thought and the Atlantic Political Tradition* (Princeton: Princeton University Press, 1975), p. 77.

31. Polybius, *The Rise of the Roman Empire*, edited by F.W. Walbank and trans. Ian-Scott Kilvert (London: Penguin 1979), p. 350.

32. Polybius, *The Rise of the Roman Empire*, p. 350.

33. Polybius, *The Rise of the Roman Empire*, p. 310.

34. Polybius, *The Rise of the Roman Empire*, p. 311.

35. Polybius, *The Rise of the Roman Empire*, p. 350.

36. Polybius, *The Rise of the Roman Empire*, p. 350.

37. On the significance of this change see Jeffrey A. Winters, *Oligarchy* (Cambridge: Cambridge University Press, 2011), pp. 26–31.

38. Peter Fraser, 'Public Petitioning and Parliament Before 1832', *History 46*, no. 158 (1961): pp. 195–211.

39. For the politics of land in Britain since the 1970s see Brett Christophers, *The New Enclosure: The Appropriation of Public Land in Neoliberal Britain* (London: Verso, 2019).

40. Richard Johnson, *The End of the Second Reconstruction* (Cambridge: Polity, 2020), pp. 40–1.

41. See John Dunn, *Setting the People Free: The Story of Democracy* (London: Atlantic Books, 2005); John Dunn, 'Conclusions' in *Democracy: The*

Unfinished Journey 508 BC to 1993, edited by John Dunn (Oxford: Oxford University Press, 1993), pp. 250–60.

42. Income tax was introduced during the Civil War and repealed in 1872.

43. Winters, *Oligarchy*, pp. 227–9. For a political history of American income tax see John Whitte, *The Politics and Development of the Federal Income Tax* (Madison: University of Wisconsin Press, 1986).

44. Scheidel, *The Great Leveller*, pp. 143–9.

45. See William H. Riker, *Liberalism Against Populism: A Confrontation Between the Theory of Democracy and the Theory of Social Choice* (San Francisco: W.H. Freeman, 1982).

46. Max Weber, 'Parliament and Government in Germany' in *Weber, Political Writings*, pp. 219–22; Max Weber, 'The Profession and Vocation of Politics' in Weber, *Political Writings*, pp. 331, 342–3.

47. Tomáš Sedláček, *Economics of Good and Evil: The Quest for Economic Meaning from Gilgamesh to Wall Street* (Oxford: Oxford University Press, 2013), pp. 76–8.

48. James Macdonald, *A Free Nation Deep in Debt: The Financial Roots of Democracy* (New York: Farrar, Straus, & Giroux, 2003), p. 373. This view was reinforced by the idea that debt had destructive consequences for the Roman Republic.

49. Macdonald, *A Free Nation Deep in Debt*, ch. 8.

50. This was strategy pioneered by Louis Napoleon to finance France's participation in the Crimean War. On the emergence from the mid-nineteenth century of a new form of citizen creditors see Macdonald, *A Free Nation Deep in Debt*, pp. 377–464.

51. Quoted in Macdonald, *A Free Nation Deep in Debt*, p. 396.

52. Machiavelli, *The Discourses*, edited by Bernard Crick and trans. Leslie Walker (London: Penguin, 1970), pp. 385 and 385–7.

53. Machiavelli, *The Discourses*, pp. 201, 202.

54. For an interpretation of Machiavelli's analysis that makes Machiavelli a supporter of the Gracchi's redistributive agenda and a critic of their prudential approach to the problem by trying to resurrect old laws see John P. McCormick, 'Machiavelli and the Gracchi: Prudence, Violence and Redistribution', *Global Crime 10*, no. 4 (2009): pp. 298–305.

55. Gregory Ablavsky, 'The Savage Constitution', *Duke Law Journal 63*, no. 5 (2014): pp. 999–1089.

56. James Madison, 'Federalist 63' in Alexander Hamilton, James Madison, and John Jay, *The Federalist: With Letters of Brutus*, edited by Terence Ball (Cambridge: Cambridge University Press 2003), p. 307.

57. Alexander Hamilton, 'Federalist 1' in Hamilton, Madison and Jay, *The Federalist*, p. 3.

58. Brutus, 'Letter IV' in Hamilton, Madison and Jay, *The Federalist: With Letters of Brutus*, p. 458.

59. See Drew R. McCoy, *The Elusive Republic: Political Economy in Jeffersonian America* (Chapel Hill: University of North Carolina Press, 1980), ch. 6;

Lance Banning, *The Jeffersonian Persuasion: Evolution of a Party Ideology* (Ithaca: Cornell University Press, 1978), chs. 5 and 6; E. James Ferguson, *The Power of the Purse: A History of American Public Finance, 1776–1790* (Chapel Hill: University of North Carolina Press, 1961).

60. The Omaha Platform. Available at http://historymatters.gmu.edu/d/ 5361/

61. See, for example, for different judgements, Thomas Frank, *The People, No: A Brief History of Anti-Populism* (New York: Metropolitan Books, 2020); Barry Eichengreen, *The Populist Temptation: Economic Grievance and Political Reaction in the Modern Era* (Oxford: Oxford University Press, 2018), ch 2.

62. On the importance of the producer class ethic to the American populists see Michael Kazin, *The Populist Persuasion: An American History*, revised edition (Ithaca: Cornell University Press, 1995), pp. 13–15.

63. Quoted in Kazin, *The Populist Persuasion*, p. 45.

64. Speech by William Jennings Bryan at the Democratic National Convention in Chicago, 9 July 1896, http://historymatters.gmu.edu/d/5354/

65. Quoted in Kazin, *The Populist Persuasion*, p. 44.

66. Rogers M. Smith, 'The "American Creed" and American Identity: The Limits of Liberal Citizenship in the United States', *Western Political Quarterly 41* no. 2 (1988): pp. 235–6, 243–5; John Higham, *Strangers in the Land: Patterns of American Nativism, 1860–1925*, revised edition (New Brunswick: Rutgers University Press, 2002).

67. Referendums did not in practice mean that corporate interests could be defeated by the democratic majority. Corporate and professional interests found means to use these direct elections to their own advantage. See Daniel A. Smith and Joseph Lubinski, 'Direct Democracy During the Progressive Era: A Crack in the Populist Veneer?', *Journal of Policy History 14*, no. 4 (2002): pp. 349–83.

68. Gary Gerstle begins his book—*American Crucible*—on American nationhood and the contest between the contradictory claims of civic nationalism and racial nationalism and the twentieth-century history of each with two chapters on Theodore Roosevelt.

69. For the argument that the Progressives were blind to class conflict in democratic politics see Shelton Stromquist, *Reinventing 'the People': The Progressive Movement, the Class Problem, and the Origins of Modern Liberalism* (Urbana: University of Illinois Press, 2006).

70. Kazin, *The Populist Persuasion*, p. 20.

71. On the importance for the New York banks of the dollar becoming an international currency see J. Lawrence Broz, *The International Origins of the Federal Reserve System* (Ithaca: Cornell University Press, 2009).

72. Liaquat Ahamed, *The Lords of Finance: 1929, The Great Depression, and the Bankers Who Broke the World* (London: Windmill Books, 2009), p. 56.

73. A 1917 act had already placed some limits on migration from Southern and Eastern Europe for the first time, but in practice they had proved

ineffective. On the 1920s immigration laws and their relationship to American nationhood see Gerstle, *American Crucible*, pp. 95–122.

74. Quoted in Boyer, *Cultural and Political Crisis in Vienna*, p. 459.

75. On the history of tax havens see Ronan Palan, Richard Murphy, and Christian Chavagneux, *Tax Havens: How Globalisation Really Works* (Ithaca: Cornell University Press, 2009), chs. 4 and 5. On the history of Jersey as a tax haven see Mark P. Hampton, 'Creating Spaces. The Political Economy of Island Offshore Finance Centres: The Case of Jersey', *Geographische Zeitschrift 84*, no. 2 (1996): pp. 103–13. On how resistance to paying taxes by some among the rich took shape in Britain see Andrea Binder, 'The Politics of the Invisible: Offshore Finance and State Power: A Country-Level Comparison', PhD Dissertation submitted to Cambridge University, January 2019, pp. 72–4.

76. On the general problem of capital flight in democracies during the interwar years see The League of Nations (Ragnar Nurske), *International Currency Experience: Lessons of the Inter-War Period* (League of Nations, Economic, Financial and Transit Department, 1944), pp. 162–3. On the problems facing French democracy in the 1920s around taxation and capital flight see Christophe Farquet, 'Capital Flight and Tax Competition After the First World War: The Political Economy of French Tax Cuts, 1922–1928', *Contemporary European History 27* no. 4 (2018): pp. 537–61. On the French financial and currency crisis and its eventual resolution see Ahamed, *The Lords of Finance*, pp. 247–69; Kenneth Mouré, *The Gold Standard Illusion: France, the Bank of France, and the International Gold Standard, 1914–1939* (Oxford: Oxford University Press, 2002), chs. 4–5.

77. Winters, *Oligarchy*, pp. 230–2.

78. Quoted in Farquet, 'Capital Flight and Tax Competition After the First World War', p. 558.

79. Frederick Taylor, *The Downfall of Money: Germany's Hyperinflation and the Destruction of the Middle Class* (London: Bloomsbury Publishing, 2013), pp. 351–2.

80. See Daniel Tost, 'German Monetary Mythology', *Handelsblatt*, 31 July 2017, https://www.handelsblatt.com/english/bundesbank-birthday-german-monetary-mythology/23571490.html?ticket=ST-510167-ZyfyCkdvtOlJWndHWxNM-ap1

81. See Robert L. Hetzel, 'German Monetary Policy in the First Half of the Twentieth Century', *Federal Reserve Bank of Richmond Economic Quarterly 88*, no. 1 (2002): pp. 4–8.

82. Gerald Feldman, *The Great Disorder: Politics, Economics, and Society in the German Inflation 1914–1924* (Oxford: Oxford University Press, 1993), p. 4.

83. Quoted Hetzel, 'German Monetary Policy in the First Half of the Twentieth Century', p. 11.

84. Quoted in Ahamed, *The Lords of Finance*, p. 462.

85. For a recent argument that treats Roosevelt as an economic populist and defends this kind of populism as necessary in an economic crisis see Dani

Rodrik, 'Is Populism Necessarily Bad Economics?', *AEA Papers and Proceedings 108* (2018): pp. 196–9.

86. Franklin Roosevelt, Inaugural speech, 4 March 1933, https://avalon.law.yale.edu/20th_century/froos1.asp. On Roosevelt's use of economic nationhood see Gerstle, *American Crucible*, pp. 128–43, 149–55.

87. Franklin Roosevelt, Speech Accepting the Democratic Party's Re-Nomination for the Presidency, 27 July 1936, https://www.presidency.ucsb.edu/documents/acceptance-speech-for-the-renomination-for-the-presidency-philadelphia-pa

88. Amy E. Hiller, 'Redlining and the Home Owners' Loan Corporation', *Journal of Urban History 29*, no. 4 (2003): pp. 394–420.

89. Katznelson, *Fear Itself*; Ira Katznelson, *When Affirmative Action Was White: An Untold History of Racial Inequality in Twentieth-Century America* (New York: W.W. Norton, 2005).

90. William Childs, *The Texas Railroad Commission: Understanding Regulation in America to the Mid-Twentieth Century* (College Station: Texas A&M University Press, 2005), pp. 217–24. This conflation continued during the attempts to open up offshore exploration and production in the Gulf of Mexico. Tyler Priest, 'The Dilemmas of Oil Empire', *Journal of American History 99*, no. 1 (2012): p. 239.

91. For a history of the Texas Railroad Commission see Childs, *The Texas Railroad Commission.*

Chapter 8

1. Quoted in B. Bryan, 'Trump wants to go after Amazon', *Business Insider*, 28 March 2018.

2. https://twitter.com/ThierryBreton/status/1285548529113595904

3. On the creation of the Federal Republic of Germany see Peter H. Merkl, *The Origin of the West German Republic* (Oxford: Oxford University Press, 1963).

4. Jan-Werner Müller, 'On the Origins of Constitutional Patriotism', *Contemporary Political Theory 5* (2006): p. 282. Peter Graf Kielmansegg, 'The Basic Law, Response to the Past or Design for the Future?' in 'Forty Years of the Grundgesetz', German Historical Institute Occasional Paper, Washington, DC, 1990, p. 11, https://www.ghdc.org/fileadmin/publications/Occasional_Papers/Forty_Years_of_the_grundgesetz.pdf. On the importance of the German Constitutional Court see Justin Collings, *Democracy's Guardians: A History of the German Federal Constitutional Court, 1951–2001* (Oxford: Oxford University Press, 2015); Michaela Hailbronner, *Traditions and Transformations: The Rise of German Constitutionalism* (Oxford: Oxford University Press, 2015).

5. Benn Steil, *The Battle of Bretton Woods: John Maynard Keynes, Harry Dexter White, and the Making of a New World Order* (Princeton: Princeton University Press, 2013).

6. See Diane Coyle, *GDP: A Brief Affectionate History* (Princeton: Princeton University Press, 2014).

7. Jürgen Habermas, 'Yet Again: German Identity: A Unified Nation of Angry DM-Burghers?' *New German Critique 52* (January 1991): p. 86.

8. Charles S. Maier, *The Unmasterable Past: History, Holocaust, and German National Identity*, revised edition (Cambridge, MA: Harvard University Press, 1998), p. 7.

9. On post-war British economic nationhood see David Edgerton, *The Rise and Fall of the British Nation: A Twentieth-Century History* (London: Allen and Lane, 2018).

10. Helen Thompson, *Might, Right, Prosperity and Consent: Representative Democracy and the International Economy 1919–2001* (Manchester: Manchester University Press, 2008), pp. 107–13.

11. See Nelson Lichtenstein, *State of the Union: A Century of American Labor* (Princeton: Princeton University Press, 2002), ch. 4.

12. Meg Jacobs, 'The Uncertain Future of American Politics, 1940–1973' in *American History Now*, edited by Eric Foner and Lisa McGirr (Philadelphia: Temple University Press, 2011), p. 160.

13. Jacobs, 'The Uncertain Future of American Politics, 1940–1973', pp. 158–62.

14. William Childs, *The Texas Railroad Commission: Understanding Regulation in America to the Mid-Twentieth Century* (College Station: Texas A&M University Press, 2005), pp. 237–40.

15. Walter Scheidel, *The Great Leveller: Violence and the History of Inequality from the Stone Age to the Twenty-First Century* (Princeton: Princeton University Press), pp. 149–59.

16. Scheidel, *The Great Leveller*, pp. 152–3.

17. Scheidel, *The Great Leveller*, p. 166.

18. On post-war taxation see Sven Steinmo, *Taxation and Democracy: Swedish, British and American Approaches to Financing the Modern State* (London: Yale University Press, 1993). There were ongoing constraints in the United States about the tax state. See Meg Jacobs and Julian E. Zelizer, 'The Democratic Experiment: New Directions in American Political History' in *The Democratic Experiment: New Directions in American Political History*, edited by Meg Jacobs, William J. Novak, and Julian E. Zelizer (Princeton: Princeton University Press), pp. 276–300. On the importance of the wartime tax regimes to post-war taxation see Thomas Picketty, *Capital in the Twenty-First Century* (Cambridge, MA: Harvard University press, 2014), pp. 146–50.

19. Ian Kershaw, 'War and Political Violence in Twentieth-Century Europe', *Contemporary European History 14*, no. 1 (2005): p. 120.

20. Although there was always a pan-German party in post-war Austrian politics, no pan-German party participated in an Austrian government until the 1980s.

21. William Safran, 'State, Nation, National Identity, and Citizenship: France as a Test Case', *International Political Science Review 12*, no. 3 (1991): p. 221.

22. On the way that the very language of the French revolution and French nationhood had long provided a political discourse to support rebellions against the French Empire see Lorelle Semley, *To Be Free and French: Citizenship in France's Atlantic Empire* (Cambridge: Cambridge University Press, 2017).

23. Safran, 'State, Nation, National Identity, and Citizenship', p. 225.

24. Safran, 'State, Nation, National Identity, and Citizenship', pp. 226–31.

25. On the historians' dispute see Maier, *The Unmasterable Past*. On how the issues around constitutional patriotism played out around unification see Jan-Werner Müller, *Another Country: German Intellectuals, Unification, and National Identity* (London: Yale University Press, 2000).

26. On the role of British citizen-creditors in financing the war see James Macdonald, *A Free Nation Deep in Debt: The Financial Roots of Democracy* (New York: Farrar, Straus, & Giroux, 2003), pp. 435–45.

27. Robert Colls, *Identity of England* (Oxford: Oxford University Press, 2004), pp. 124–6. For the role of the idea of 'the people's war' in British perceptions of the Second World War see Angus Calder, *The People's War: Britain 1939–45* (London: Pimlico, 1992).

28. For an influential later version of this argument set in a broader Marxist framework see Tom Nairn, *The Break-up of Britain* (London: Verso, 1981).

29. Gary Gerstle, *American Crucible: Race and Nation in the Twentieth Century*, revised edition (Princeton: Princeton University Press, 2016), pp. 197–9. Lawrence R. Samuel, *Pledging Allegiance: American Identity and the Bond Drive of World War II* (Washington, DC: Smithsonian Institution Press, 1997).

30. Martin Luther King Jr, Speech in Atlanta, 10 May 1967, https://www.theatlantic.com/magazine/archive/2018/02/martin-luther-king-hungry-club-forum/552533/

31. See Gerstle, *American Crucible*, ch. 7. The most powerful statement of black nationalism is Malcolm X's autobiography: Malcom X and Alex Haley, *The Autobiography of Malcolm X* (London: Penguin, 2007). (Originally published by Grove Press, 1965.)

32. Gerstle, *American Crucible*, pp. 349–57. As an example of the pessimistic take see Bruce D. Porter, 'Can American Democracy Survive?', *Commentary 96* (November 1993): pp. 37–40, https://www.commentarymagazine.com/articles/bruce-porter/can-american-democracy-survive/

33. Robert Kaplan sees the end of the draft in 1973 as bringing 'the United States back to its roots as a weakly governed, brawling, fractious society' comparable to what prevailed before the Civil War. Robert D. Kaplan, 'Fort Leavenworth and the Eclipse of Nationhood', *Atlantic Monthly*, September 1996, https://www.theatlantic.com/magazine/archive/1996/09/fort-leavenworth-and-the-eclipse-of-nationhood/376665/

34. Some intellectuals used the democratic excess argument to explain the American failure in Vietnam. David Runciman, *The Confidence Trap: A History of Democracy in Crisis from World War I to the Present*, updated edition (Princeton: Princeton University Press, 2017), pp. 189–95.

35. Michael J. Crozier, Samuel P. Huntington, and Jojo Watanuki, *The Crisis of Democracy: Report on the Governability of Democracies to the Trilateral Commission* (New York: New York University Press, 1975), p. 2.

36. Crozier, Huntington, and Watanuki, *The Crisis of Democracy*, p. 113.

37. Crozier, Huntington, and Watanuki, *The Crisis of Democracy*, p. 164.

38. Mark Blyth and Matthias Matthijs, 'Black Swans, Lame Ducks, and the Mystery of IPE's Missing Macro-Economy', *Review of International Political Economy 24*, no. 2 (2017): pp. 210–11.

39. Meg Jacobs, *Panic at the Pump: The Energy Crisis and the Transformation of American Politics in the 1970s* (New York: Hill and Wang, 2017), p. 94.

40. Jacobs, *Panic at the Pump*, 33. Stefan Eich and Adam Tooze make a similar argument to mine here against the claim that it was a democratic excess that sustained inflation. Stefan Eich and Adam Tooze, 'The Great Inflation' in *Vorgeschichte der Gegenwa: Dimensionen des Strukturbruchs nach dem Boom*, edited by Anselm Doering-Manteuffel, Lutz Raphael, and Thomas Schlemmer (Göttingen: Vandenhoeck and Ruprecht, 2016). In English at https://mk0adamtoozept2ql1eh.kinstacdn.com/wp-content/uploads/2020/05/The_Great_Inflation_w_Adam:Tooze_2016.pdf

41. Meg Jacobs, *Panic at the Pump*, pp. 33–4. On the democratic strength of the idea that governments should stop price increases see Meg Jacobs, *Pocketbook Politics: Economic Citizenship in Twentieth Century America* (Princeton: Princeton University Press, 2007).

42. The 1979 Conservative Party General Election Manifesto, http://www.conservativemanifesto.com/1979/1979-conservative-manifesto.shtml

43. Crozier, Huntington, and Watanuki, *Crisis of Democracy*, p. 9.

44. Scott Lash, 'The End of Neo-Corporatism? The Breakdown of Centralised Bargaining in Sweden', *British Journal of Industrial Relations 23*, no. 2 (1985): pp. 215–39.

45. Quoted Jacobs, *Panic at the Pump*, p. 35.

46. Quoted Jacobs, *Panic at the Pump*, p. 44.

47. James Schlesinger, 'Will War Yield Oil Security?' *Challenge 34*, no. 2 (1991): p. 30.

48. Ronald Reagan, Address to the Nation on the Iran Arms and Contra Aid Controversy, 13 November 1986, https://www.reaganlibrary.gov/archives/speech/address-nation-iran-arms-and-contra-aid-controversy-november-13-1986

49. Richard Nixon, Address to the Nation About National Energy Policy, 7 November 1973, https://www.presidency.ucsb.edu/documents/address-the-nation-about-national-energy-policy

50. Jimmy Carter, Address to the Nation: Energy and the National Goals, 15 July 1979, https://www.jimmycarterlibrary.gov/assets/documents/speeches/energy-crisis.phtml

51. Jacobs, *Panic at the Pump*, ch. 5.

52. Jon Henley, 'Gigantic Sleaze Scandal Winds up as Former Elf Oil Chiefs are Jailed', *Guardian*, 13 November 2003, https://www.theguardian.com/business/2003/nov/13/france.oilandpetrol

53. On the use of offshore financing by the Christian Democrats see Andrea Binder, 'The Politics of the Invisible: Offshore Finance and State Power, a Country Level Comparison', PhD Dissertation submitted to Cambridge University, January 2019, pp. 81–3.

54. Address by President Eisenhower, 17 January 1961. https://www.eisenhowerlibrary.gov/sites/default/files/research/online-documents/farewell-address/1961-01-17-press-release.pdf

55. Michael Howard, 'War and the Nation-state', *Daedalus 108*, no. 4 (1979): pp. 106–7.

56. On the importance of constitutionalism with a strong distrust of any claim to popular sovereignty and the later weight of this for the EU via the German Constitutional Court see Jan-Werner Müller, 'Beyond Militant Democracy?', *New Left Review 73* (January/February 2012): pp. 39–47.

57. See Wolfram Kaiser, *Christian Democracy and the Origins of European Union* (Cambridge: Cambridge University Press, 2007).

58. Friedrich A. Hayek, 'The Economic Conditions of Interstate Federalism' in Friedrich A. Hayek, *Individualism and Economic Order* (Chicago: Chicago University Press, 1948), pp. 255–72.

59. Craig Parsons, *A Certain Idea of Europe* (Ithaca: Cornell University Press, 2006), pp. 52–66.

60. See Eric O'Connor, 'European Democracy Deferred: de Gaulle and the Dehousse Plan,1960', *Modern and Contemporary France 25*, no. 2 (2017): pp. 209–24.

61. Wolfgang Streeck, 'Progressive Regression', *New Left Review 118* (July/August 2019): p. 121.

62. See Alan Milward, *The European Rescue of the Nation-State* (London: Routledge, 1992).

63. On the advantages of finance to Western governments in the 1970s and 1980s see Greta Krippner, *Capitalising on Crisis: The Political Origins of the Rise of Finance* (Cambridge, MA: Harvard University Press, 2011). For the argument that debt staved off what would have been a full-scale crisis of capitalism and democracy in the 1970s see Wolfgang Streeck, *Buying Time: The Delayed Crisis of Democratic Capitalism* (London: Verso, 2014).

64. On the limited impact of open international capital flows on most European welfare states see Duane Swank, *Global Capital, Political Institutions, and Policy Change in Developed Welfare States* (New York: Cambridge University Press, 2002).

65. For a comparative study of competitive tax reform see Duane Swank, 'Taxing Choices: International Competition, Domestic Institutions, and the Transformation of Corporate Tax Policy', *Journal of European Public Policy 23*, no. 4 (2016): pp. 571–603.

66. On why small democratic states drove corporation tax competition see Philipp Genschel, Hanna Lierse, and Laura Seelkopf, 'Dictators Don't Compete: Autocracy, Democracy and Tax Competition', *Review of International Political Economy 23*, no. 2 (2016): pp. 290–315.

67. Philipp Genschel, 'Globalization and the Transformation of the Tax State', *European Review 13*, no. 1 (2005): p. 66.

68. Jacob Burckhardt, *The Age of Constantine the Great* (Berkeley: University of California Press, 1992), p. 70.

69. On the place of tax havens in the world economy see Ronen Palan, Richard Murphy, and Christian Chavagneux, *Tax Havens: How Globalization Really Works* (Ithaca: Cornell University Press, 2010); Gabriel Zucman, *The Hidden Wealth of Nations: The Scourge of Tax Havens* (Chicago: University of Chicago Press, 2015).

70. On this point see Binder, 'The Politics of the Invisible', pp. 166–8. On the rise of offshore banking see Gary Burn, 'The State, the City and the Euromarkets', *Review of International Political Economy 6* no. 2 (1999): pp. 225–61. Robert N. McCauley, Patrick M. McGuire, and Vladyslav Sushko, 'Global Dollar Credit: Links to US Monetary Policy and Leverage', January 2015, BIS Working Paper, no. 483, https://ssrn.com/abstract=2552576

71. Jacob Hacker and Paul Pierson, 'Winner-Takes-All-Politics: Public Policy, Political Organisation, and the Precipitous Rise of Top Incomes in the United States', *Politics and Society 38*, no. 2 (2010): pp. 193–6.

72. Hacker and Pierson, 'Winner-Takes-All-Politics', pp. 157–9.

73. Hacker and Pierson, 'Winner-Takes-All-Politics', pp. 176–9.

74. Jacobs, *Pocketbook Politics*, pp. 267–8.

75. Wolfgang Streeck and Philippe C. Schmitter, 'From National Corporatism to Transnational Pluralism: Organised Interests in the Single European Market', *Politics and Society 19*, no. 2 (1991): pp. 133–64 For further discussion see Blyth and Matthijs, 'Black Swans', pp. 216–17.

76. James Macdonald in his history of the citizen creditor and its relationship to democratic politics sees the peacetime debt of the 1970s financed predominantly in international capital markets as itself a manifestation of the breakdown of nationhood and 'a house divided into warring economic interest groups'. Macdonald, *A Free Nation Deep in Debt*, p. 471.

77. Wolfgang Streeck draws a distinction between a tax state, which is a *Staatsvolk*, and a *Marktvolk*, which is a debt state. The *Staatsvolk* rests on a national people of citizens and the *Marktvolk* on an international people of investors. But the concept of the people only makes sense in relation to a

political community, not to banks, pension funds, and individuals with no sense of political commonality. Wolfgang Streeck, *Buying Time*, pp. 80–6.

78. On the impact of falling inflation from the 1980s on creditor–debtor politics see Mark Blyth, 'Will the Politics or Economics of Deflation Prove More Harmful?', *Intereconomics: Review of European Economic Policy 50*, no. 2 (2015): pp. 115–16.

79. Blyth and Matthijs, 'Black Swans', p. 216. On the way in which private debt temporarily stabilized democracies from the 1970s see Colin Crouch, 'Privatised Keynesianism: An Unacknowledged Policy Regime', *British Journal of Politics and International Relations 11*, no. 3 (2009): pp. 382–99.

80. Heath was, nonetheless, reliant on sixty-nine Labour MPs breaking their party whip to support the government.

81. Robert Saunders, *Yes to Europe!: The 1975 Referendum and Seventies Britain* (Cambridge: Cambridge University Press, 2018), pp. 63–76.

82. The clear constraints on parliamentary sovereignty in the British constitution before accession to the EC materialized around the Union and matters pertaining to Scotland, Wales, and Northern Ireland. For further discussion of this point see Helen Thompson, 'Consent: The Dynamite at the Heart of the British Constitution', *Prospect*, 9 June 2021, https://www. prospectmagazine.co.uk/essays/consent-british-constitution-referendums-brexit-europe

83. Streeck and Schmitter, 'From National Corporatism to Transnational Pluralism', p. 152. On the failures of European trade union federation see Streeck, 'Progressive Regression', pp. 122–4; Parsons, *A Certain Idea of Europe*, pp. 52–66.

84. Streeck and Schmitter, 'From National Corporatism to Transnational Pluralism', pp. 134–5. For an argument that the EU was less conducive to business lobbying than the American republic see Christine Mahoney, 'Lobbying Success in the United States and the European Union', *Journal of Public Policy 27*, no. 1 (2007): pp. 35–56.

85. See Neil Fligstein, *Euroclash: The EU, European Identity, and the Future of Europe* (Oxford: Oxford University Press, 2009). On the class implications of cosmopolitan identity see Craig Calhoun, 'The Class Consciousness of Frequent Travelers: Toward a Critique of Actually Existing Cosmopolitanism', *South Atlantic Quarterly 101*, no. 4 (2002): pp. 869–97.

86. For a discussion of the implications of the difference between the Bundesbank's legitimating authority and the ECB's authority, and the implications for representation and legitimacy, see Hjalte Lokdam, 'Banking on Sovereignty: A Genealogy of the European Central Bank's Independence', PhD dissertation submitted to the London School of Economics, 2019. For the argument that there was a broader anti-inflationary monetary consensus behind monetary union see Kathleen McNamara, *The Currency of Ideas: Monetary Politics in the European Union* (Ithaca: Cornell University Press, 1998).

Chapter 9

1. Quoted in Jon Schwarz, 'Jimmy Carter: The US is an "Oligarchy with Unlimited Political Bribery"', *Intercept*, 31 July 2015, https://theintercept.com/2015/07/30/jimmy-carter-u-s-oligarchy-unlimited-political-bribery/

2. Bernie Sanders, 'Democracy Versus Oligarchy', speech on 31 March 2014, https://www.commondreams.org/views/2014/04/01/democracy-vs-oligarchy

3. Bernie Sanders, 'Bernie's Announcement', speech on 26 May 2015. Published as Ezra Klein, 'Read Bernie Sander's populist, policy-heavy speech kicking off his campaign', *Vox*, 26 May 2015, https://www.vox.com/2015/5/26/8662903/bernie-sanders-full-text-speech-presidential-campaign

4. Quoted in David Frum, 'If Liberals Won't Enforce Borders, Fascists Will', *Atlantic*, April 2019, https://www.theatlantic.com/magazine/archive/2019/04/david-frum-how-much-immigration-is-too-much/583252/

5. Quoted in Ezra Klein, 'Bernie Sanders, The Vox Conversation', *Vox*, 28 July 2015, https://www.vox.com/2015/7/28/9014491/bernie-sanders-vox-conversation

6. CNN Politics, Transcript of Republican Debate in Miami, Full Text, 15 March 2016, https://edition.cnn.com/2016/03/10/politics/republican-debate-transcript-full-text/index.html

7. See Ivan Krastev, *After Europe* (Philadelphia: University of Pennsylvania Press, 2017).

8. Matthew Goodwin and Caitlin Milazzo, 'Taking Back Control: Investigating the Role of Immigration in the 2016 Vote for Brexit', *British Journal of Politics and International Relations 19*, no. 3 (2017): pp. 450–64.

9. Bundesverfassungsgericht, Judgment of the Second Senate of 5 May 2020–2 BvR 859/15, para 104, https://www.bundesverfassungsgericht.de/SharedDocs/Entscheidungen/EN/2020/05/rs20200505_2bvr085915en.html;jsessionid=8407F8BD54CB01E168426940040ADD26.1_cid386

10. Kenneth Dyson and Kevin Featherstone, *The Road to Maastricht: Negotiating Economic and Monetary Union* (Oxford: Oxford University Press, 1999), p. 93.

11. Matt Qvortrup, 'The Three Referendums on the European Constitution Treaty in 2005', *Political Quarterly 77*, no. 1 (2006): p. 95. On the divisions among Gaullists see Benjamin Leruth and Nicholas Startin, 'Between Euro-Federalism, Euro-Pragmatism and Euro-Populism: The Gaullist Movement Divided Over Europe', *Modern Contemporary France 25*, no. 2 (2017): pp. 153–69.

12. Craig Parsons, *A Certain Idea of Europe* (Ithaca: Cornell University Press, 2006), pp. 225–7.

13. Parsons, *A Certain Idea of Europe*, pp. 242–3.

14. On the gap between French politicians' rhetoric on Europe and the difficulty political reality see Vivien A. Schmidt, 'Trapped by their

Ideas: French Elites' Discourses of European Integration and Globalization', *Journal of European Public Policy 20*, no. 4 (2006): pp. 992–1009.

15. Bundesverfassungsgericht, *57 Manfred Brunner and others v. the European Union treaty, para 55, http://www.proyectos.cchs.csic.es/euroconstitution/library/Brunner_Sentence.pdf

16. Bundesverfassungsgericht, *57 Manfred Brunner and others v. the European Union treaty, para 44. On this point in the Court's judgment see Matthias Mahlman, 'Constitutional Identity and the Politics of Homogeneity', *German Law Journal 6*, no. 2 (2005): pp. 307–18.

17. Martin J. Bull and James L. Newell, *Italian Politics: Adjustment Under Duress* (Cambridge: Polity Press, 2006), pp. 14–15.

18. Kenneth Dyson and Kevin Featherstone, 'Italy and EMU as a *"Vincolo Esterno"*: Empowering the Technocrats, Transforming the State', *South European Society and Politics 1*, no. 2 (1996): p. 277.

19. Dyson and Featherstone, 'Italy and EMU as a *"Vincolo Esterno"* ', pp. 278–9. Carli himself was old and seriously ill when the negotiations began. He was also a technocratic minister, who had been governor of the *Banca d'Italia*.

20. Martin J. Bull, 'In the Eye of the Storm: The Italian Economy and the Eurozone Crisis', *South European Society and Politics 23*, no. 1 (2018): p. 18; Dyson and Featherstone, 'Italy and EMU as a *"Vincolo Esterno"* ': p. 295.

21. On the rise of the Northern League see Francesco Cavatorta, 'The Role of the Northern League in Transforming the Italian Political System: From Economic Federalism to Ethnic Politics and Back', *Contemporary Politics 7*, no. 1 (2001): pp. 27–40.

22. Wolfgang Streeck, 'Markets and Peoples: Democratic Capitalism and European Integration', *New Left Review 73* (Jan/Feb 2012): pp. 68–9.

23. Quoted in Guardian Staff and Agencies, 'The Euro has Screwed Everybody—Berlusconi', *Guardian*, 29 July 2005, https://www.theguardian.com/world/2005/jul/29/euro.italy

24. See Nicolas Jabko, 'The Importance of Being Nice: An Institutionalist Analysis of French Preferences on the Future of Europe', *Comparative European Politics 2*, no. 3 (2004): pp. 282–301.

25. Chirac had complained at one point during the latter stage of the Nice negotiations that 'every solution presents horrendous problems.' Quoted in 'So That's All Agreed Then', *Economist*, 14 December 2000, https://www.economist.com/special/2000/12/14/so-thats-all-agreed-then

26. European Council Meeting in Laeken, 14 and 15 December 2001, Annex 1, https://www.consilium.europa.eu/media/20950/68827.pdf. For an account of the constitutional convention and subsequent treaty negotiations see Peter Norman, *The Accidental Constitution: The Making of Europe's Constitutional Treaty*, second edition (Eurocomment: 2005).

27. On the emergence of a democratic constraint on the EU's development see Liesbet Hooghe and Gary Marks, 'A Postfunctionalist Theory of European Integration: From Permissive Consensus to Constraining Dissensus', *British Journal of Political Science 39*, no. 1 (2009): pp. 1–17; Vivien A. Schmidt, *Democracy in Europe: The EU and National Polities* (Oxford: Oxford University Press, 2007).

28. 'So Much for Stability', *Economist*, 15 July 2004, https://www.economist.com/news/2004/07/15/so-much-for-stability. Qvortrup, 'The Three Referendums', pp. 89–97.

29. On the 2005 French referendum see Colette Mazzucelli, 'The French Rejection of the Constitutional Treaty' in *The Rise and Fall of the EU's Constitutional Treaty*, edited by Finn Laursen (Leiden and Boston: Martinus Nijhoff Publications, 2008), pp. 161–80.

30. On the divisions within the French Socialist Party see Markus Wagner, 'Debating Europe in the French Socialist Party: The 2004 Internal Referendum on the EU Constitution', *French Politics 6*, no. 3 (2008): pp. 257–79.

31. Qvortrup, 'The Three Referendums', pp. 94–6.

32. BBC News, 'Lisbon Treaty: What They Said', 30 September 2009, http://news.bbc.co.uk/1/hi/world/europe/8282241.stm

33. Bundesverfassungsgericht, Judgment of the Second Senate of 30 June 2009 BvE 2/08, preamble, https://www.bundesverfassungsgericht.de/SharedDocs/Entscheidungen/EN/2009/06/es20090630_2bve000208en.html

34. Bundesverfassungsgericht, Judgment of the Second Senate of 30 June 2009, para 2c.

35. Bundesverfassungsgericht, Judgment of the Second Senate of 30 June 2009, para 2d. For a frontal attack on the Court's reasoning about democracy and the nation see Jo Eric Khushal Murkens, 'Identity Trumps Integration: The Lisbon Treaty in the German Federal Constitutional Court', *Der Staat 48*, no. 4 (2009): pp. 517–34.

36. Bruno Waterfield, 'EU Polls Would Be Lost, Says Nicolas Sarkozy', *Daily Telegraph*, 14 November 2007, https://www.telegraph.co.uk/news/worldnews/1569342/EU-polls-would-be-lost-says-Nicolas-Sarkozy.html

37. Emmanuel Macron, 'Initiative for Europe', speech at the Sorbonne, 26 September 2017, http://international.blogs.ouest-france.fr/archive/2017/09/29/macron-sorbonne-verbatim-europe-18583.html

38. Bruno Waterfield and Toby Helm, 'Gordon Brown Rules Out EU Treaty Referendum', *Daily Telegraph*, 18 October 2007, https://www.telegraph.co.uk/news/uknews/1566537/Gordon-Brown-rules-out-EU-treaty-referendum.html Vaughne Miller, The Treaty of Lisbon: Government and Parliamentary Views on a Referendum, House of Commons Library SN/IA/5071, 15 May 2009, p. 9, https://commonslibrary.parliament.uk/research-briefings/sn05071/

39. Quoted in George Parker and Alex Barker, 'David Cameron's Adventures in Europe', *Financial Times*, 22 January 2016, https://www.ft.com/content/26cbc524-bfb4-11e5-846f-79b0e3d20eaf

40. Quoted in Ben Hall and Joshua Chaffin, 'Sarkozy Smarts at Cameron's Snub on Europe', *Financial Times*, 15 June 2009, https://www.ft.com/content/10f18dde-56ab-11de-9a1c-00144feabdc0

41. Quoted in Vaughne Miller, *The Treaty of Lisbon*, p. 19.

42. Quoted in Gavin Hewitt, 'Greece: The Dangerous Game', *BBC News*, 1 February 2015, https://www.bbc.co.uk/news/world-europe-31082656

43. David Cameron, Speech at Bloomberg, 23 January 2013, https://www.gov.uk/government/speeches/eu-speech-at-bloomberg

44. See for different versions of this argument Albert Weale, 'The Democratic Duty to Oppose Brexit', *Political Quarterly 88*, no. 2 (2017): pp. 170–81; Anthony Barnett, 'Brexit has Killed the Sovereignty of Parliament', *Open Democracy*, 4 December 2016, https://www.opendemocracy.net/en/opendemocracyuk/brexit-has-killed-sovereignty-of-parliament/ For a similar argument from outside Britain see Kenneth Rogoff, 'Britain's Democratic Failure', *Project Syndicate*, 24 June 2016, https://www.project-syndicate.org/commentary/brexit-democratic-failure-for-uk-by-kenneth-rogoff-2016-06?barrier=accesspaylog

45. On fiscal austerity as a bait and switch response to the banking crisis see Mark Blyth, *Austerity: The History of a Dangerous Idea* (New York: Oxford University Press, 2013). In some cases, especially Britain, which had a particularly large budget deficit and where the bank bailouts were managed off-balance sheet, the charge that fiscal austerity was a response to the banking crisis is hard to sustain: see Helen Thompson, 'UK Debt in Comparative Perspective: The Pernicious Legacy of Financial Sector Debt', *British Journal of Politics and International Relations 15*, no. 3 (2013): pp. 476–92.

46. For the argument that all the left and right populist parties are anti-creditor parties see Mark Blyth and Matthias Matthijs, 'Black Swans, Lame Ducks, and the Mystery of IPE's Missing Macro-Economy', *Review of International Political Economy 24*, no. 2 (2017): pp. 203–21. For an argument that these were not class-based protests but directionless disruption see Ivan Krastev, *Democracy Disrupted: The Politics of Global Protest* (Philadelphia: University of Pennsylvania Press, 2014).

47. In Slovakia in particular, there was resentment that, with lower standards of living than Greece and having accepted much tighter fiscal surveillance than Greece over qualifying for monetary union, it had to act as a creditor to Greece, albeit it was in fact acting as much to support Northern European banks. For a discussion of the broad implications here in a historical perspective about nationalism see Stefan Auer, 'Richard Sulik: A Provincial or a European Slovak Politician?', *Humanities Research Journal 19*, no. 1 (2013): pp. 81–100.

48. For this argument see Hans Kundnani, 'Europe and the Return of History', *Journal of Modern European History 11*, no. 3 (2013): pp. 279–86.

49. Alexandros Kioupkiolis, 'Podemos: The Ambiguous Promises of Left-Wing Populism in Contemporary Spain', *Journal of Political Ideologies 21*,

no. 2 (2016): p. 104. For an example of this political language see Diego Beas, 'How Spain's 15-M Movement Is Redefining Politics', *Guardian*, 15 October 2011, https://www.theguardian.com/commentisfree/2011/oct/15/spain-15-m-movement-activism Pablo Iglesias, 'Understanding Podemos', *New Left Review 93* (May/June 2015): pp. 7–22. While there was much in Podemos' rhetoric that had echoes of the American People's party, it also had elements of the American progressives as a reaction against class-based politics. See Christopher J. Bickerton and Carlo Invernizzi Accetti, '"Techno-Populism" as a New Party Family: The Case of the Five Star Movement and Podemos', *Contemporary Italian Politics 10*, no. 2 (2018): pp. 132–50.

50. Kioupkiolis, 'Podemos', p. 101.

51. On the effect of Spain's economic crisis on the 2012 Catalan parliamentary election see Guillem Rico and Robert Liñeira, 'Bringing Secessionism into the Mainstream: The 2012 Regional Election in Catalonia', *South European Society and Politics 19*, no. 2 (2014): pp. 257–80.

52. On the complex political choices facing the German government see Wade Jacoby, 'Europe's New German Problem: The Timing of Politics and the Politics of Timing' in *The Future of the Euro*, edited by Matthias Matthijs and Mark Blyth (New York: Oxford University Press, 2015).

53. Jacoby, 'Europe's New German Problem', p. 198.

54. On the OMT decision see Mehrdad Payandeh, 'The OMT Judgement of the German Federal Constitutional Court: Repositioning the Court Within the EU's Constitutional Architecture', *European Constitutional Law Review 13*, no. 2 (2017): pp. 400–16.

55. Quoted in Eric Maurice, 'EU Judges Examine ECB Bond Buying Scheme', *EUobserver*, 11 July 2018, https://euobserver.com/economic/142345

56. Alternative für Deutschland, Manifesto for the 2017 General Election, https://www.afd.de/wp-content/uploads/sites/111/2017/04/2017-04-12_afd-grundsatzprogramm-englisch_web.pdf

57. Stefan Wagstyl and Claire Jones, 'Germany Blames Mario Draghi for Rise of Rightwing Afd Party', *Financial Times*, 10 April 2016, https://www.ft.com/content/bc0175c4-ff2b-11e5-9cc4-27926f2b110c

58. Martin Arnold and Guy Chazan, 'Bundesbank to Keep Buying Bonds After Court Challenge', *Financial Times*, 6 July 2000, https://www.ft.com/content/99447f21-46db-465b-8ed0-9a214a898a74

59. On the AfD in terms of German Euroscepticism see Robert Grimm, 'The Rise of the Eurosceptic Party Alternative für Deutschland, Between Ordoliberal Critique and Popular Anxiety', *International Political Science Review 36*, no. 3 (2015): pp. 264–78.

60. On the breach of a long-held taboo for the Christian Democrats see Der Spiegel staff, 'Aftershocks Continue After Germany's Massive Political Earthquake', *Spiegel International*, 10 February 2020, https://www.spiegel.de/

international/germany/a-dark-day-for-democracy-the-political-earthquake-that-shook-germany-a-01847ef8-beb3-45aa-bdbb-f0fda7d87806

61. On France's structural position between Germany and the Southern European states in the Eurozone crisis see Mark I. Vail, 'Europe's Middle Child: France's Statist Liberalism and the Conflicted Politics of the Euro' in *The Future of the Euro*, edited by Blyth and Matthijs, pp. 136–60.

62. Quoted in Julian Coman, 'France's Socialist Hopeful Promises to Storm the Financial Bastille', *Guardian*, 11 February 2012, https://www.theguardian.com/world/2012/feb/11/francois-hollande-presidential-election-sarkozy

63. Quoted in Vail, 'Europe's Middle Child', p. 153.

64. Hugh Carnegy, 'Merkel Swings Behind Sarkozy Poll Bid', *Financial Times*, 6 February 2020, https://www.ft.com/content/83fed6a6-50d6-11e1-ab40-00144feabdc0

65. On Hollande's difficulties in regard to Europe as a party management problem see David Hanley, 'From "La Petite Europe Vaticane" to the Club Med: The French Socialist Party and the Challenges of European Integration', *Modern and Contemporary France 25*, no. 2 (2017): pp. 135–51.

66. Macron reportedly stated before the German election that 'if the FDP gets into the German government, I'll be dead.' Quoted in Wolfgang Streeck, 'Europe Under Merkel IV: Balance of Impotence', *American Affairs II*, no. 2 (2018), https://americanaffairsjournal.org/2018/05/europe-under-merkel-iv-balance-of-impotence/

67. See Stefano Sacchi, 'Conditionality by Other Means: EU Involvement in Italy's Structural Reforms in the Sovereign Debt Crisis', *Comparative European Politics 13*, no. 1 (2015): pp. 77–92.

68. Paolo Franzosi, Francesco Marone, and Eugenio Salvati, 'Populism and Euroscepticism in the Italian Five Star Movement', *International Spectator 50*, no. 2 (2015): p. 110.

69. Quoted in Franzosi, Marone and Salvati, 'Populism and Euroscepticism in the Italian Five Star Movement', p. 114.

70. Martin J. Bull, 'In the Eye of the Storm: The Italian Economy and the Eurozone Crisis', *South European Society and Politics 23*, no. 1 (2018): pp. 3–28.

71. Stefano Sacchi and Jungho Roh, 'Conditionality, Austerity, and Welfare: Financial Crisis and Its Impact on Welfare in Italy and Korea', *Journal of European Social Policy 26* no. 4 (2016): p. 370, endnote 25; Georg Picot and Arianna Tassinari, 'Politics in a Transformed Labour Market: Renzi's Labour Market Reform', *Italian Politics 30*, no. 1 (2015): p. 130.

72. Sacchi and Roh, 'Conditionality, Austerity, and Welfare', pp. 363–7.

73. Quoted in James Politi and Jim Brunsden, 'Matteo Renzi Defends Italy's Budget Plan', *Financial Times*, 20 October 2016, https://www.ft.com/content/3b436b2a-96b8-11e6-a1dc-bdf38d484582

74. Tom Knowles, 'Upheaval in Italy Keeps Europe Addicted to QE', *Times*, 5 December 2016, https://www.thetimes.co.uk/article/european-bank-may-extend-qe-after-italian-poll-n8d9dkh5x Jeff Black, 'Renzi's Italian

Fate Also Overshadows Draghi's Route for QE', *Bloomberg*, 5 December 2016, https://www.bloomberg.com/news/articles/2016-12-05/renzi-s -italian-fate-also-overshadows-draghi-s-path-ahead-for-qe

75. For a different way of reaching similar judgements that sees German politics moving from stability into imbalance see Sidney A. Rothstein and Tobias Schulze-Cleven, 'Germany After the Social Democratic Century: The Political Economy of Imbalance', *German Politics 29*, no. 3 (2020): pp. 297–318; Adam Tooze, 'Which is Worse?: Germany Divided', *London Review of Books 41*, no. 14 (19 July 2019), https://www.lrb.co.uk/the-paper/v41/n14/adam-tooze/which-is-worse

76. United States Census Bureau, Housing Vacancies and Home Ownership, Data, Historical Tables, Table 16, https://www.census.gov/housing/ hvs/data/histtabs.html

77. On the domestic politics of Fannie Mae and Freddie Mac see Helen Thompson, *China and the Mortgaging of America: Domestic Politics and Economic Interdependence* (London: Palgrave, 2010), chs. 3–4.

78. On the implications of the domestic conflicts in the United States around the US–China economic relationship see Naná de Graaff and Bastiaan van Apeldoorn, 'US-China Relations and the Liberal World Order: Contending Elites, Colliding Visions?', *International Affairs 94*, no. 1 (2018): pp. 113–31. On American business lobbying operations on China see Robert Dreyfuss, 'The New China Lobby', *American Prospect*, 19 December 2001, https://prospect.org/world/new-china-lobby/ On distributional influence on American foreign policy more generally see Lawrence R. Jacobs and Benjamin I. Page, 'Who Influences U.S. Foreign Policy?' *American Political Science Review 99*, no. 1 (2005): pp. 107–23. On the effect of China's own pressure on American lobbying during the Clinton administration see Ho-fung Hung, 'The Periphery in the Making of Globalization: The China Lobby and the Reversal of Clinton's China Trade Policy, 1993–1994', *Review of International Political Economy*, published online 13 April 2020, https://doi.org/10.1080/09692290.2020.1749105

79. Bob Woodward, 'Findings Link Chinese Allies to Chinese Intelligence', *Washington Post*, 10 February 1998, https://www.washingtonpost.com/ archive/politics/1998/02/10/findings-link-clinton-allies-to-chinese-intel ligence/87265d5d-7452-41f2-ad2f-aa4abe7e579e/

80. Jeff Colgan and Robert O. Keohane, 'The Liberal Order is Rigged. Fix it Now or Watch it Wither', *Foreign Affairs 96*, no. 3 (May–June 2017): p. 39.

81. There was also a growth in foreign national overstaying their visas. On the politics of the border see Peter Andreas, 'The Escalation of US Immigration Control in the Post-NAFTA Era', *Political Science Quarterly 113*, no. 4 (1998–99): pp. 591–615.

82. Jens Manuel Krogstad, Jeffrey S. Passel, and D'Vera Cohn, 'Five Facts About Illegal Immigration in the United States', Pew Research Centre, 12 June 2019, https://www.pewresearch.org/fact-tank/2019/06/12/ 5-facts-about-illegal-immigration-in-the-u-s/

83. On the impact of both business group and trade union lobbying on migration in different sectors see Giovanni Facchini, Anna Maria Mayda, and Prachi Mishra, 'Do Interest Groups Affect US Immigration Policy?' IMF Working Paper, WP/08/244, October 2008, https://www.imf.org/external/pubs/ft/wp/2008/wp08244.pdf

84. Daniel B. Wood, 'Legal Fight Over Illegal Aliens', *Christian Science Monitor*, 12 May 1994, https://www.csmonitor.com/1994/0512/12012.html

85. Royce Crocker, Congressional Redistricting: An Overview, Congressional Research Service, 21 November 2012, pp. 9–10, https://fas.org/sgp/crs/misc/R42831.pdf

86. Quoted in Eric W. Orts, 'The Path to Give California 12 Senators and Vermont Just One', *Atlantic*, 2 January 2019, https://www.theatlantic.com/ideas/archive/2019/01/heres-how-fix-senate/579172/

87. Sean Trende, *The Lost Majority: Why the Future of Government is up for Grabs and Who Will Take It* (London: Palgrave, 2012), introduction and part II.

88. Gary Gerstle, *American Crucible: Race and Nation in the Twentieth Century*, revised edition (Princeton: Princeton University Press, 2016), pp. 385–93.

89. Barack Obama, Declaration speech, Springfield, Illinois, February 2007, https://www.cbsnews.com/news/transcript-of-barack-obamas-speech/

90. Gerstle, *American Crucible*, pp. 393–409.

91. Andrew Clark, 'Bankers and Academics at the Top of Donor List', *Guardian*, 8 November 2008, https://www.theguardian.com/world/2008/nov/08/barackobama-wallstreet-bankers-campaign-donations-goldmansachs

92. The F-35 fighter jet programme became the poster-child for this problem. See Valerie Insinna, 'Inside America's Dysfunctional Trillion Dollar Fighter-Jet Program, *New York Times*, 21 August 2019, https://www.nytimes.com/2019/08/21/magazine/f35-joint-strike-fighter-program.html

93. See, for example, John M. Broder, 'Oil and Gas Aid Bush Bid for President', *New York Times*, 23 June 2000, https://www.nytimes.com/2000/06/23/us/oil-and-gas-aid-bush-bid-for-president.html

94. On the Bush administration's energy policies and their political fallout see Meg Jacobs, 'Wreaking Havoc from Within: George W. Bush's Energy Policy in Historical Perspective' in *The Presidency of George W. Bush: A First Historical Assessment*, edited by Julian E. Zelizer (Princeton: Princeton University Press, 2011), pp. 139–68.

95. Quoted Jacobs, 'Wreaking Havoc from Within', p. 139.

96. Jacobs, Wreaking Havoc from Within', p. 167.

97. Elizabeth Kolbert, 'Changing Lanes', *New Yorker*, 4 August 2008, https://www.newyorker.com/magazine/2008/08/11/changing-lanes

98. Statement by the President on the Keystone XL pipeline, 6 November 2015, https://obamawhitehouse.archives.gov/the-press-office/2015/11/06/statement-president-keystone-xl-pipeline

99. Richard Valdmanis and Grant Smith, 'Oil Industry Bet Big on Jeb Bush, Reuter Review Shows. Now What?', *Reuters*, 19 February 2016, https://www.reuters.com/article/us-usa-election-oil-donors/oil-industry-bet-big-on-jeb-bush-for-president-reuters-review-shows-now-what-idUKKCN0VS279

100. On one occasion he declaimed that when he was 'elected president, the academics and political hacks are going to take the back seat. The people taking the decisions will be ones with real world experience.' Quoted in Dan Roberts, 'Jeb Bush Lays Out Energy Plan with Call to Relax Environmental Rules', *Guardian*, 29 September 2015, https://www.theguardian.com/us-news/2015/sep/29/jeb-bush-energy-policy-environment

101. Theda Skocpol and Vanessa Williamson, *The Tea Party and the Remaking of American Conservatism* (New York: Oxford University Press, 2013).

102. Vanessa Williamson, Theda Skocpol, and John Coggin, 'The Tea Party and the Remaking of American Conservatism', *Perspective on Politics 9*, no. 1 (2019): p. 33.

103. For a critique of the Koch brothers' influence on the Tea Party see Jane Mayer, 'Covert Operations', *New Yorker*, 23 August 2010, https://www.newyorker.com/magazine/2010/08/30/covert-operations

104. One Tea Party activist who campaigned for Marco Rubio in Florida in 2010 said of his membership of the Gang of Eight: 'He lied to us first and then he went around and repeated that lie from the panhandle to the keys. That's why he got elected. That really angered me.' Quoted in Leigh Ann Caldwell, 'Marco Rubio's record on immigration is more complicated than you think', *NBC News*, 12 January 2016, https://www.nbcnews.com/politics/2016-election/marco-rubio-s-record-immigration-more-complicated-you-think-n488601

105. On the political fallout of the foreclosures crisis see Alan Blinder, *After the Music Stopped: The Financial Crisis, the Response, and the Work Ahead* (London: Penguin, 2013), ch. 12. For the story of how three people who lost their homes uncovered the fraud at work see David Dayen, *Chain of Title: How Three Ordinary Americans Uncovered Wall Street's Great Foreclosure Fraud* (London: New Press, 2013).

106. Jeffrey P. Thompson and Gustavo A. Suarez, 'Exploring the Racial Wealth Gap Using the Survey of Consumer Finances', Finance and Economics Discussion Series Divisions of Research and Statistics and Monetary Affairs, Federal Reserve Board, Washington, DC, 2015, p. 9, https://www.federalreserve.gov/econresdata/feds/2015/files/2015076pap.pdf

107. See Richard Johnson, *The End of the Second Reconstruction* (Cambridge: Polity Press, 2020), ch. 4.

108. Quoted in Elena Shor, 'Oil-Industry Dreads Trump-Clinton Choice', *Politico*, 18 March 2016, https://www.politico.com/story/2016/03/oil-industry-donald-trump-hillary-clinton-choice-220947

109. Quoted in Ben Jacobs, 'Donald Trump Would Allow Keystone XL Pipeline and End Paris Climate Deal', *Guardian*, 26 May 2016, https://www.theguardian.com/us-news/2016/may/26/donald-trump-environmental-policy-climate-change-keystone-xl

110. Justin Worland, 'Donald Trump Promises Oil and Gas Industry Big But Scepticism Remains', *Time*, 22 September 2016, https://time.com/4504617/donald-trump-oil-gas-environment/

111. Susan Phillips, 'Why the Oil and Gas Industry is Not Giving to Trump', NPR, StateImpact Pennsylvania, 20 September 2016, https://stateimpact.npr.org/pennsylvania/2016/09/20/why-the-oil-and-gas-industry-is-not-giving-to-trump/

112. The White House, 'Fact Sheet: President Donald J. Trump is Unleashing American Energy Dominance', 14 May 2019, https://www.presidency.ucsb.edu/documents/fact-sheet-president-donald-j-trump-unleashing-american-energy-dominance

113. For the argument that Trump's election showed how democratic excess led to chaos see Jonathan Rauch and Ray La Raja, 'Too Much Democracy is Bad for Democracy' *Atlantic*, December 2019, https://www.theatlantic.com/magazine/archive/2019/12/too-much-democracy-is-bad-for-democracy/600766/

114. For class-based analysis of the divisions in Western democracies, not just the United States, that concentrates on the previously excessive political influence of those classes that benefited from the post-1970s international economy see Michael Lind, *The New Class War: Saving Democracy from the Metropolitan Elite* (London: Atlantic Books, 2020).

115. On the part the Trump's presidency played in hollowing out the American administrative state see Michael Lewis, *The Fifth Risk: Undoing Democracy* (London: Allen Lane, 2018).

116. Quoted in Todd S. Purdum, 'Gavin Newsom's Nation-State', *Atlantic*, 21 April 2020, https://www.theatlantic.com/politics/archive/2020/04/coronavirus-california-gavin-newsom/610006/

117. Quoted in Spencer Kimball, 'New York Governor Cuomo Says Trump has No Authority to Impose Quarantine: "It Would Be Illegal"', CNBC, 28 March 2020, https://www.cnbc.com/2020/03/28/ny-gov-cuomo-says-trump-has-no-authority-to-impose-quarantine.html

118. For the argument that the Eurozone can accommodate much more economic divergence than was supposed by its critics who argued that it was not an optimal currency area see Waltraud Schelkle, *The Political Economy of Monetary Solidarity: Understanding the Euro Experiment* (Oxford: Oxford University Press, 2017).

119. For a different starting place for the same argument that the Eurozone democracies are burdened by too little democratic political competition see Sheri Berman and Hans Kundnani, 'The Cost of Convergence', *Journal of Democracy 32*, no. 1 (2021): pp. 22–36.

Conclusion

1. Adam Tooze, *Crashed: How a Decade of Financial Crises Changed the World* (London: Penguin, 2018), p. 13.

2. David Brunnstom, Alexandra Alper, and Yew Lun Tian, 'China Will "Eat Our Lunch", Biden Warns After Clashing With Xi On Most Fronts', *Reuters*, 11 February 2021, https://www.reuters.com/article/us-usa-china-idUSKBN2AB06A

3. See European Commission, Second Report on the State of the Energy Union, 1 February 2017, https://ec.europa.eu/info/publications/2nd-report-state-energy-union_en

4. Austria too is an anti-nuclear power state. As a harbinger of likely conflicts to come, frustration with nuclear power's exclusion from the Commission's pathway to carbon neutrality led Macron in early 2021 to make common cause with six Eastern European and Balkan member states. Frédéric Simon, 'Macron, Orban Urge EU to "Actively Support" Nuclear Power', *Euractiv*, 25 March 2021, https://www.euractiv.com/section/energy-environment/news/macron-orban-urge-eu-to-actively-support-nuclear-power/

5. Michaël Tanchum, 'The Logic Beyond Lausanne: A Geopolitical Perspective on the Congruence Between Turkey's New Hard Power and its Strategic Reorientation', *Insight Turkey 22*, no. 3 (2020): p. 42.

6. Speech by Angela Merkel at 2020 Annual Meeting of the World Economy Forum in Davos, 23 January 2020, https://www.bundeskanzlerin.de/bkin-en/news/speech-by-federal-chancellor-dr-angela-merkel-at-the-2020-annual-meeting-of-the-world-economic-forum-in-davos-on-23-january-2020-1716620

7. For a discussion of the politics of the rise of the car see David Gartman, 'Three Ages of the Automobile: The Cultural Logics of the Car', *Theory, Culture, and Society 21*, nos. 4–5 (2004): pp. 169–95.

8. Martin Williams, 'Why it is Feared Scotland's Wind Power Boom is All Hot Air', *Herald*, 29 November 2019, https://www.heraldscotland.com/news/18067837.feared-scotlands-wind-power-economic-boom-hot-air/

9. Ralph Vartabedian, 'How California's Faltering High-Speed Rail Project Was "Captured" by Costly Consultants', *Los Angeles Times*, 26 April 2019, https://www.latimes.com/local/california/la-me-california-high-speed-rail-consultants-20190426-story.html

10. On the density issue see Vaclav Smil, *Power Density: A Key to Understanding Energy Sources and Uses* (Cambridge, MA: MIT Press, 2015).

11. Our World in Data, Energy Mix, Global Primary Energy Consumption by Source, https://ourworldindata.org/energy-mix

12. Vaclav Smil, Gradual Greening: Power Density and the Hydrocarbon Habit, Blue Books, CLSA Investment Group, 13 September 2016, pp. 9–14, http://vaclavsmil.com/wp-content/uploads/2016/12/CLSA-U-Blue-Books-Gradual-greening_-Power-density-and-the-hydrocarbon-habit-20160913–1.pdf

Afterword 2022: War

1. Andrea Shalal, Andreas Rinke, and Jeff Mason, 'Biden Pledges End to Nord Stream 2 if Russia Invades Ukraine', *Reuters*, 8 February 2022, https://www.reuters.com/world/biden-germanys-scholz-stress-unified-front-against-any-russian-aggression-toward-2022-02-07/

2. Quoted in Piotr Buras, 'Olaf Scholz: Tweeting on Thin Ice', *European Council on Foreign Relations Commentary*, 21 February 2022, https://ecfr.eu/article/olaf-scholz-tweeting-on-thin-ice/

3. Matthew Karnitschnig, Hans von der Burchard, Florian Eder, and Andrew Desiderio, 'Inside Olaf Scholz's Historic Shift on Defence, Ukraine and Russia', *Politico*, 5 March 2022, https://www.politico.eu/article/olaf-scholz-historic-shift-defense-ukraine-russia-war/

4. Policy Statement by Olaf Scholz, chancellor of the Federal Republic of Germany and member of the German Bundestag, 27 February 2022, Berlin, https://www.bundesregierung.de/breg-en/news/policy-statement-by-olaf-scholz-chancellor-of-the-federal-republic-of-germany-and-member-of-the-german-bundestag-27-february-2022-in-berlin-2008378

5. On the relationship of the first independent Ukrainian states and their merger in 1919 to wartime Europe, see Borislav Chernev, *Twilight of Empire: The Brest-Litovsk Conference and the Remaking of East-Central Europe, 1917–18* (Toronto, ON: University of Toronto Press, 2017), ch. 4.

6. Karnitschnig et al., 'Inside Olaf Scholz's Historic Shift'.

7. Quoted in Kira Taylor, 'EU Rolls Out Plan to Slash Russian Gas Imports by Two Thirds Before Year End', *Euractiv*, 9 March 2022, https://www.euractiv.com/section/energy/news/eu-rolls-out-plan-to-slash-russian-gas-imports-by-two-thirds-before-year-end/

8. Speech by Viktor Orbán at the 31st Bálványos Summer Free University and Student Camp, 23 July 2022, https://abouthungary.hu/speeches-and-remarks/speech-by-prime-minister-viktor-orban-at-the-31-st-balvanyos-summer-free-university-and-student-camp

9. Yongchang Chin and Rakesh Sharma, 'Oil's New Map: How India Turns Russia Crude into the West's Fuel', *Bloomberg UK*, 5 February 2023, https://www.bloomberg.com/news/articles/2023-02-05/oil-s-new-map-how-india-turns-russia-crude-into-the-west-s-fuel

10. Shotaro Tani, 'Europe's Imports of Russian Seaborne Gas Jump to Record High', 28 November 2022, https://www.ft.com/content/81db1e45-6ef9-4034-879b-82597e2b87f9

11. Vladimir Afanasiev, 'Erdogan Steps Up Backing for Russia's Turkish Gas Hub Plan', *Upstream Energy Explored*, 20 October 2022, https://www.upstreamonline.com/politics/erdogan-steps-up-backing-for-russia-s-turkish-gas-hub-plan/2-1-1338137

12. Quoted in Nektaria Stamouli, 'Greece to Allies: Crack Down on Turkey or Risk Another Ukraine', *Politico*, 7 September 2022, https://www.

politico.eu/article/greece-turkey-eu-crack-down-or-risk-another-ukraine-russia-war/

13. Milan Kundera, 'The Tragedy of Central Europe', in *Thoughts on Europe: Past, Present, and Future*, ed. Yoeri Albrecht and Mathieu Segers (Amsterdam: Amsterdam University Press, 2021), p. 209.

14. For reflections from a German Russian scholar on what he sees as a common German unwillingness to focus on Ukraine's history, see Karl Schlögel, *Ukraine: A Nation on the Borderland*, trans. Gerrit Jackson (London: Reaktion Books, 2018), ch. 3.

15. Tony Judt, *Postwar: A History of Europe Since 1945* (London: Vintage Books, digital edition), pp. 933–4.

16. For Biden blaming Putin's war for energy prices, see 'Remarks by President Biden on Gas Prices and Putin's Price Hike', 22 June 2022, https://www.whitehouse.gov/briefing-room/speeches-remarks/2022/06/22/remarks-by-president-biden-on-gas-prices-and-putins-price-hike/

17. Trading Economics, 'EU Natural Gas', https://tradingeconomics.com/commodity/eu-natural-gas

18. Demand in China, India, Pakistan, and Bangladesh fell sharply. Sam Reynolds, 'Asia's Lower LNG Demand in 2022 Highlights Challenges for Industry Growth', *Institute for Energy Economics and Financial Analysis*, 11 January 2023, https://ieefa.org/resources/asias-lower-lng-demand-2022-highlights-challenges-industry-growth

19. US Energy Information Administration, 'International Data, Petroleum and Other Liquids', https://www.eia.gov/international/data/world

20. US Energy Information Administration, 'Petroleum and Other Liquids', https://www.eia.gov/dnav/pet/hist/LeafHandler.ashx?n=PET&s=MCRFPUS2&f=M

21. US Department of the Treasury, 'Statistics. A2: Major Foreign Holders of Treasury Securities, Historical Data and Statistics; B2 Monthly Holdings of US Long-Term Securities at Current Market Value by Foreign Residents, Holdings by Country (China)', https://home.treasury.gov/data/treasury-international-capital-tic-system-home-page/tic-forms-instructions/securities-b-portfolio-holdings-of-us-and-foreign-securities

22. Notably, in early 2023, the Biden administration persuaded the Netherlands, where there are companies indispensable to the supply chain, to join its semi-conductor ban.

23. Patricia Nilsson, 'BASF to Downsize "Permanently" in Europe', *Financial Times*, 26 October 2022, https://www.ft.com/content/f6d2fe70-16fb-4d81-a26a-3afb93e0bf57

24. Andy Bounds, 'EU Accuses US of Breaking WTO Rules with Green Energy Incentives', *Financial Times*, 6 November 2022, https://www.ft.com/content/de1ec769-a76c-474a-927c-b7e5aeff7d9e

25. Doug Palmer, 'WTO Says Trump's Steel Tariffs Violated Global Trade Rules', *Politico*, 9 December 2022, https://www.politico.com/news/2022/12/09/wto-ruling-trump-tariffs-violate-rules-00073282

26. Quoted in Amy Kazmin, 'Revulsion at Ukraine War Ends Rome's Old Amity with Moscow,' *Financial Times*, 2 May 2022, https://www.ft.com/content/70d99402-98c4-4f1b-a693-2f25739b2455

27. 'Remarks by President Biden Announcing US Ban on Imports of Russian Oil, Liquefied Natural Gas, and Coal', 8 March 2022, https://www.whitehouse.gov/briefing-room/speeches-remarks/2022/03/08/remarks-by-president-biden-announcing-u-s-ban-on-imports-of-russian-oil-liquefied-natural-gas-and-coal/

28. On Pakistan's loss of contracted LNG supply, see Shotaro Tani, 'Europe's Appetite for LNG Leaves Developing Nations Starved of Gas', *Financial Times*, 23 September 2022, https://www.ft.com/content/752b1285-3174-4cf1-83c0-b1151888bf4e

Index